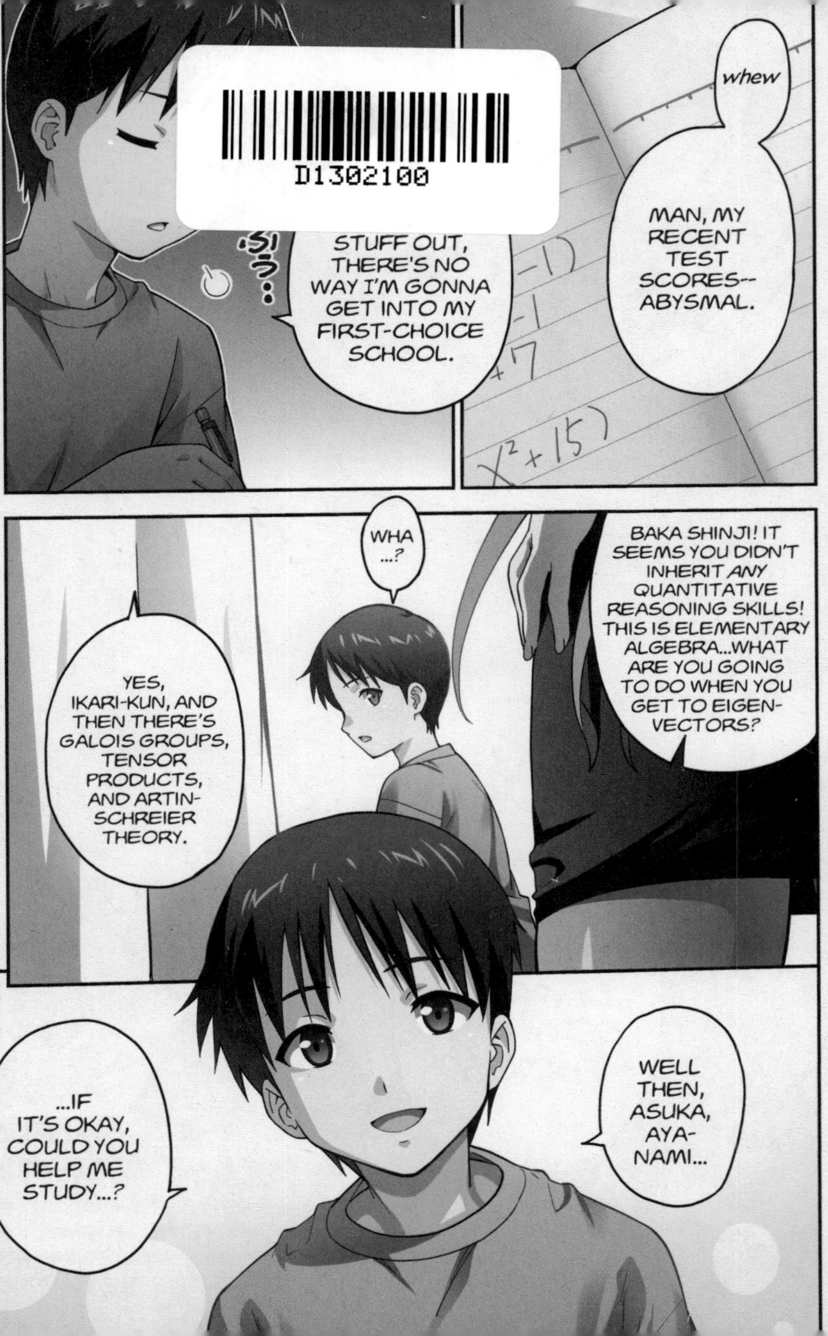
whew
MAN, MY RECENT TEST SCORES--ABYSMAL.
STUFF OUT, THERE'S NO WAY I'M GONNA GET INTO MY FIRST-CHOICE SCHOOL.
ふぅ..
BAKA SHINJI! IT SEEMS YOU DIDN'T INHERIT *ANY* QUANTITATIVE REASONING SKILLS! THIS IS ELEMENTARY ALGEBRA...WHAT ARE YOU GOING TO DO WHEN YOU GET TO EIGEN-VECTORS?
WHA ...?
YES, IKARI-KUN, AND THEN THERE'S GALOIS GROUPS, TENSOR PRODUCTS, AND ARTIN-SCHREIER THEORY.
WELL THEN, ASUKA, AYA-NAMI...
...IF IT'S OKAY, COULD YOU HELP ME STUDY...?

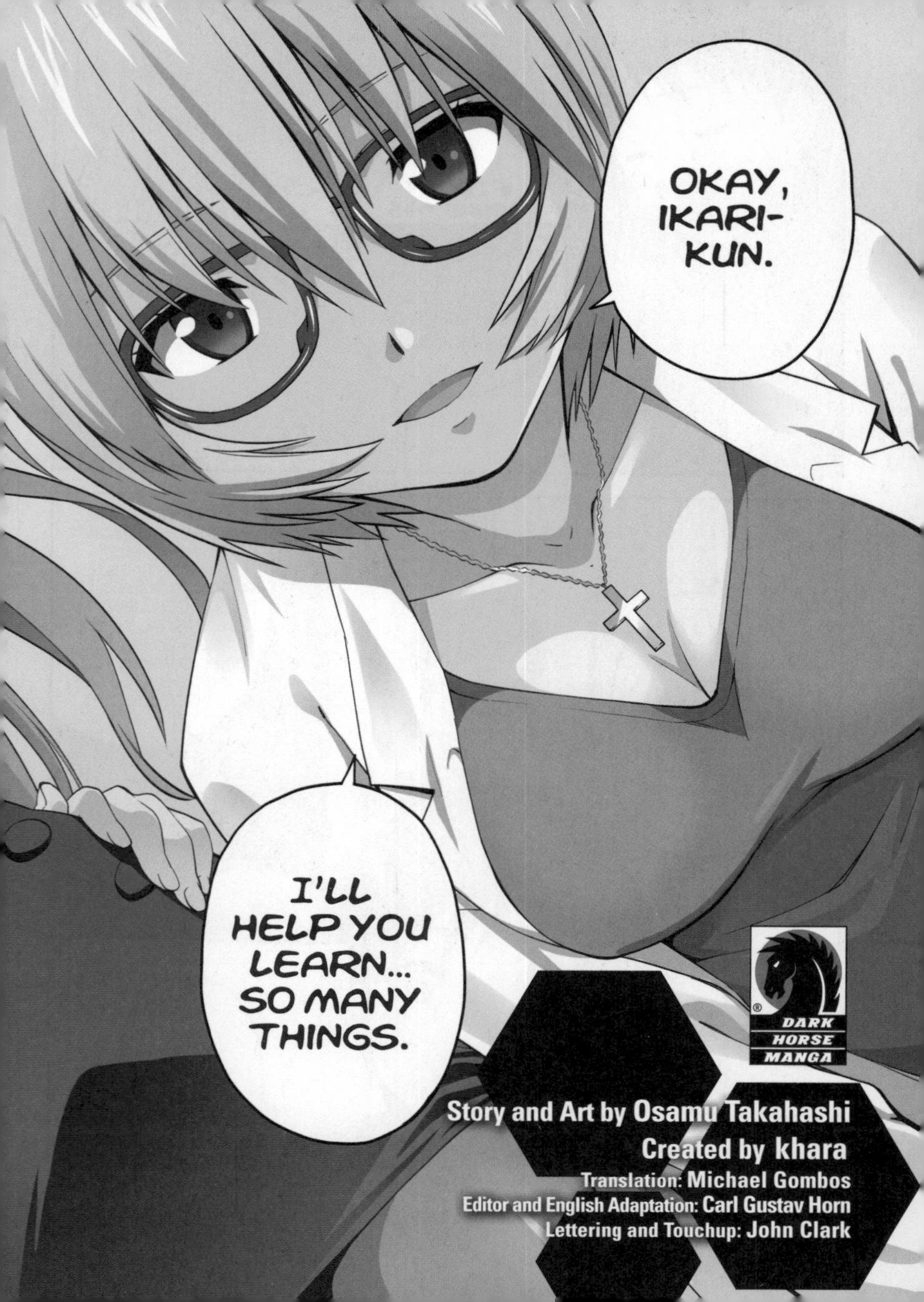
OKAY, IKARI-KUN.
I'LL HELP YOU LEARN... SO MANY THINGS.
DARK HORSE MANGA

Story and Art by Osamu Takahashi
Created by khara
Translation: Michael Gombos
Editor and English Adaptation: Carl Gustav Horn
Lettering and Touchup: John Clark

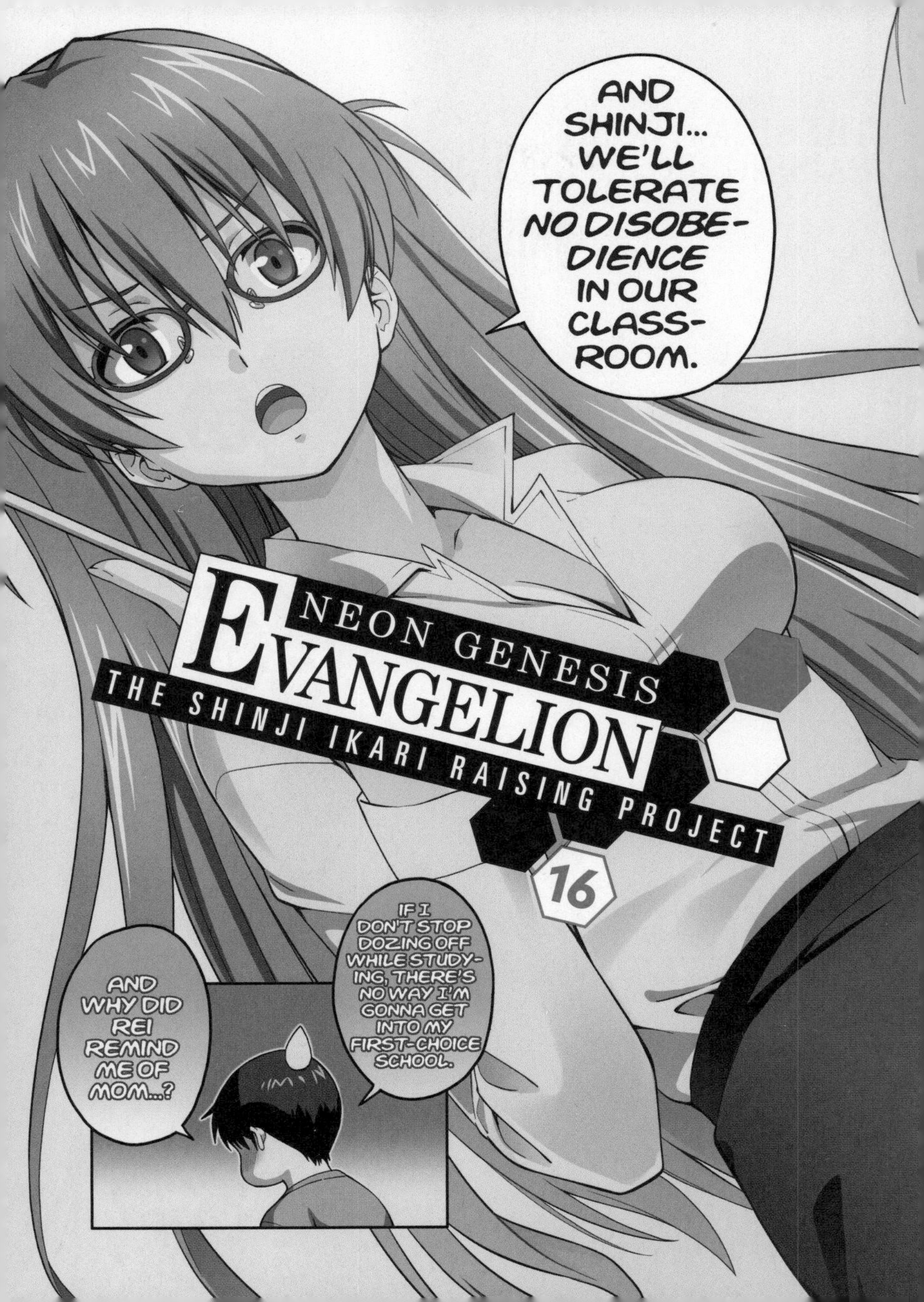
AND SHINJI... WE'LL TOLERATE NO DISOBE-DIENCE IN OUR CLASS-ROOM.
NEON GENESIS EVANGELION
THE SHINJI IKARI RAISING PROJECT
16
IF I DON'T STOP DOZING OFF WHILE STUDY-ING, THERE'S NO WAY I'M GONNA GET INTO MY FIRST-CHOICE SCHOOL.
AND WHY DID REI REMIND ME OF MOM...?

NEON GENESIS EVANGELION

# THE SHINJI IKARI RAISING PROJECT

CONTENTS



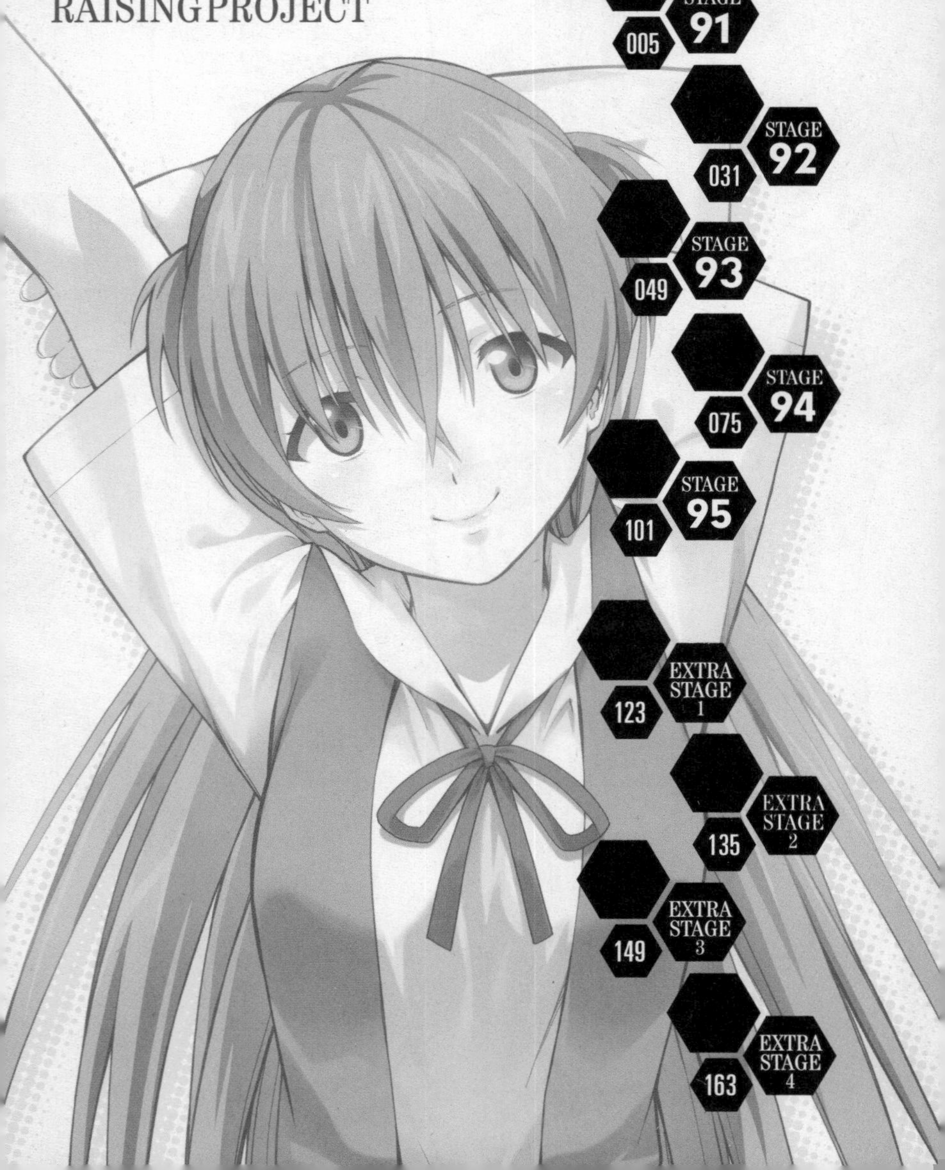

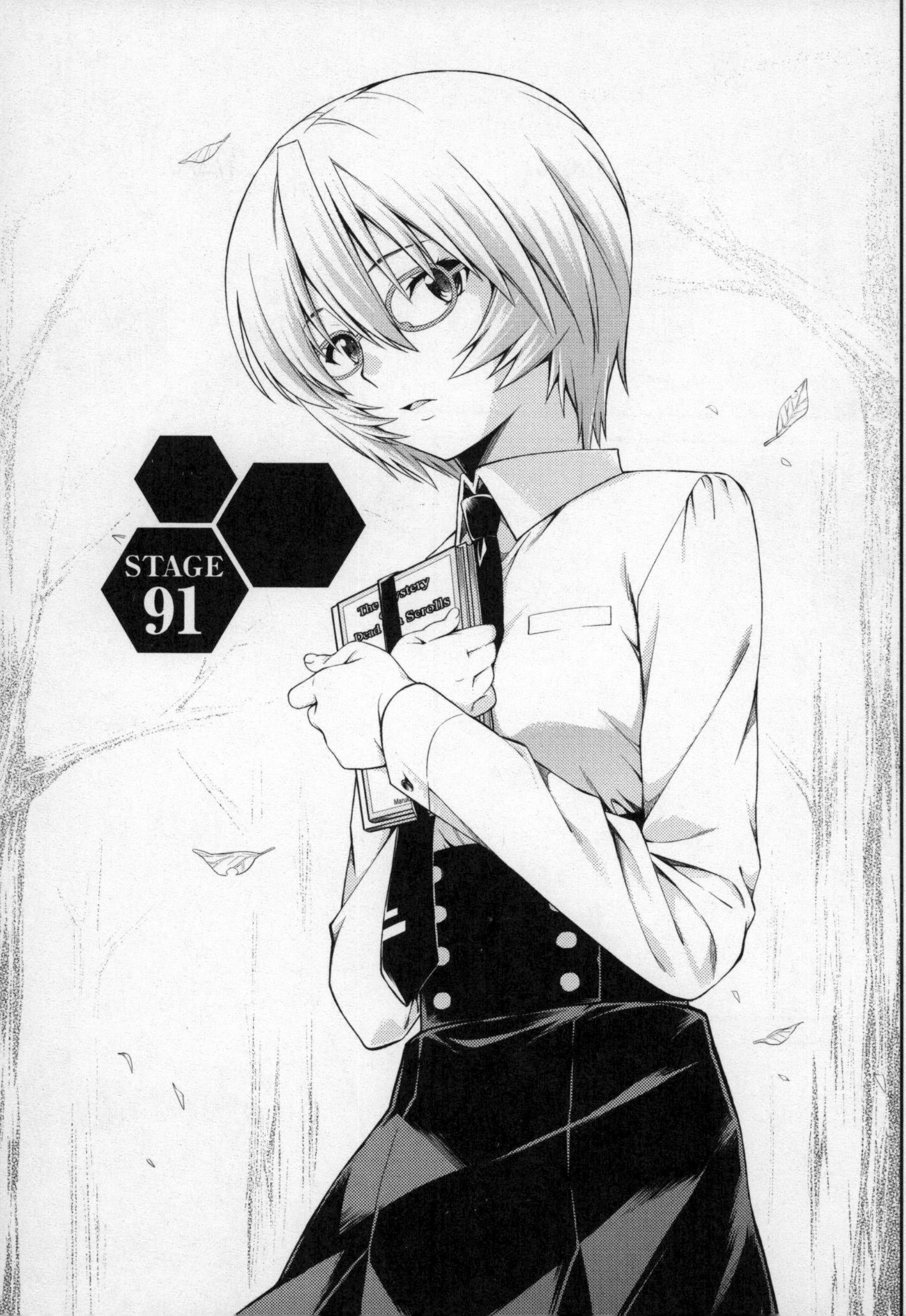
STAGE
91

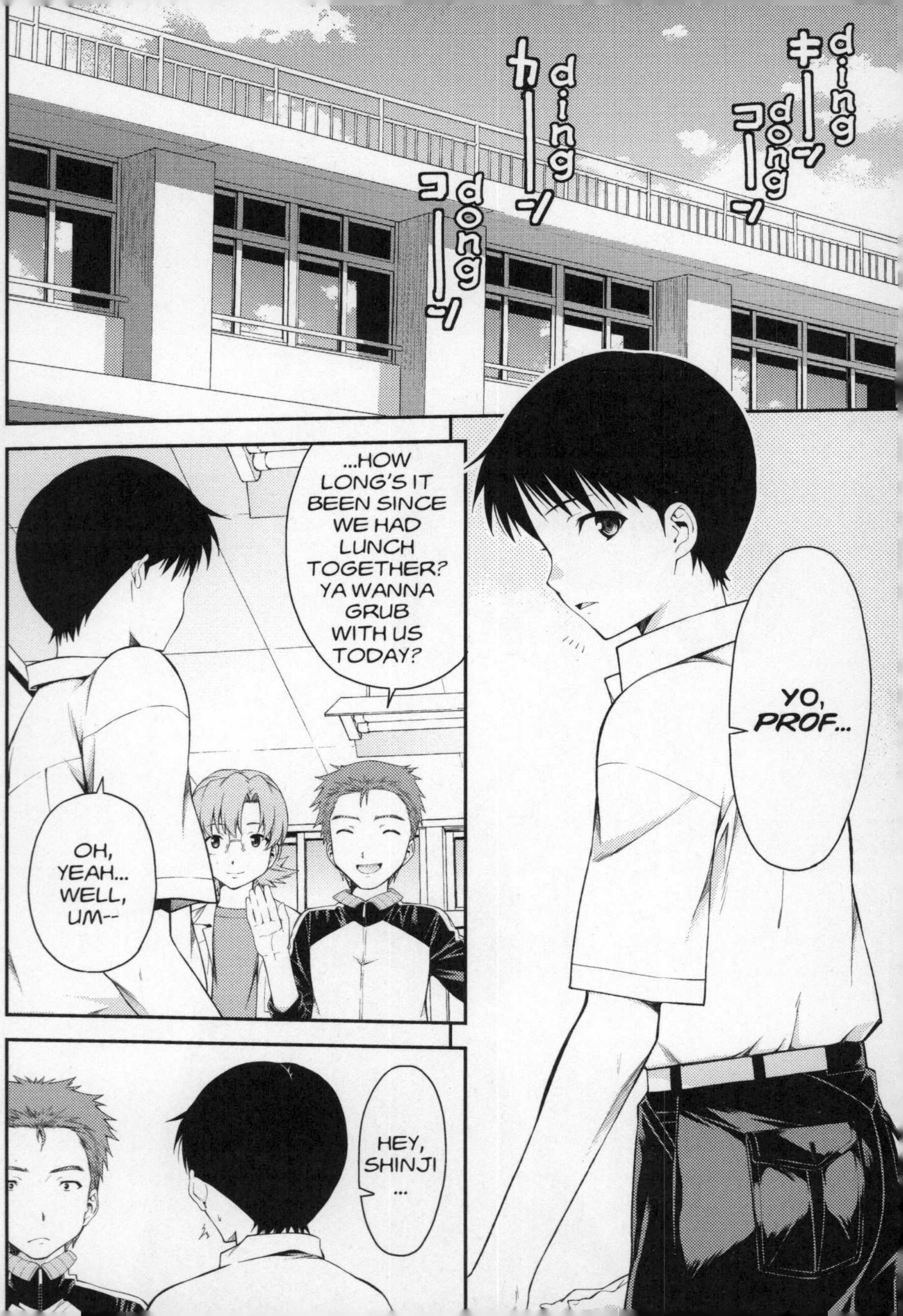

ding キー dong コー
ding カー dong コー
YO, PROF...
...HOW LONG'S IT BEEN SINCE WE HAD LUNCH TOGETHER? YA WANNA GRUB WITH US TODAY?
OH, YEAH... WELL, UM--
HEY, SHINJI ...

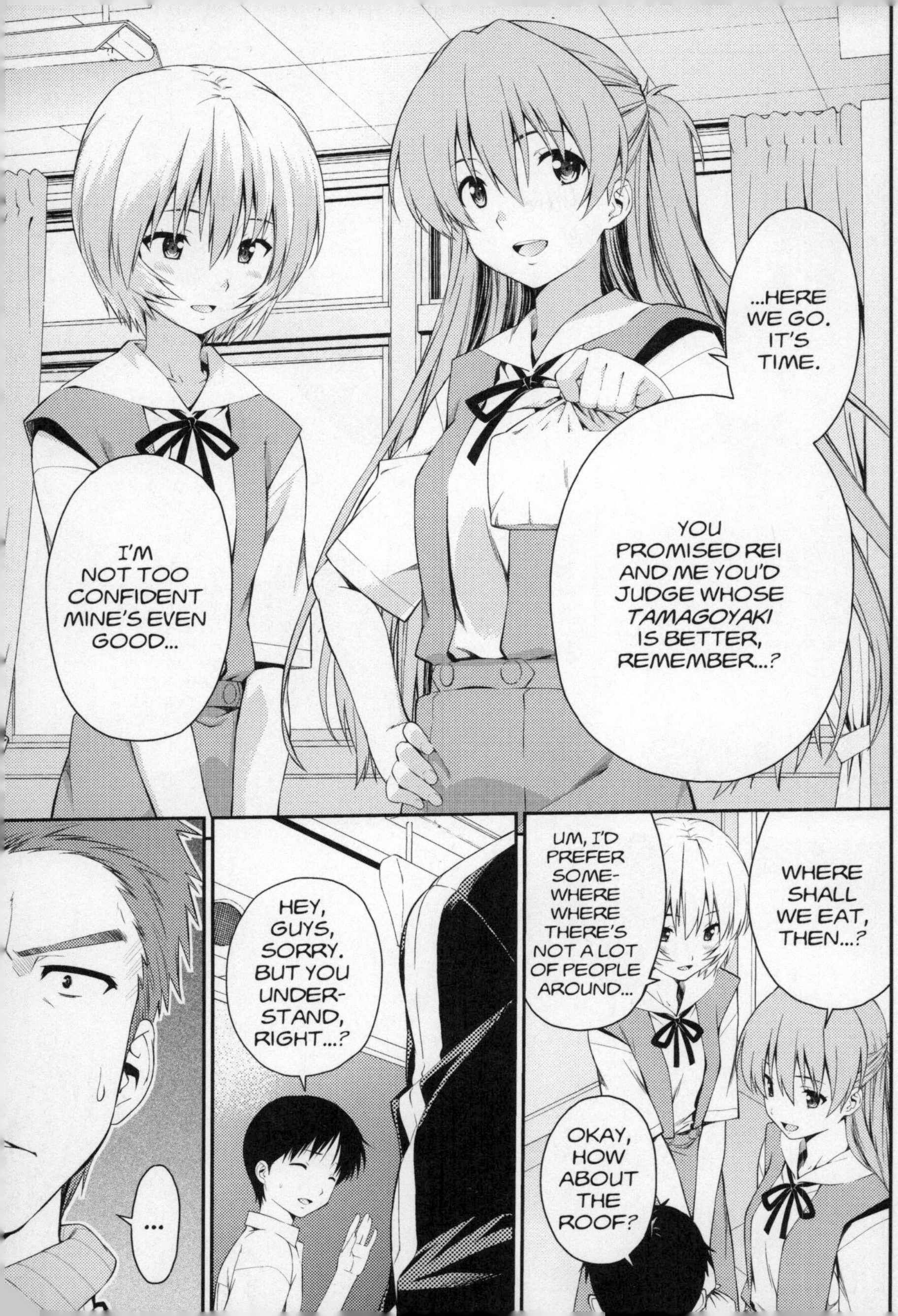
...HERE WE GO. IT'S TIME.
YOU PROMISED REI AND ME YOU'D JUDGE WHOSE *TAMAGOYAKI* IS BETTER, REMEMBER...?
I'M NOT TOO CONFIDENT MINE'S EVEN GOOD...
WHERE SHALL WE EAT, THEN...?
UM, I'D PREFER SOME-WHERE WHERE THERE'S NOT A LOT OF PEOPLE AROUND...
OKAY, HOW ABOUT THE ROOF?
HEY, GUYS, SORRY. BUT YOU UNDER-STAND, RIGHT...?
...

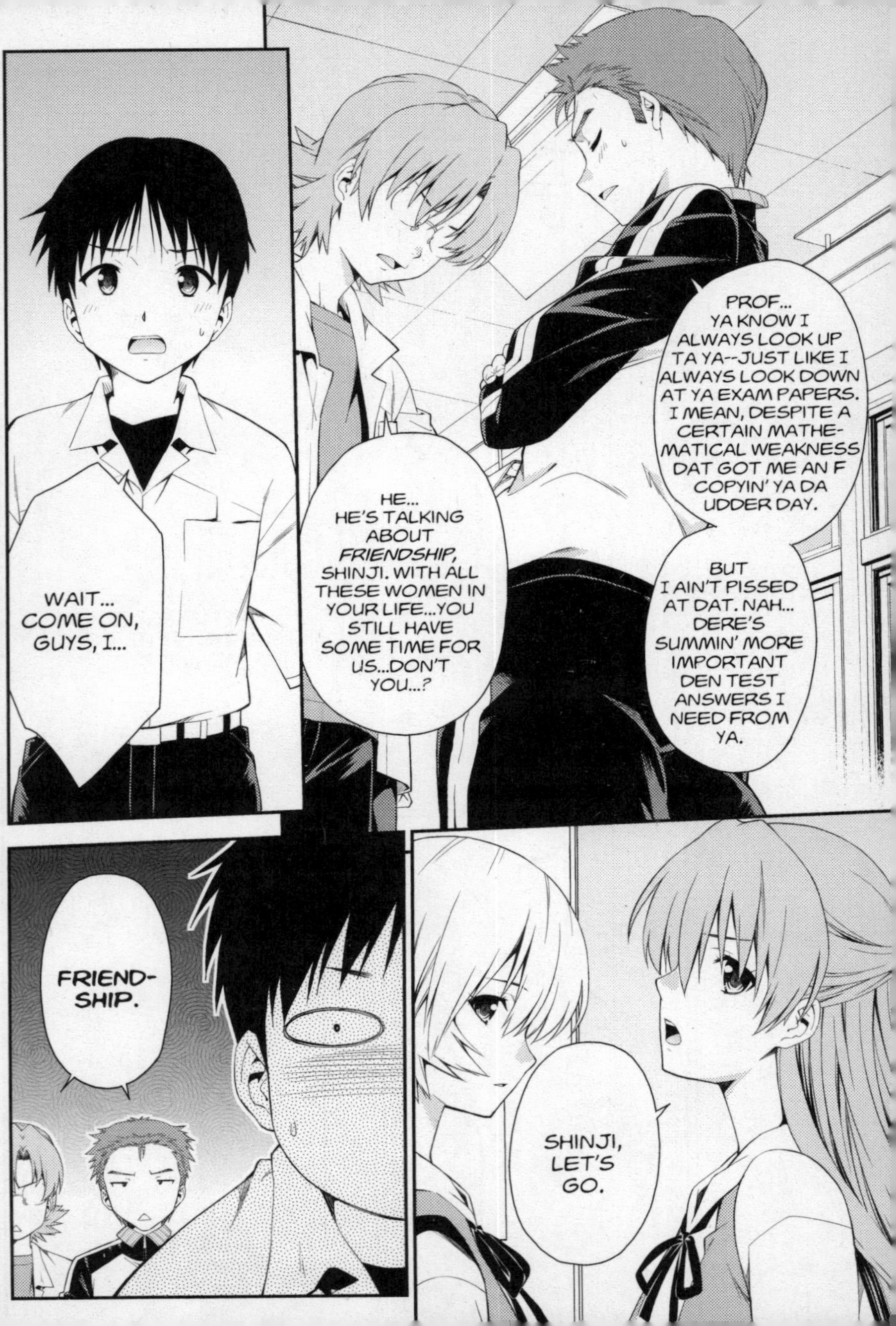
PROF... YA KNOW I ALWAYS LOOK UP TA YA--JUST LIKE I ALWAYS LOOK DOWN AT YA EXAM PAPERS. I MEAN, DESPITE A CERTAIN MATHE-MATICAL WEAKNESS DAT GOT ME AN F COPYIN' YA DA UDDER DAY.
BUT I AIN'T PISSED AT DAT. NAH... DERE'S SUMMIN' MORE IMPORTANT DEN TEST ANSWERS I NEED FROM YA.
HE... HE'S TALKING ABOUT *FRIENDSHIP,* SHINJI. WITH ALL THESE WOMEN IN YOUR LIFE...YOU STILL HAVE SOME TIME FOR US...DON'T YOU...?
WAIT... COME ON, GUYS, I...
SHINJI, LET'S GO.
FRIEND-SHIP.

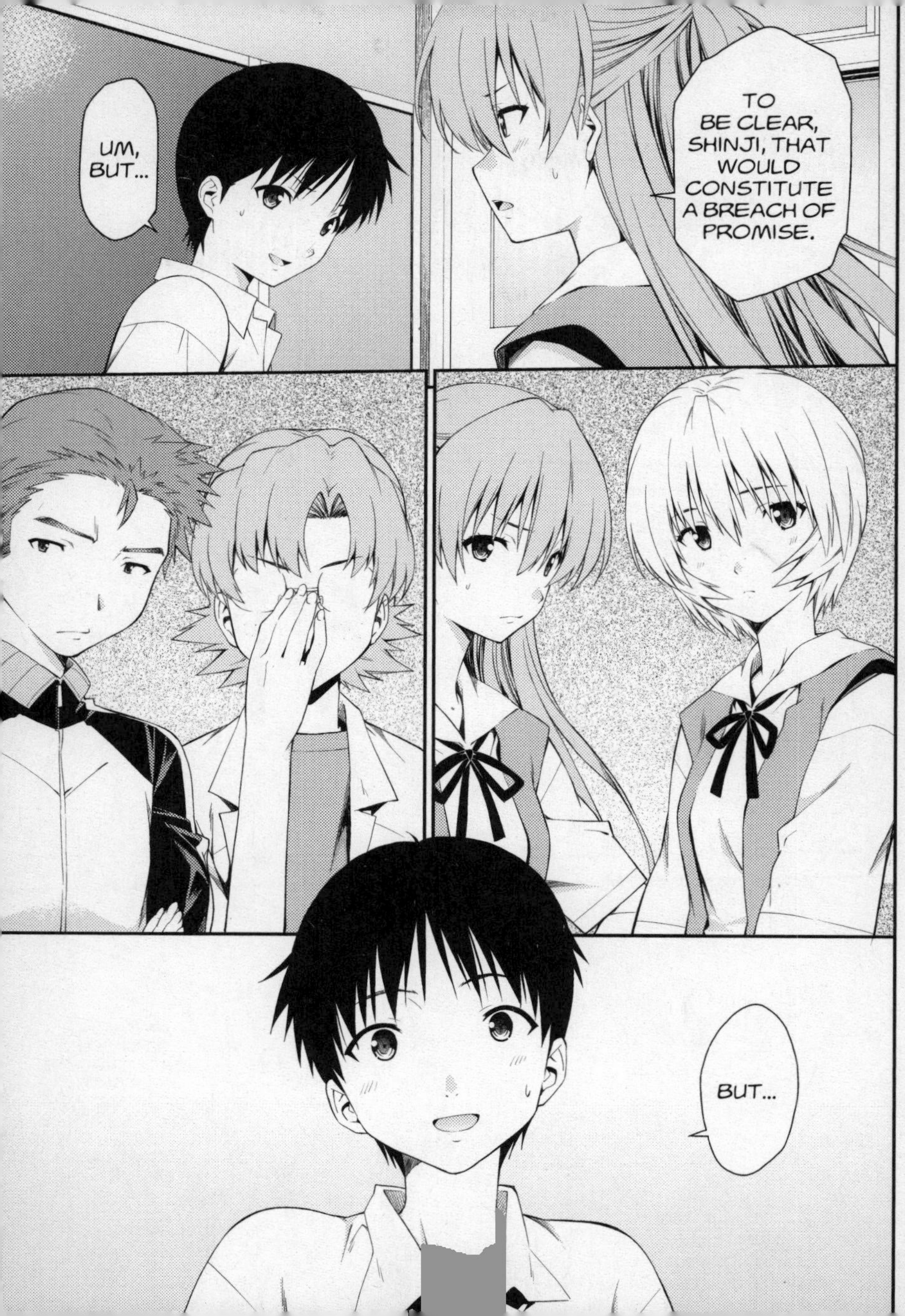
TO BE CLEAR, SHINJI, THAT WOULD CONSTITUTE A BREACH OF PROMISE.
UM, BUT...
BUT...

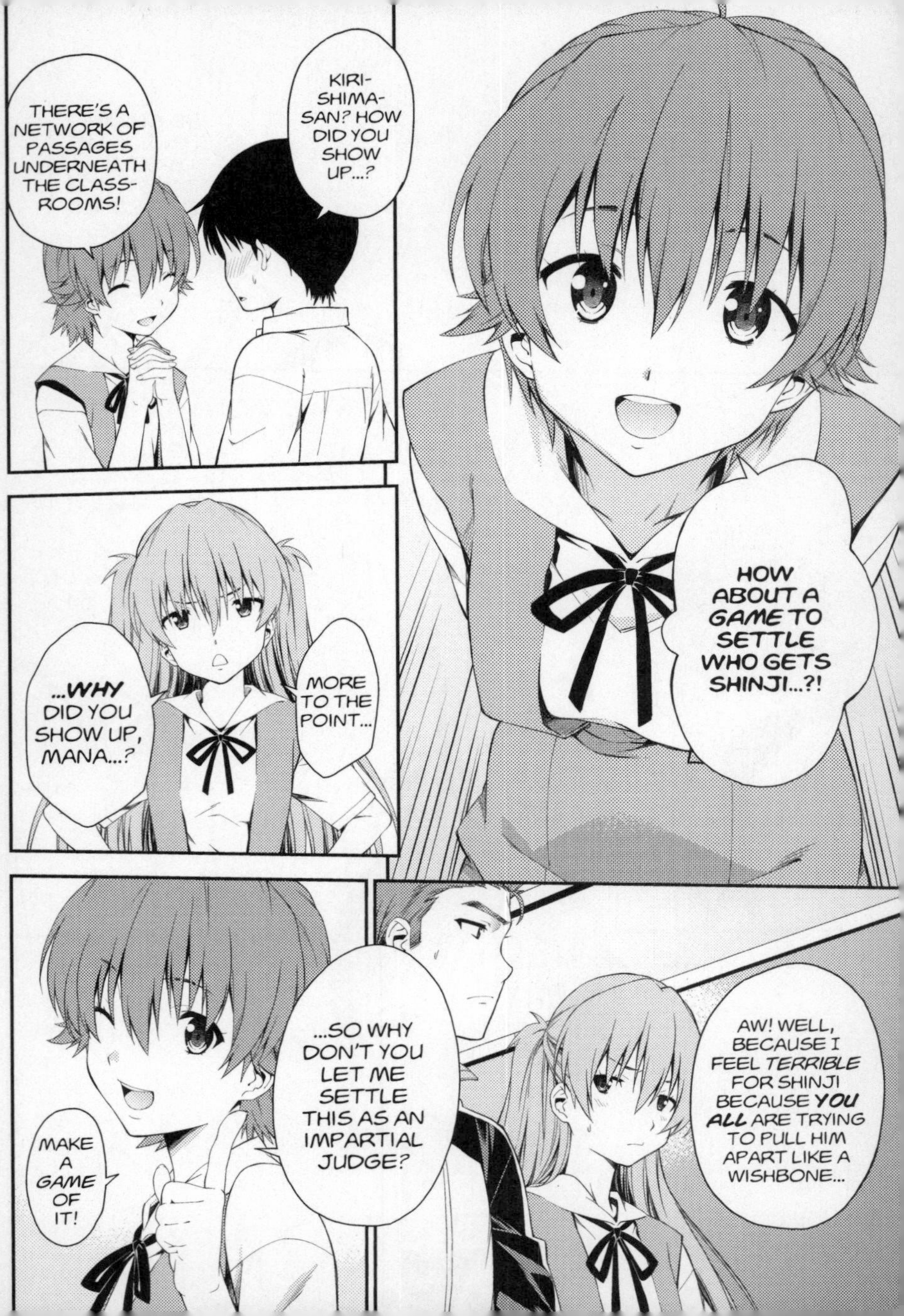
KIRI-SHIMA-SAN? HOW DID YOU SHOW UP...?
THERE'S A NETWORK OF PASSAGES UNDERNEATH THE CLASS-ROOMS!
MORE TO THE POINT...
...***WHY*** DID YOU SHOW UP, MANA...?
HOW ABOUT A *GAME* TO SETTLE WHO GETS SHINJI...?!
AW! WELL, BECAUSE I FEEL *TERRIBLE* FOR SHINJI BECAUSE ***YOU ALL*** ARE TRYING TO PULL HIM APART LIKE A WISHBONE...
...SO WHY DON'T YOU LET ME SETTLE THIS AS AN IMPARTIAL JUDGE?
MAKE A *GAME* OF IT!

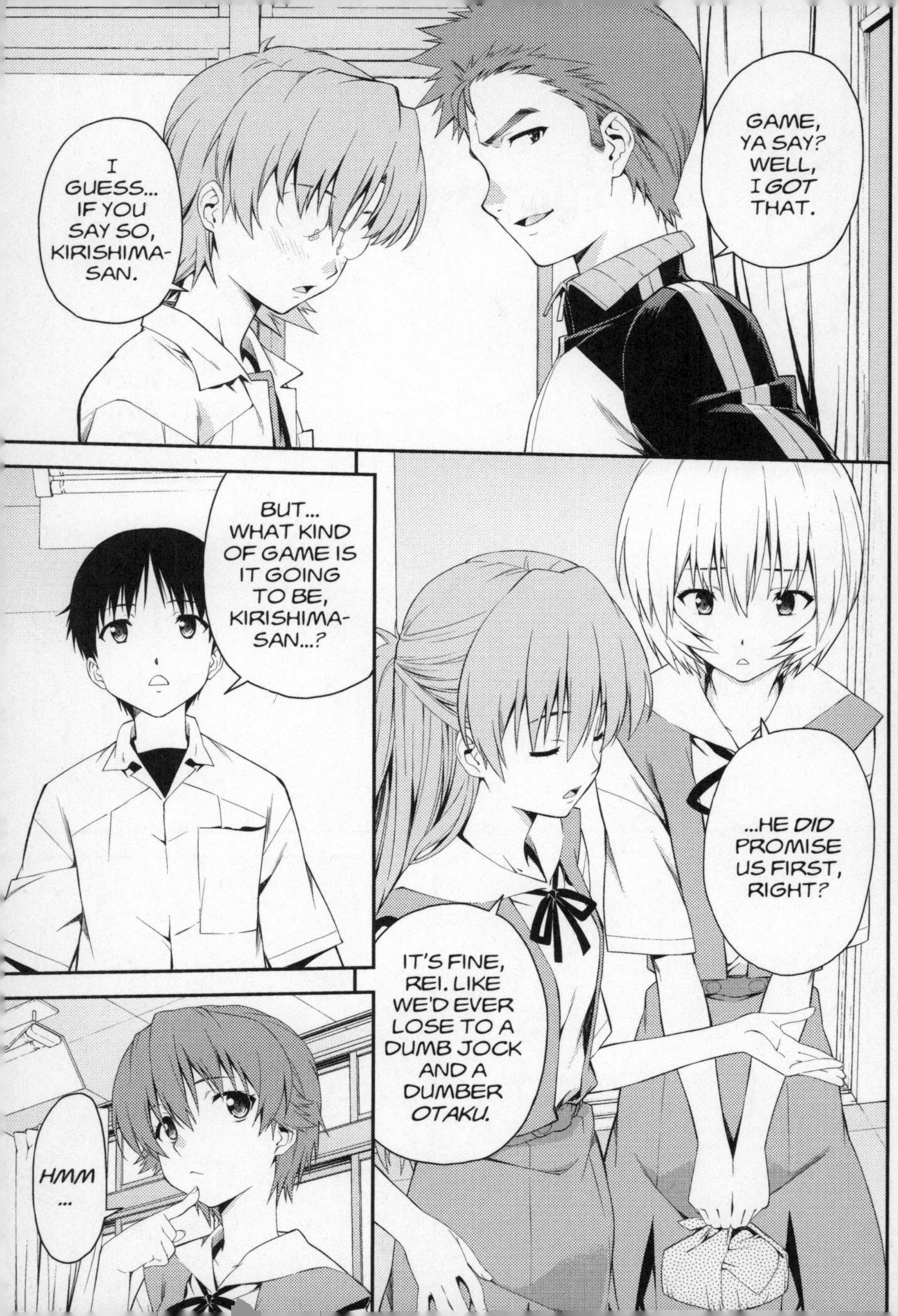
GAME, YA SAY? WELL, I GOT THAT.
I GUESS... IF YOU SAY SO, KIRISHIMA-SAN.
...HE *DID* PROMISE US FIRST, RIGHT?
IT'S FINE, REI. LIKE WE'D EVER LOSE TO A DUMB JOCK AND A DUMBER *OTAKU.*
BUT... WHAT KIND OF GAME IS IT GOING TO BE, KIRISHIMA-SAN...?
*HMM* ...

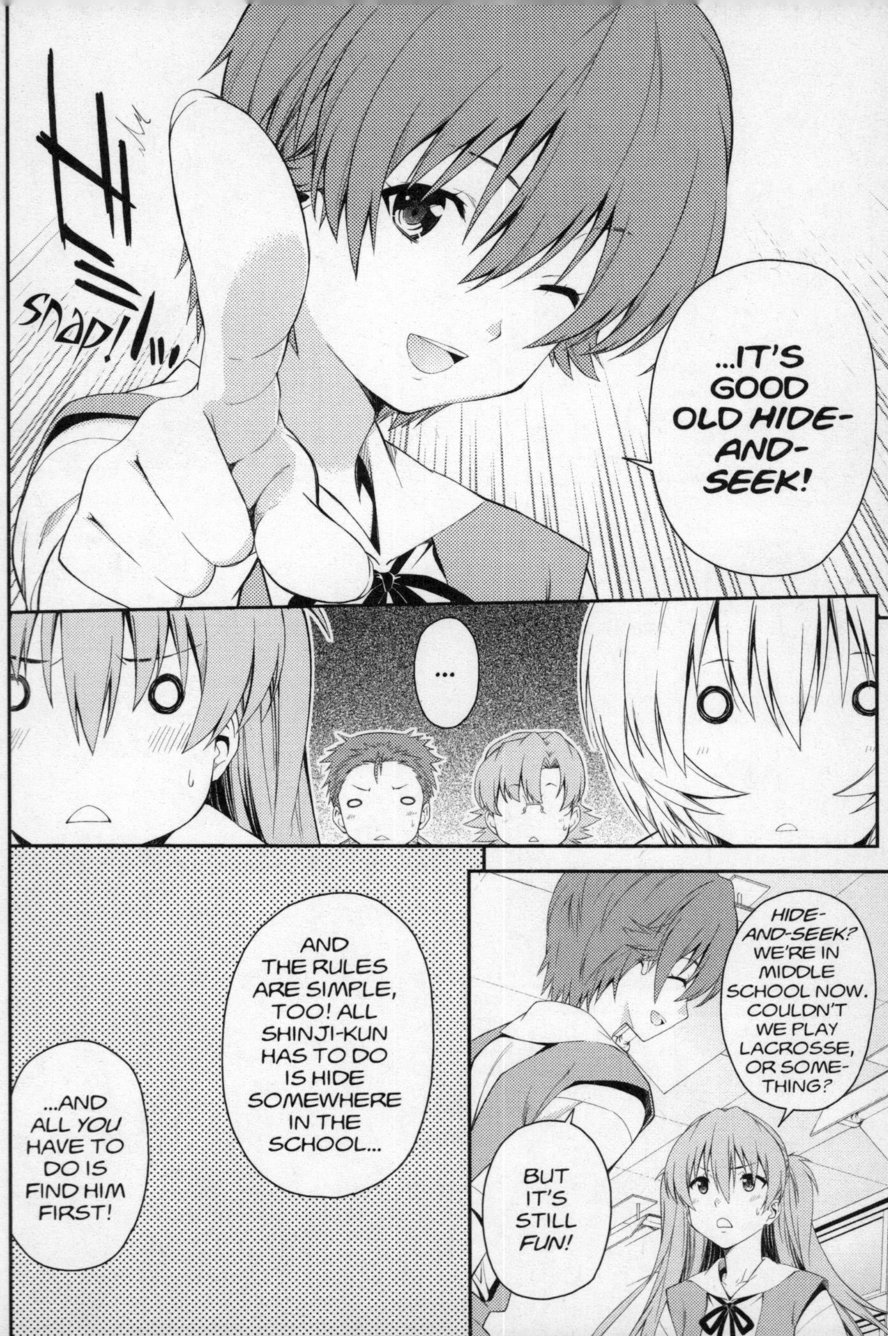
...IT'S GOOD OLD HIDE-AND-SEEK!
snap!
...
HIDE-AND-SEEK? WE'RE IN MIDDLE SCHOOL NOW. COULDN'T WE PLAY LACROSSE, OR SOMETHING?
BUT IT'S STILL *FUN*!
AND THE RULES ARE SIMPLE, TOO! ALL SHINJI-KUN HAS TO DO IS HIDE SOMEWHERE IN THE SCHOOL...
...AND ALL *YOU* HAVE TO DO IS FIND HIM FIRST!

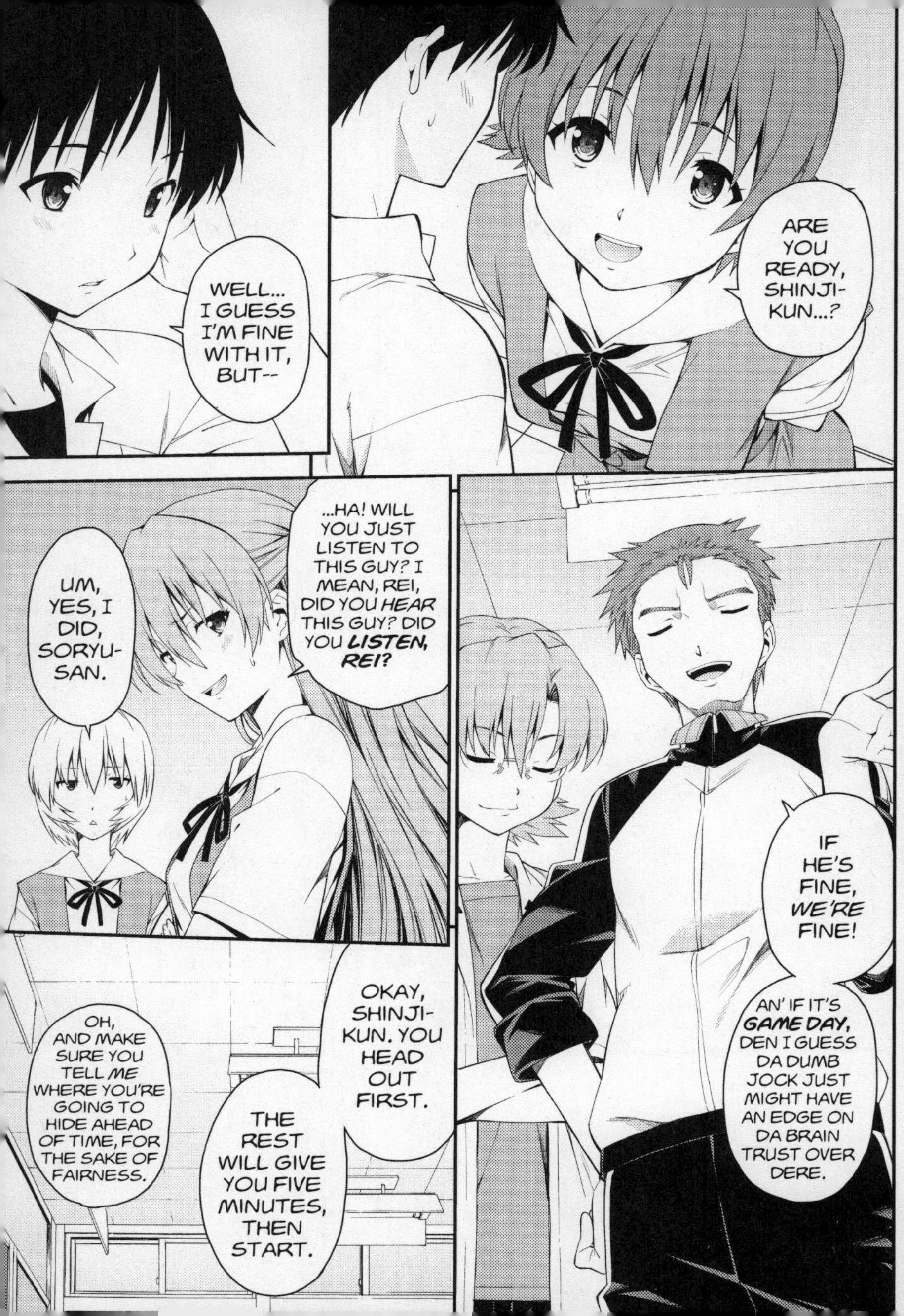
ARE YOU READY, SHINJI-KUN...?
WELL... I GUESS I'M FINE WITH IT, BUT--
IF HE'S FINE, *WE'RE* FINE!
AN' IF IT'S **GAME DAY,** DEN I GUESS DA DUMB JOCK JUST MIGHT HAVE AN EDGE ON DA BRAIN TRUST OVER DERE.
...HA! WILL YOU JUST LISTEN TO THIS GUY? I MEAN, REI, DID YOU *HEAR* THIS GUY? DID YOU ***LISTEN, REI?***
UM, YES, I DID, SORYU-SAN.
OKAY, SHINJI-KUN. YOU HEAD OUT FIRST.
THE REST WILL GIVE YOU FIVE MINUTES, THEN START.
OH, AND MAKE SURE YOU TELL *ME* WHERE YOU'RE GOING TO HIDE AHEAD OF TIME, FOR THE SAKE OF FAIRNESS.

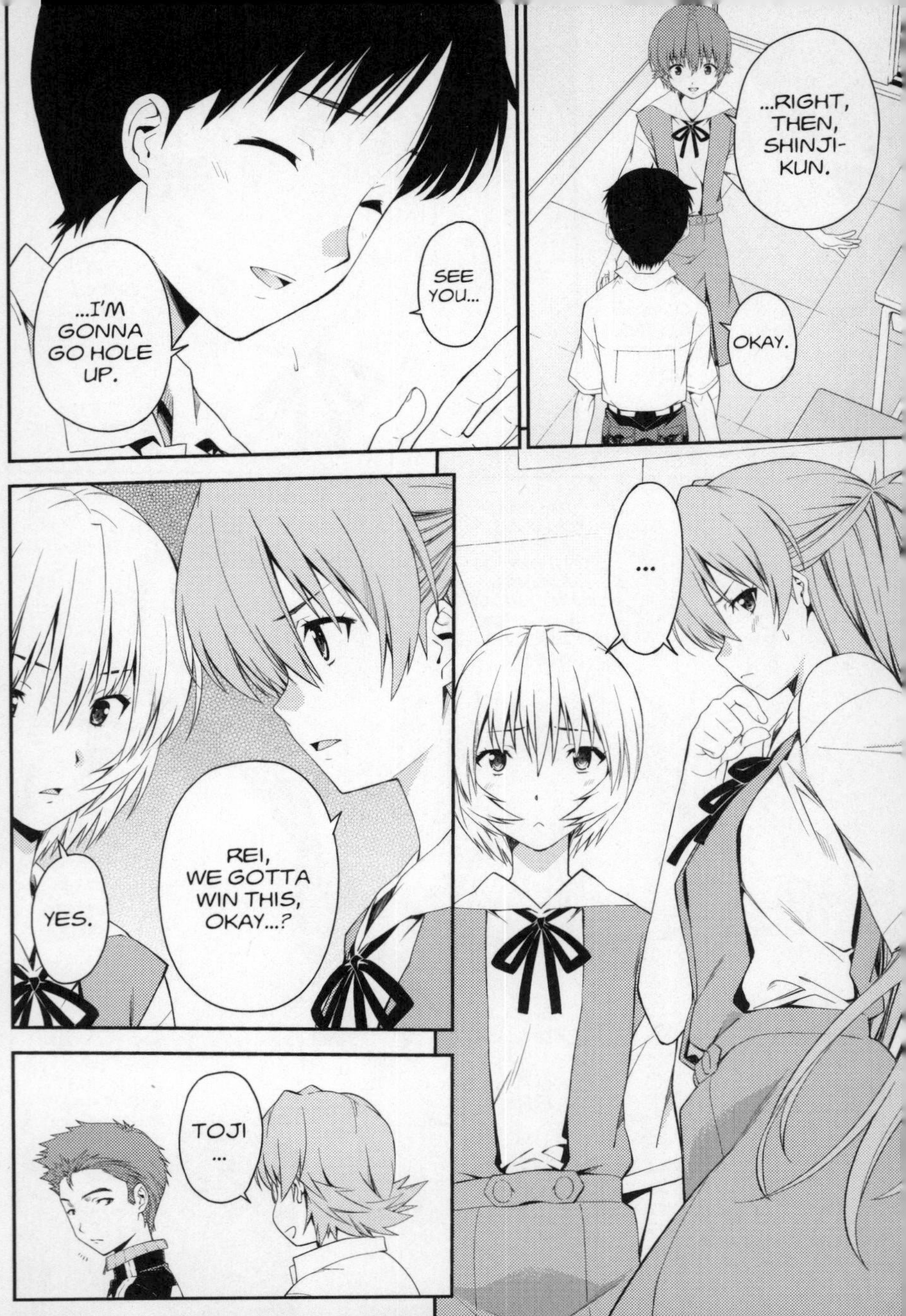
...RIGHT, THEN, SHINJI-KUN.
OKAY.
SEE YOU...
...I'M GONNA GO HOLE UP.
...
REI, WE GOTTA WIN THIS, OKAY...?
YES.
TOJI ...

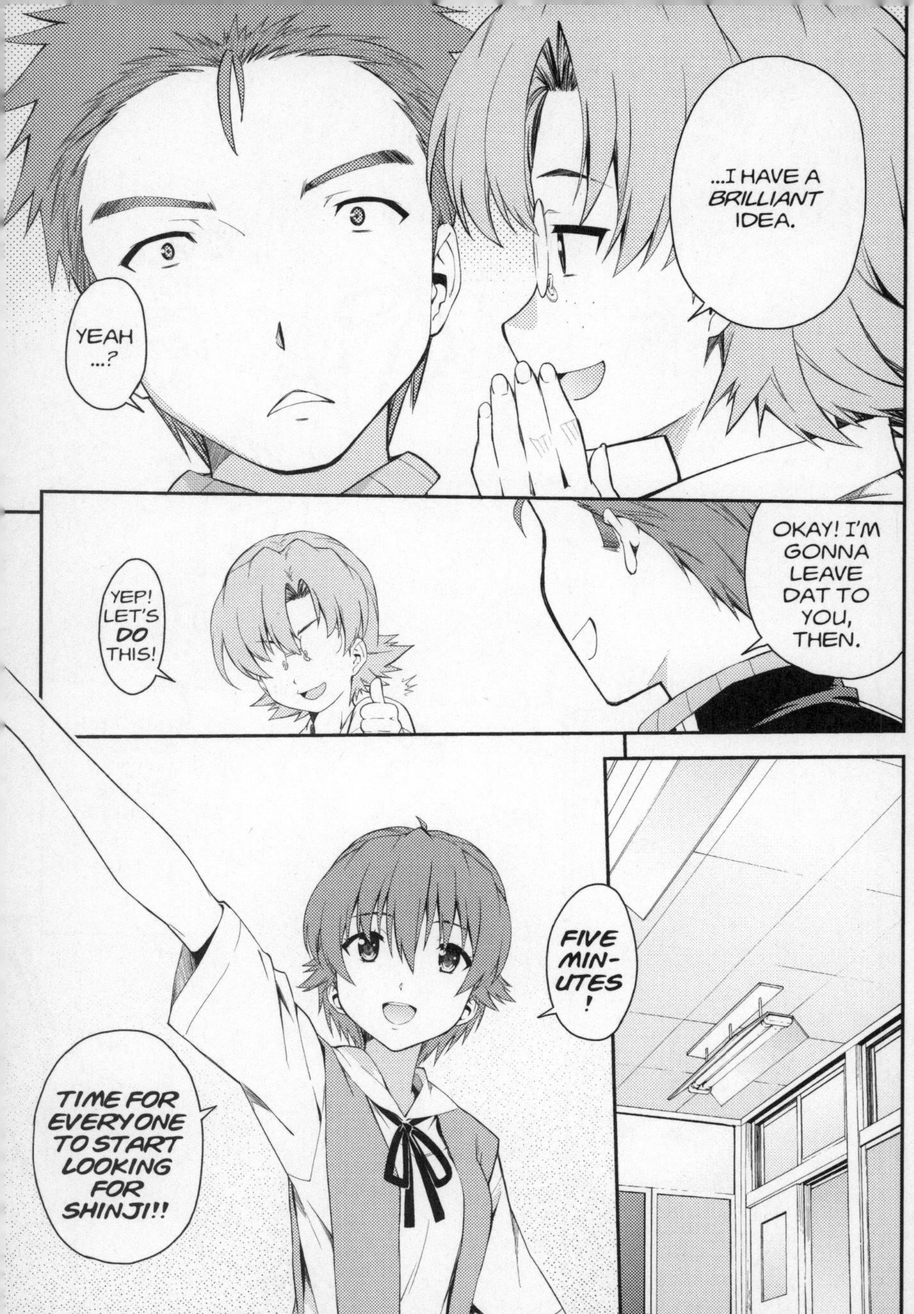
...I HAVE A BRILLIANT IDEA.
YEAH ...?
OKAY! I'M GONNA LEAVE DAT TO YOU, THEN.
YEP! LET'S DO THIS!
FIVE MIN-UTES!
TIME FOR EVERYONE TO START LOOKING FOR SHINJI!!

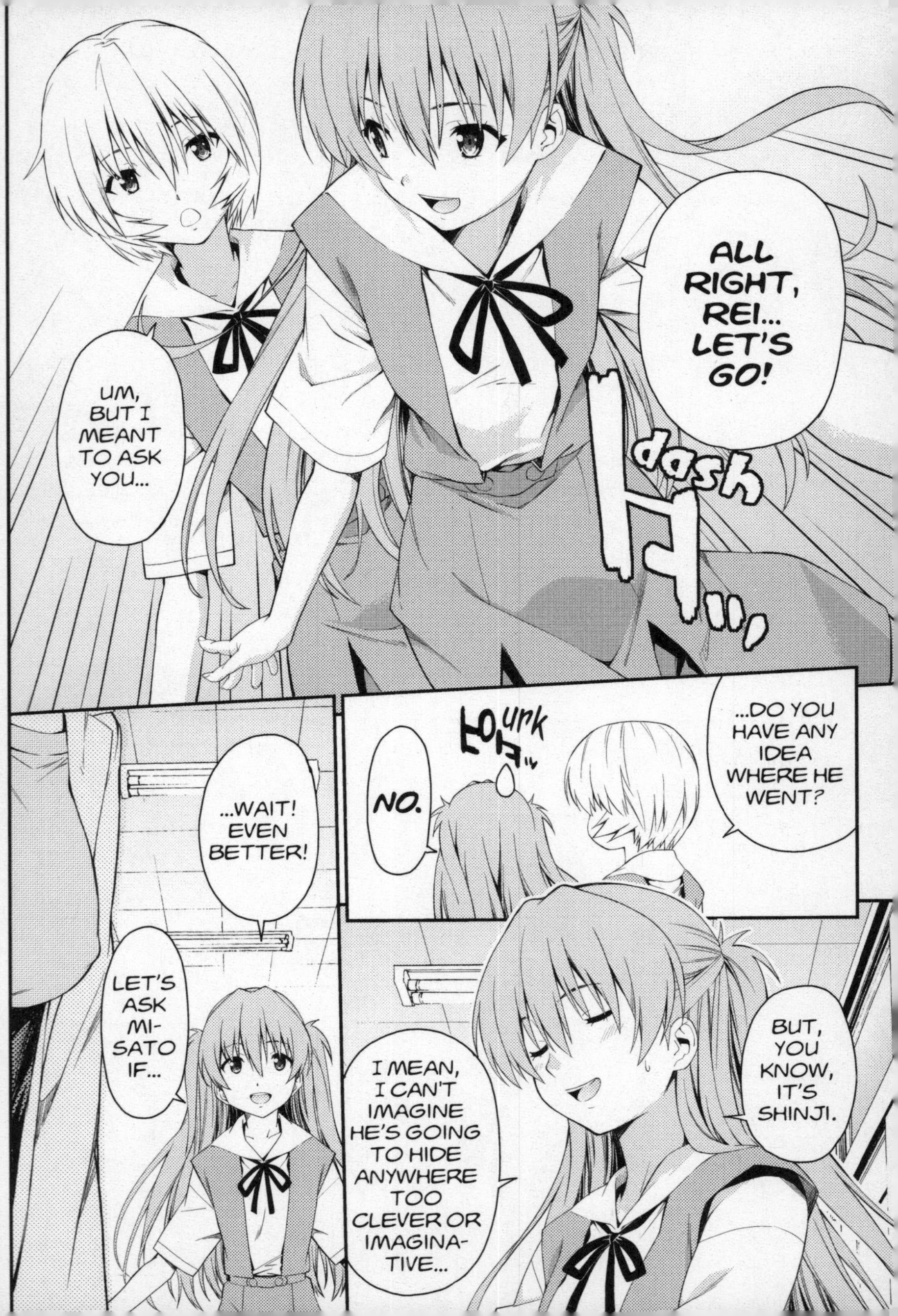
ALL RIGHT, REI... LET'S GO!
dash
UM, BUT I MEANT TO ASK YOU...
...DO YOU HAVE ANY IDEA WHERE HE WENT?
urk
NO.
BUT, YOU KNOW, IT'S SHINJI.
I MEAN, I CAN'T IMAGINE HE'S GOING TO HIDE ANYWHERE TOO CLEVER OR IMAGINA-TIVE...
...WAIT! EVEN BETTER!
LET'S ASK MI-SATO IF...

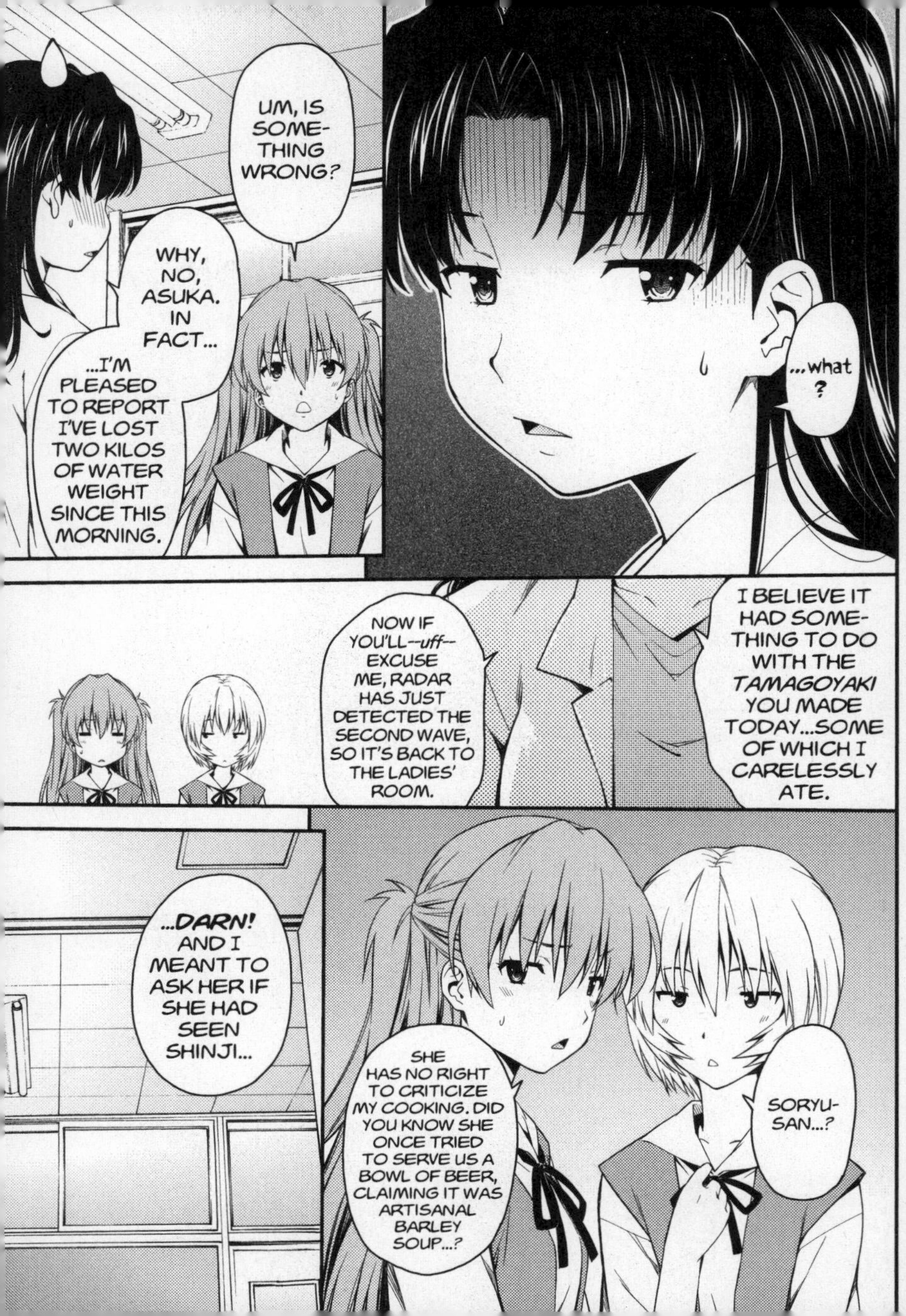
...what?
UM, IS SOMETHING WRONG?
WHY, NO, ASUKA. IN FACT...
...I'M PLEASED TO REPORT I'VE LOST TWO KILOS OF WATER WEIGHT SINCE THIS MORNING.
I BELIEVE IT HAD SOMETHING TO DO WITH THE *TAMAGOYAKI* YOU MADE TODAY...SOME OF WHICH I CARELESSLY ATE.
NOW IF YOU'LL--*uff*--EXCUSE ME, RADAR HAS JUST DETECTED THE SECOND WAVE, SO IT'S BACK TO THE LADIES' ROOM.
SHE HAS NO RIGHT TO CRITICIZE MY COOKING. DID YOU KNOW SHE ONCE TRIED TO SERVE US A BOWL OF BEER, CLAIMING IT WAS ARTISANAL BARLEY SOUP...?
SORYU-SAN...?
...**DARN!** AND I MEANT TO ASK HER IF SHE HAD SEEN SHINJI...

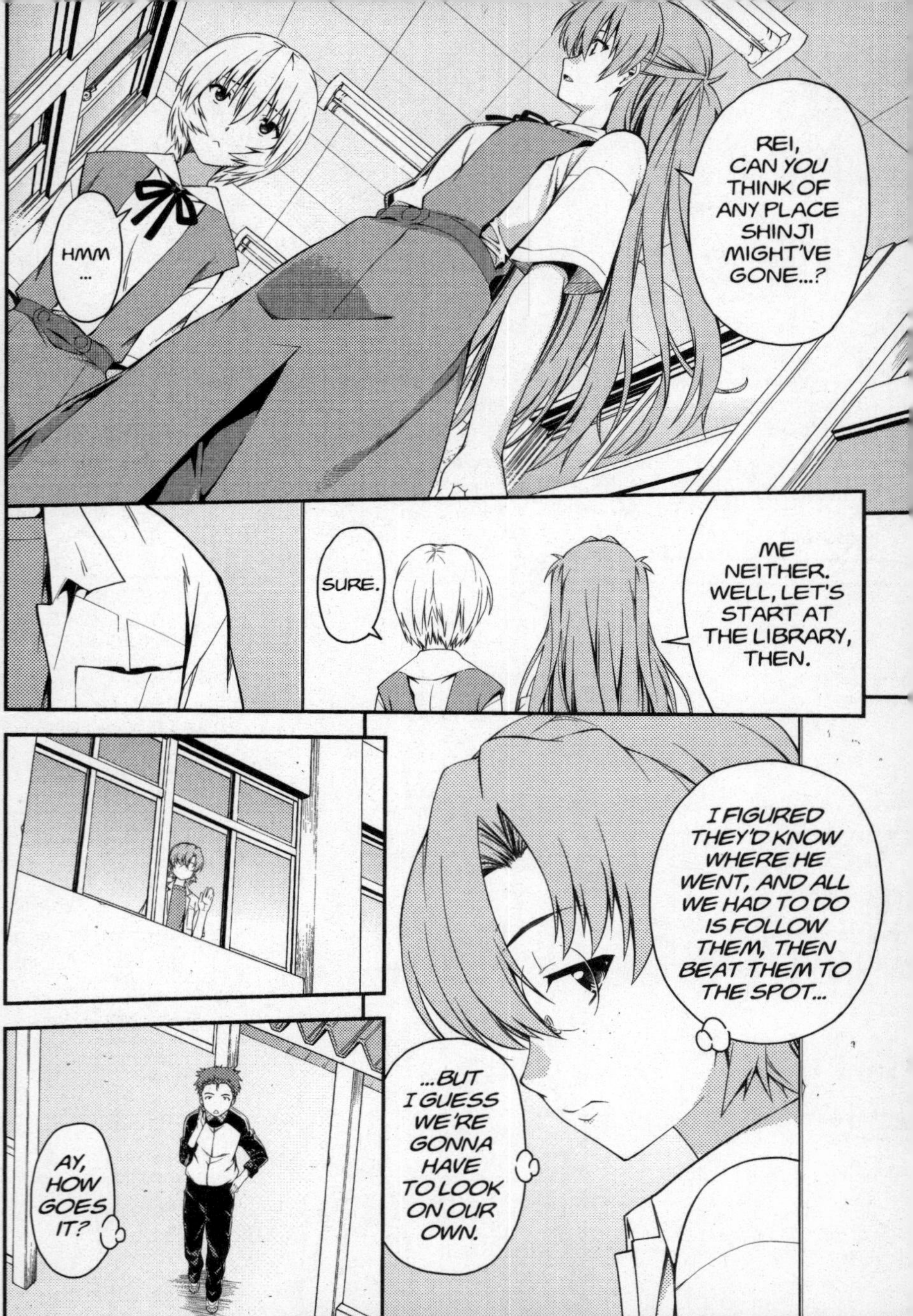
REI, CAN YOU THINK OF ANY PLACE SHINJI MIGHT'VE GONE...?
HMM ...
ME NEITHER. WELL, LET'S START AT THE LIBRARY, THEN.
SURE.
I FIGURED THEY'D KNOW WHERE HE WENT, AND ALL WE HAD TO DO IS FOLLOW THEM, THEN BEAT THEM TO THE SPOT...
...BUT I GUESS WE'RE GONNA HAVE TO LOOK ON OUR OWN.
AY, HOW GOES IT?

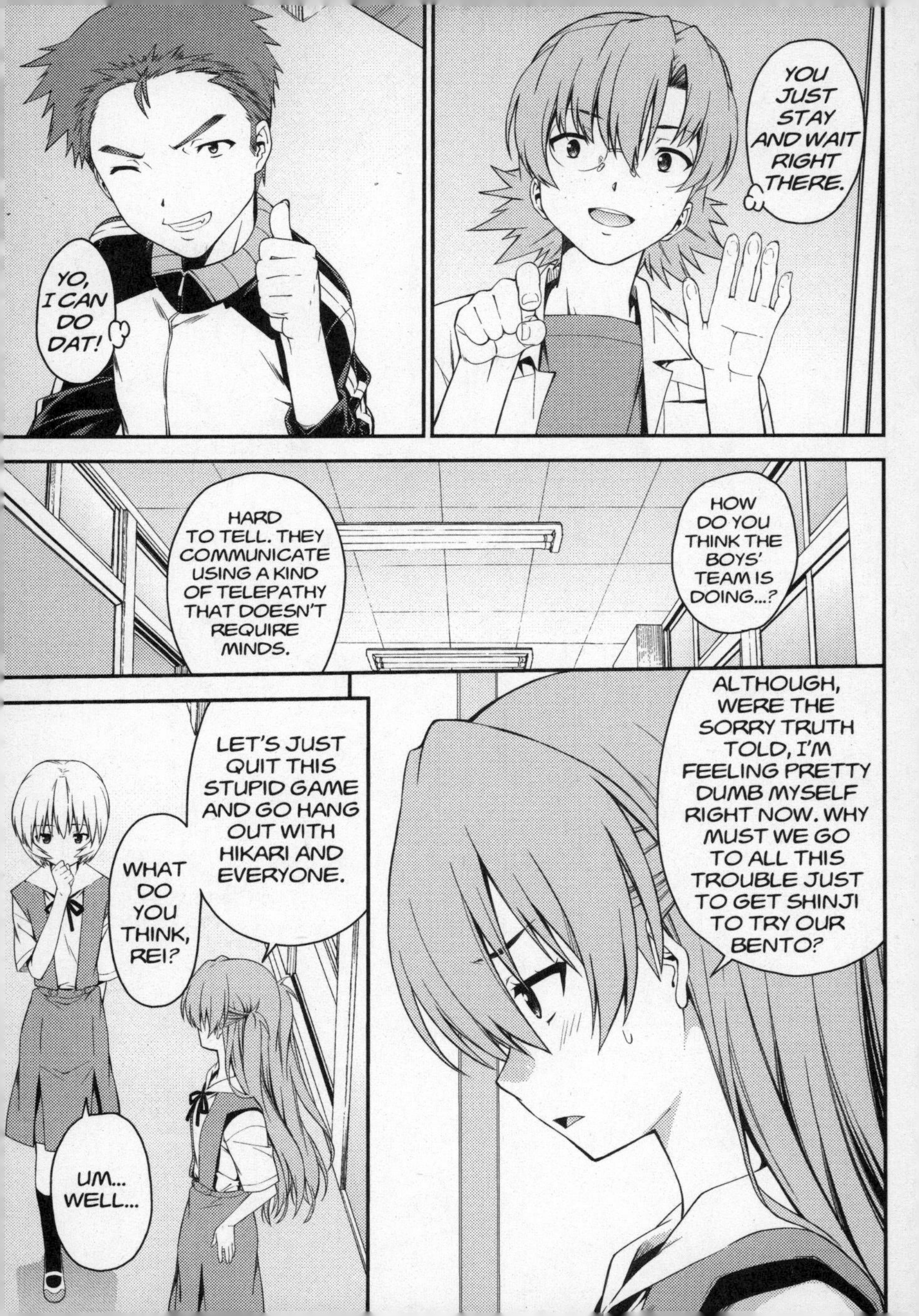
YOU JUST STAY AND WAIT RIGHT THERE.
YO, I CAN DO DAT!
HOW DO YOU THINK THE BOYS' TEAM IS DOING...?
HARD TO TELL. THEY COMMUNICATE USING A KIND OF TELEPATHY THAT DOESN'T REQUIRE MINDS.
ALTHOUGH, WERE THE SORRY TRUTH TOLD, I'M FEELING PRETTY DUMB MYSELF RIGHT NOW. WHY MUST WE GO TO ALL THIS TROUBLE JUST TO GET SHINJI TO TRY OUR BENTO?
LET'S JUST QUIT THIS STUPID GAME AND GO HANG OUT WITH HIKARI AND EVERYONE.
WHAT DO YOU THINK, REI?
UM... WELL...

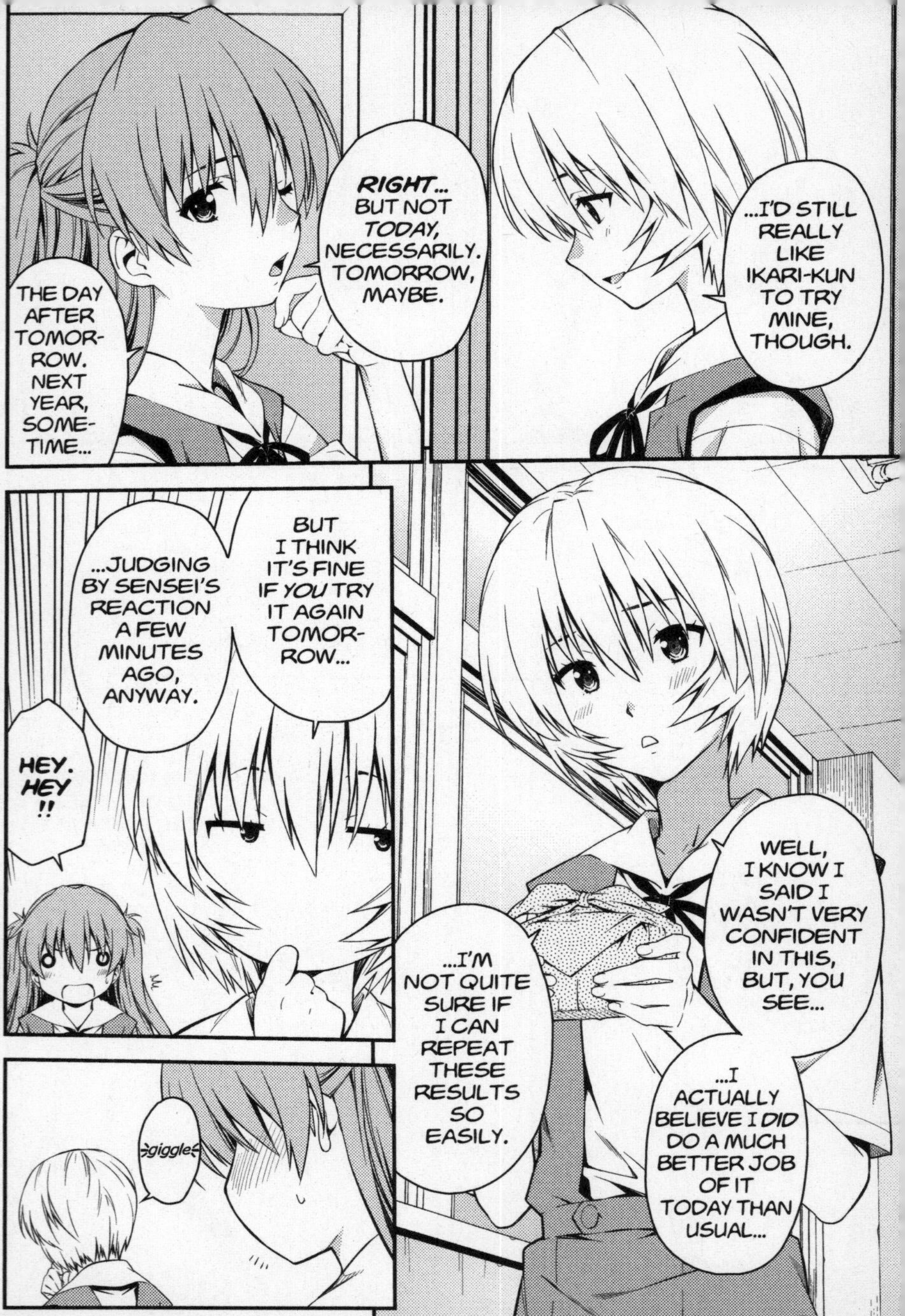
...I'D STILL REALLY LIKE IKARI-KUN TO TRY MINE, THOUGH.
RIGHT... BUT NOT TODAY, NECESSARILY. TOMORROW, MAYBE.
THE DAY AFTER TOMORROW. NEXT YEAR, SOMETIME...
WELL, I KNOW I SAID I WASN'T VERY CONFIDENT IN THIS, BUT, YOU SEE...
...I ACTUALLY BELIEVE I DID DO A MUCH BETTER JOB OF IT TODAY THAN USUAL...
...I'M NOT QUITE SURE IF I CAN REPEAT THESE RESULTS SO EASILY.
BUT I THINK IT'S FINE IF YOU TRY IT AGAIN TOMORROW...
...JUDGING BY SENSEI'S REACTION A FEW MINUTES AGO, ANYWAY.
HEY. HEY!!
giggle

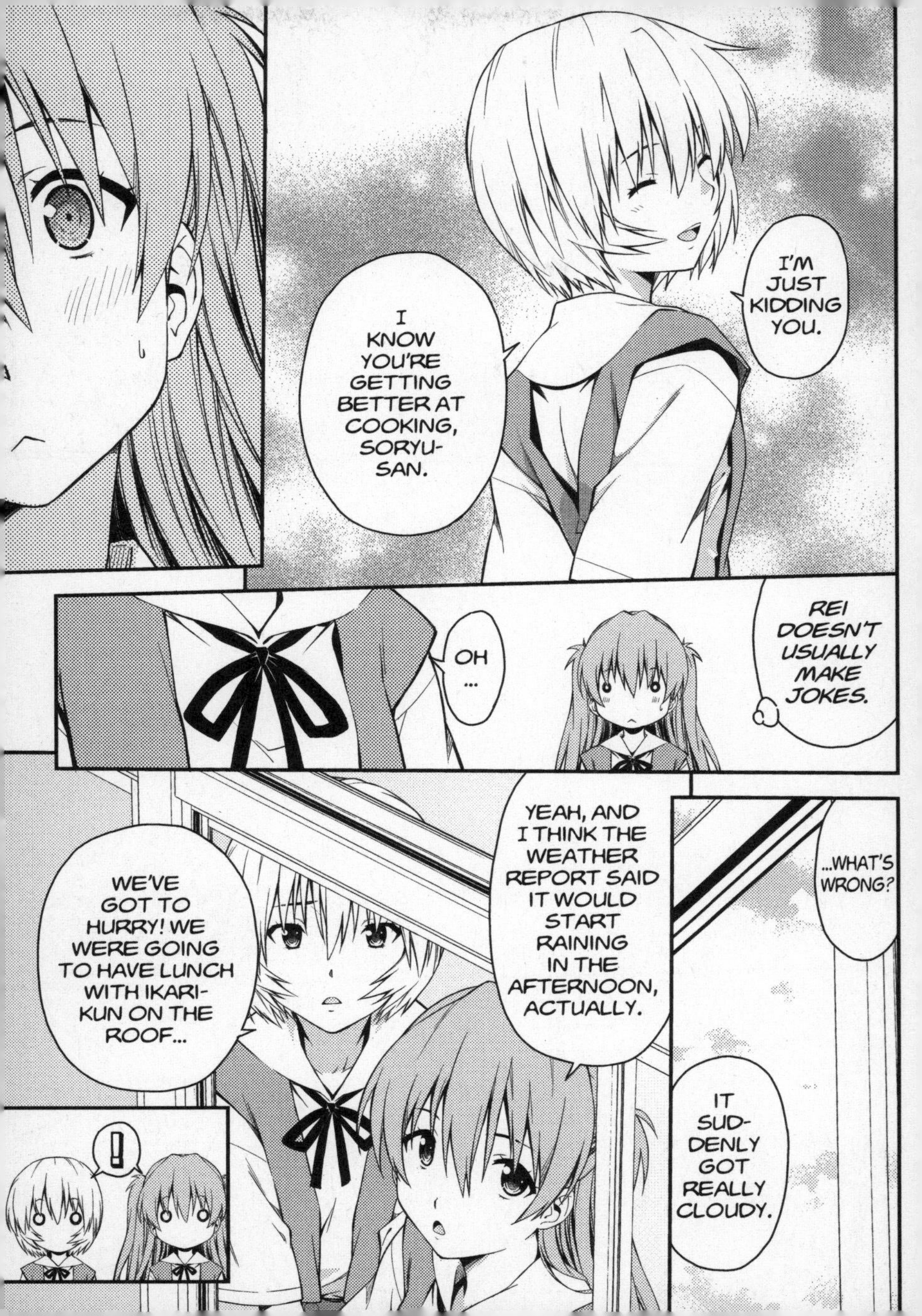
I'M JUST KIDDING YOU.
I KNOW YOU'RE GETTING BETTER AT COOKING, SORYU-SAN.
REI DOESN'T USUALLY MAKE JOKES.
OH ...
...WHAT'S WRONG?
IT SUD-DENLY GOT REALLY CLOUDY.
YEAH, AND I THINK THE WEATHER REPORT SAID IT WOULD START RAINING IN THE AFTERNOON, ACTUALLY.
WE'VE GOT TO HURRY! WE WERE GOING TO HAVE LUNCH WITH IKARI-KUN ON THE ROOF...
!

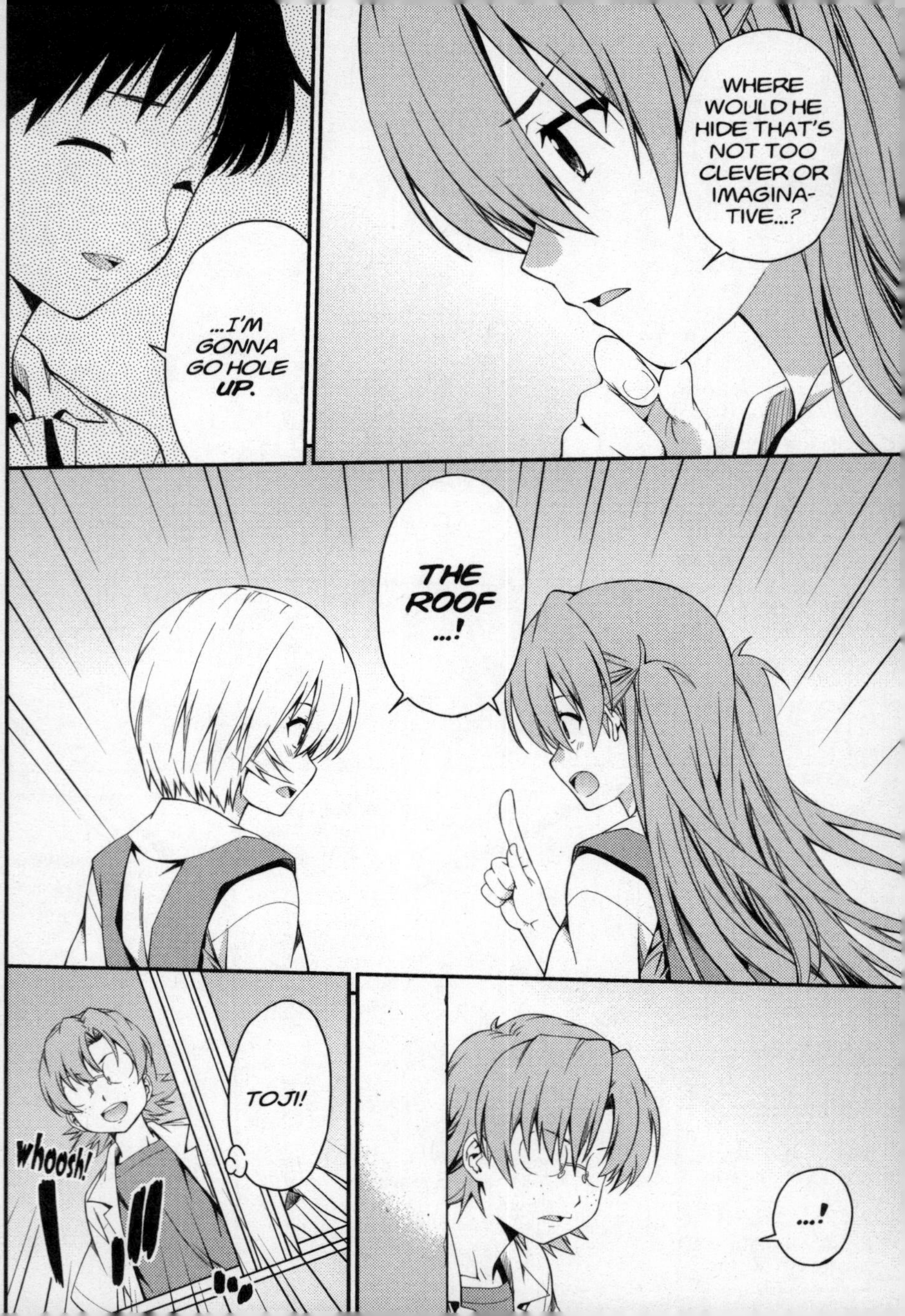
WHERE WOULD HE HIDE THAT'S NOT TOO CLEVER OR IMAGINA-TIVE...?
...I'M GONNA GO HOLE UP.
THE ROOF ...!
...!
TOJI!
whoosh!

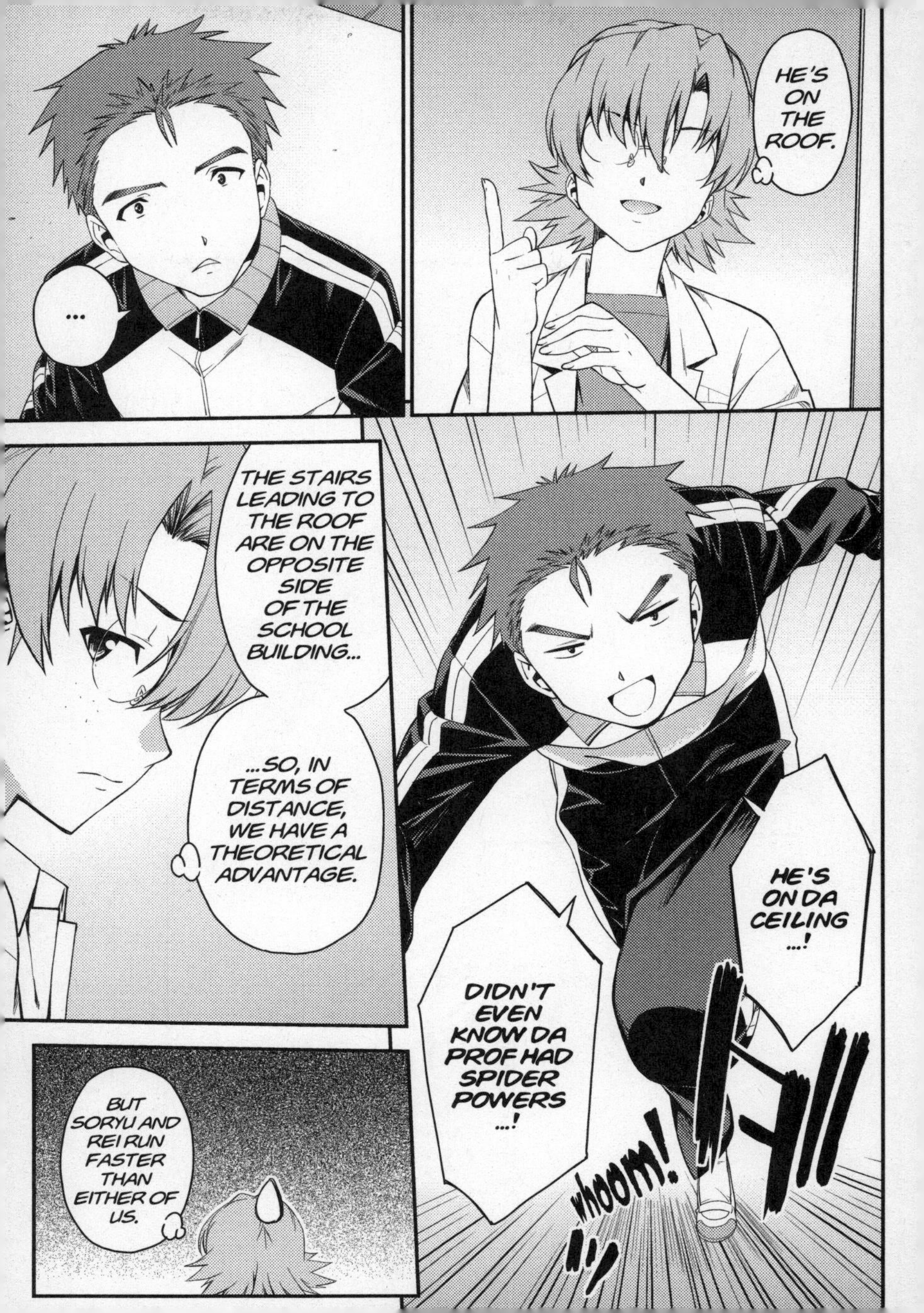
HE'S ON THE ROOF.
...
HE'S ON DA CEILING ...!
DIDN'T EVEN KNOW DA PROF HAD SPIDER POWERS ...!
whoom!!
THE STAIRS LEADING TO THE ROOF ARE ON THE OPPOSITE SIDE OF THE SCHOOL BUILDING...
...SO, IN TERMS OF DISTANCE, WE HAVE A THEORETICAL ADVANTAGE.
BUT SORYU AND REI RUN FASTER THAN EITHER OF US.

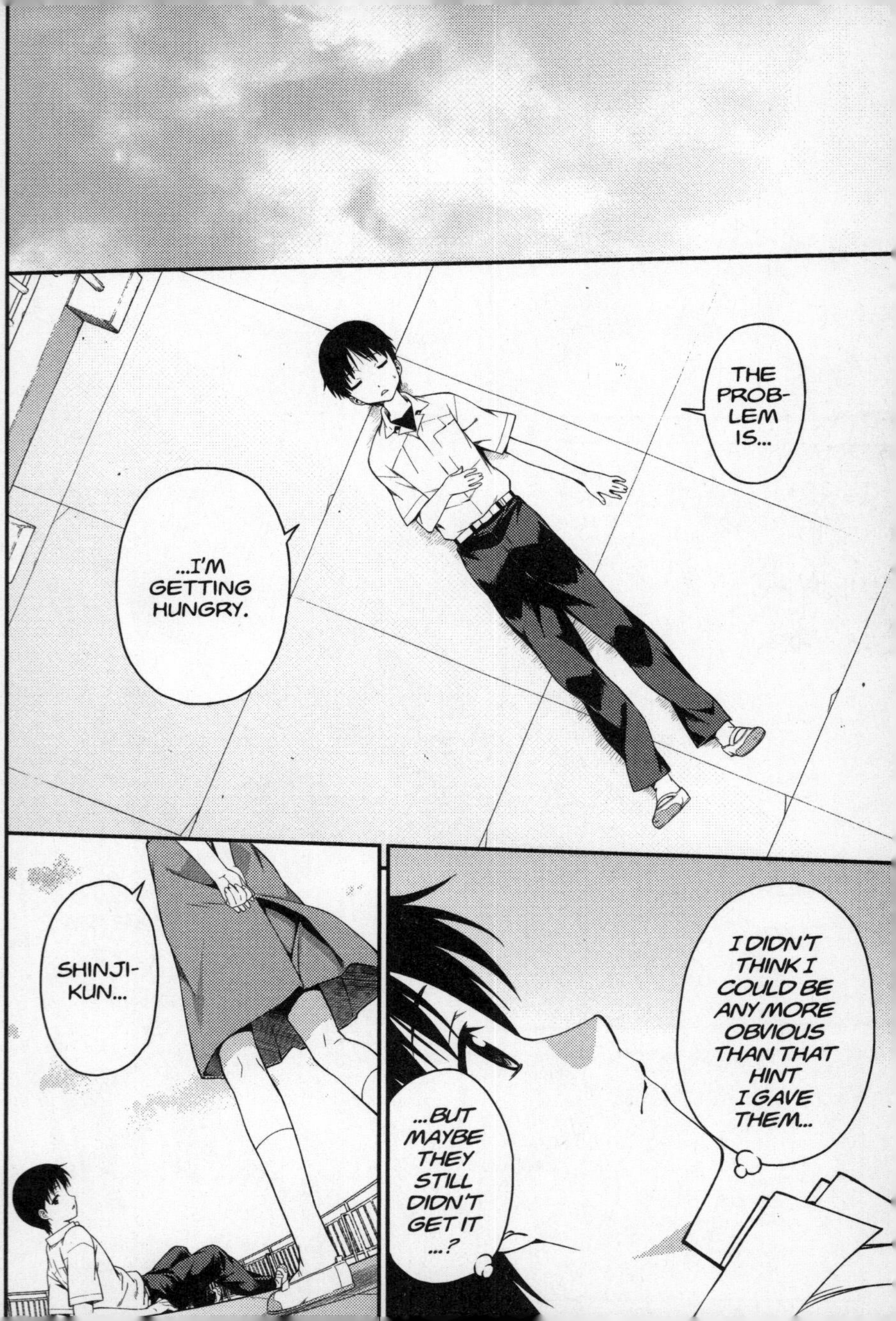
THE PROB-LEM IS...
...I'M GETTING HUNGRY.
I DIDN'T THINK I COULD BE ANY MORE OBVIOUS THAN THAT HINT I GAVE THEM...
...BUT MAYBE THEY STILL DIDN'T GET IT ...?
SHINJI-KUN...

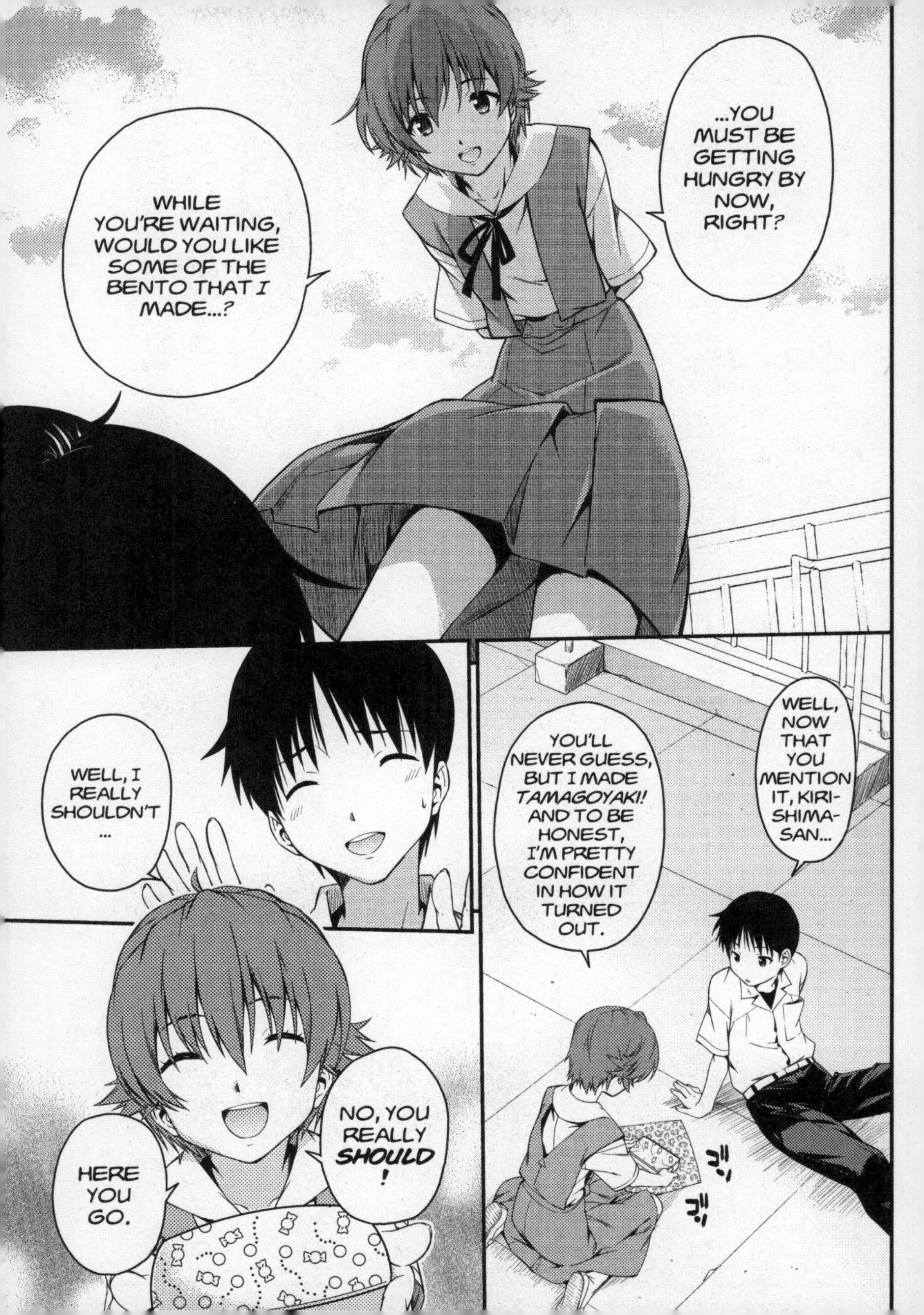
...YOU MUST BE GETTING HUNGRY BY NOW, RIGHT?
WHILE YOU'RE WAITING, WOULD YOU LIKE SOME OF THE BENTO THAT *I* MADE...?
WELL, NOW THAT YOU MENTION IT, KIRI-SHIMA-SAN...
YOU'LL NEVER GUESS, BUT I MADE *TAMAGOYAKI!* AND TO BE HONEST, I'M PRETTY CONFIDENT IN HOW IT TURNED OUT.
WELL, I REALLY SHOULDN'T ...
NO, YOU REALLY ***SHOULD***!
HERE YOU GO.

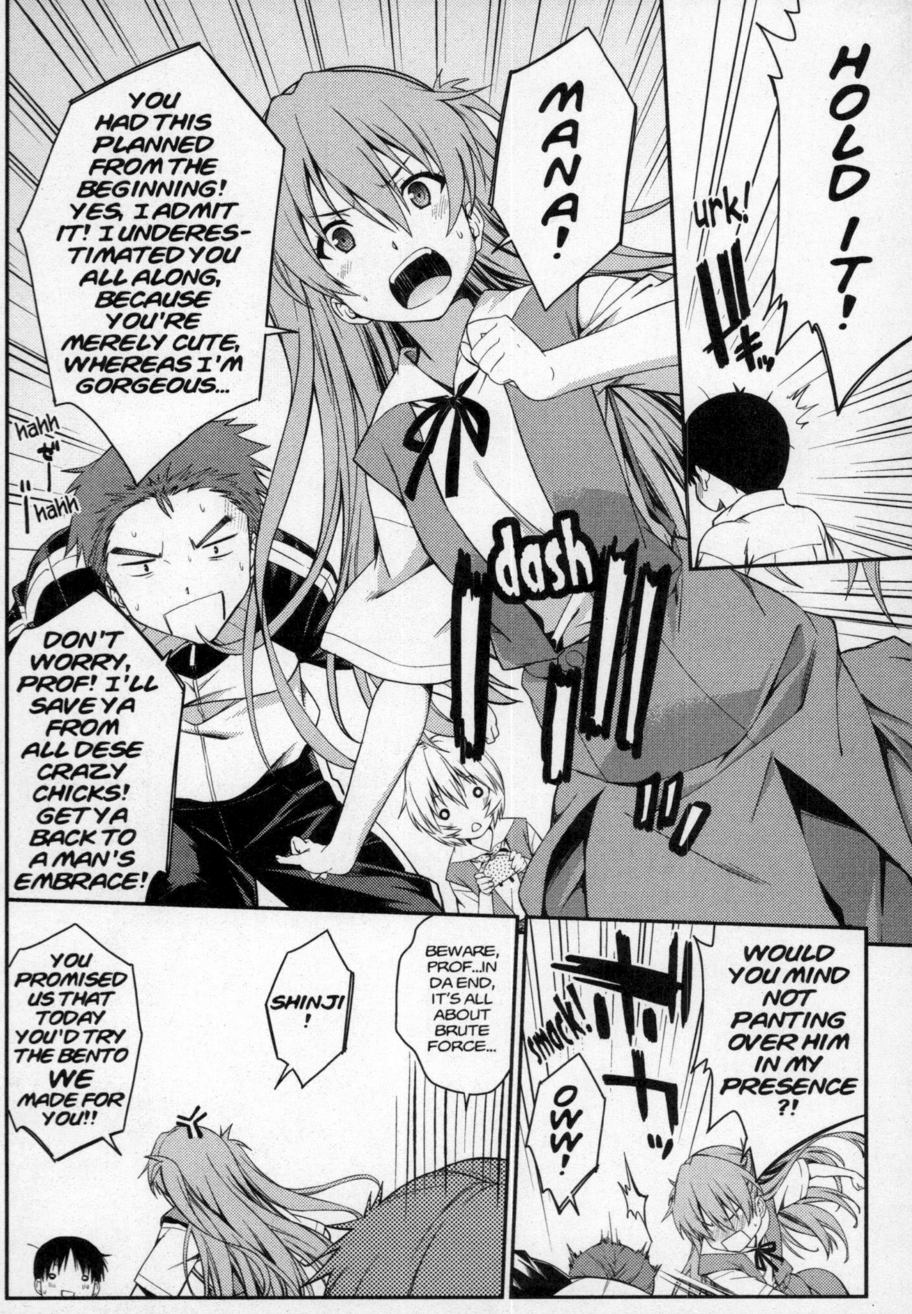
HOLD IT!
urk!
MANA!
YOU HAD THIS PLANNED FROM THE BEGINNING! YES, I ADMIT IT! I UNDERES-TIMATED YOU ALL ALONG, BECAUSE YOU'RE MERELY CUTE, WHEREAS I'M GORGEOUS...
hahh
hahh
dash
DON'T WORRY, PROF! I'LL SAVE YA FROM ALL DESE CRAZY CHICKS! GET YA BACK TO A MAN'S EMBRACE!
WOULD YOU MIND NOT PANTING OVER HIM IN MY PRESENCE?!
smack!
OWW!
BEWARE, PROF...IN DA END, IT'S ALL ABOUT BRUTE FORCE...
SHINJI!
YOU PROMISED US THAT TODAY YOU'D TRY THE BENTO WE MADE FOR YOU!!

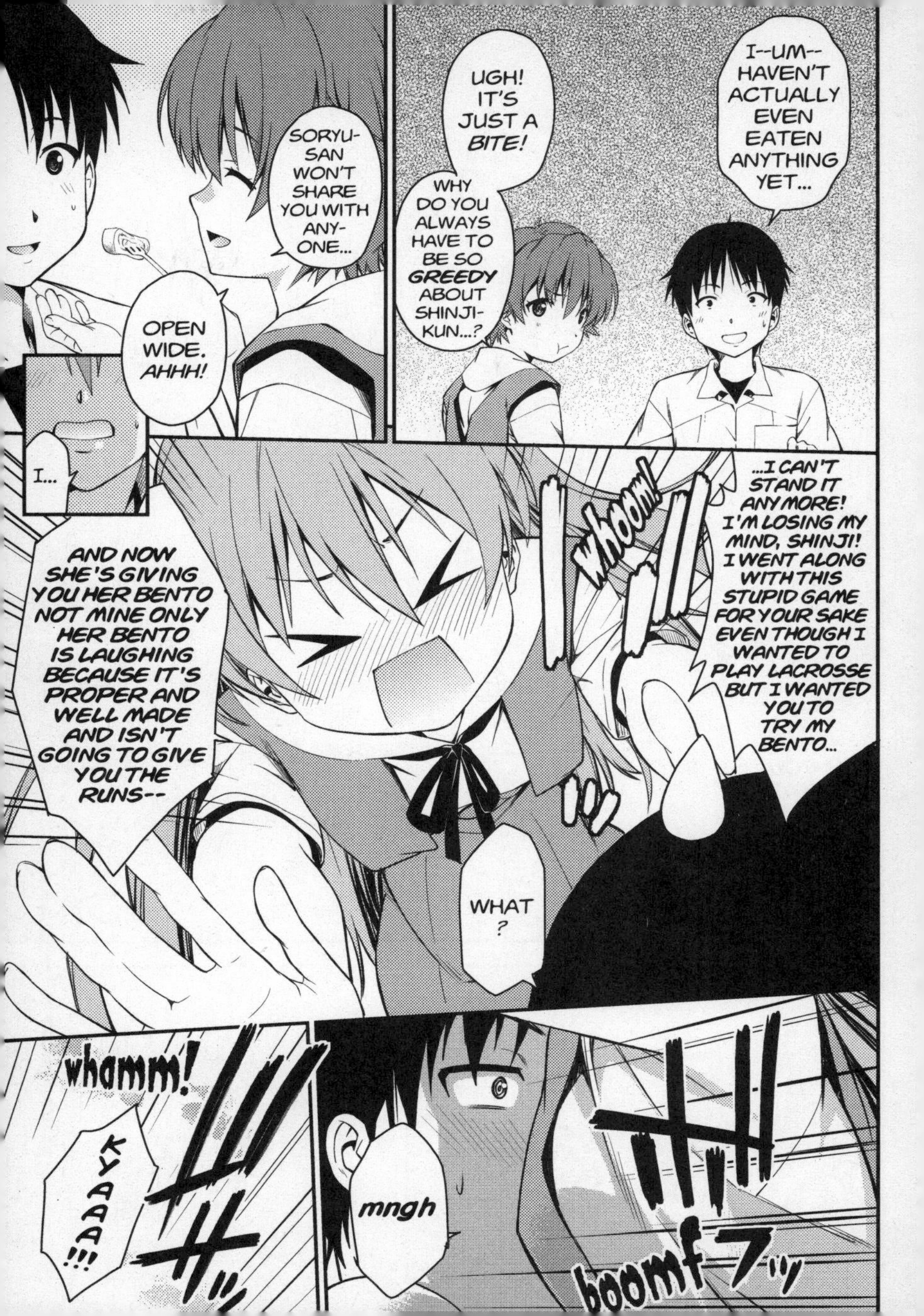
I--UM-- HAVEN'T ACTUALLY EVEN EATEN ANYTHING YET...
UGH! IT'S JUST A *BITE!*
WHY DO YOU ALWAYS HAVE TO BE SO **GREEDY** ABOUT SHINJI-KUN...?
SORYU-SAN WON'T SHARE YOU WITH ANY-ONE...
OPEN WIDE. *AHHH!*
I...
...I CAN'T STAND IT ANYMORE! I'M LOSING MY MIND, SHINJI! I WENT ALONG WITH THIS STUPID GAME FOR YOUR SAKE EVEN THOUGH I WANTED TO PLAY LACROSSE BUT I WANTED YOU TO TRY MY BENTO...
whoom!
AND NOW SHE'S GIVING YOU HER BENTO NOT MINE ONLY HER BENTO IS LAUGHING BECAUSE IT'S PROPER AND WELL MADE AND ISN'T GOING TO GIVE YOU THE RUNS--
WHAT?
boomf
mngh
whamm!
KYAAAA!!!

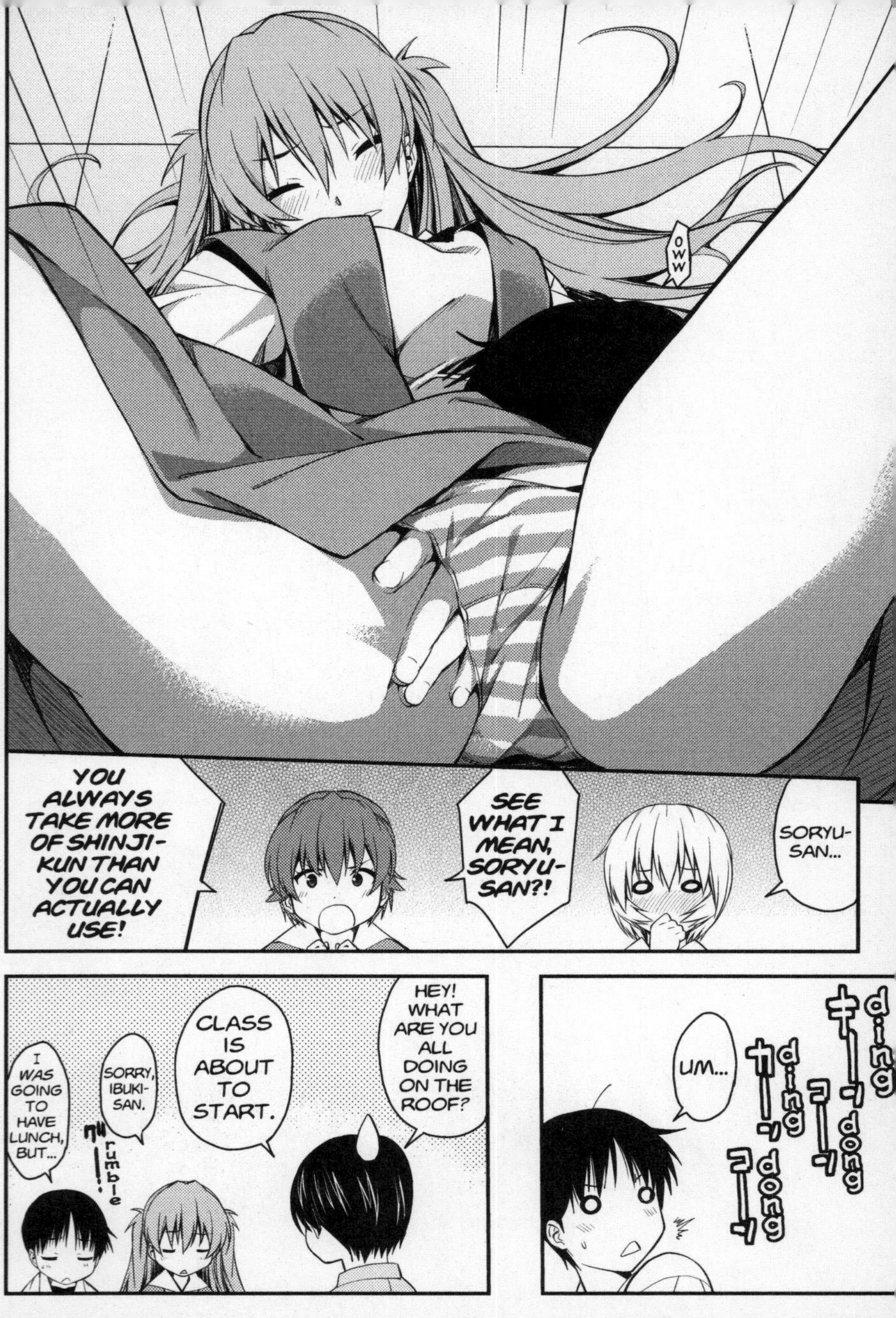
OWW
SORYU-SAN...
SEE WHAT I MEAN, SORYU-SAN?!
YOU ALWAYS TAKE MORE OF SHINJI-KUN THAN YOU CAN ACTUALLY USE!
ding dong ding dong
UM...
HEY! WHAT ARE YOU ALL DOING ON THE ROOF?
CLASS IS ABOUT TO START.
SORRY, IBUKI-SAN.
I WAS GOING TO HAVE LUNCH, BUT...
rumble

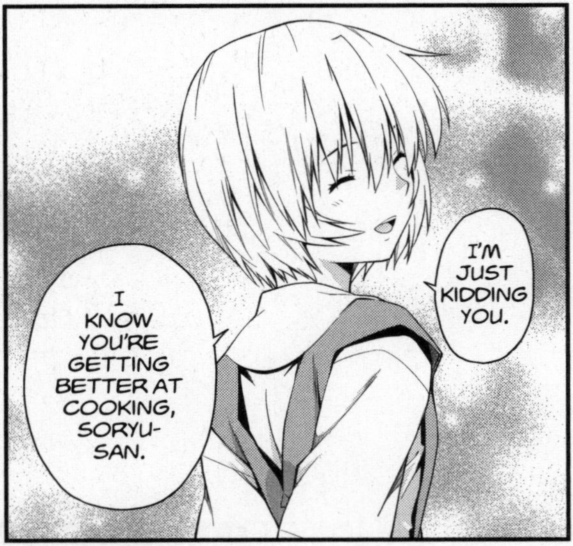
I'M JUST KIDDING YOU.
I KNOW YOU'RE GETTING BETTER AT COOKING, SORYU-SAN.

NEON GENESIS
EVANGELION
THE SHINJI IKARI RAISING PROJECT

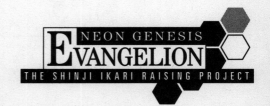

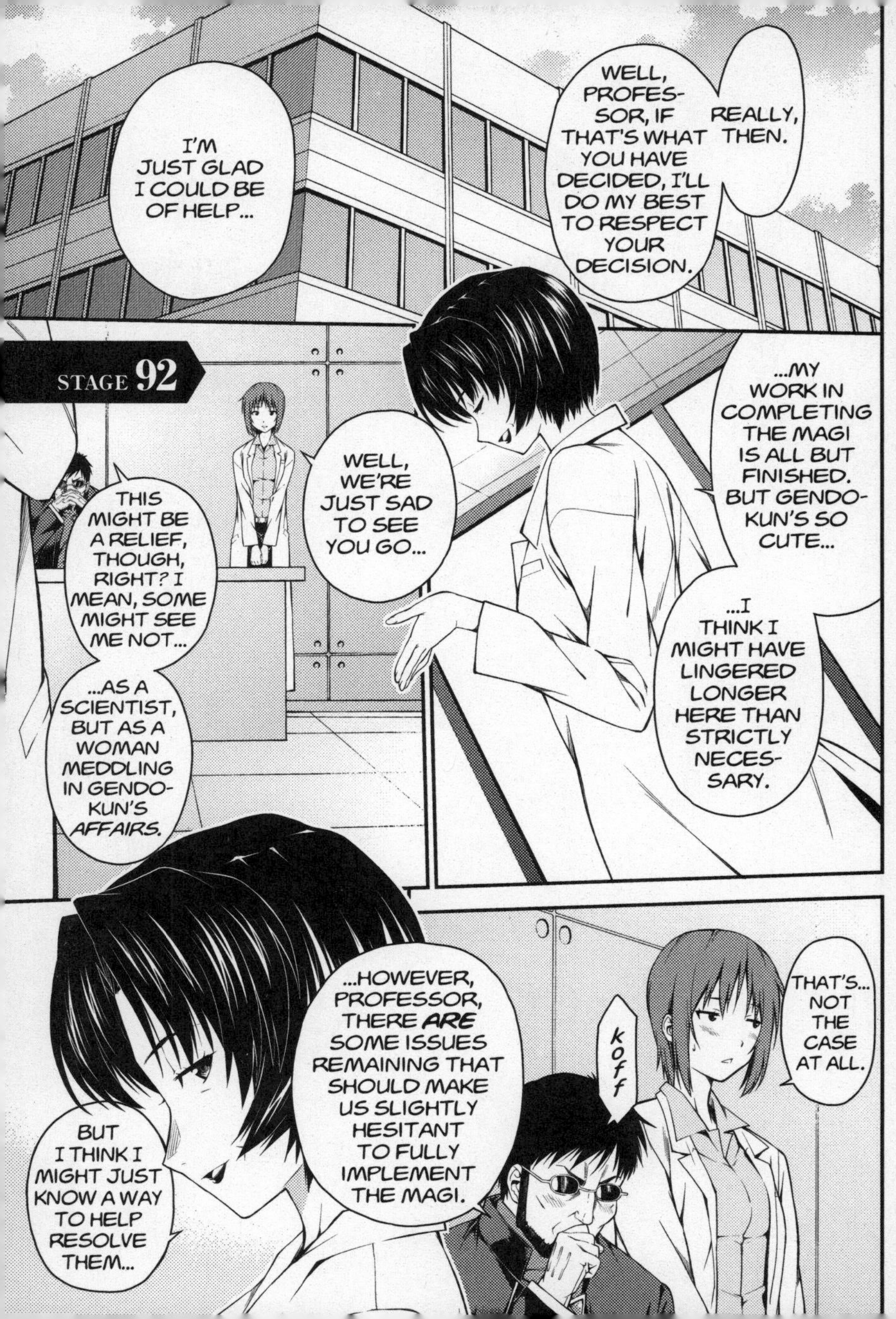
REALLY, THEN.
WELL, PROFESSOR, IF THAT'S WHAT YOU HAVE DECIDED, I'LL DO MY BEST TO RESPECT YOUR DECISION.
I'M JUST GLAD I COULD BE OF HELP...
STAGE 92
...MY WORK IN COMPLETING THE MAGI IS ALL BUT FINISHED. BUT GENDO-KUN'S SO CUTE...
...I THINK I MIGHT HAVE LINGERED LONGER HERE THAN STRICTLY NECESSARY.
WELL, WE'RE JUST SAD TO SEE YOU GO...
THIS MIGHT BE A RELIEF, THOUGH, RIGHT? I MEAN, SOME MIGHT SEE ME NOT...
...AS A SCIENTIST, BUT AS A WOMAN MEDDLING IN GENDO-KUN'S *AFFAIRS.*
THAT'S... NOT THE CASE AT ALL.
koff
...HOWEVER, PROFESSOR, THERE ***ARE*** SOME ISSUES REMAINING THAT SHOULD MAKE US SLIGHTLY HESITANT TO FULLY IMPLEMENT THE MAGI.
BUT I THINK I MIGHT JUST KNOW A WAY TO HELP RESOLVE THEM...

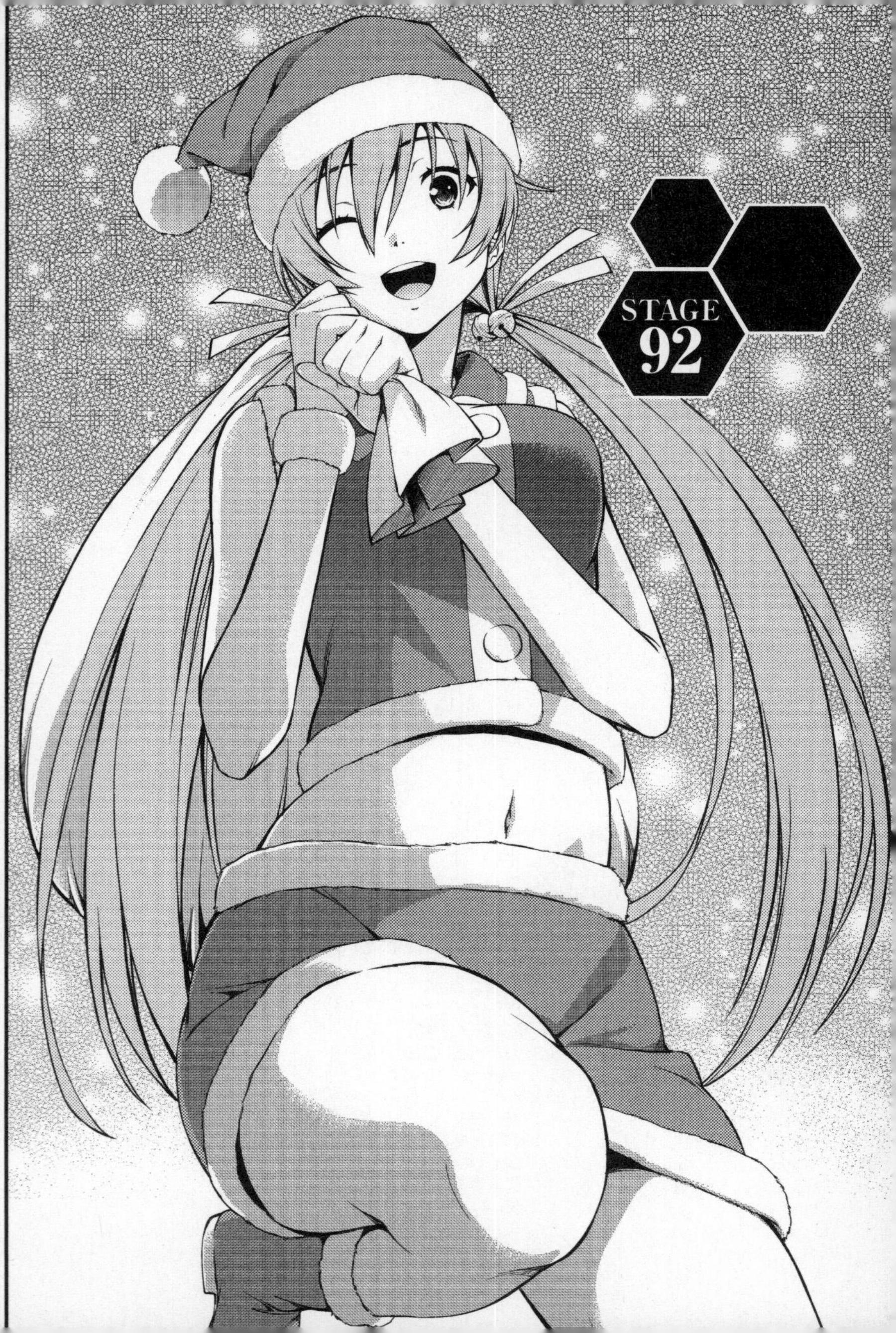
STAGE
92

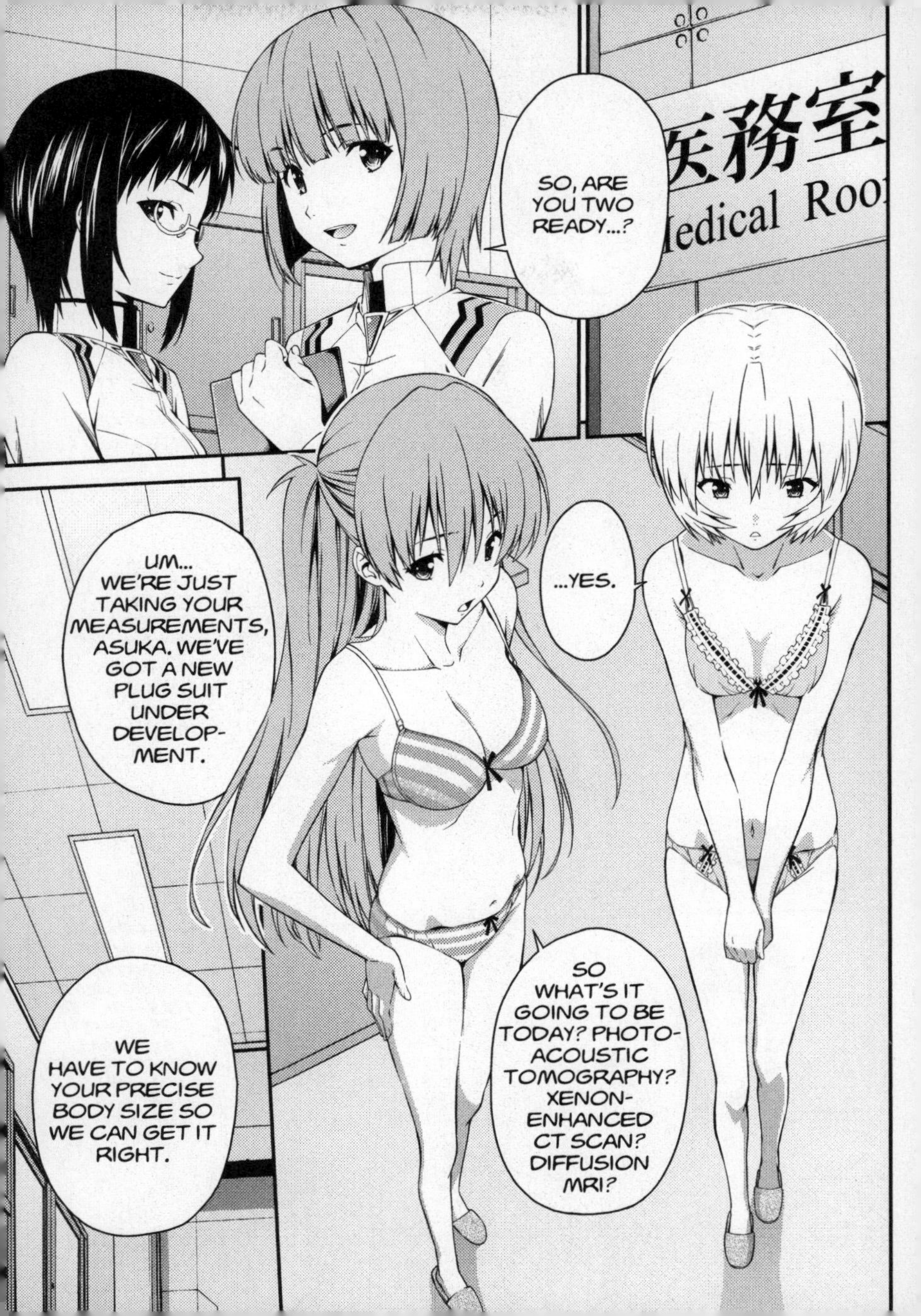

務室
edical Roo
SO, ARE YOU TWO READY...?
...YES.
SO WHAT'S IT GOING TO BE TODAY? PHOTO-ACOUSTIC TOMOGRAPHY? XENON-ENHANCED CT SCAN? DIFFUSION MRI?
UM... WE'RE JUST TAKING YOUR MEASUREMENTS, ASUKA. WE'VE GOT A NEW PLUG SUIT UNDER DEVELOP-MENT.
WE HAVE TO KNOW YOUR PRECISE BODY SIZE SO WE CAN GET IT RIGHT.

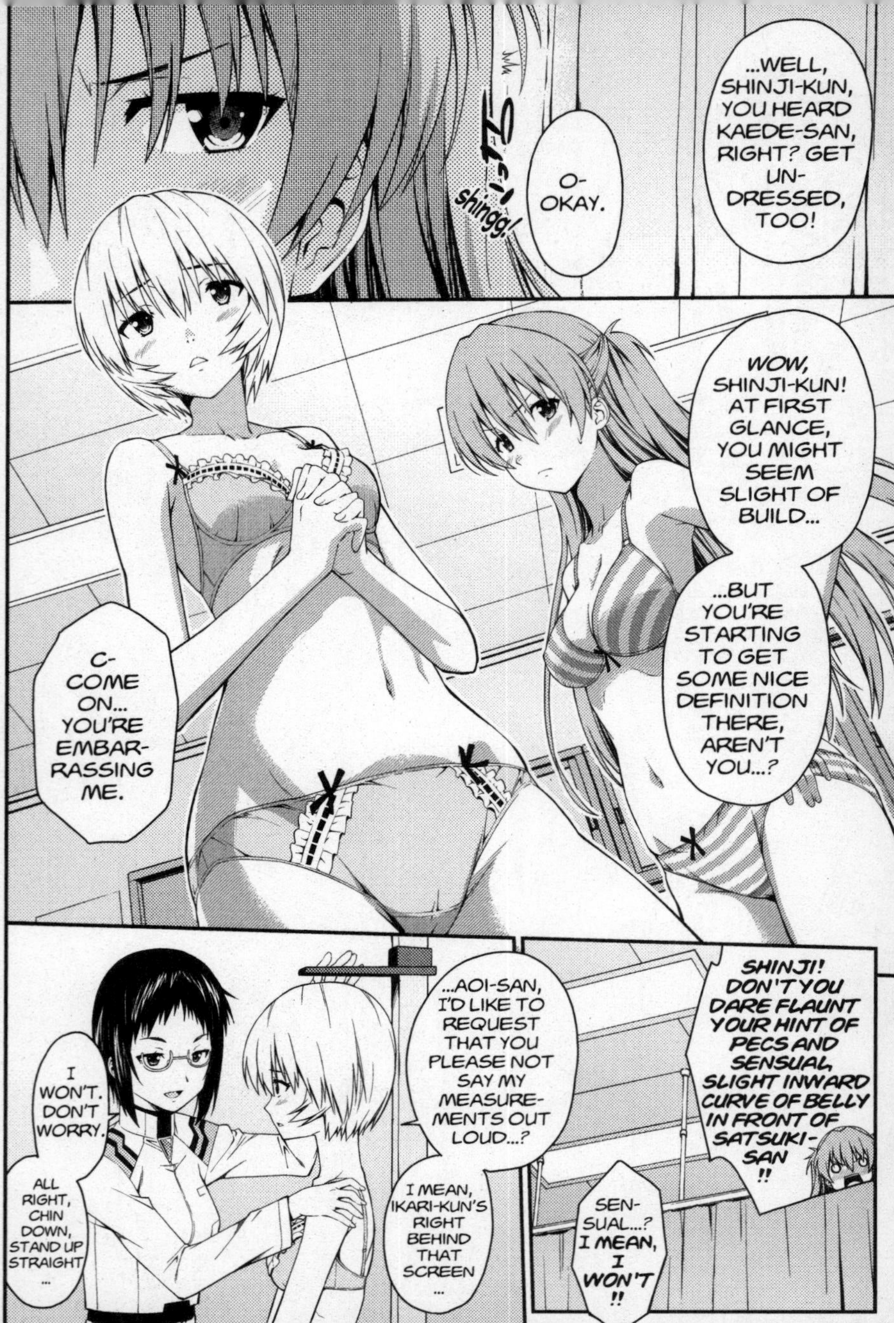
...WELL, SHINJI-KUN, YOU HEARD KAEDE-SAN, RIGHT? GET UN-DRESSED, TOO!
O-OKAY.
shinggg!
WOW, SHINJI-KUN! AT FIRST GLANCE, YOU MIGHT SEEM SLIGHT OF BUILD...
...BUT YOU'RE STARTING TO GET SOME NICE DEFINITION THERE, AREN'T YOU...?
C-COME ON... YOU'RE EMBARRASSING ME.
SHINJI! DON'T YOU DARE FLAUNT YOUR HINT OF PECS AND SENSUAL, SLIGHT INWARD CURVE OF BELLY IN FRONT OF SATSUKI-SAN!!
SEN-SUAL...? I MEAN, I WON'T!!
...AOI-SAN, I'D LIKE TO REQUEST THAT YOU PLEASE NOT SAY MY MEASUREMENTS OUT LOUD...?
I WON'T. DON'T WORRY.
I MEAN, IKARI-KUN'S RIGHT BEHIND THAT SCREEN...
ALL RIGHT, CHIN DOWN, STAND UP STRAIGHT...

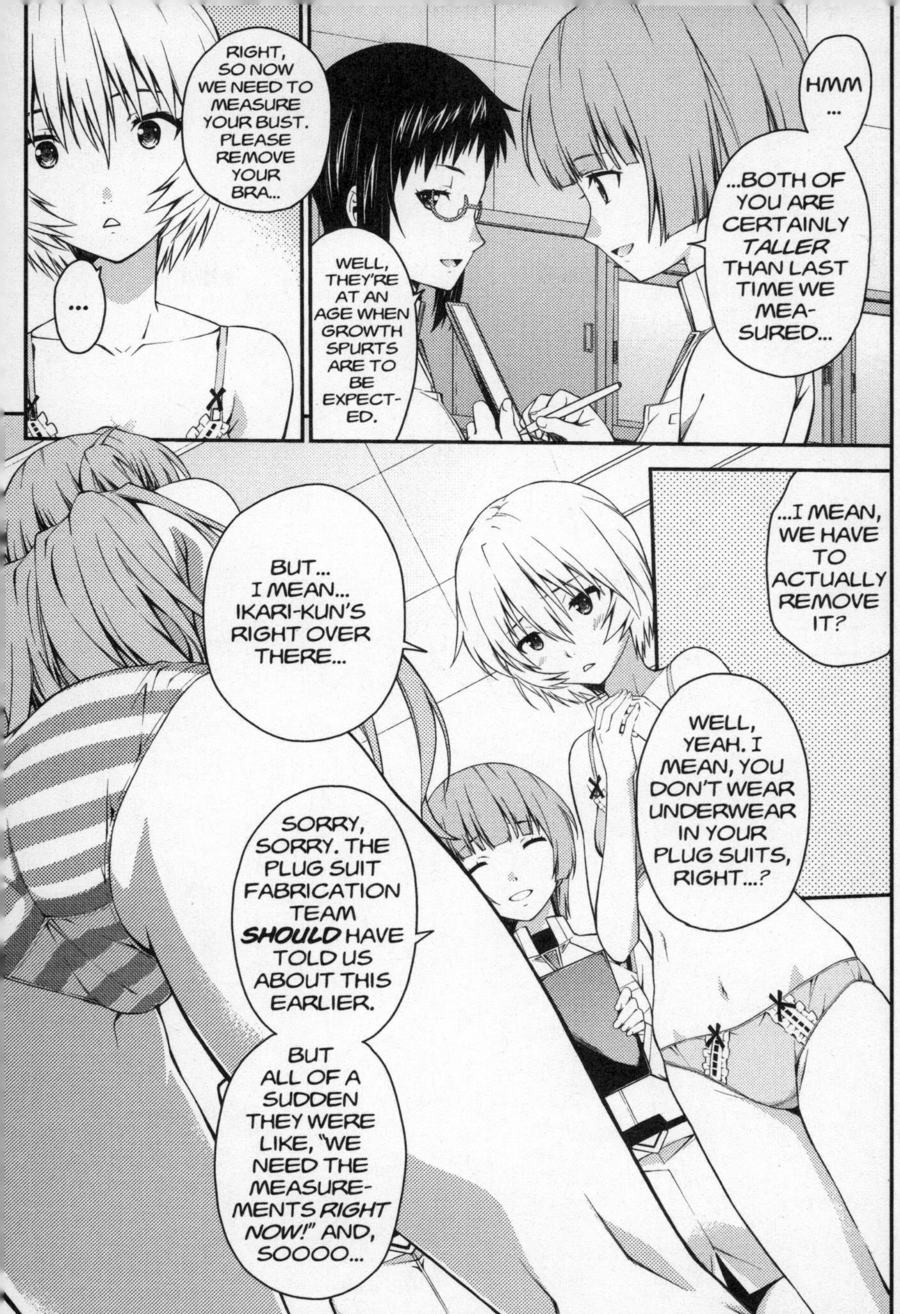
HMM ...
...BOTH OF YOU ARE CERTAINLY *TALLER* THAN LAST TIME WE MEA-SURED...
WELL, THEY'RE AT AN AGE WHEN GROWTH SPURTS ARE TO BE EXPECT-ED.
RIGHT, SO NOW WE NEED TO MEASURE YOUR BUST. PLEASE REMOVE YOUR BRA...
...
...I MEAN, WE HAVE TO ACTUALLY REMOVE IT?
WELL, YEAH. I MEAN, YOU DON'T WEAR UNDERWEAR IN YOUR PLUG SUITS, RIGHT...?
BUT... I MEAN... IKARI-KUN'S RIGHT OVER THERE...
SORRY, SORRY. THE PLUG SUIT FABRICATION TEAM ***SHOULD*** HAVE TOLD US ABOUT THIS EARLIER.
BUT ALL OF A SUDDEN THEY WERE LIKE, "WE NEED THE MEASURE-MENTS *RIGHT NOW!*" AND, SOOOO...

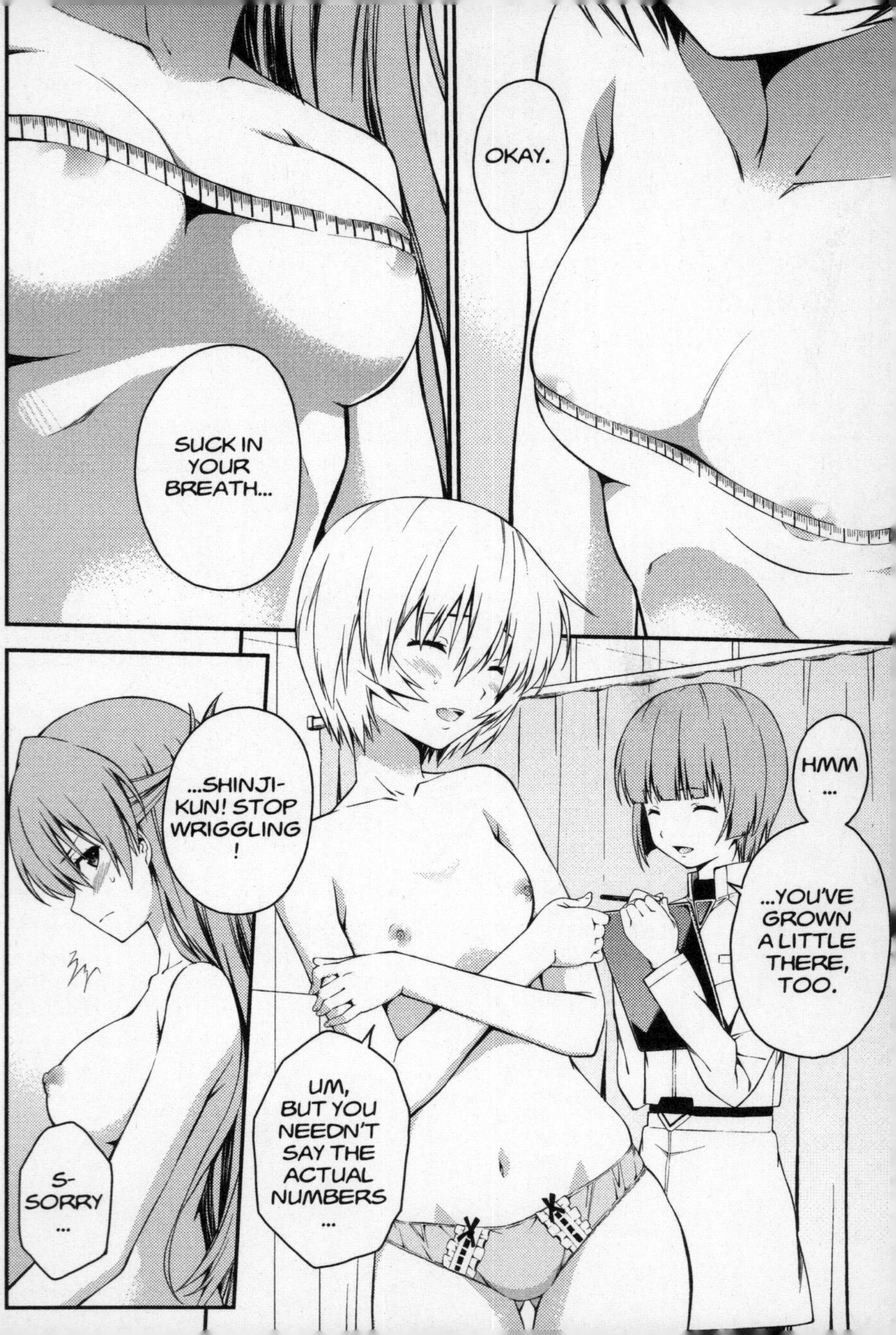
OKAY.
SUCK IN YOUR BREATH...
HMM ...
...YOU'VE GROWN A LITTLE THERE, TOO.
UM, BUT YOU NEEDN'T SAY THE ACTUAL NUMBERS ...
...SHINJI-KUN! STOP WRIGGLING !
S-SORRY ...

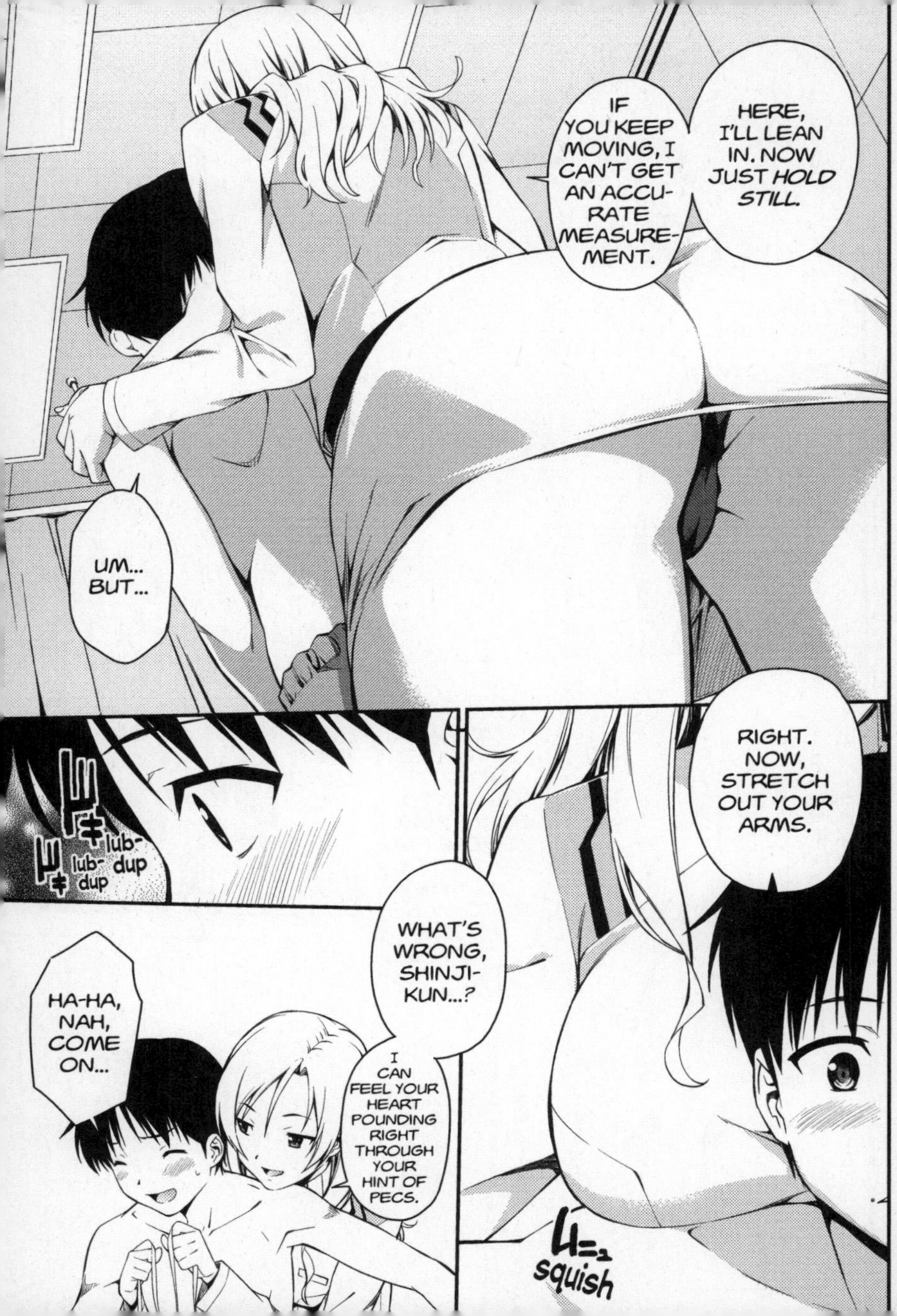
HERE, I'LL LEAN IN. NOW JUST HOLD STILL.
IF YOU KEEP MOVING, I CAN'T GET AN ACCURATE MEASUREMENT.
UM... BUT...
RIGHT. NOW, STRETCH OUT YOUR ARMS.
squish
lub-dup lub-dup
WHAT'S WRONG, SHINJI-KUN...?
I CAN FEEL YOUR HEART POUNDING RIGHT THROUGH YOUR HINT OF PECS.
HA-HA, NAH, COME ON...

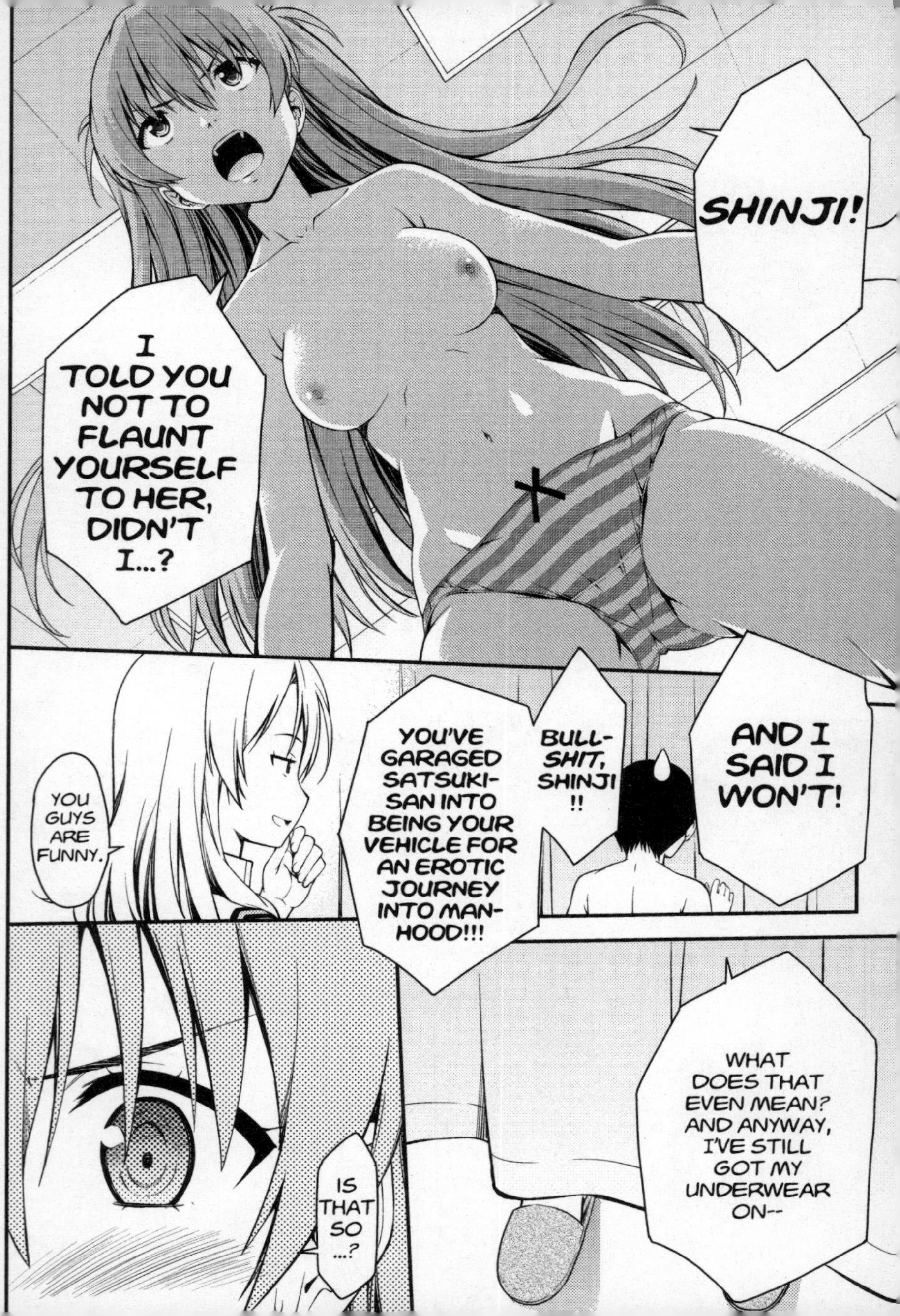
SHINJI!
I TOLD YOU NOT TO FLAUNT YOURSELF TO HER, DIDN'T I...?
AND I SAID I WON'T!
BULL-SHIT, SHINJI!!
YOU'VE GARAGED SATSUKI-SAN INTO BEING YOUR VEHICLE FOR AN EROTIC JOURNEY INTO MAN-HOOD!!!
YOU GUYS ARE FUNNY.
WHAT DOES THAT EVEN MEAN? AND ANYWAY, I'VE STILL GOT MY UNDERWEAR ON--
IS THAT SO ...?

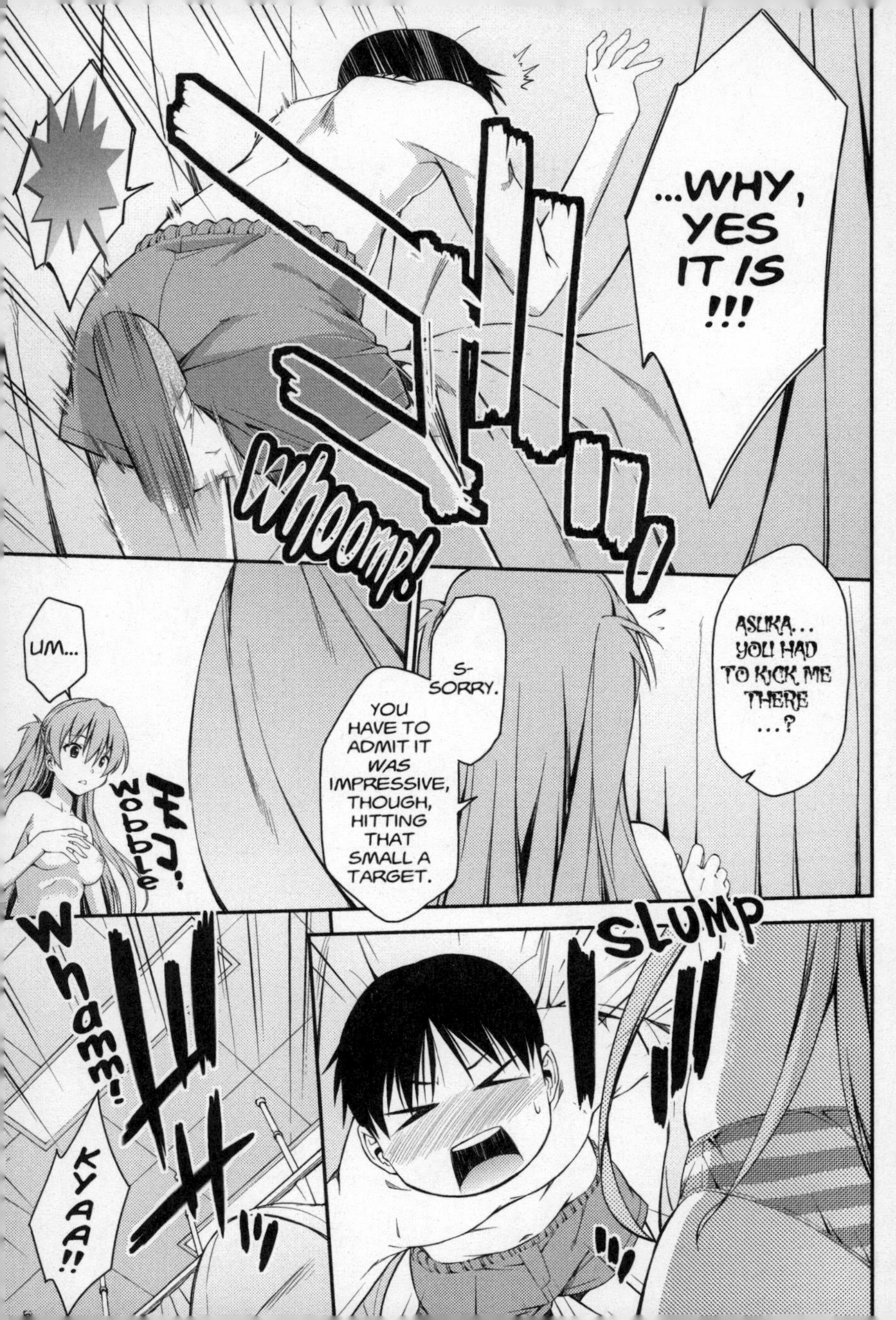
...WHY, YES IT IS !!!
Whoomp!
ASUKA... YOU HAD TO KICK ME THERE ...?
S- SORRY.
YOU HAVE TO ADMIT IT WAS IMPRESSIVE, THOUGH, HITTING THAT SMALL A TARGET.
UM...
wobble
SLUMP
Whamm!
KYAA!!

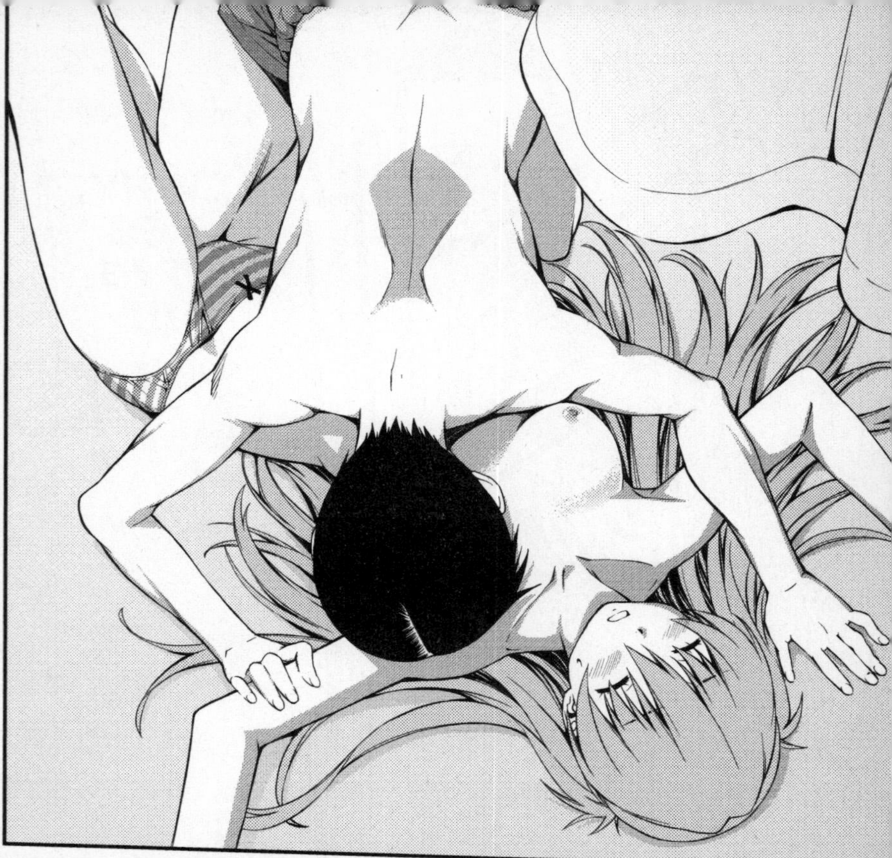

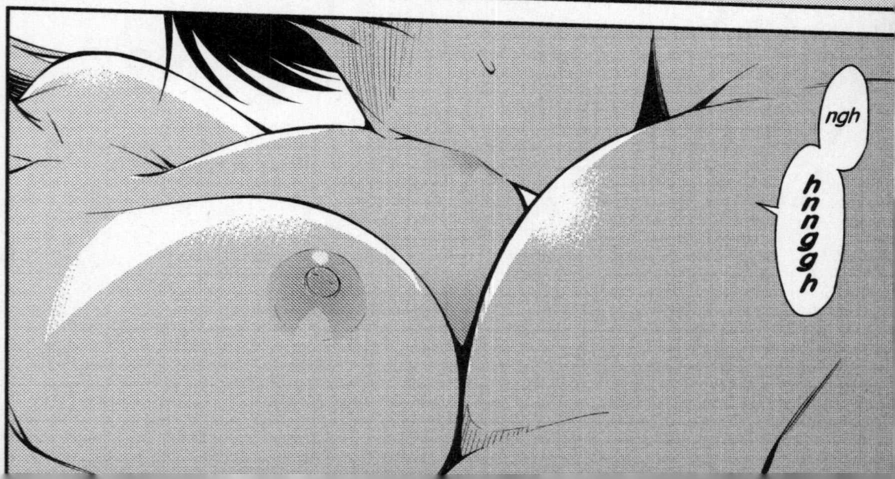
ngh
hnnggh

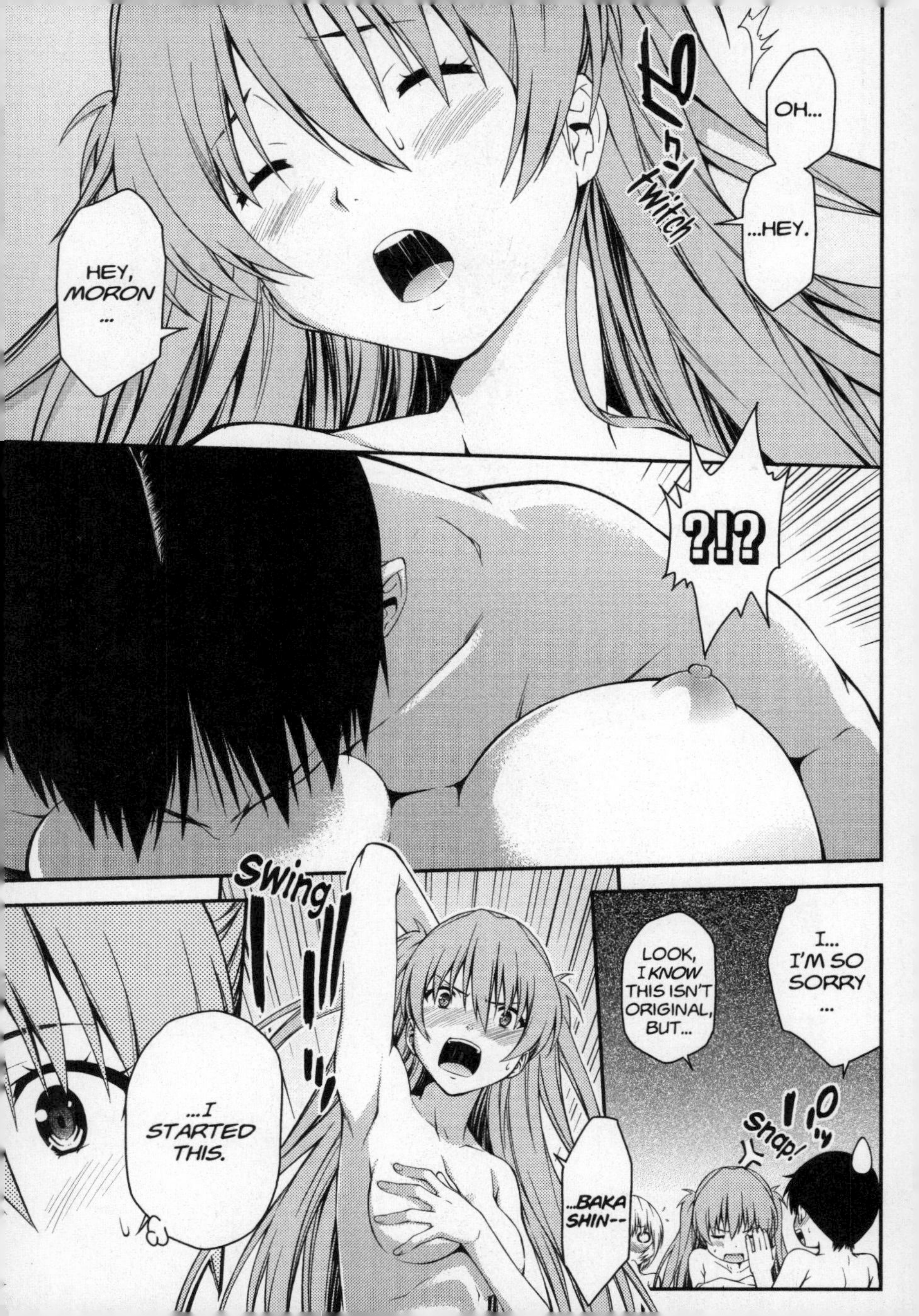
OH...
...HEY.
twitch
HEY, MORON ...
?!?
I... I'M SO SORRY ...
LOOK, I KNOW THIS ISN'T ORIGINAL, BUT...
snap!
swing
...BAKA SHIN--
...I STARTED THIS.

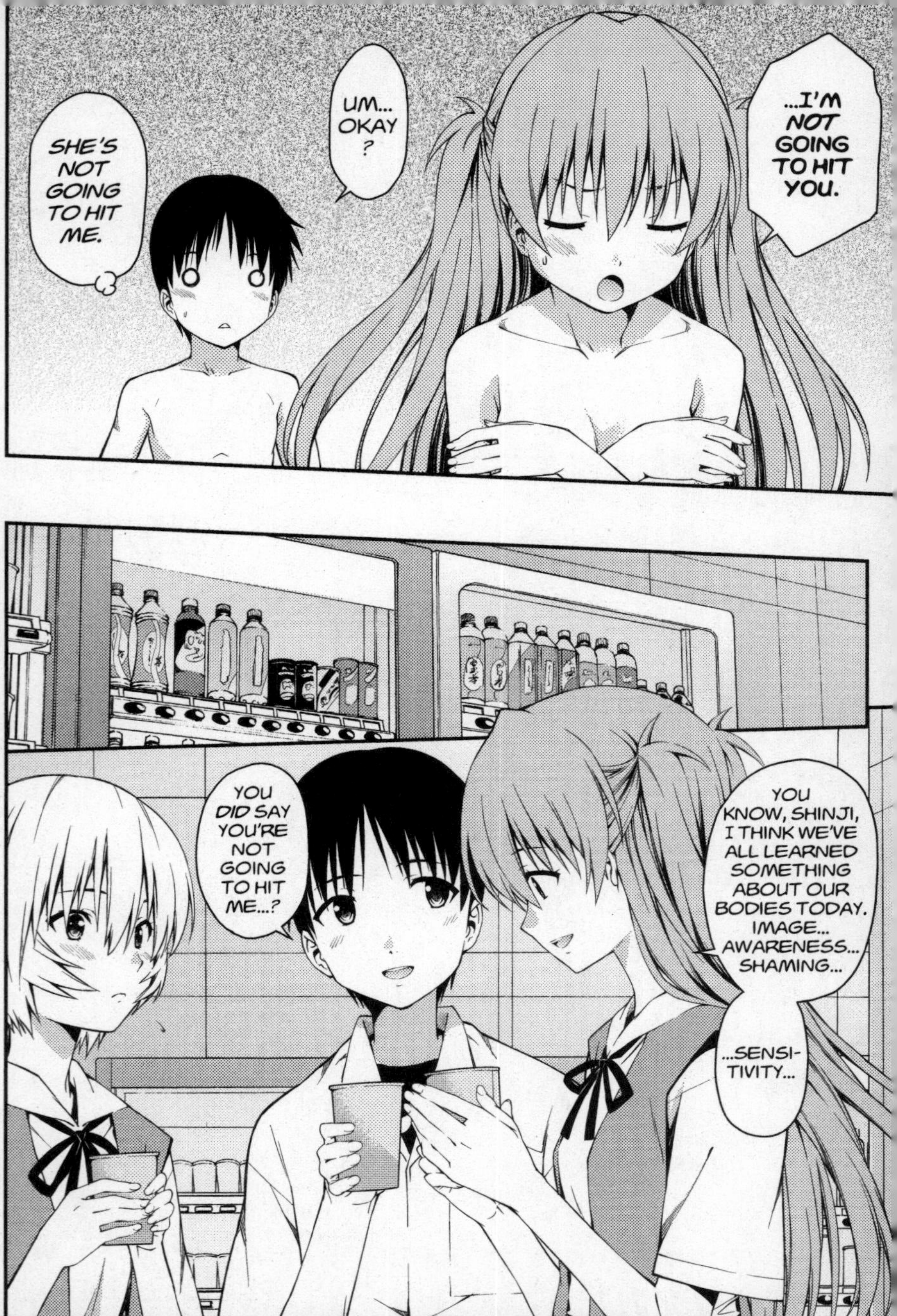
...I'M NOT GOING TO HIT YOU.
UM... OKAY ?
SHE'S NOT GOING TO HIT ME.
YOU KNOW, SHINJI, I THINK WE'VE ALL LEARNED SOMETHING ABOUT OUR BODIES TODAY. IMAGE... AWARENESS... SHAMING...
...SENSI-TIVITY...
YOU DID SAY YOU'RE NOT GOING TO HIT ME...?

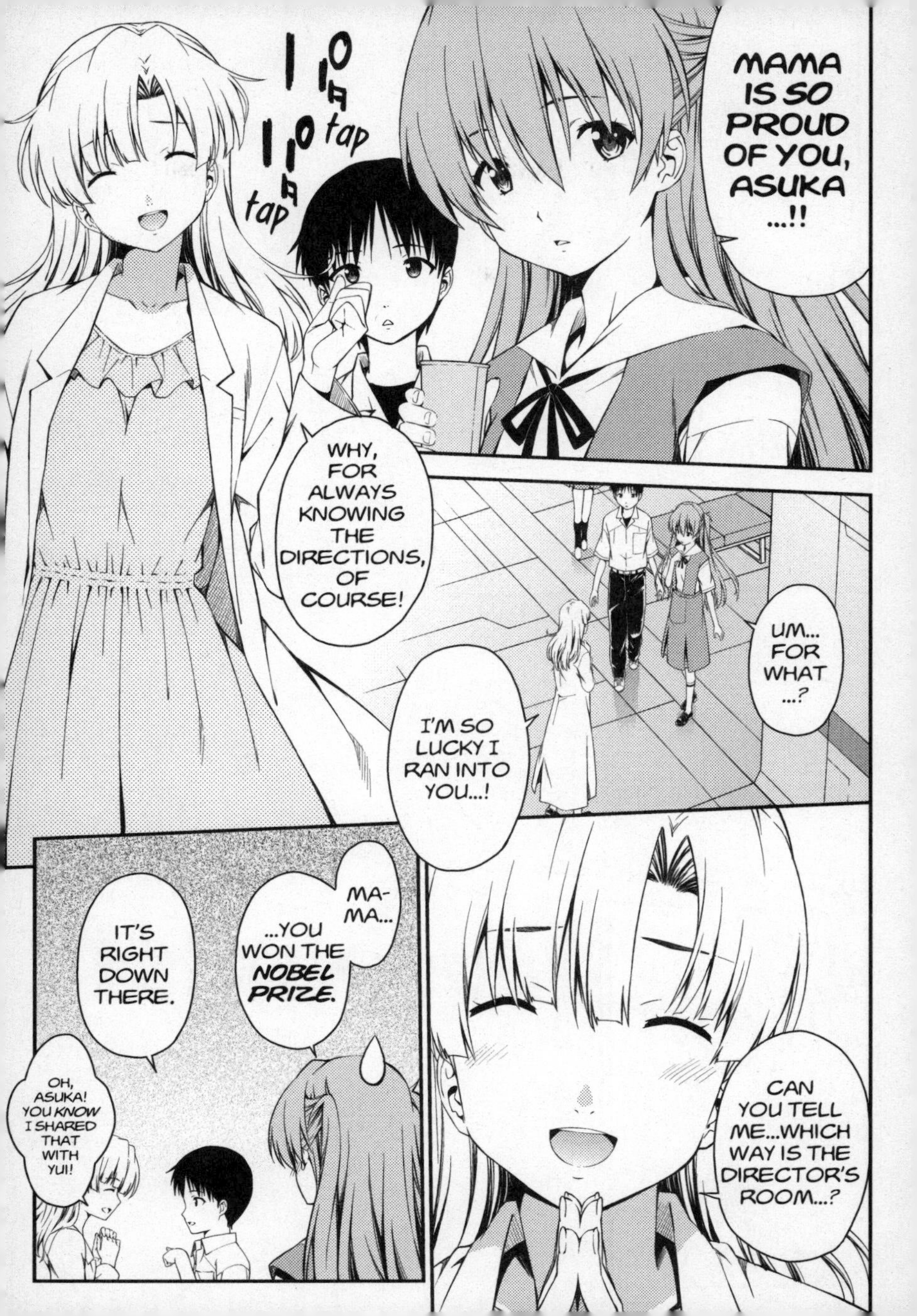
MAMA IS SO PROUD OF YOU, ASUKA ...!!
tap tap
WHY, FOR ALWAYS KNOWING THE DIRECTIONS, OF COURSE!
UM... FOR WHAT ...?
I'M SO LUCKY I RAN INTO YOU...!
CAN YOU TELL ME...WHICH WAY IS THE DIRECTOR'S ROOM...?
MA-MA... ...YOU WON THE NOBEL PRIZE.
IT'S RIGHT DOWN THERE.
OH, ASUKA! YOU KNOW I SHARED THAT WITH YUI!

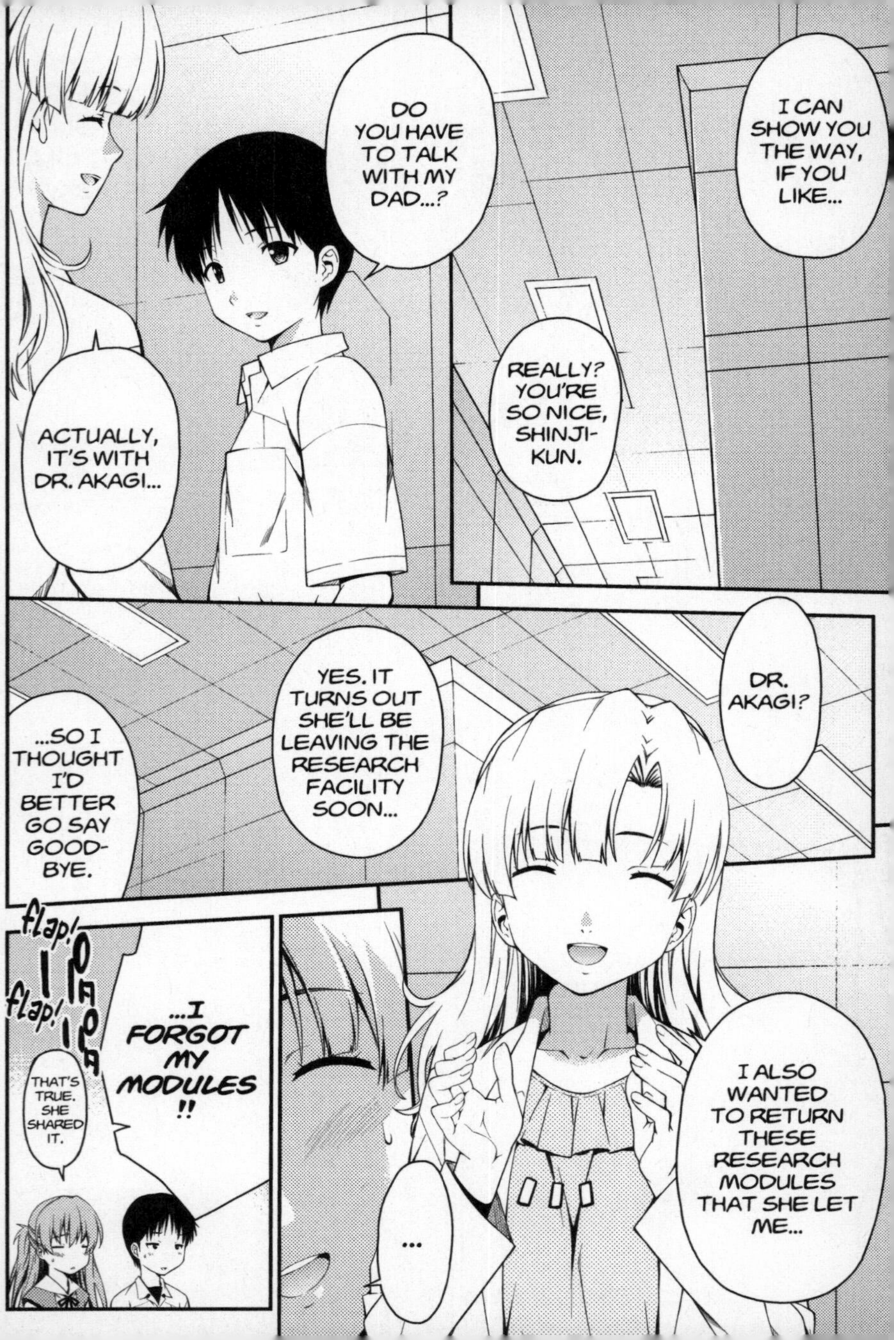
I CAN SHOW YOU THE WAY, IF YOU LIKE...
REALLY? YOU'RE SO NICE, SHINJI-KUN.
DO YOU HAVE TO TALK WITH MY DAD...?
ACTUALLY, IT'S WITH DR. AKAGI...
DR. AKAGI?
YES. IT TURNS OUT SHE'LL BE LEAVING THE RESEARCH FACILITY SOON...
...SO I THOUGHT I'D BETTER GO SAY GOOD-BYE.
I ALSO WANTED TO RETURN THESE RESEARCH MODULES THAT SHE LET ME...
...
flap! flap!
...I FORGOT MY MODULES !!
THAT'S TRUE. SHE SHARED IT.

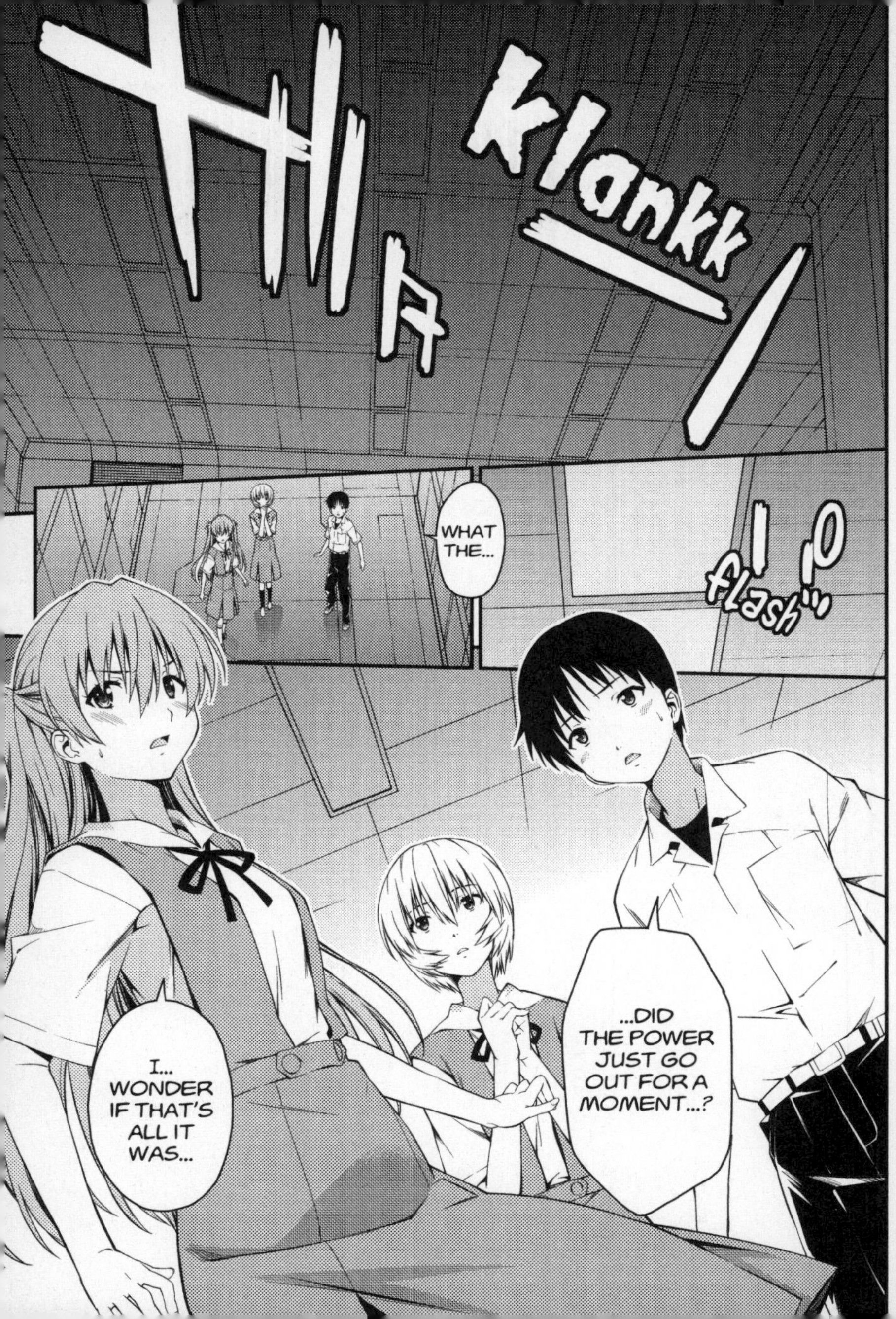
klankk
flash
WHAT THE...
...DID THE POWER JUST GO OUT FOR A MOMENT...?
I... WONDER IF THAT'S ALL IT WAS...

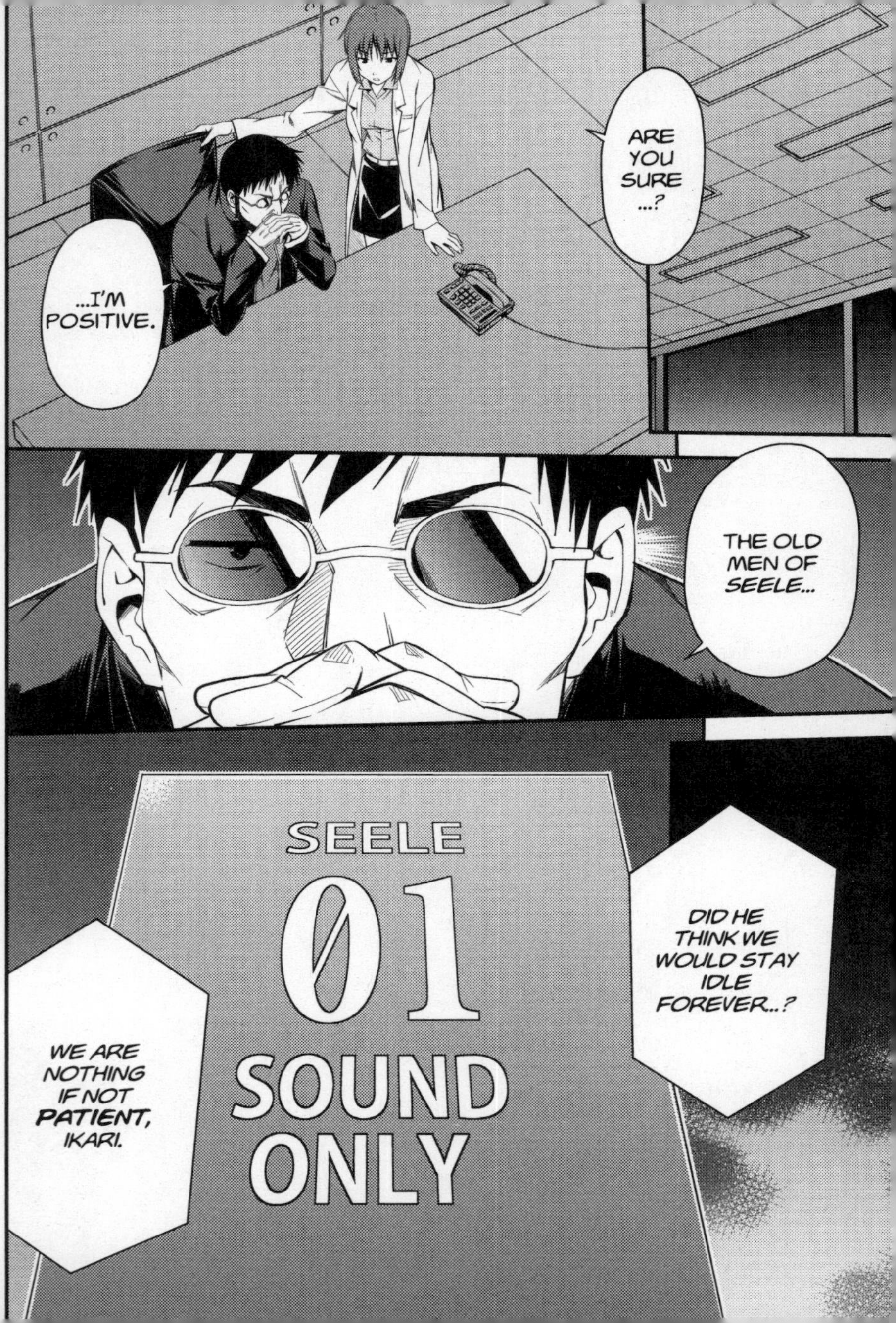
ARE YOU SURE ...?
...I'M POSITIVE.
THE OLD MEN OF SEELE...
SEELE 01 SOUND ONLY
DID HE THINK WE WOULD STAY IDLE FOREVER...?
WE ARE NOTHING IF NOT PATIENT, IKARI.

the shinji ikari raising project

NEON GENESIS EVANGELION
THE SHINJI IKARI RAISING PROJECT

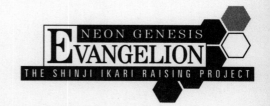

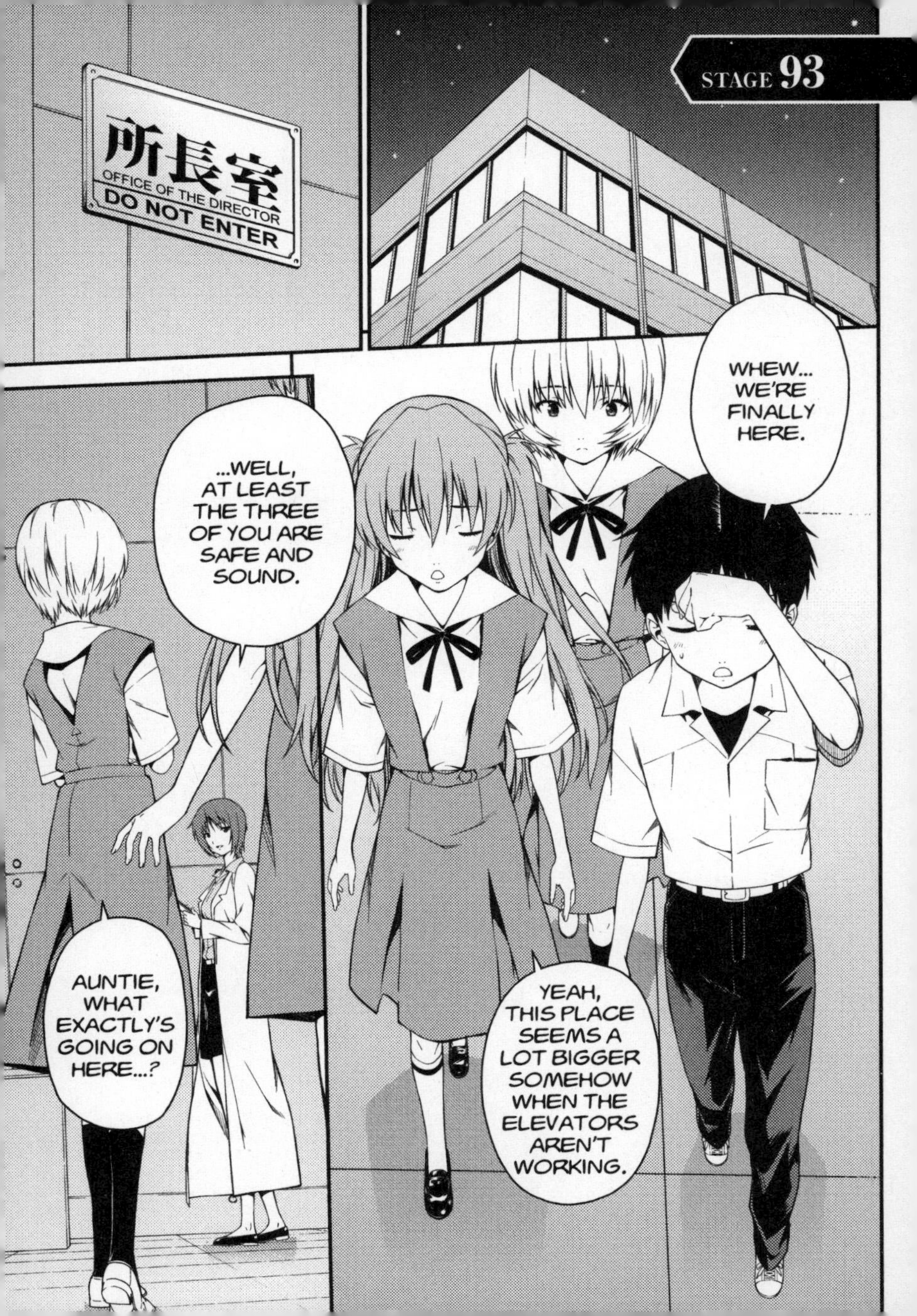
STAGE 93
所長室
OFFICE OF THE DIRECTOR
DO NOT ENTER
WHEW... WE'RE FINALLY HERE.
YEAH, THIS PLACE SEEMS A LOT BIGGER SOMEHOW WHEN THE ELEVATORS AREN'T WORKING.
...WELL, AT LEAST THE THREE OF YOU ARE SAFE AND SOUND.
AUNTIE, WHAT EXACTLY'S GOING ON HERE...?

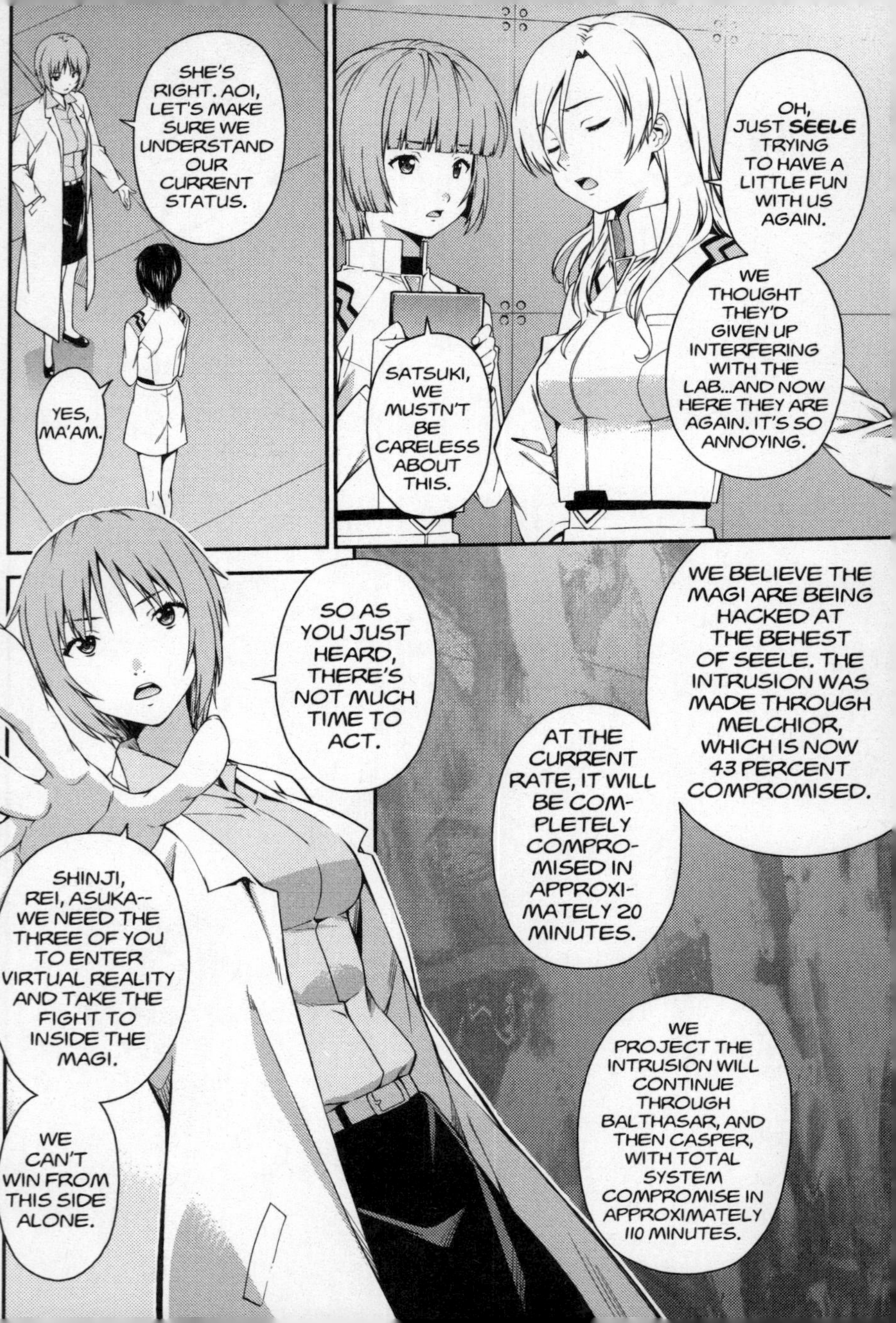
OH, JUST SEELE TRYING TO HAVE A LITTLE FUN WITH US AGAIN.
WE THOUGHT THEY'D GIVEN UP INTERFERING WITH THE LAB...AND NOW HERE THEY ARE AGAIN. IT'S SO ANNOYING.
SATSUKI, WE MUSTN'T BE CARELESS ABOUT THIS.
SHE'S RIGHT. AOI, LET'S MAKE SURE WE UNDERSTAND OUR CURRENT STATUS.
YES, MA'AM.
WE BELIEVE THE MAGI ARE BEING HACKED AT THE BEHEST OF SEELE. THE INTRUSION WAS MADE THROUGH MELCHIOR, WHICH IS NOW 43 PERCENT COMPROMISED.
AT THE CURRENT RATE, IT WILL BE COM-PLETELY COMPRO-MISED IN APPROXI-MATELY 20 MINUTES.
WE PROJECT THE INTRUSION WILL CONTINUE THROUGH BALTHASAR, AND THEN CASPER, WITH TOTAL SYSTEM COMPROMISE IN APPROXIMATELY 110 MINUTES.
SO AS YOU JUST HEARD, THERE'S NOT MUCH TIME TO ACT.
SHINJI, REI, ASUKA--WE NEED THE THREE OF YOU TO ENTER VIRTUAL REALITY AND TAKE THE FIGHT TO INSIDE THE MAGI.
WE CAN'T WIN FROM THIS SIDE ALONE.

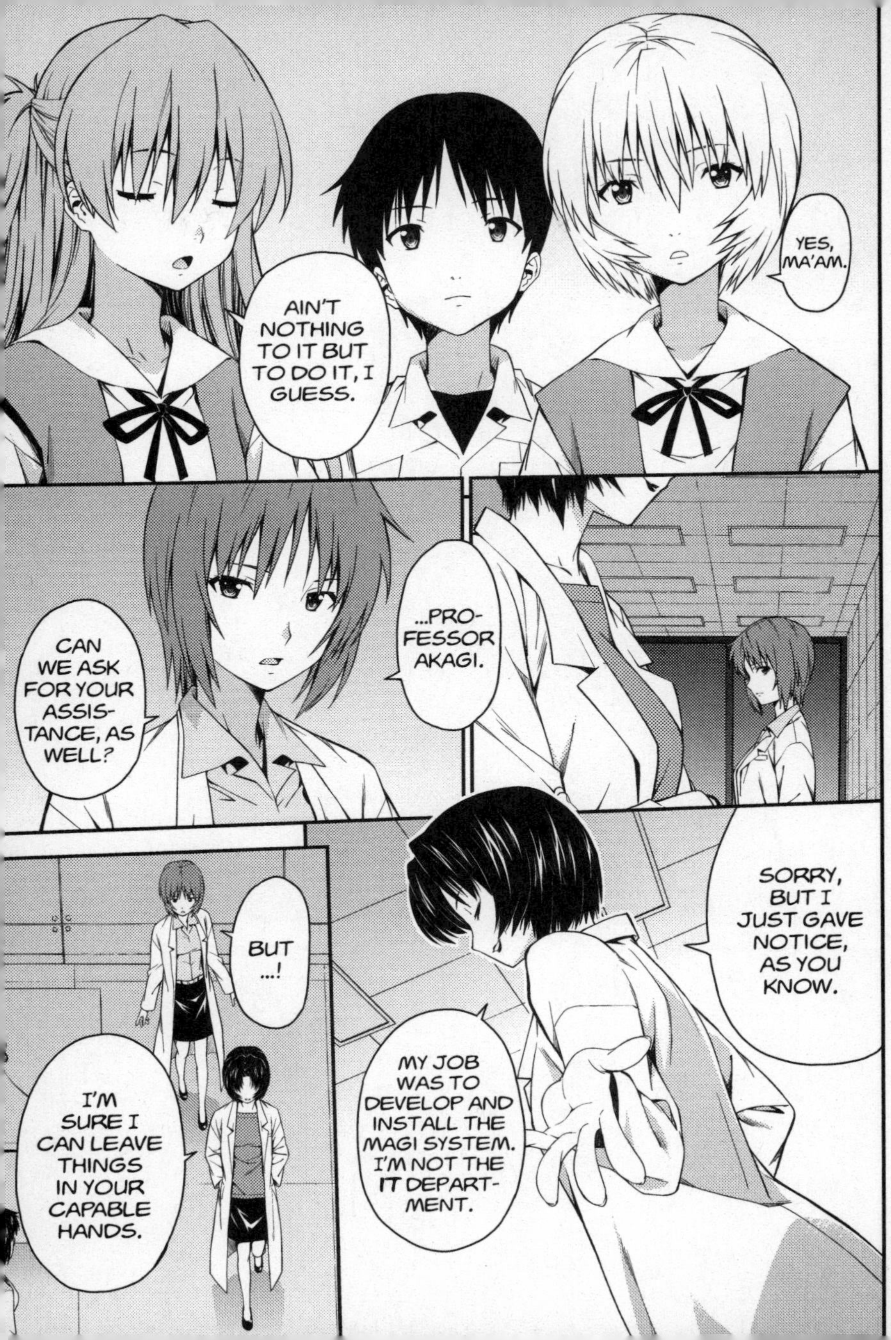
YES, MA'AM.
AIN'T NOTHING TO IT BUT TO DO IT, I GUESS.
...PRO-FESSOR AKAGI.
CAN WE ASK FOR YOUR ASSIS-TANCE, AS WELL?
SORRY, BUT I JUST GAVE NOTICE, AS YOU KNOW.
MY JOB WAS TO DEVELOP AND INSTALL THE MAGI SYSTEM. I'M NOT THE IT DEPART-MENT.
BUT ...!
I'M SURE I CAN LEAVE THINGS IN YOUR CAPABLE HANDS.

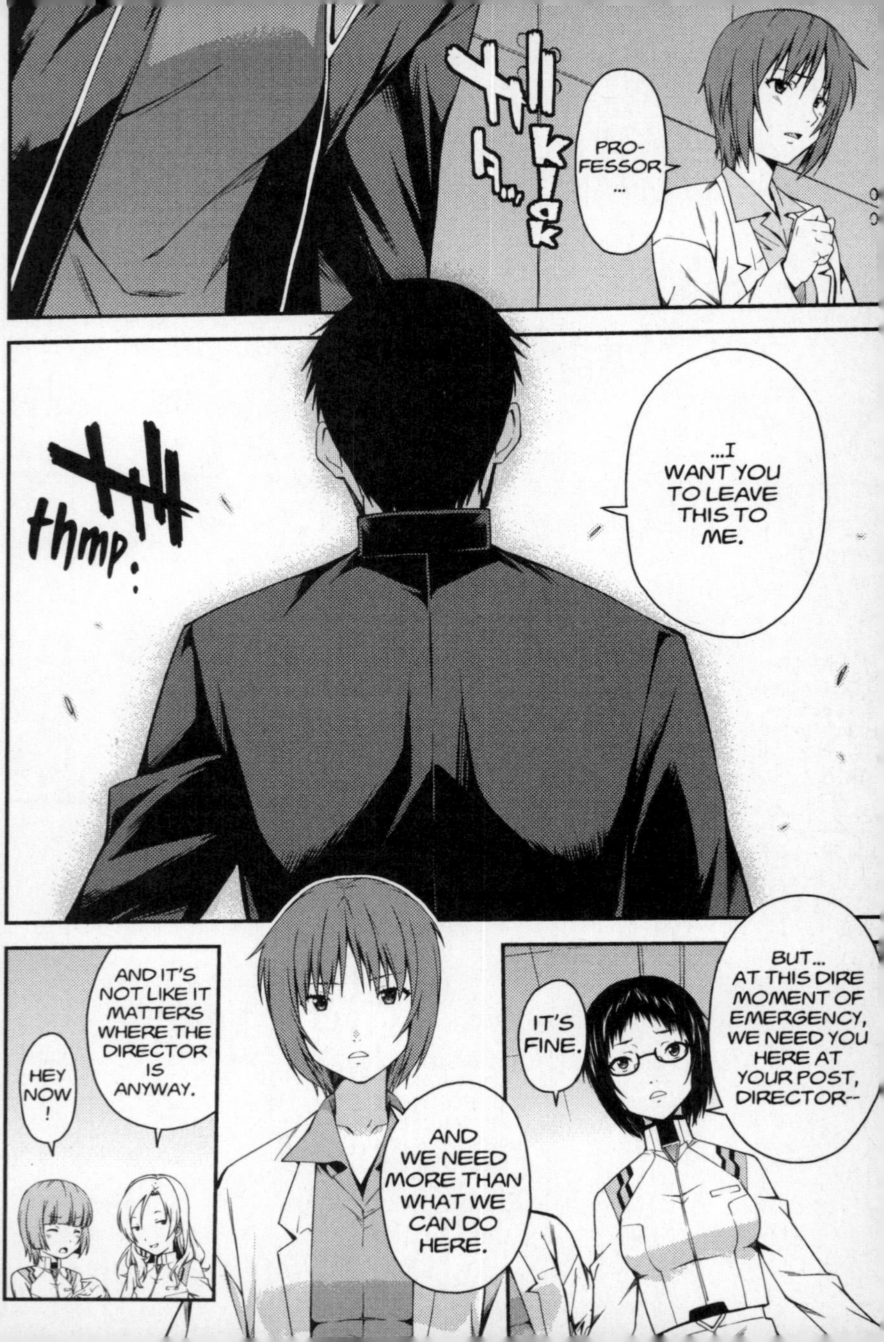
klak
PRO-FESSOR ...
...I WANT YOU TO LEAVE THIS TO ME.
thmp
BUT... AT THIS DIRE MOMENT OF EMERGENCY, WE NEED YOU HERE AT YOUR POST, DIRECTOR--
IT'S FINE.
AND WE NEED MORE THAN WHAT WE CAN DO HERE.
AND IT'S NOT LIKE IT MATTERS WHERE THE DIRECTOR IS ANYWAY.
HEY NOW!

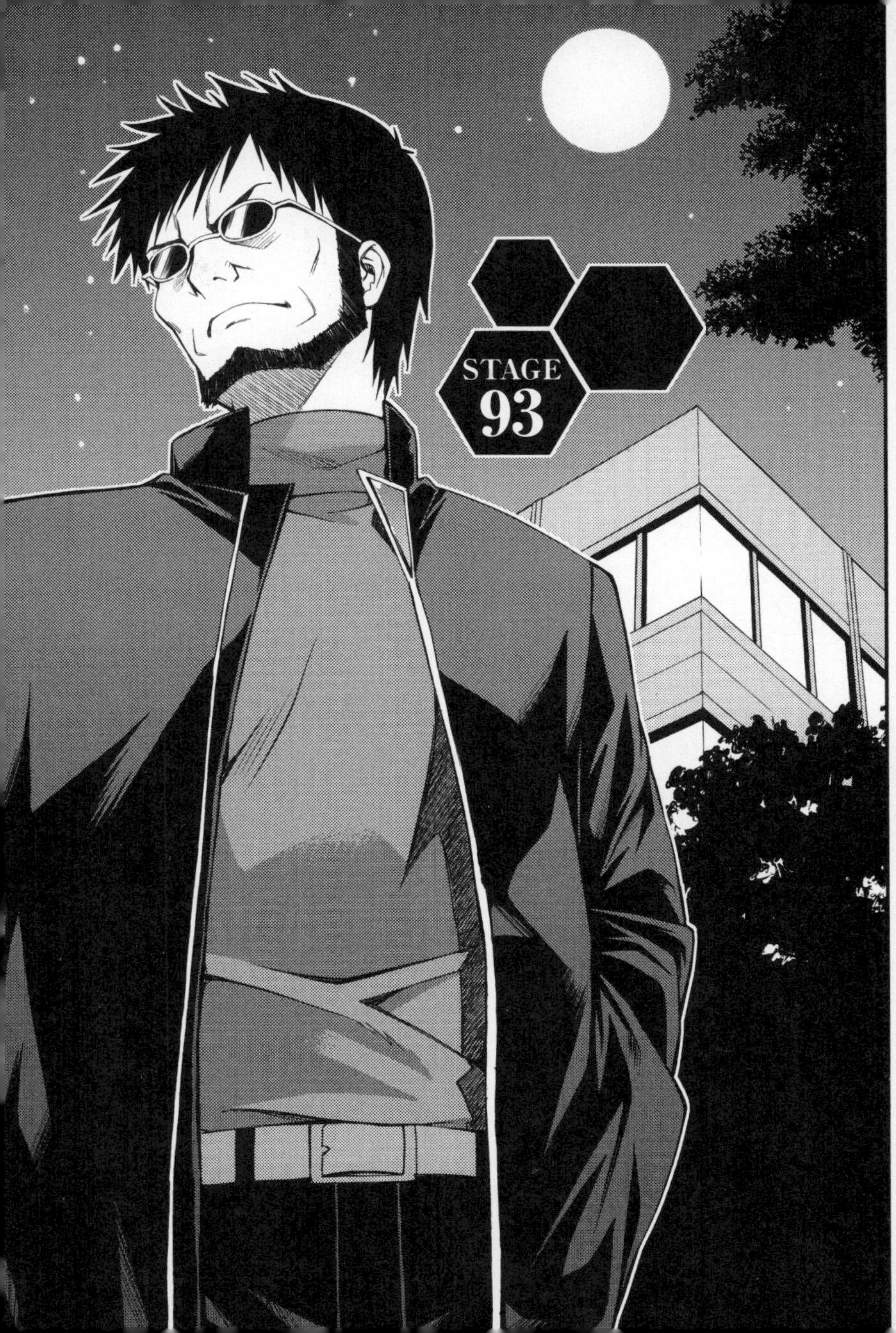
STAGE
93

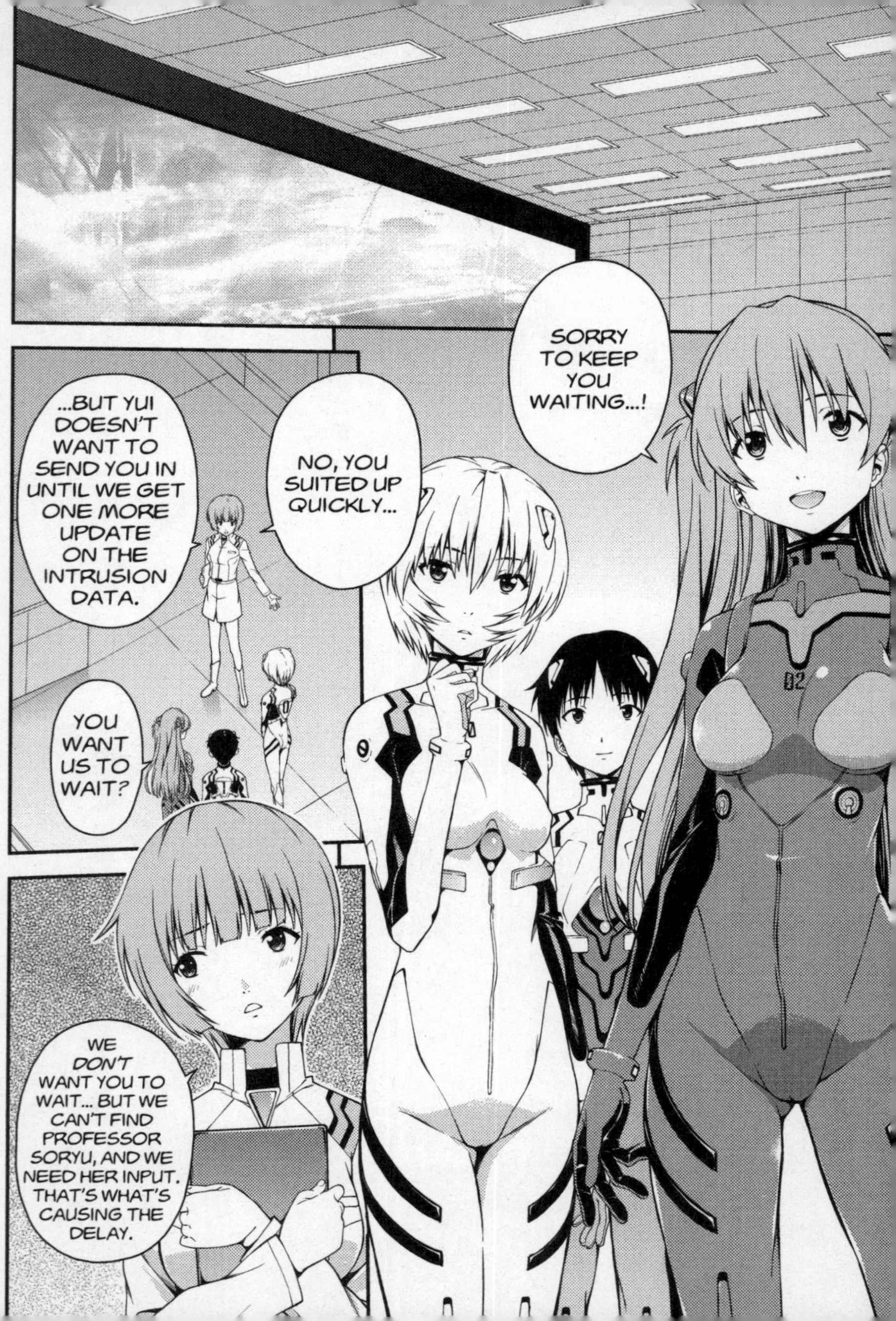
SORRY TO KEEP YOU WAITING...!
NO, YOU SUITED UP QUICKLY...
...BUT YUI DOESN'T WANT TO SEND YOU IN UNTIL WE GET ONE MORE UPDATE ON THE INTRUSION DATA.
YOU WANT US TO WAIT?
WE *DON'T* WANT YOU TO WAIT... BUT WE CAN'T FIND PROFESSOR SORYU, AND WE NEED HER INPUT. THAT'S WHAT'S CAUSING THE DELAY.

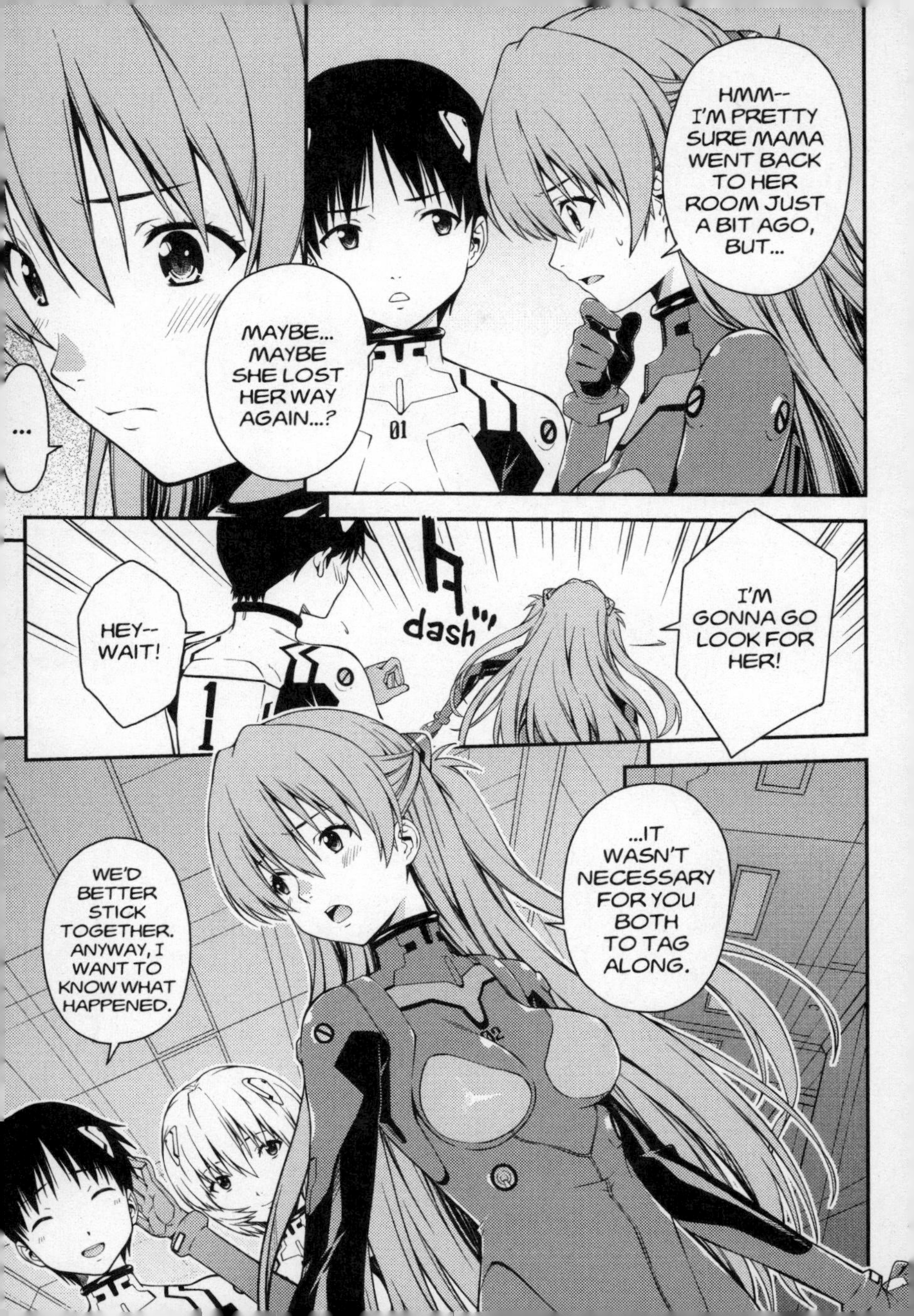
HMM-- I'M PRETTY SURE MAMA WENT BACK TO HER ROOM JUST A BIT AGO, BUT...
MAYBE... MAYBE SHE LOST HER WAY AGAIN...?
...
01
I'M GONNA GO LOOK FOR HER!
dash
HEY-- WAIT!
...IT WASN'T NECESSARY FOR YOU BOTH TO TAG ALONG.
WE'D BETTER STICK TOGETHER. ANYWAY, I WANT TO KNOW WHAT HAPPENED.

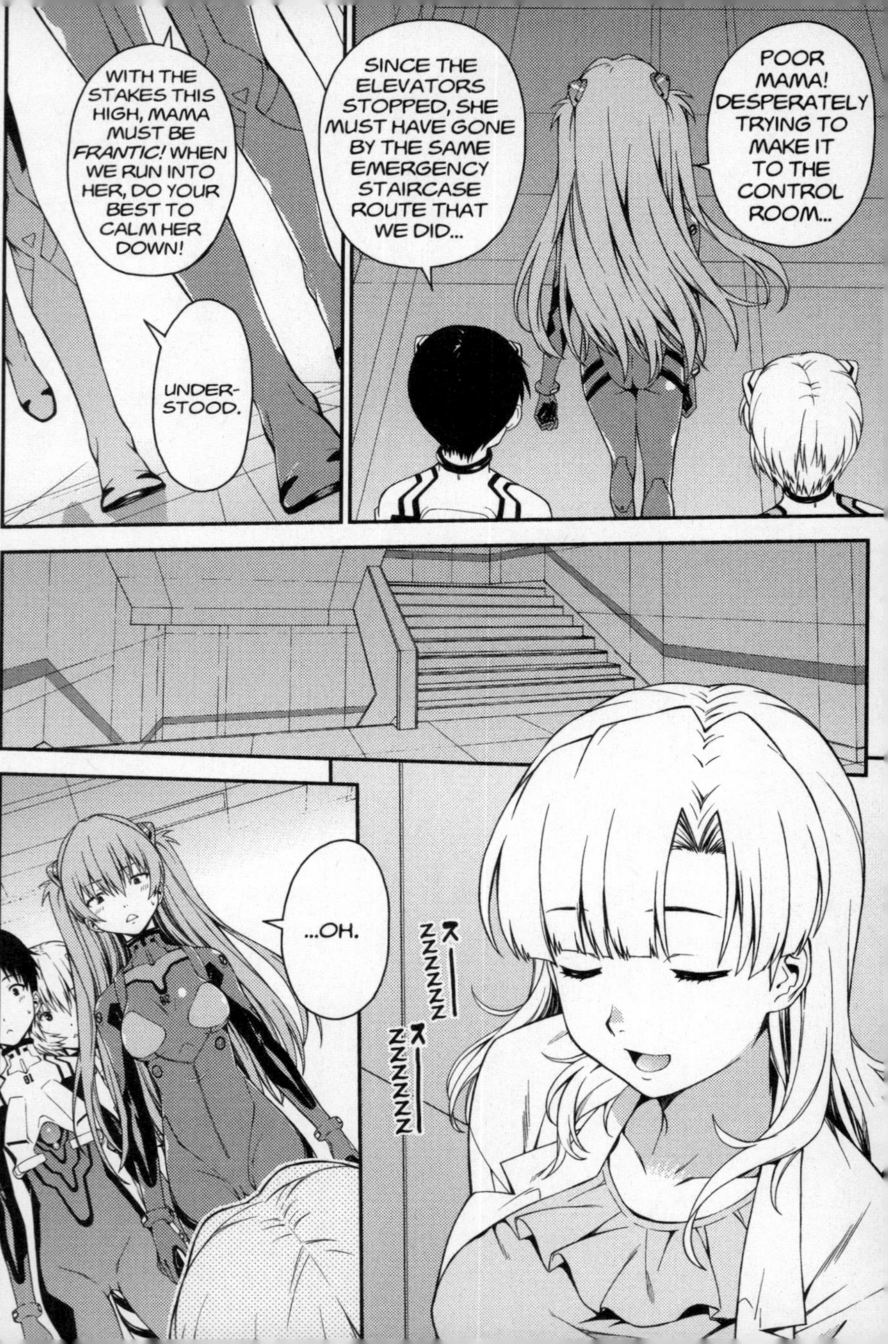
POOR MAMA! DESPERATELY TRYING TO MAKE IT TO THE CONTROL ROOM...
SINCE THE ELEVATORS STOPPED, SHE MUST HAVE GONE BY THE SAME EMERGENCY STAIRCASE ROUTE THAT WE DID...
WITH THE STAKES THIS HIGH, MAMA MUST BE *FRANTIC!* WHEN WE RUN INTO HER, DO YOUR BEST TO CALM HER DOWN!
UNDER-STOOD.
ス—— ZZZZZZ
ス—— ZZZZZZ
...OH.

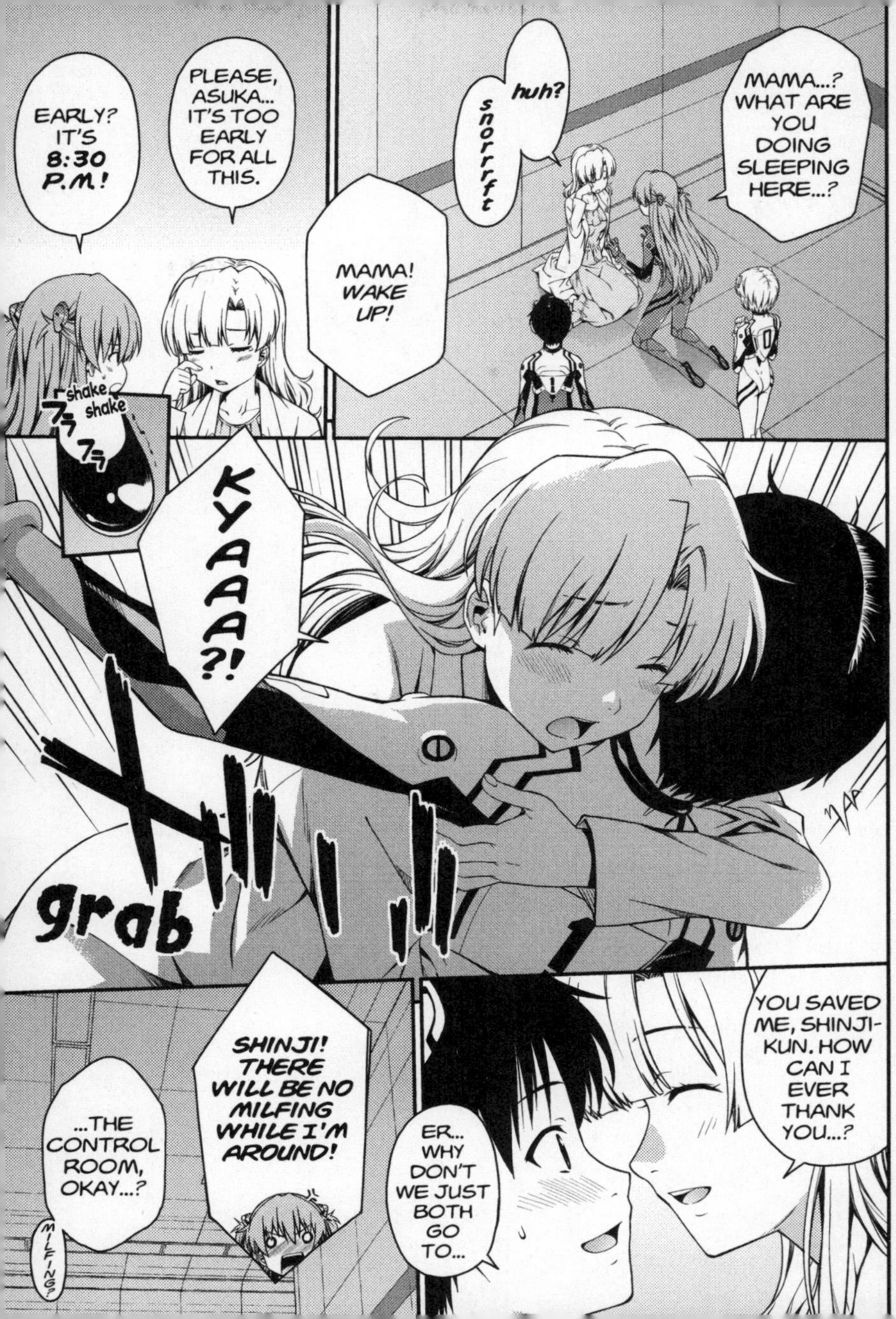
MAMA...? WHAT ARE YOU DOING SLEEPING HERE...?
huh?
snorrrfft
MAMA! WAKE UP!
shake shake
PLEASE, ASUKA... IT'S TOO EARLY FOR ALL THIS.
EARLY? IT'S 8:30 P.M.!
KYAAAA?!
grab
YOU SAVED ME, SHINJI-KUN. HOW CAN I EVER THANK YOU...?
ER... WHY DON'T WE JUST BOTH GO TO...
SHINJI! THERE WILL BE NO MILFING WHILE I'M AROUND!
...THE CONTROL ROOM, OKAY...?
MILFING?

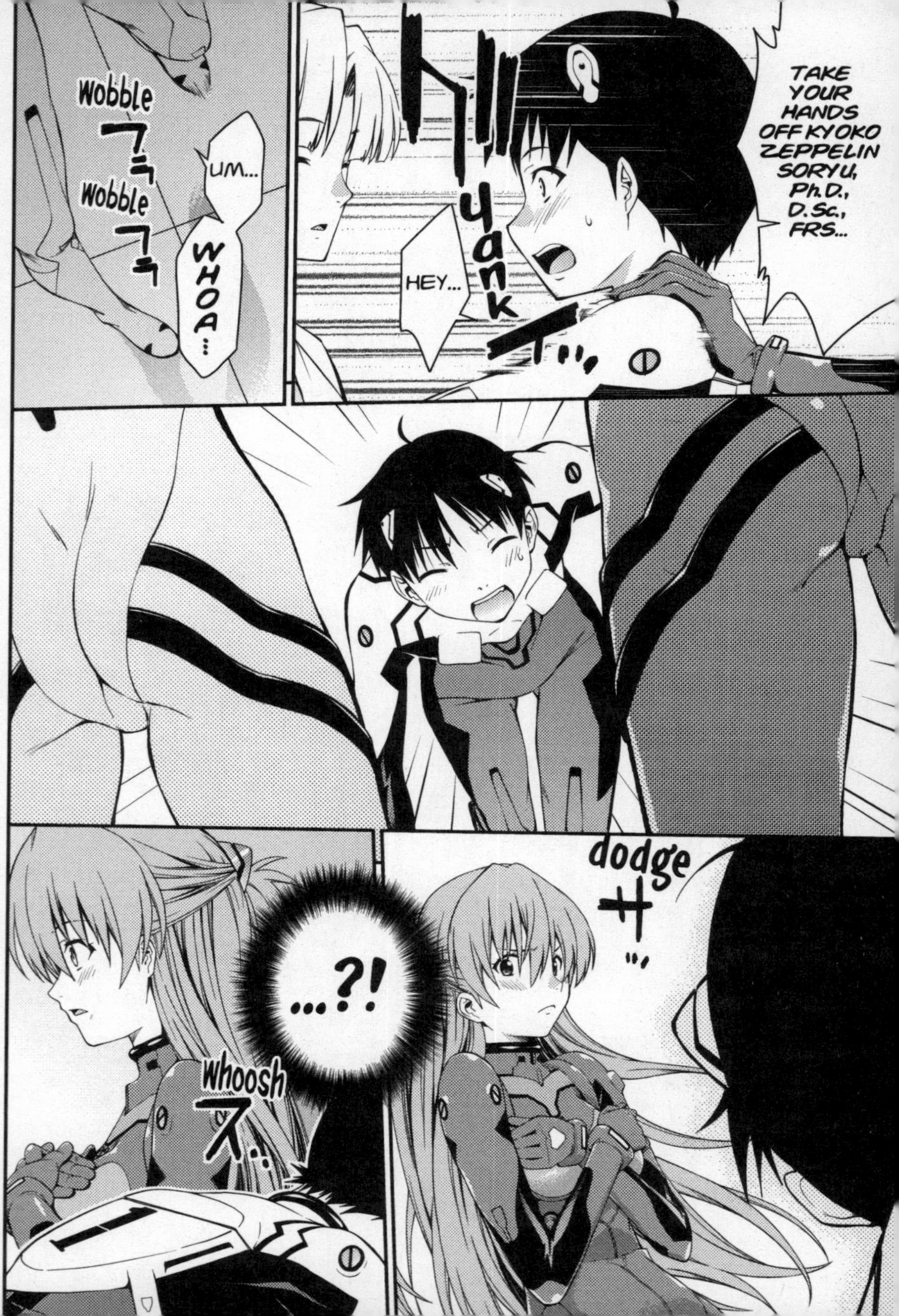
TAKE YOUR HANDS OFF KYOKO ZEPPELIN SORYU, Ph.D., D.Sc., FRS...
yank
HEY...
UM...
wobble
wobble
WHOA...
dodge
サ
...?!
whoosh
ス

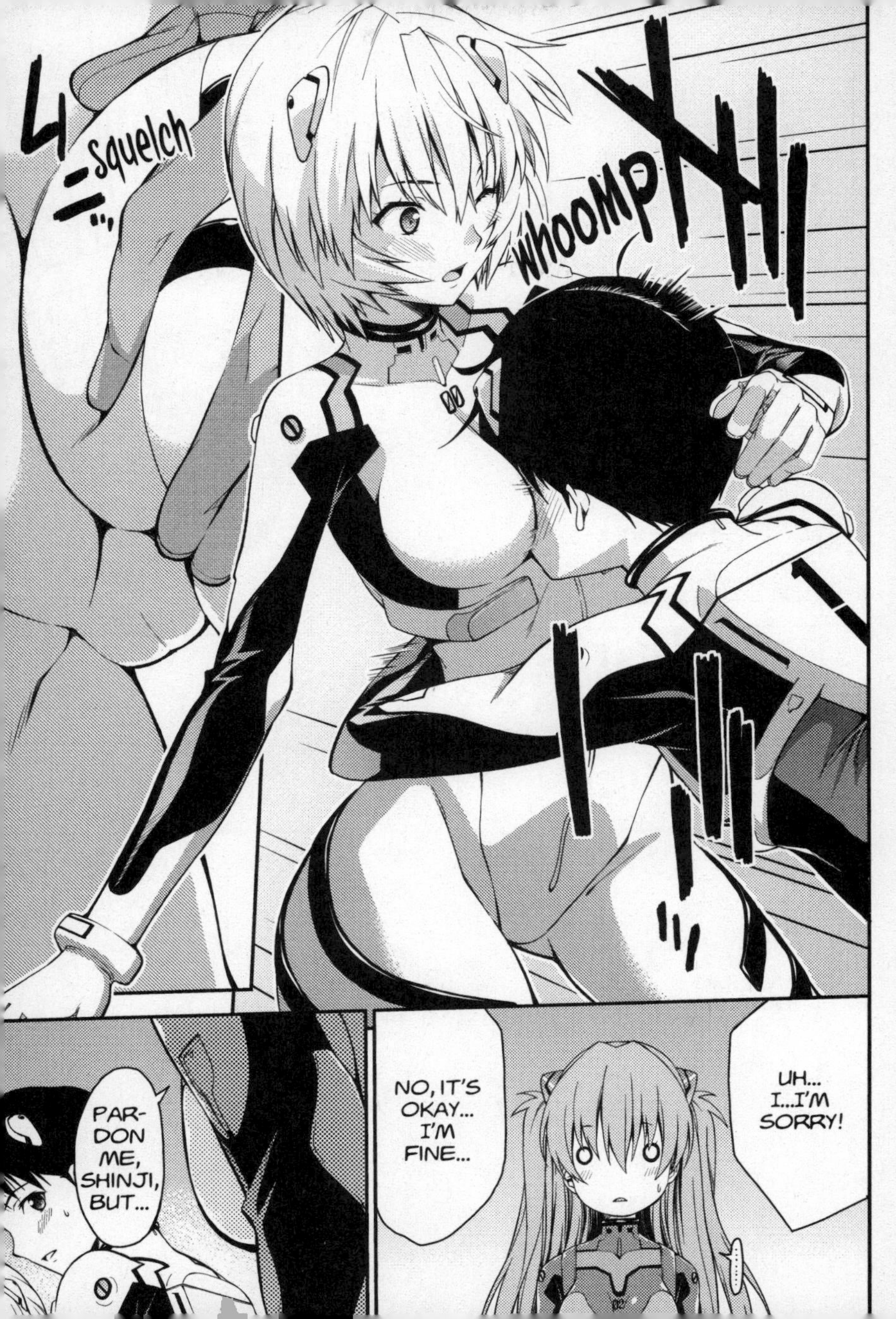
WHOOMP
SQUELCH
UH... I...I'M SORRY!
NO, IT'S OKAY... I'M FINE...
PAR-DON ME, SHINJI, BUT...

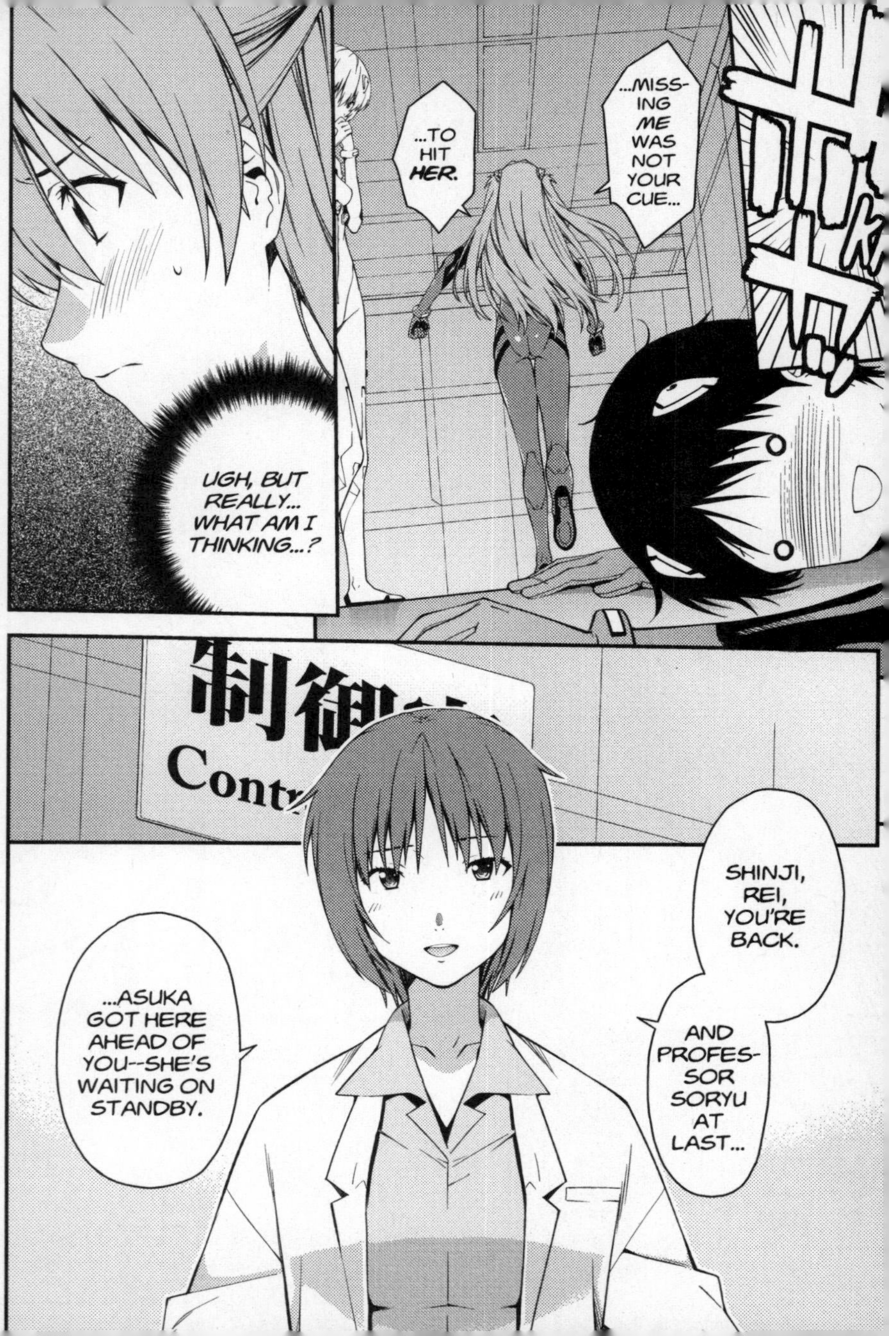
...MISS-ING ME WAS NOT YOUR CUE...
...TO HIT HER.
UGH, BUT REALLY... WHAT AM I THINKING...?
SHINJI, REI, YOU'RE BACK.
AND PROFES-SOR SORYU AT LAST...
...ASUKA GOT HERE AHEAD OF YOU--SHE'S WAITING ON STANDBY.

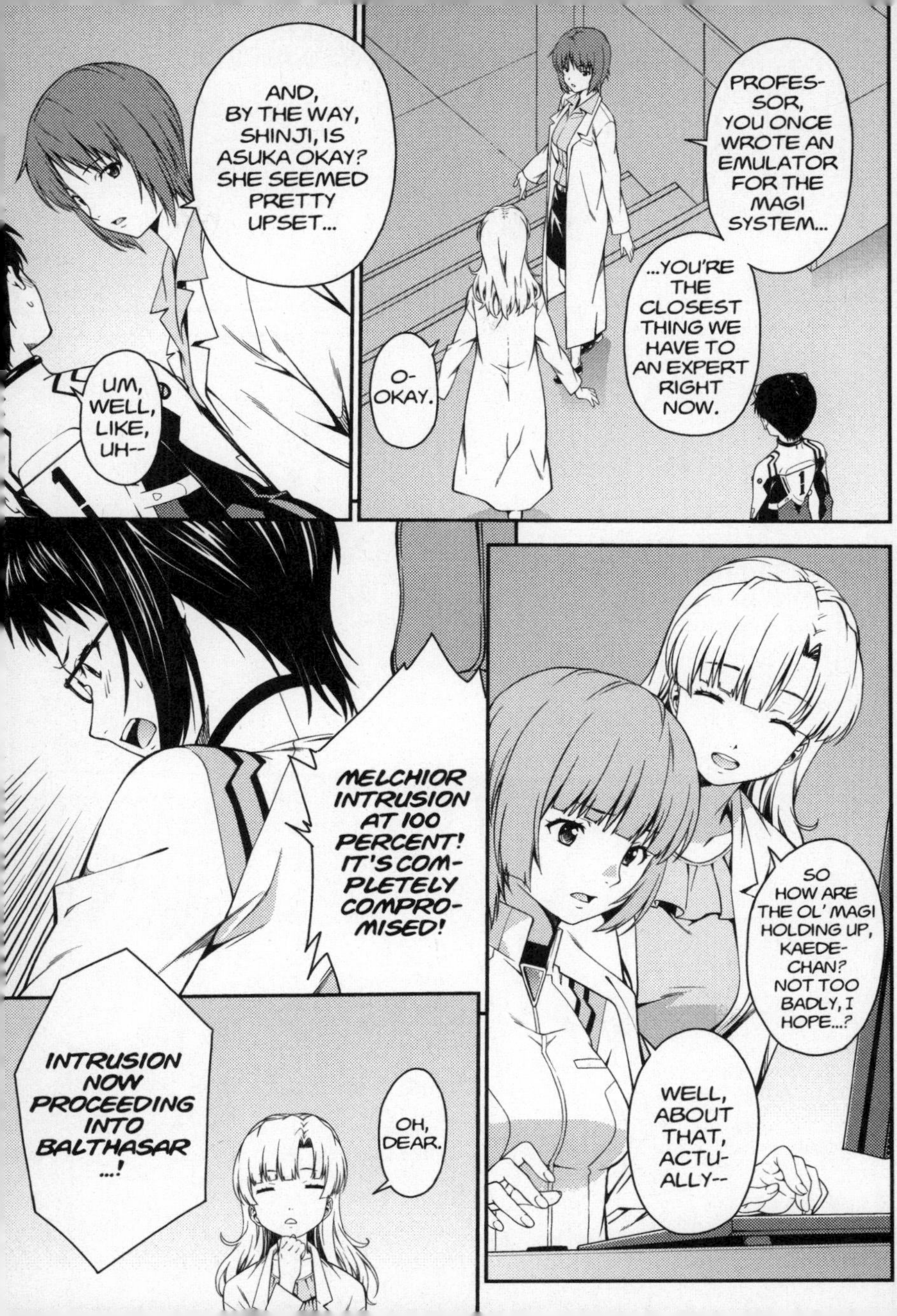
PROFES-SOR, YOU ONCE WROTE AN EMULATOR FOR THE MAGI SYSTEM...
...YOU'RE THE CLOSEST THING WE HAVE TO AN EXPERT RIGHT NOW.
O-OKAY.
AND, BY THE WAY, SHINJI, IS ASUKA OKAY? SHE SEEMED PRETTY UPSET...
UM, WELL, LIKE, UH--
SO HOW ARE THE OL' MAGI HOLDING UP, KAEDE-CHAN? NOT TOO BADLY, I HOPE...?
WELL, ABOUT THAT, ACTU-ALLY--
MELCHIOR INTRUSION AT 100 PERCENT! IT'S COM-PLETELY COMPRO-MISED!
INTRUSION NOW PROCEEDING INTO BALTHASAR ...!
OH, DEAR.

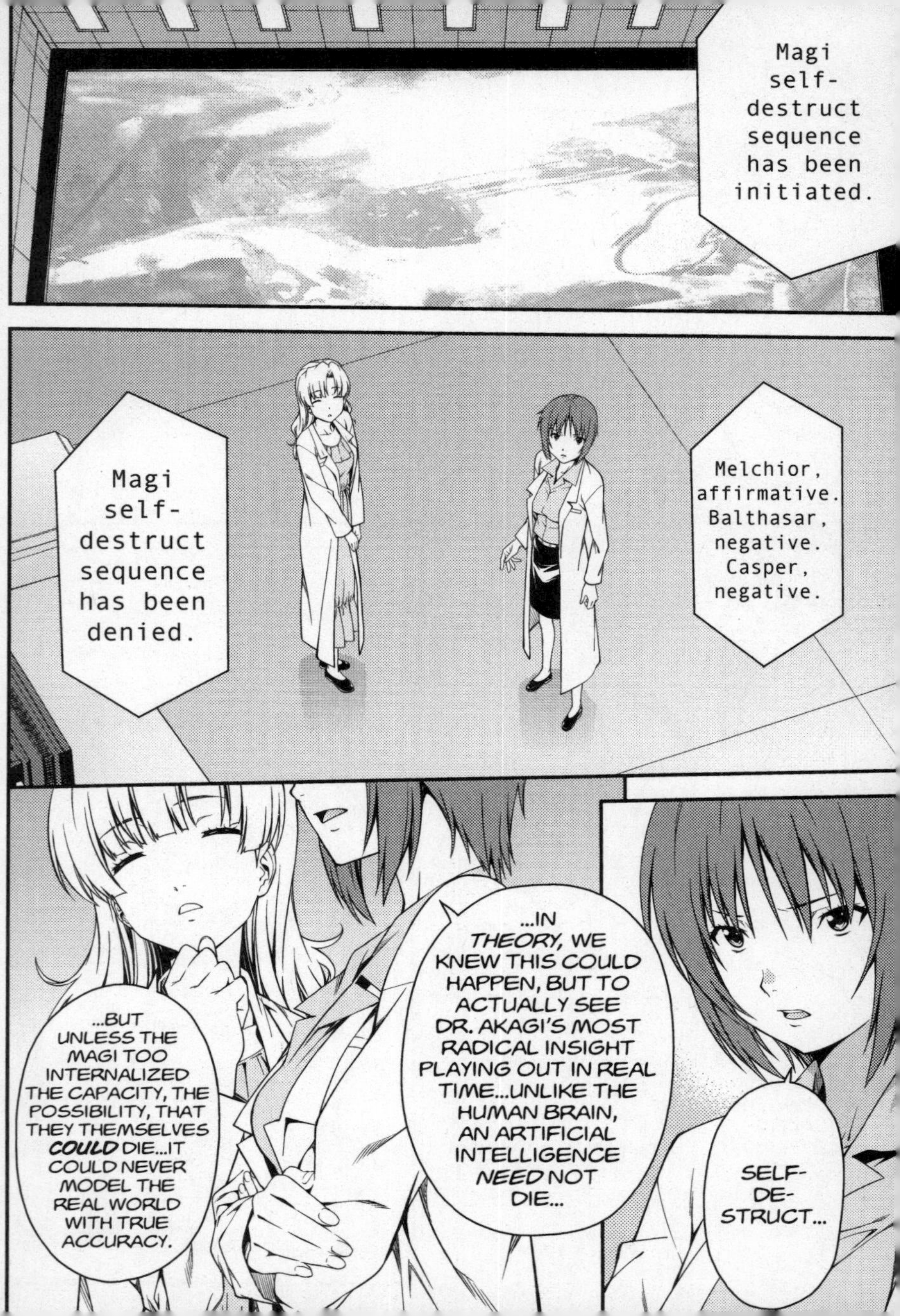
Magi self-destruct sequence has been initiated.
Melchior, affirmative. Balthasar, negative. Casper, negative.
Magi self-destruct sequence has been denied.
SELF-DESTRUCT...
...IN *THEORY*, WE KNEW THIS COULD HAPPEN, BUT TO ACTUALLY SEE DR. AKAGI'S MOST RADICAL INSIGHT PLAYING OUT IN REAL TIME...UNLIKE THE HUMAN BRAIN, AN ARTIFICIAL INTELLIGENCE *NEED* NOT DIE...
...BUT UNLESS THE MAGI TOO INTERNALIZED THE CAPACITY, THE POSSIBILITY, THAT THEY THEMSELVES ***COULD*** DIE...IT COULD NEVER MODEL THE REAL WORLD WITH TRUE ACCURACY.

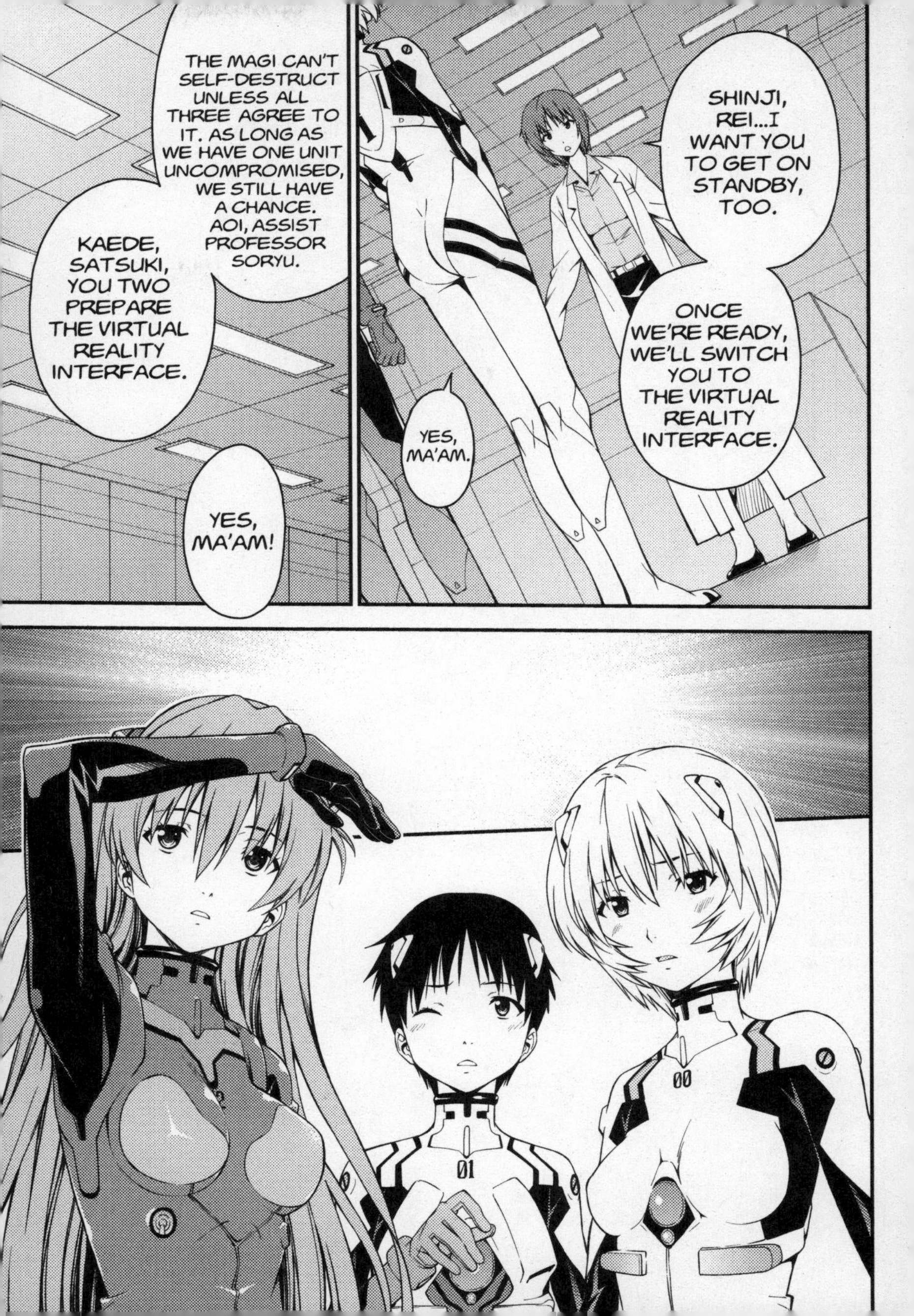
SHINJI, REI...I WANT YOU TO GET ON STANDBY, TOO.
ONCE WE'RE READY, WE'LL SWITCH YOU TO THE VIRTUAL REALITY INTERFACE.
YES, MA'AM.
THE MAGI CAN'T SELF-DESTRUCT UNLESS ALL THREE AGREE TO IT. AS LONG AS WE HAVE ONE UNIT UNCOMPROMISED, WE STILL HAVE A CHANCE. AOI, ASSIST PROFESSOR SORYU.
KAEDE, SATSUKI, YOU TWO PREPARE THE VIRTUAL REALITY INTERFACE.
YES, MA'AM!

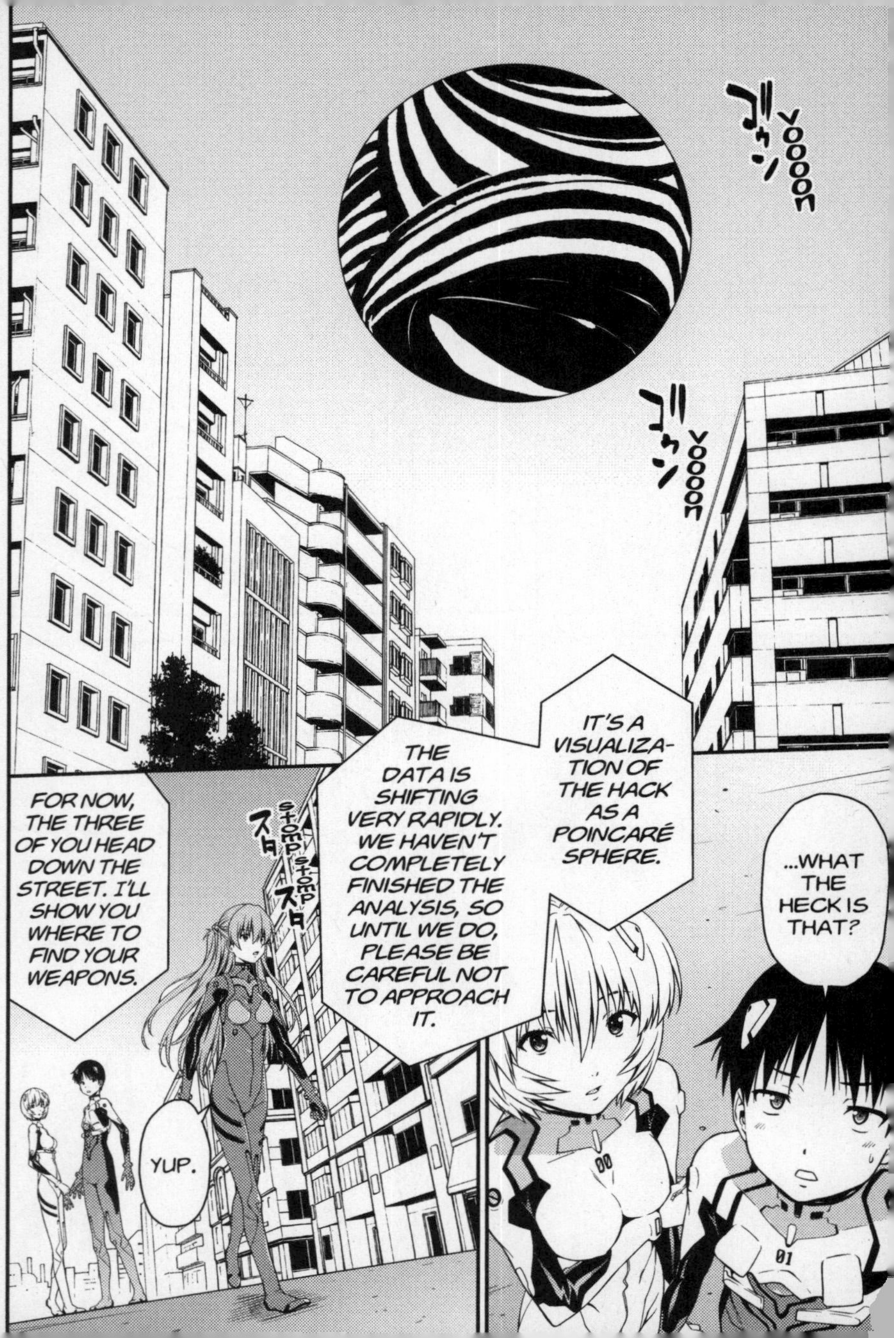
VOOOOON
VOOOOON
...WHAT THE HECK IS THAT?
IT'S A VISUALIZATION OF THE HACK AS A POINCARÉ SPHERE.
THE DATA IS SHIFTING VERY RAPIDLY. WE HAVEN'T COMPLETELY FINISHED THE ANALYSIS, SO UNTIL WE DO, PLEASE BE CAREFUL NOT TO APPROACH IT.
FOR NOW, THE THREE OF YOU HEAD DOWN THE STREET. I'LL SHOW YOU WHERE TO FIND YOUR WEAPONS.
STOMP STOMP
YUP.

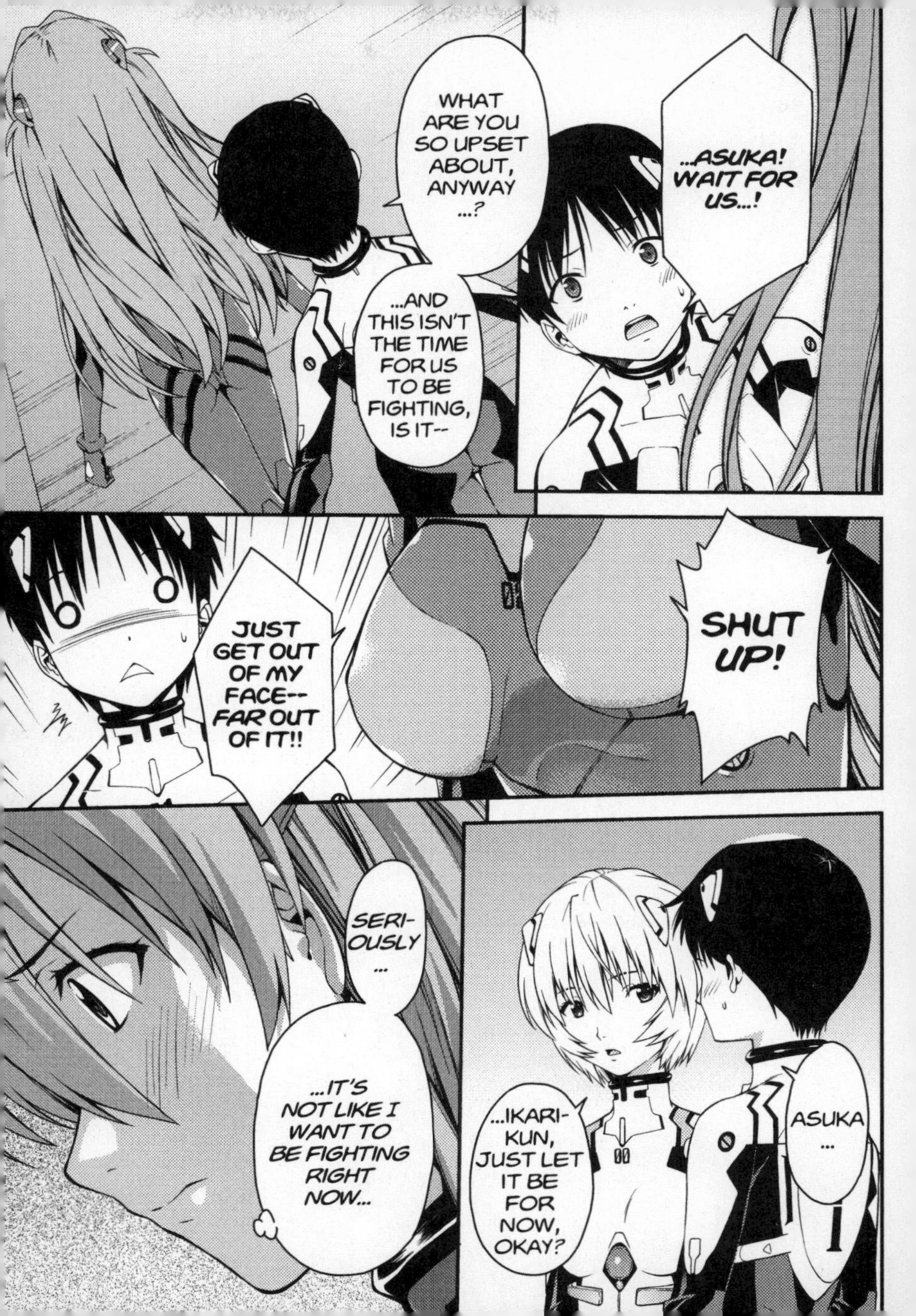
...ASUKA! WAIT FOR US...!
WHAT ARE YOU SO UPSET ABOUT, ANYWAY ...?
...AND THIS ISN'T THE TIME FOR US TO BE FIGHTING, IS IT--
SHUT UP!
JUST GET OUT OF MY FACE-- FAR OUT OF IT!!
ASUKA ...
...IKARI-KUN, JUST LET IT BE FOR NOW, OKAY?
SERI-OUSLY ...
...IT'S NOT LIKE I WANT TO BE FIGHTING RIGHT NOW...

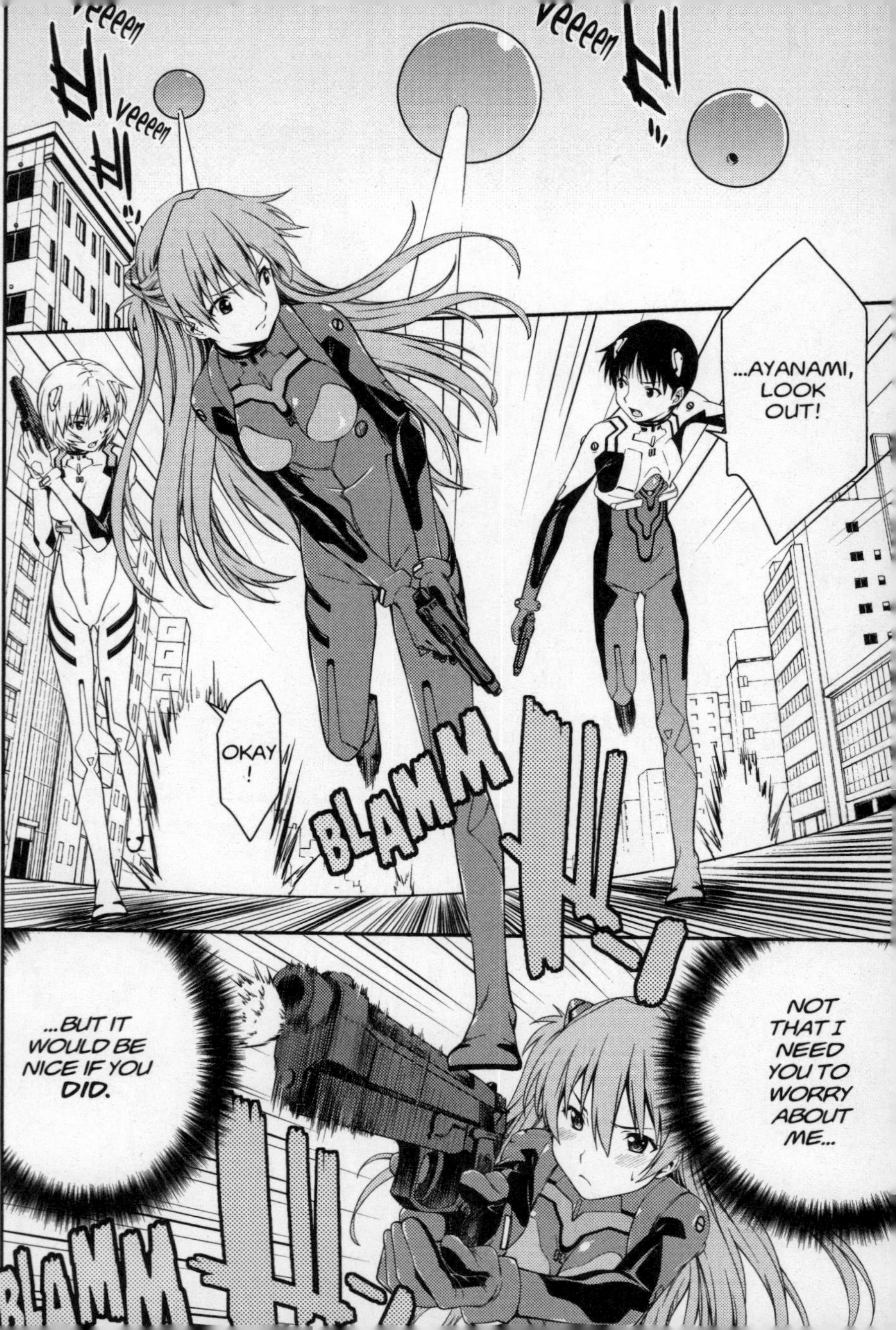
veeeen
veeeen
veeeen
...AYANAMI, LOOK OUT!
OKAY!
BLAMM
NOT THAT I NEED YOU TO WORRY ABOUT ME...
...BUT IT WOULD BE NICE IF YOU DID.
BLAMM

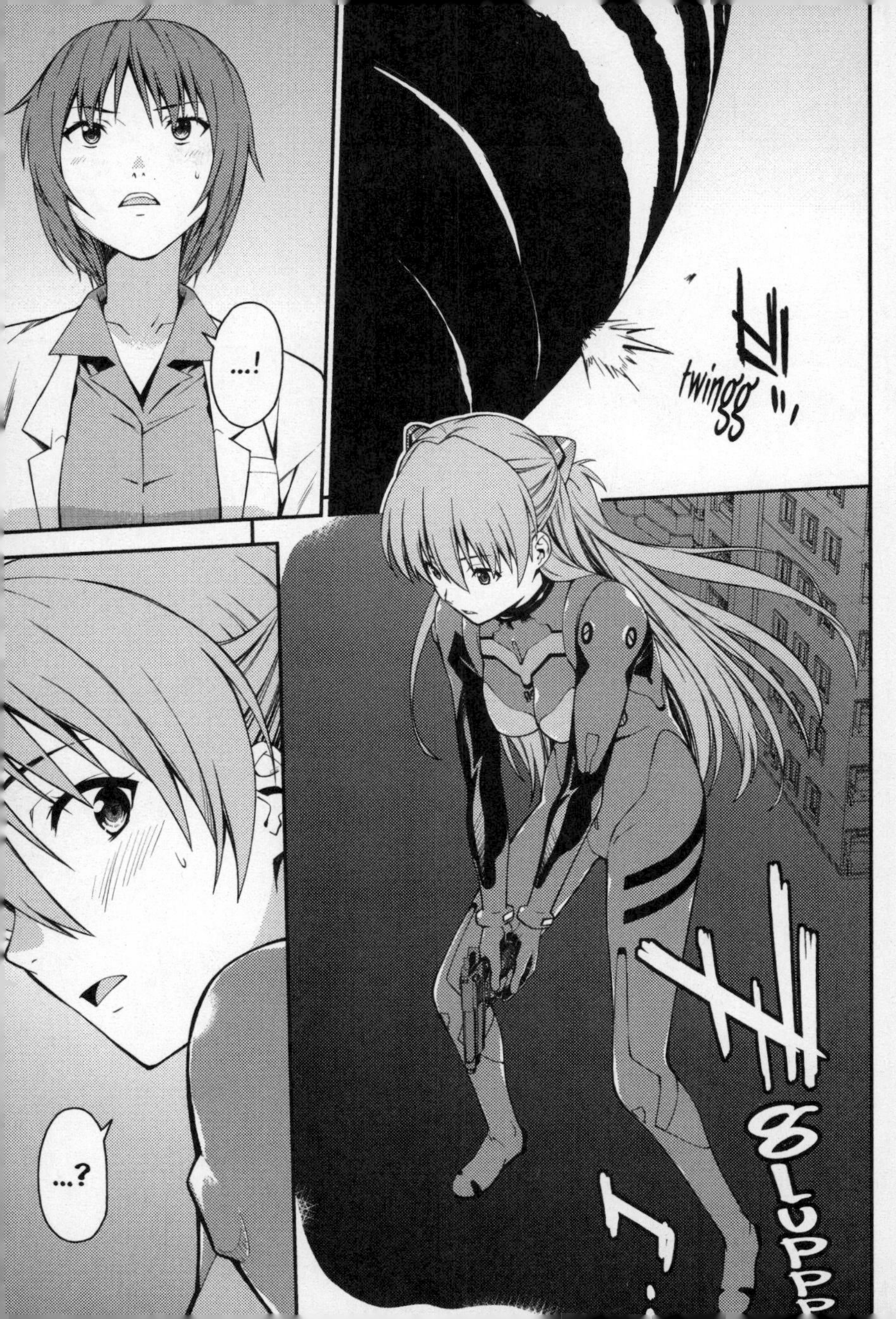
twingg
...!
SLUPP
...?

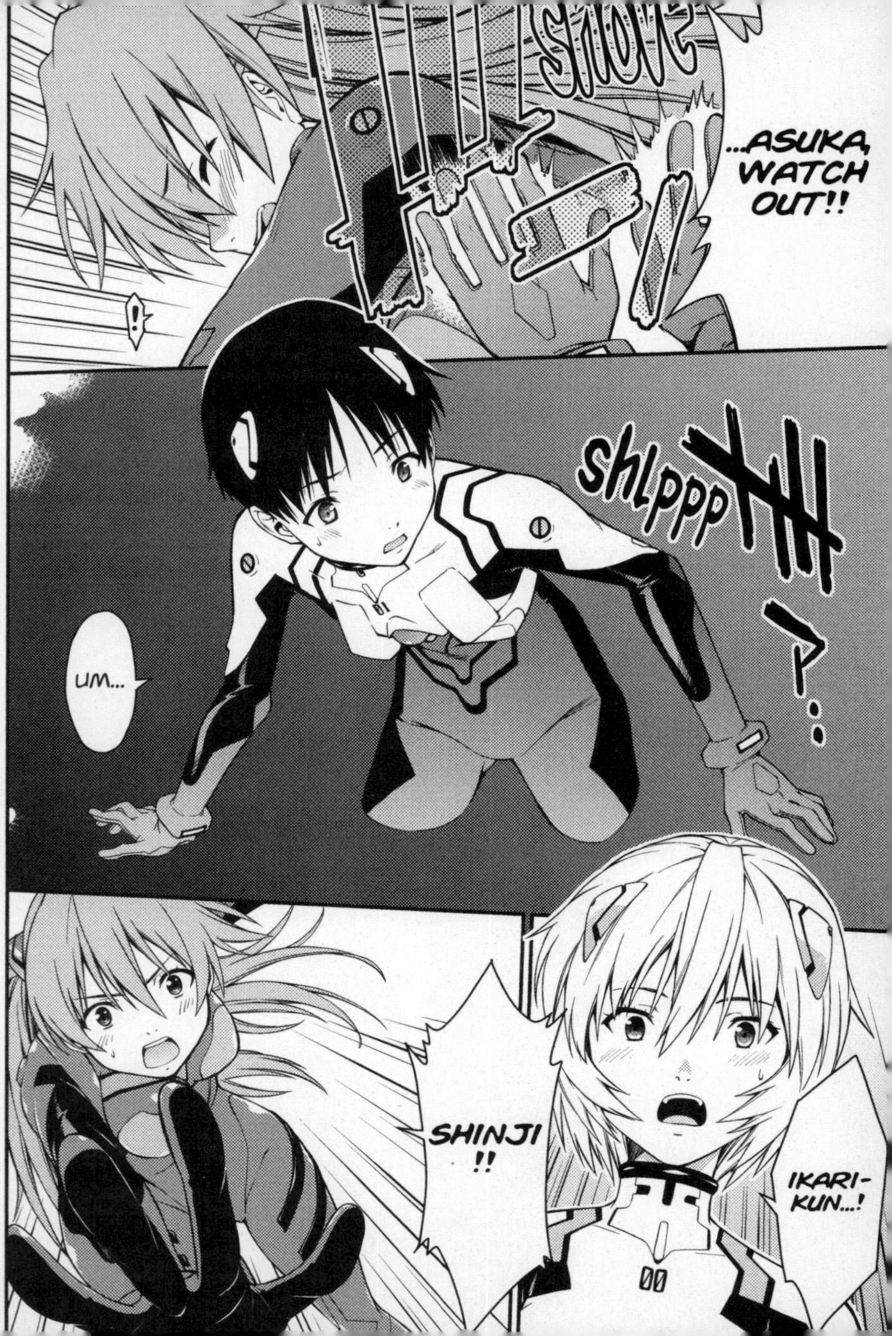
shove
...ASUKA, WATCH OUT!!
!
shlppp
?..
UM...
IKARI-KUN...!
SHINJI!!

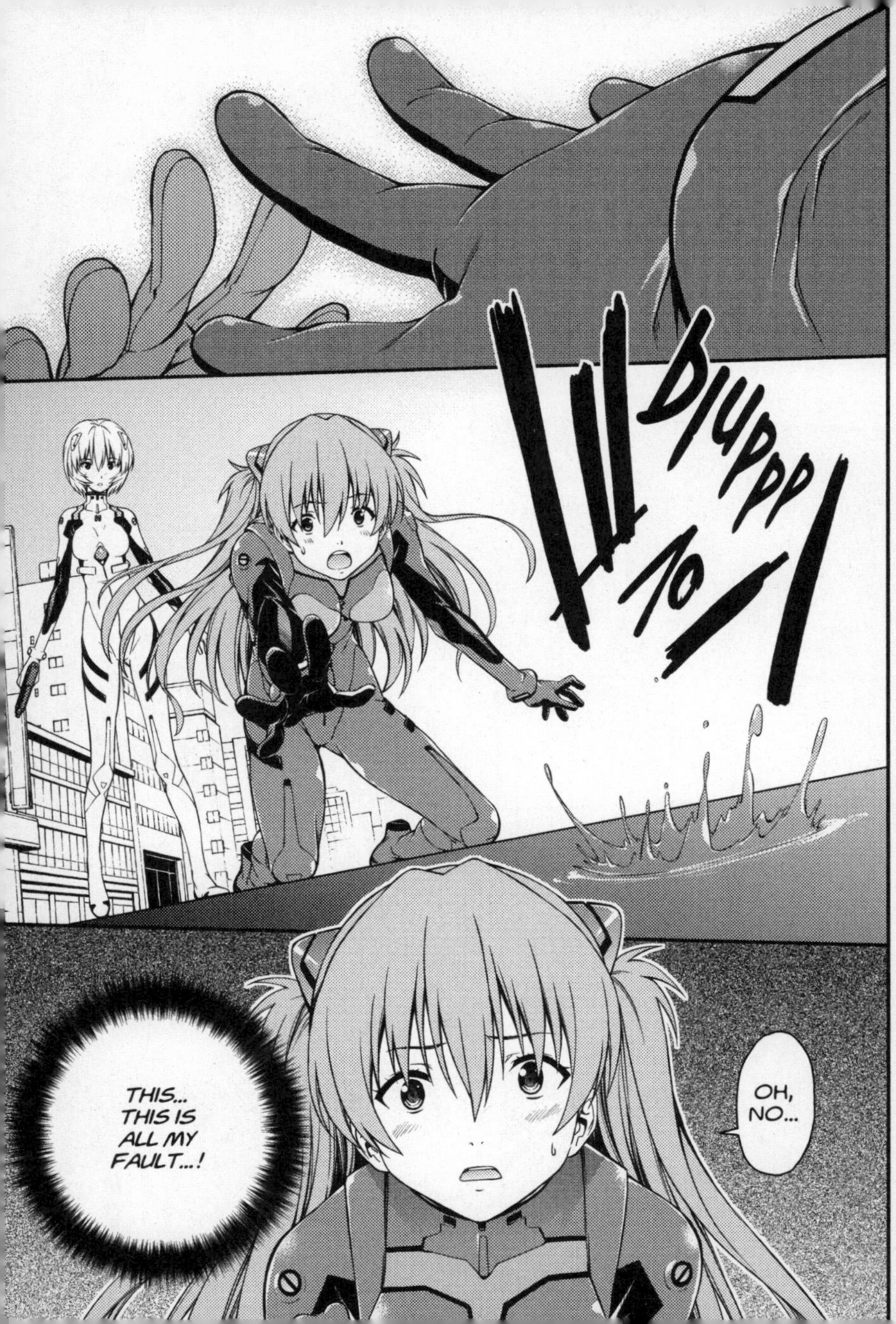
OH, NO...
THIS... THIS IS ALL MY FAULT...!

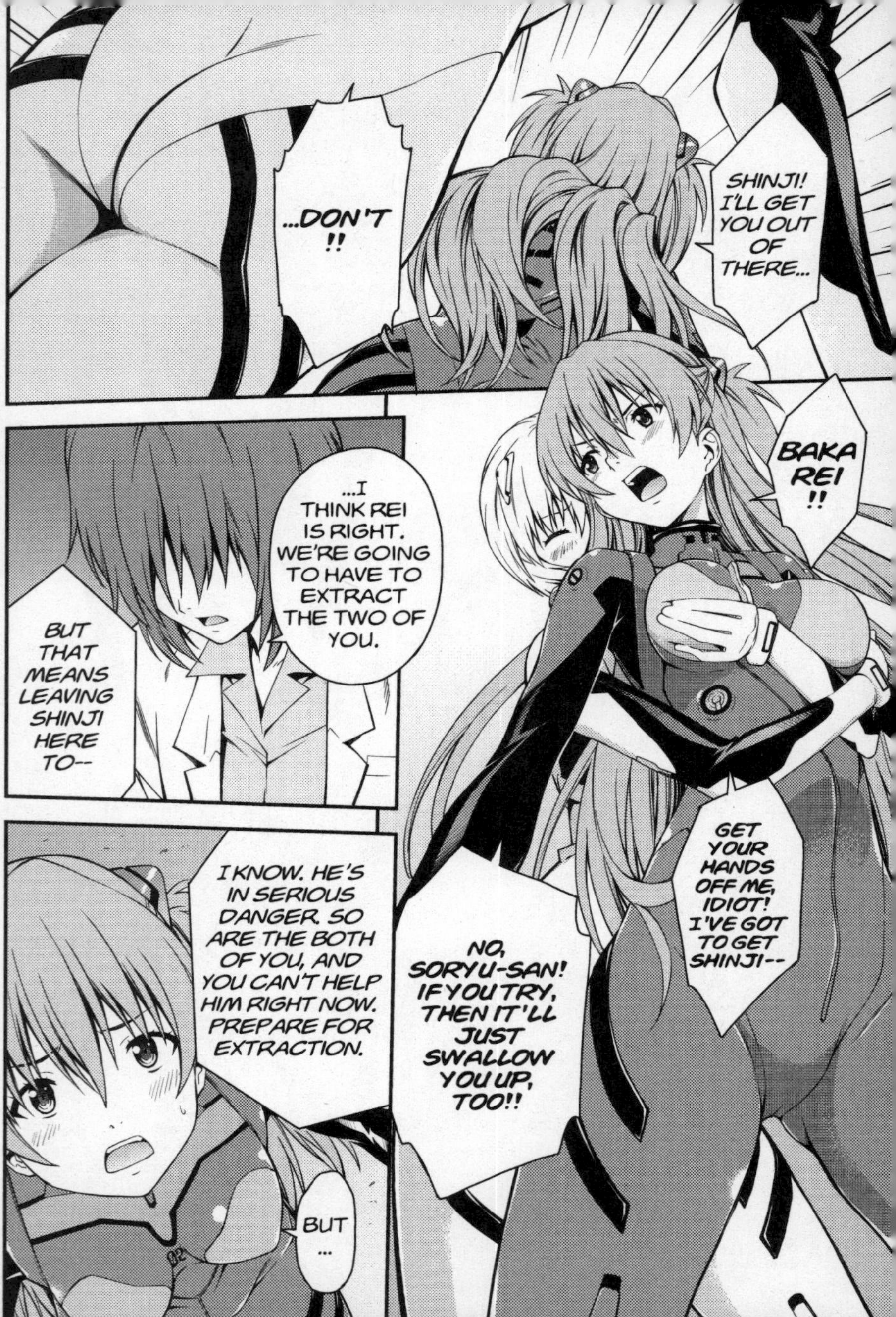
SHINJI! I'LL GET YOU OUT OF THERE...
...DON'T !!
BAKA REI !!
GET YOUR HANDS OFF ME, IDIOT! I'VE GOT TO GET SHINJI--
NO, SORYU-SAN! IF YOU TRY, THEN IT'LL JUST SWALLOW YOU UP, TOO!!
...I THINK REI IS RIGHT. WE'RE GOING TO HAVE TO EXTRACT THE TWO OF YOU.
BUT THAT MEANS LEAVING SHINJI HERE TO--
I KNOW. HE'S IN SERIOUS DANGER. SO ARE THE BOTH OF YOU, AND YOU CAN'T HELP HIM RIGHT NOW. PREPARE FOR EXTRACTION.
BUT ...

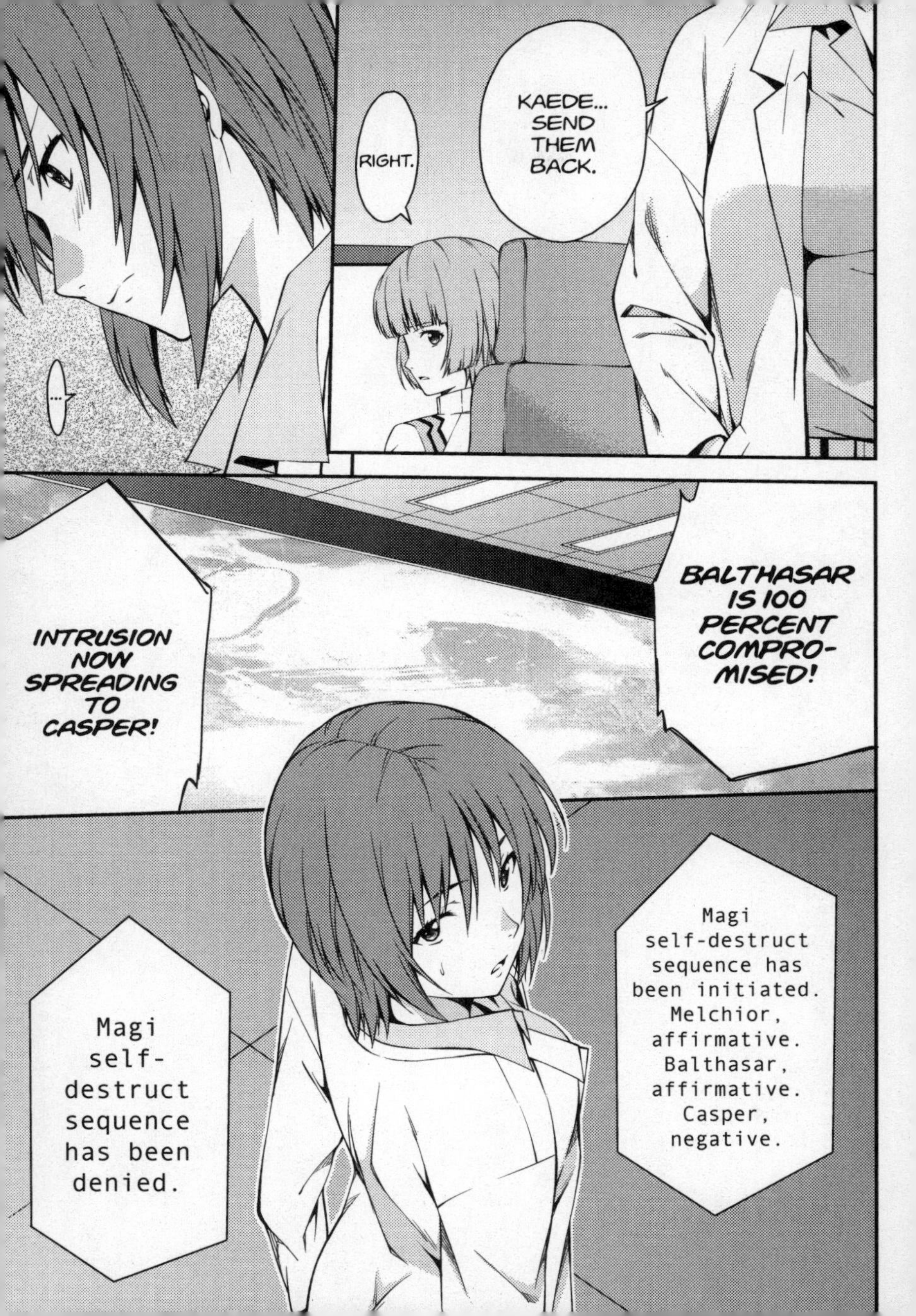
KAEDE... SEND THEM BACK.
RIGHT.
...
BALTHASAR IS 100 PERCENT COMPRO-MISED!
INTRUSION NOW SPREADING TO CASPER!
Magi self-destruct sequence has been initiated. Melchior, affirmative. Balthasar, affirmative. Casper, negative.
Magi self-destruct sequence has been denied.

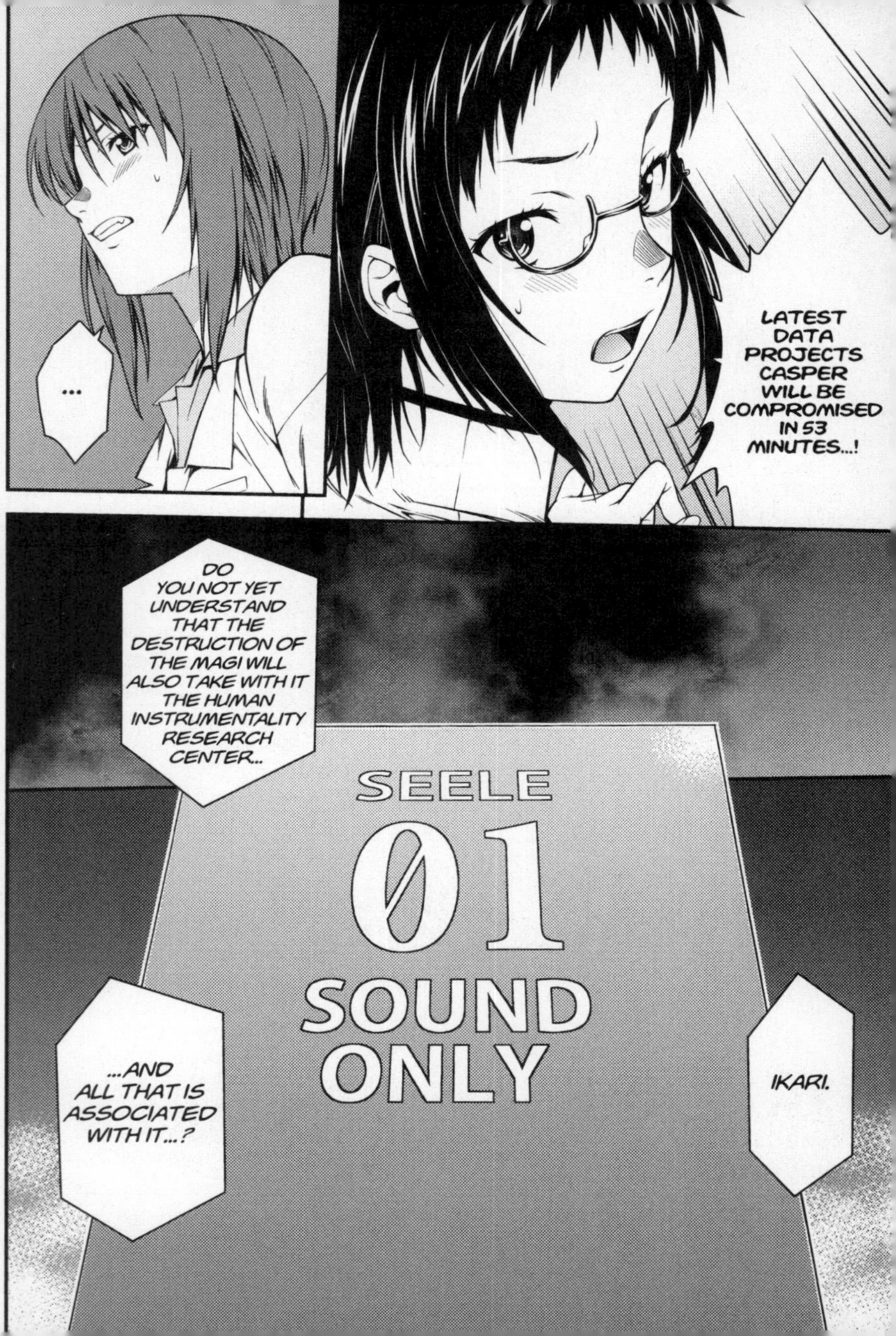
LATEST DATA PROJECTS CASPER WILL BE COMPROMISED IN 53 MINUTES...!
...
DO YOU NOT YET UNDERSTAND THAT THE DESTRUCTION OF THE MAGI WILL ALSO TAKE WITH IT THE HUMAN INSTRUMENTALITY RESEARCH CENTER...
SEELE
01
SOUND ONLY
IKARI.
...AND ALL THAT IS ASSOCIATED WITH IT...?

the shinji ikari raising project

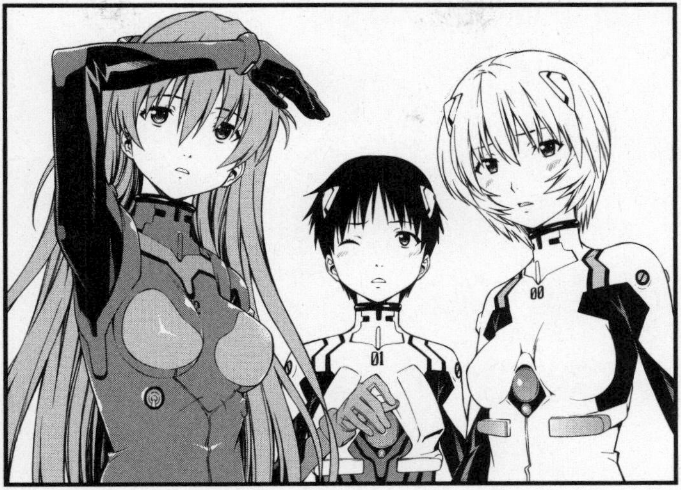

NEON GENESIS
EVANGELION
THE SHINJI IKARI RAISING PROJECT

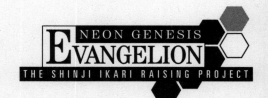

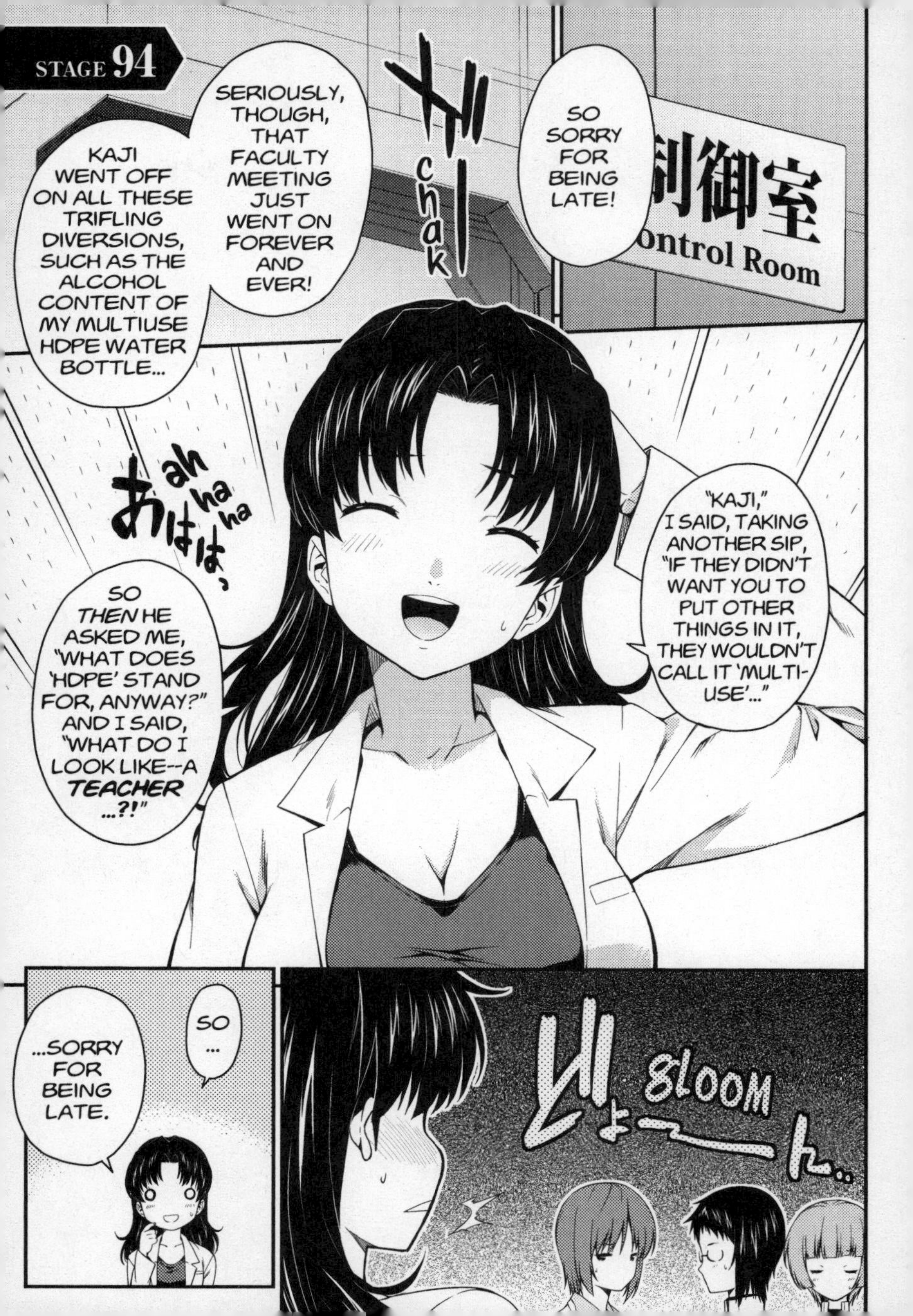
STAGE 94
SO SORRY FOR BEING LATE!
chak
SERIOUSLY, THOUGH, THAT FACULTY MEETING JUST WENT ON FOREVER AND EVER!
KAJI WENT OFF ON ALL THESE TRIFLING DIVERSIONS, SUCH AS THE ALCOHOL CONTENT OF MY MULTIUSE HDPE WATER BOTTLE...
"KAJI," I SAID, TAKING ANOTHER SIP, "IF THEY DIDN'T WANT YOU TO PUT OTHER THINGS IN IT, THEY WOULDN'T CALL IT 'MULTI-USE'..."
あははは
ah ha ha
SO *THEN* HE ASKED ME, "WHAT DOES 'HDPE' STAND FOR, ANYWAY?" AND I SAID, "WHAT DO I LOOK LIKE--A ***TEACHER*** ...?!"
GLOOM
SO ...
...SORRY FOR BEING LATE.

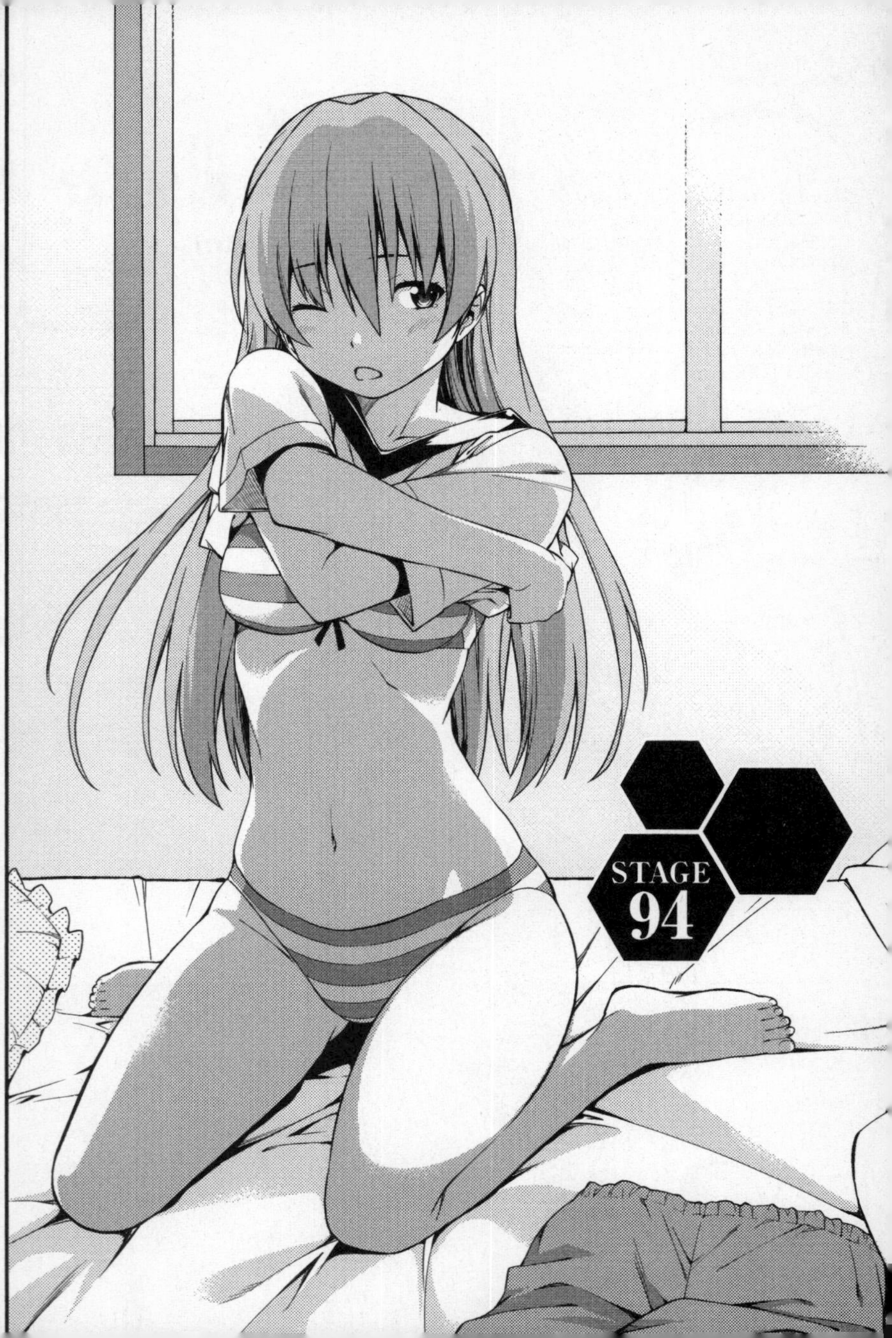
STAGE
94

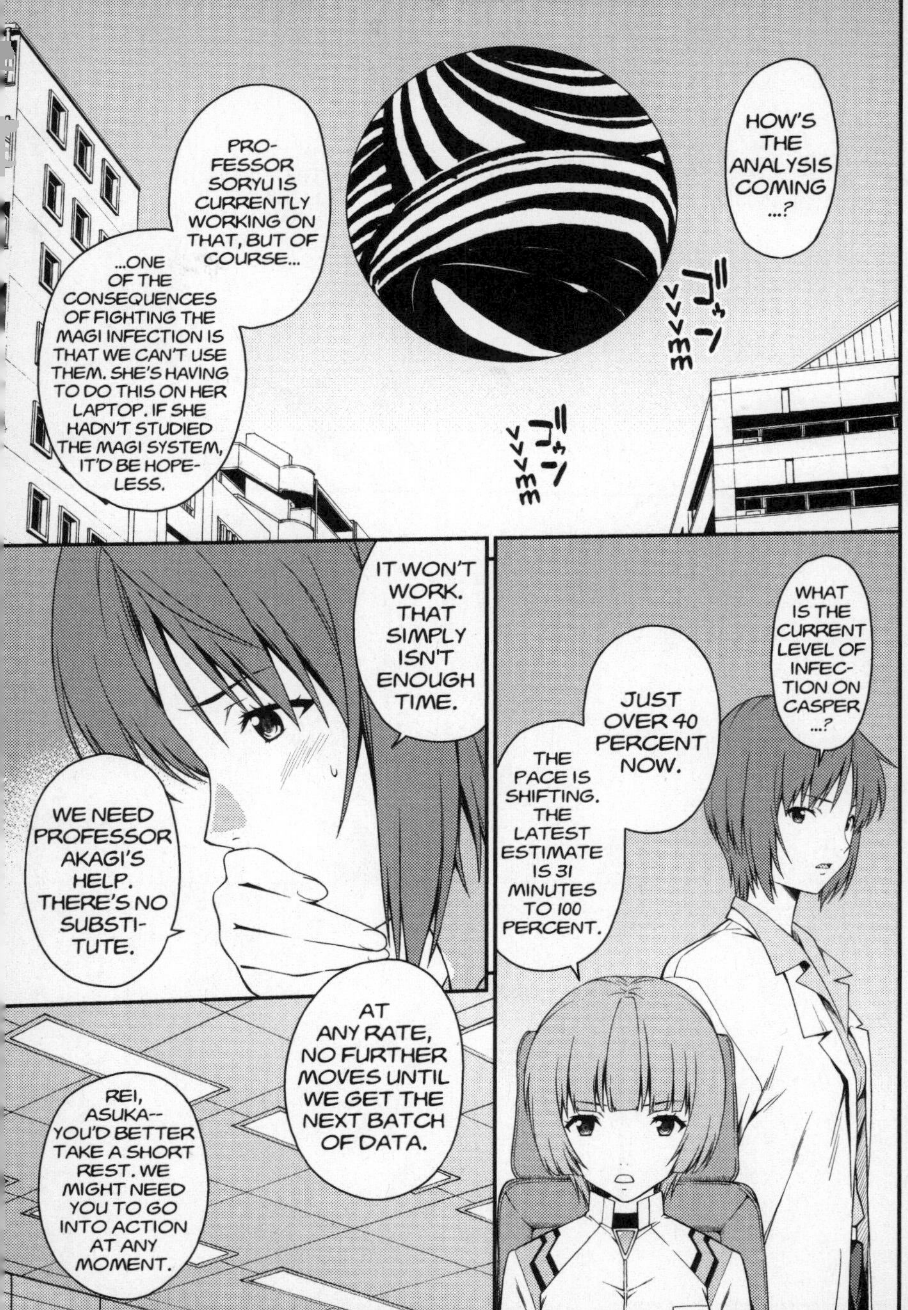
HOW'S THE ANALYSIS COMING ...?
PRO-FESSOR SORYU IS CURRENTLY WORKING ON THAT, BUT OF COURSE...
...ONE OF THE CONSEQUENCES OF FIGHTING THE MAGI INFECTION IS THAT WE CAN'T USE THEM. SHE'S HAVING TO DO THIS ON HER LAPTOP. IF SHE HADN'T STUDIED THE MAGI SYSTEM, IT'D BE HOPE-LESS.
WHAT IS THE CURRENT LEVEL OF INFEC-TION ON CASPER ...?
JUST OVER 40 PERCENT NOW.
THE PACE IS SHIFTING. THE LATEST ESTIMATE IS 31 MINUTES TO 100 PERCENT.
IT WON'T WORK. THAT SIMPLY ISN'T ENOUGH TIME.
WE NEED PROFESSOR AKAGI'S HELP. THERE'S NO SUBSTI-TUTE.
AT ANY RATE, NO FURTHER MOVES UNTIL WE GET THE NEXT BATCH OF DATA.
REI, ASUKA-- YOU'D BETTER TAKE A SHORT REST. WE MIGHT NEED YOU TO GO INTO ACTION AT ANY MOMENT.

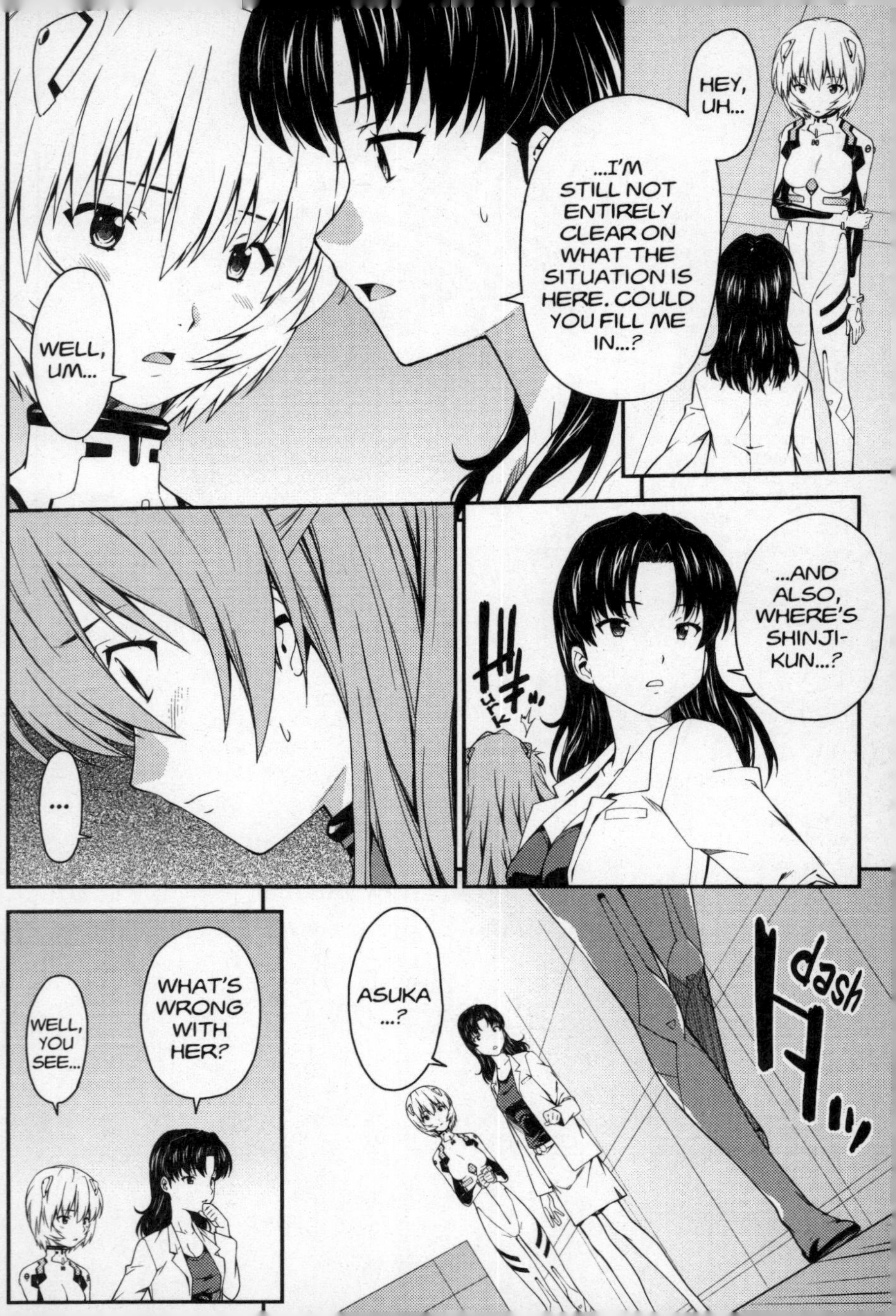
HEY, UH...
...I'M STILL NOT ENTIRELY CLEAR ON WHAT THE SITUATION IS HERE. COULD YOU FILL ME IN...?
WELL, UM...
...AND ALSO, WHERE'S SHINJI-KUN...?
...
dash
ASUKA ...?
WHAT'S WRONG WITH HER?
WELL, YOU SEE...

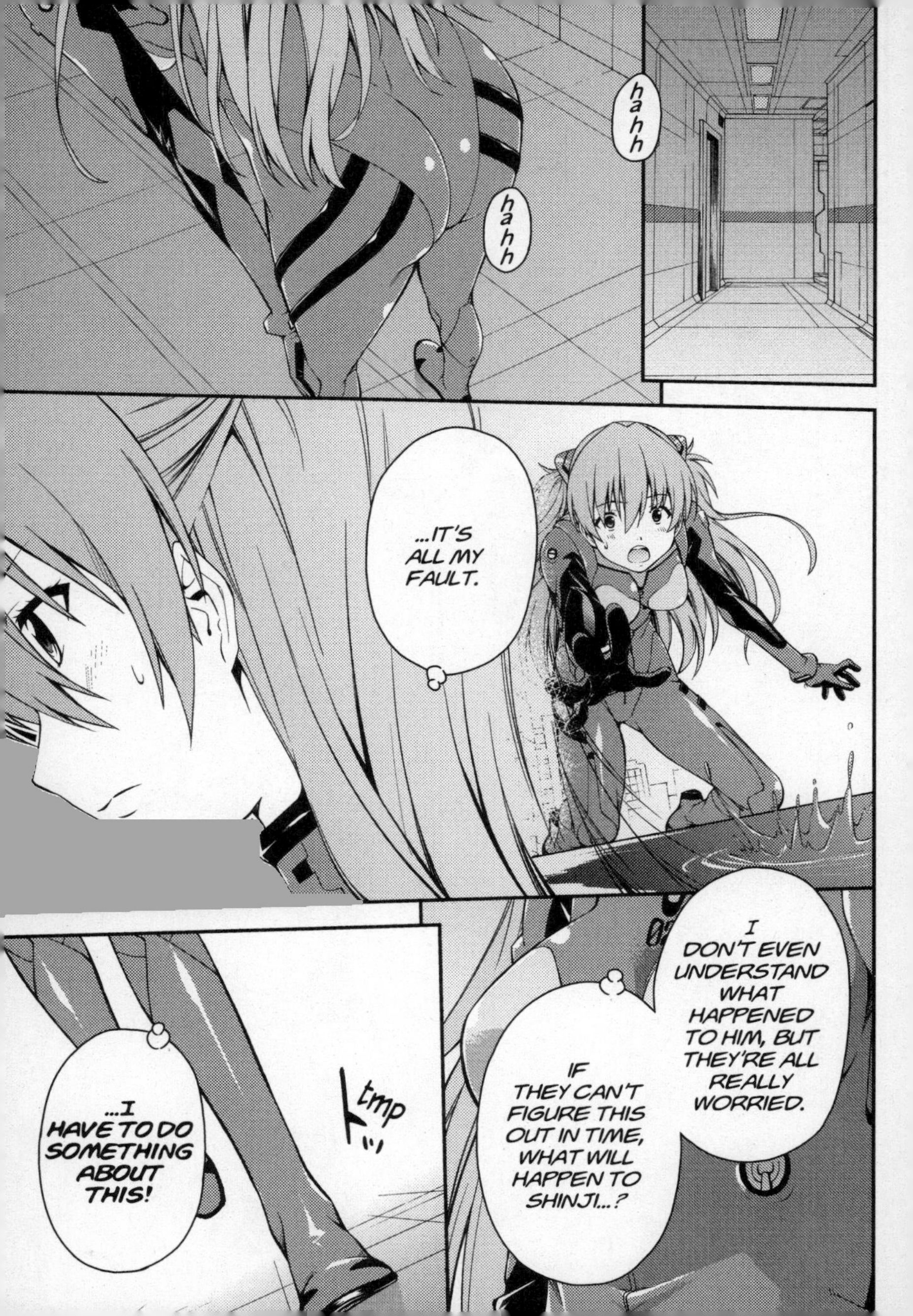
hahh
hahh
...IT'S ALL MY FAULT.
I DON'T EVEN UNDERSTAND WHAT HAPPENED TO HIM, BUT THEY'RE ALL REALLY WORRIED.
IF THEY CAN'T FIGURE THIS OUT IN TIME, WHAT WILL HAPPEN TO SHINJI...?
tmp
...I HAVE TO DO SOMETHING ABOUT THIS!

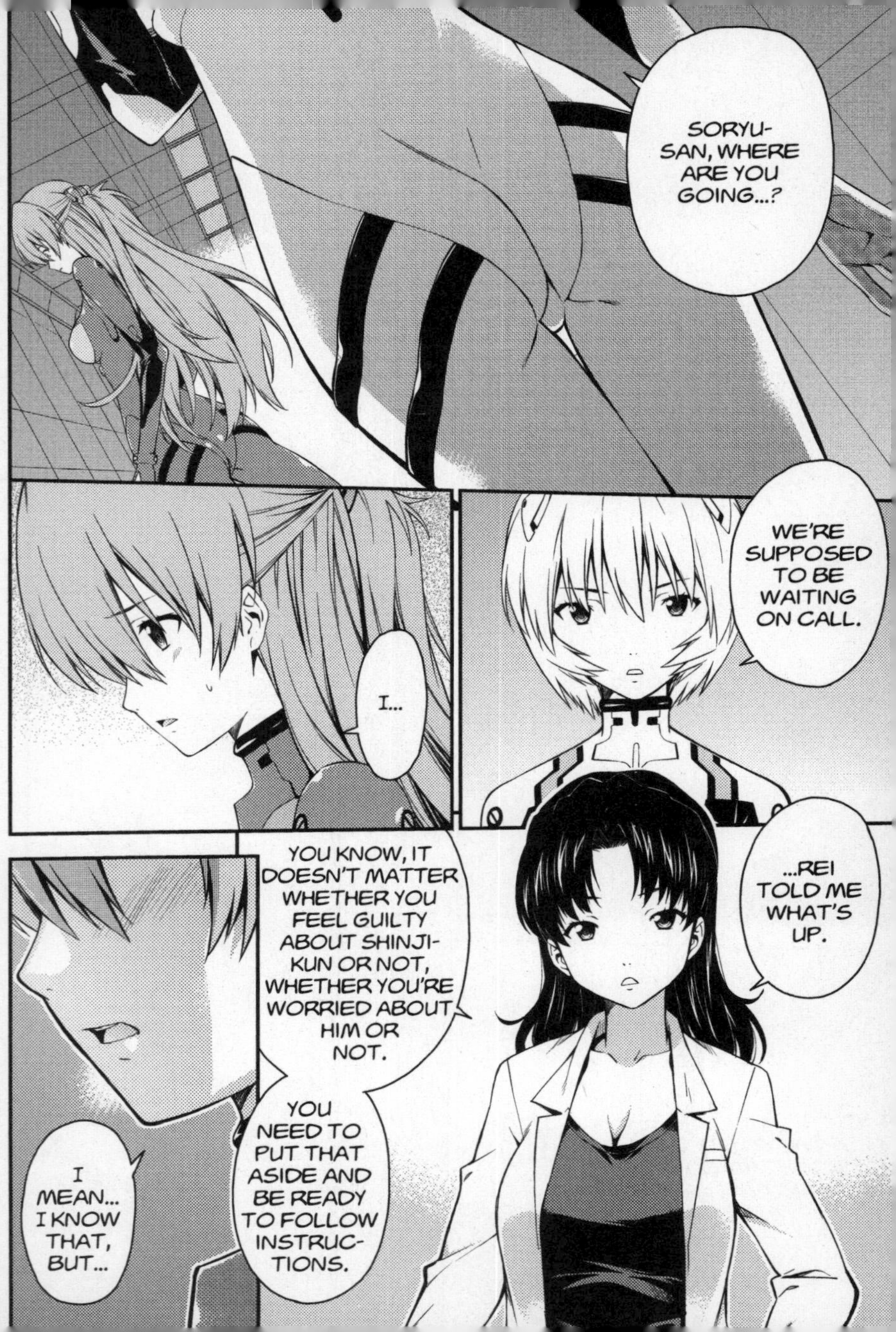
SORYU-SAN, WHERE ARE YOU GOING...?
WE'RE SUPPOSED TO BE WAITING ON CALL.
I...
...REI TOLD ME WHAT'S UP.
YOU KNOW, IT DOESN'T MATTER WHETHER YOU FEEL GUILTY ABOUT SHINJI-KUN OR NOT, WHETHER YOU'RE WORRIED ABOUT HIM OR NOT.
YOU NEED TO PUT THAT ASIDE AND BE READY TO FOLLOW INSTRUC-TIONS.
I MEAN... I KNOW THAT, BUT...

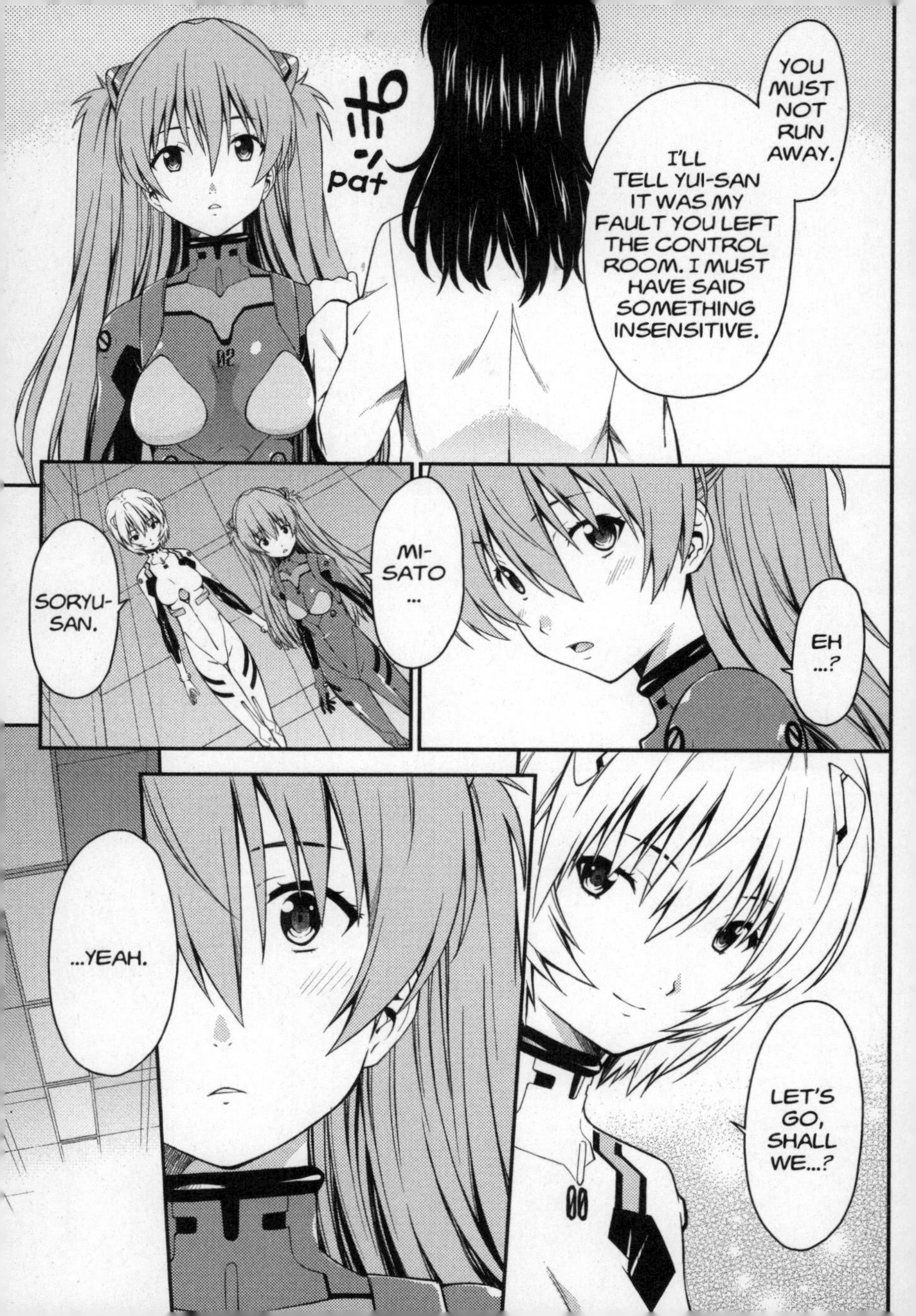
YOU MUST NOT RUN AWAY.
I'LL TELL YUI-SAN IT WAS MY FAULT YOU LEFT THE CONTROL ROOM. I MUST HAVE SAID SOMETHING INSENSITIVE.
pat
EH ...?
MI-SATO ...
SORYU-SAN.
LET'S GO, SHALL WE...?
...YEAH.

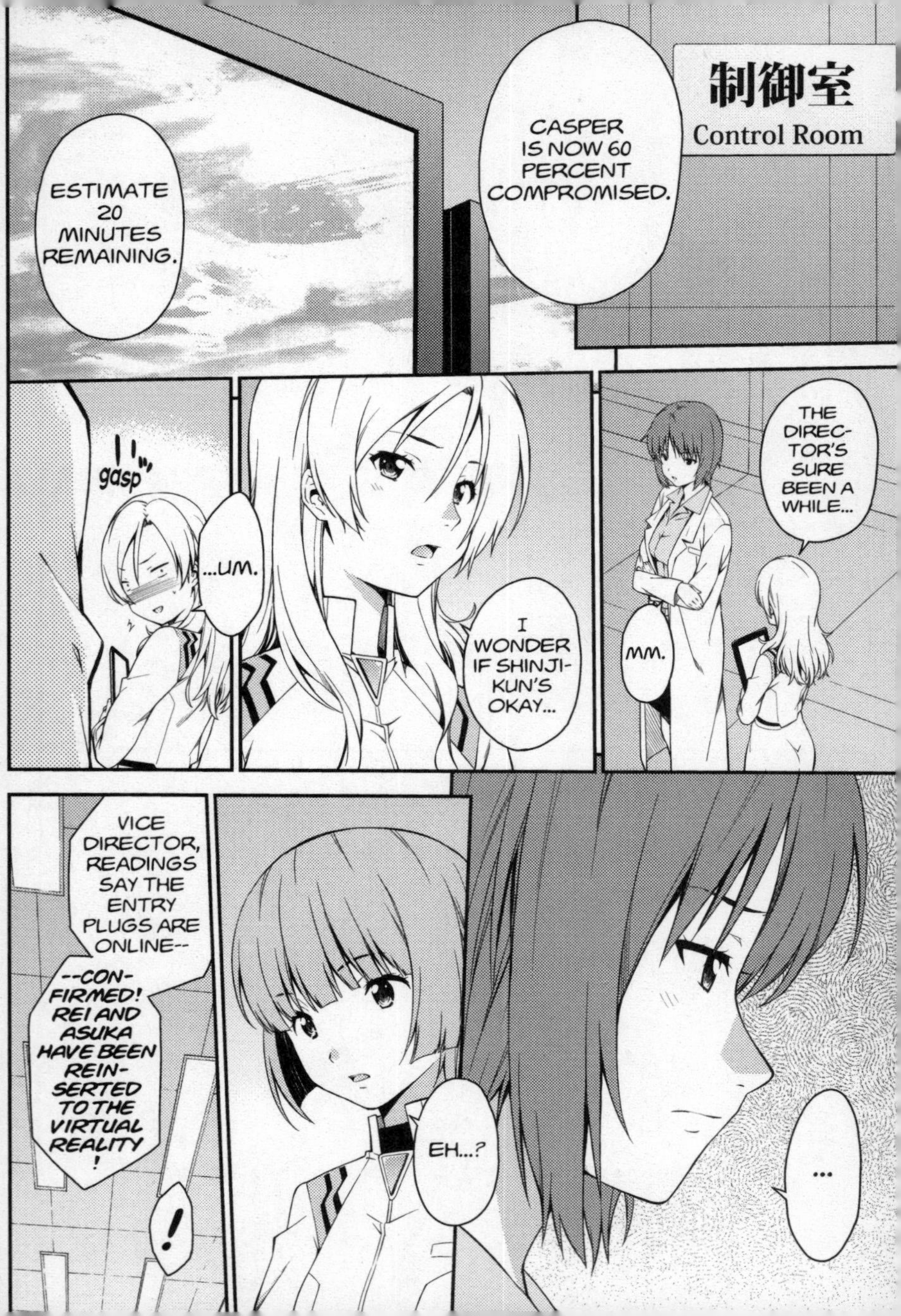
制御室
Control Room
CASPER IS NOW 60 PERCENT COMPROMISED.
ESTIMATE 20 MINUTES REMAINING.
THE DIRECTOR'S SURE BEEN A WHILE...
MM.
I WONDER IF SHINJI-KUN'S OKAY...
gasp
...UM.
...
EH...?
VICE DIRECTOR, READINGS SAY THE ENTRY PLUGS ARE ONLINE--
--CONFIRMED! REI AND ASUKA HAVE BEEN REINSERTED TO THE VIRTUAL REALITY!
!

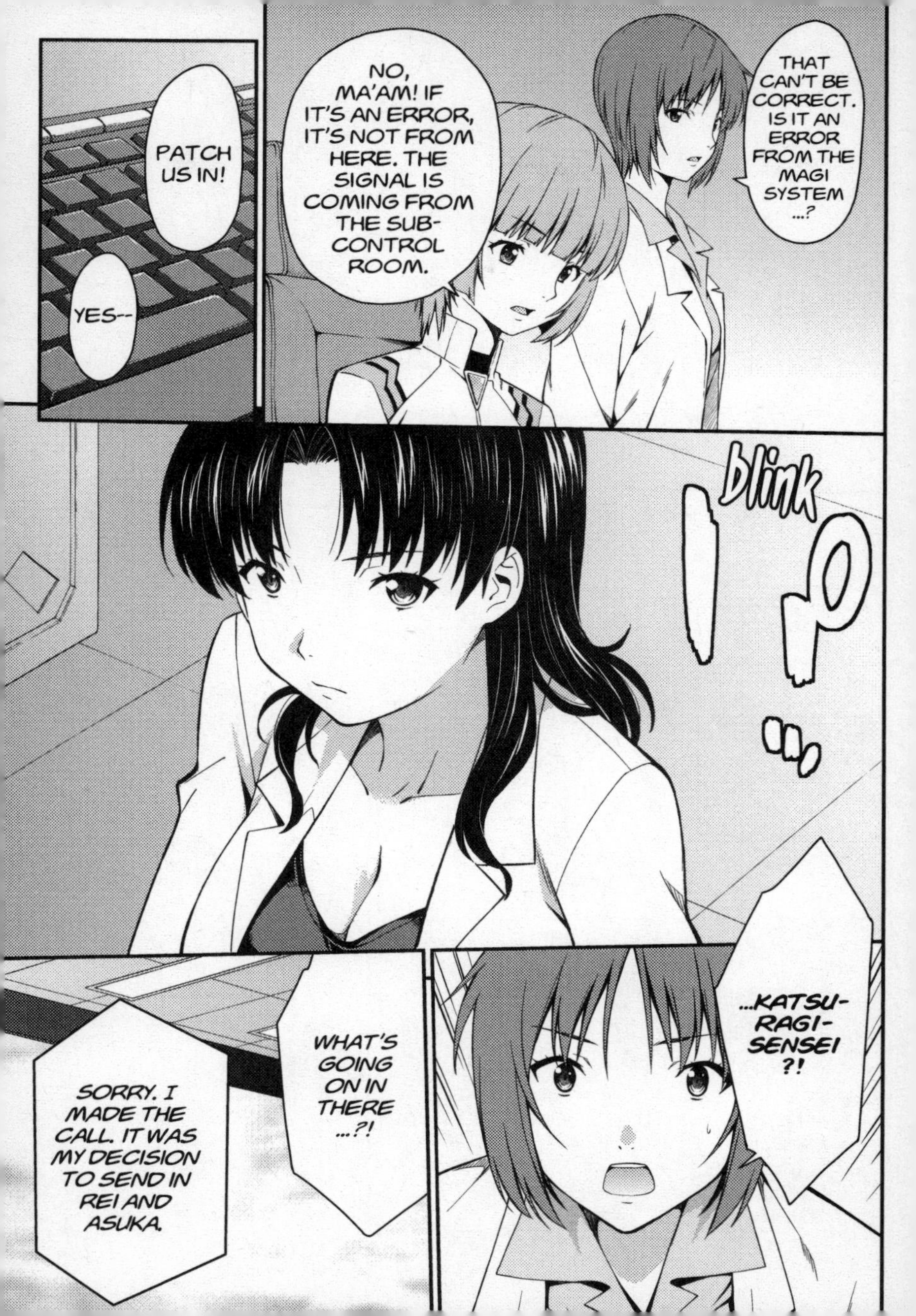
THAT CAN'T BE CORRECT. IS IT AN ERROR FROM THE MAGI SYSTEM ...?
NO, MA'AM! IF IT'S AN ERROR, IT'S NOT FROM HERE. THE SIGNAL IS COMING FROM THE SUB-CONTROL ROOM.
PATCH US IN!
YES--
blink
...KATSURAGI-SENSEI?!
WHAT'S GOING ON IN THERE ...?!
SORRY. I MADE THE CALL. IT WAS MY DECISION TO SEND IN REI AND ASUKA.

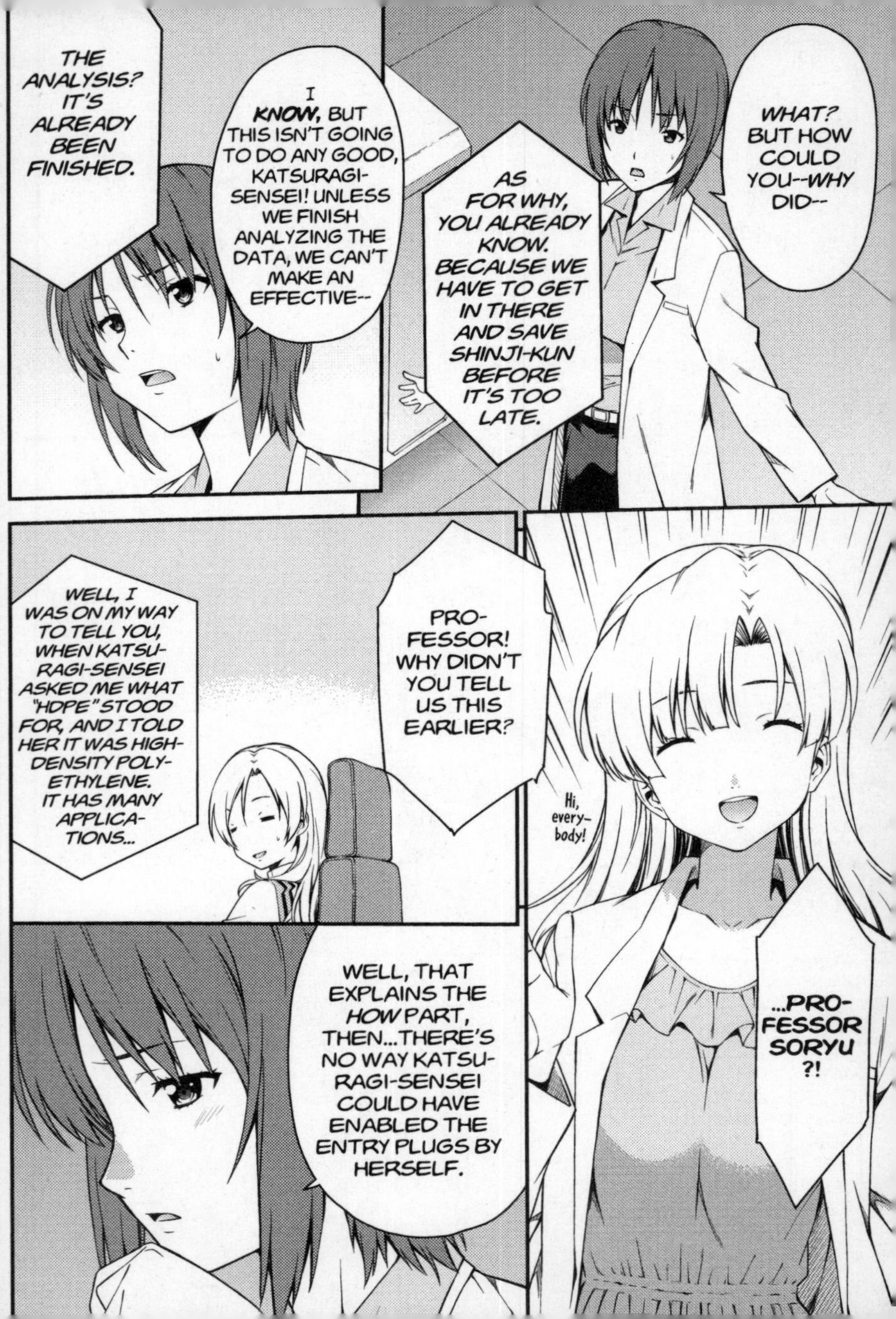
WHAT? BUT HOW COULD YOU--WHY DID--
AS FOR WHY, YOU ALREADY KNOW. BECAUSE WE HAVE TO GET IN THERE AND SAVE SHINJI-KUN BEFORE IT'S TOO LATE.
I *KNOW*, BUT THIS ISN'T GOING TO DO ANY GOOD, KATSURAGI-SENSEI! UNLESS WE FINISH ANALYZING THE DATA, WE CAN'T MAKE AN EFFECTIVE--
THE ANALYSIS? IT'S ALREADY BEEN FINISHED.
Hi, every-body!
...PRO-FESSOR SORYU?!
PRO-FESSOR! WHY DIDN'T YOU TELL US THIS EARLIER?
WELL, I WAS ON MY WAY TO TELL YOU, WHEN KATSU-RAGI-SENSEI ASKED ME WHAT "HDPE" STOOD FOR, AND I TOLD HER IT WAS HIGH-DENSITY POLY-ETHYLENE. IT HAS MANY APPLICA-TIONS...
WELL, THAT EXPLAINS THE *HOW* PART, THEN...THERE'S NO WAY KATSU-RAGI-SENSEI COULD HAVE ENABLED THE ENTRY PLUGS BY HERSELF.

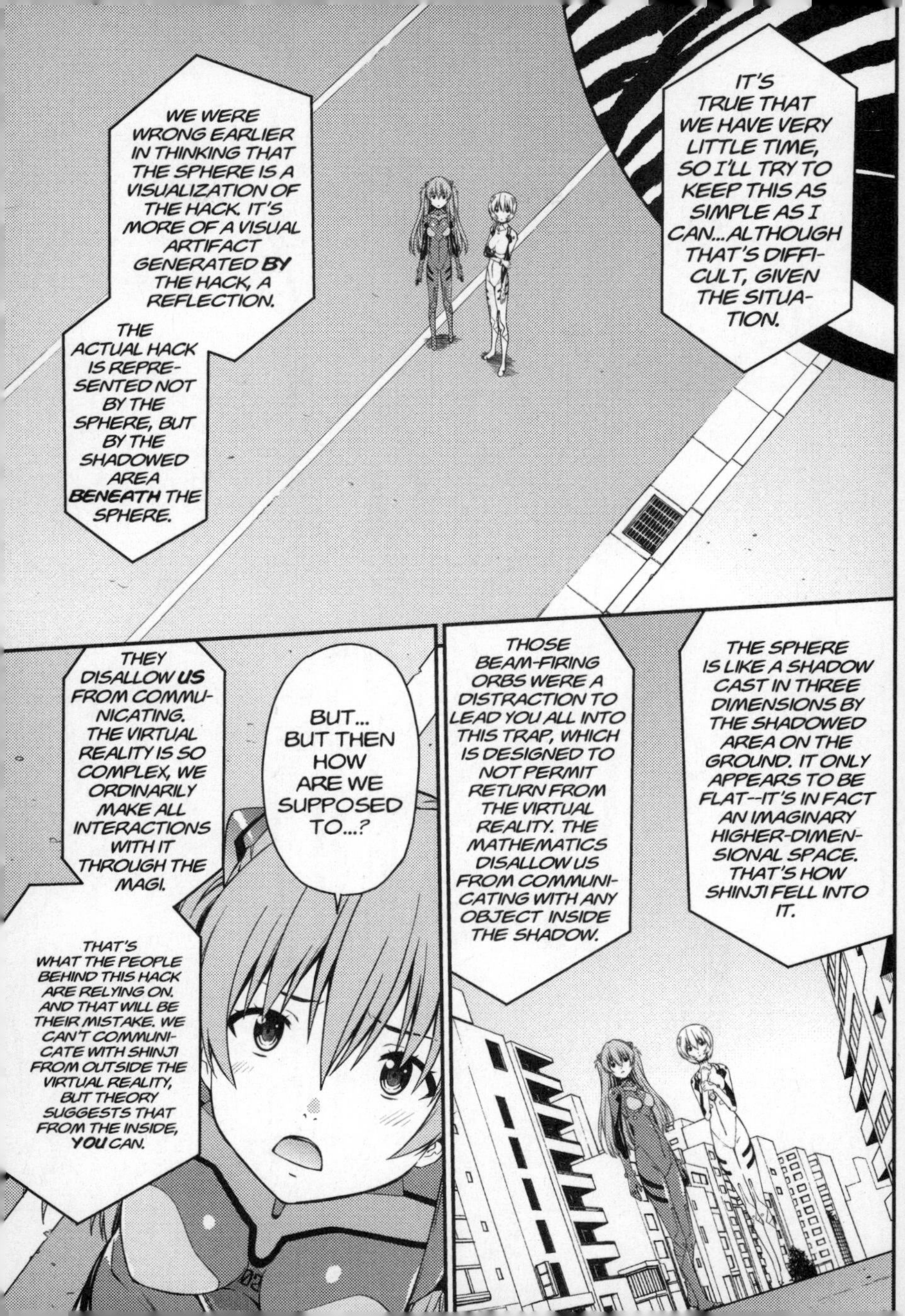
IT'S TRUE THAT WE HAVE VERY LITTLE TIME, SO I'LL TRY TO KEEP THIS AS SIMPLE AS I CAN...ALTHOUGH THAT'S DIFFI-CULT, GIVEN THE SITUA-TION.
WE WERE WRONG EARLIER IN THINKING THAT THE SPHERE IS A VISUALIZATION OF THE HACK. IT'S MORE OF A VISUAL ARTIFACT GENERATED **BY** THE HACK, A REFLECTION.
THE ACTUAL HACK IS REPRE-SENTED NOT BY THE SPHERE, BUT BY THE SHADOWED AREA **BENEATH** THE SPHERE.
THE SPHERE IS LIKE A SHADOW CAST IN THREE DIMENSIONS BY THE SHADOWED AREA ON THE GROUND. IT ONLY APPEARS TO BE FLAT--IT'S IN FACT AN IMAGINARY HIGHER-DIMEN-SIONAL SPACE. THAT'S HOW SHINJI FELL INTO IT.
THOSE BEAM-FIRING ORBS WERE A DISTRACTION TO LEAD YOU ALL INTO THIS TRAP, WHICH IS DESIGNED TO NOT PERMIT RETURN FROM THE VIRTUAL REALITY. THE MATHEMATICS DISALLOW US FROM COMMUNI-CATING WITH ANY OBJECT INSIDE THE SHADOW.
BUT... BUT THEN HOW ARE WE SUPPOSED TO...?
THEY DISALLOW **US** FROM COMMU-NICATING. THE VIRTUAL REALITY IS SO COMPLEX, WE ORDINARILY MAKE ALL INTERACTIONS WITH IT THROUGH THE MAGI.
THAT'S WHAT THE PEOPLE BEHIND THIS HACK ARE RELYING ON. AND THAT WILL BE THEIR MISTAKE. WE CAN'T COMMUNI-CATE WITH SHINJI FROM OUTSIDE THE VIRTUAL REALITY, BUT THEORY SUGGESTS THAT FROM THE INSIDE, **YOU** CAN.

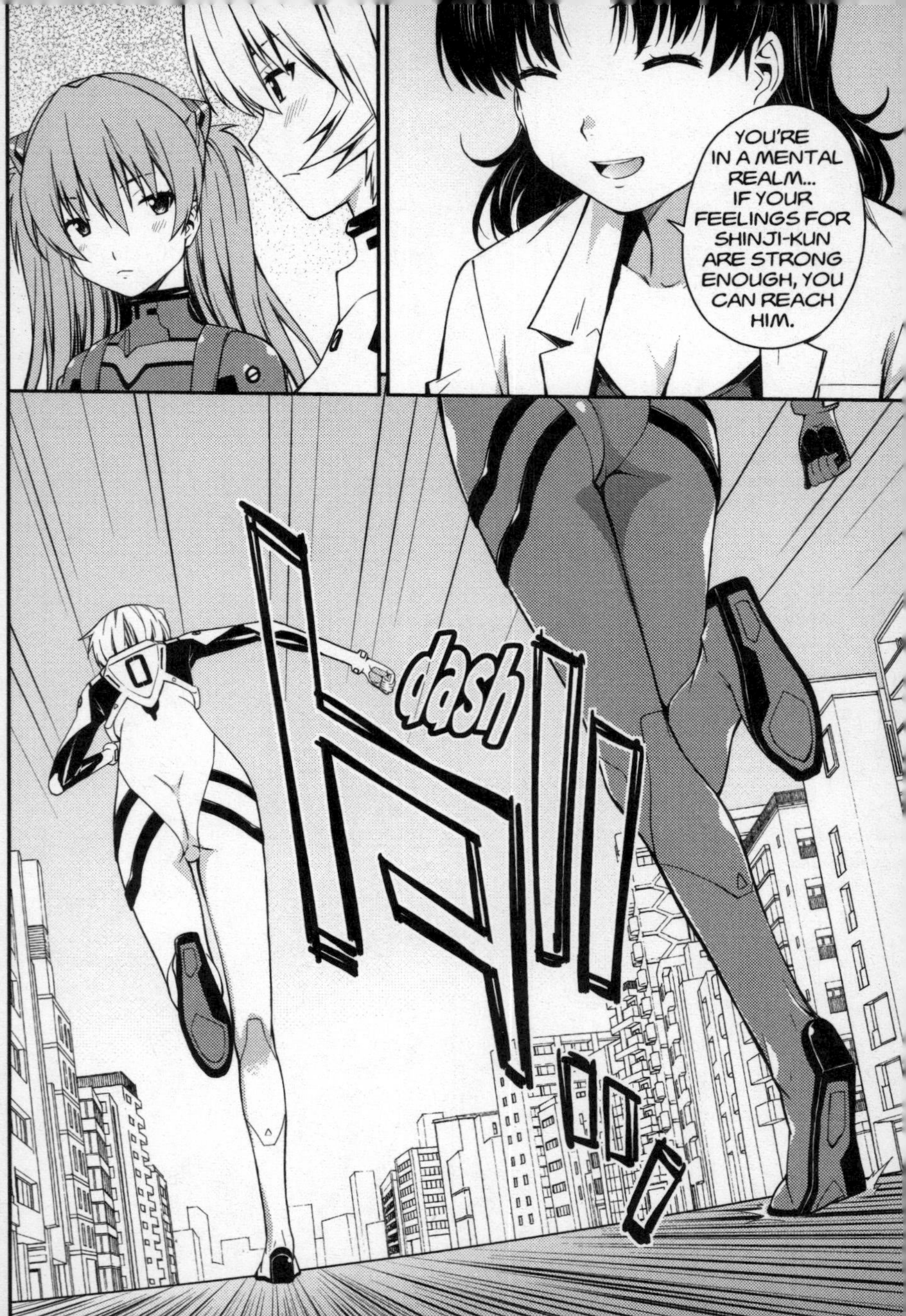
YOU'RE IN A MENTAL REALM... IF YOUR FEELINGS FOR SHINJI-KUN ARE STRONG ENOUGH, YOU CAN REACH HIM.
dash

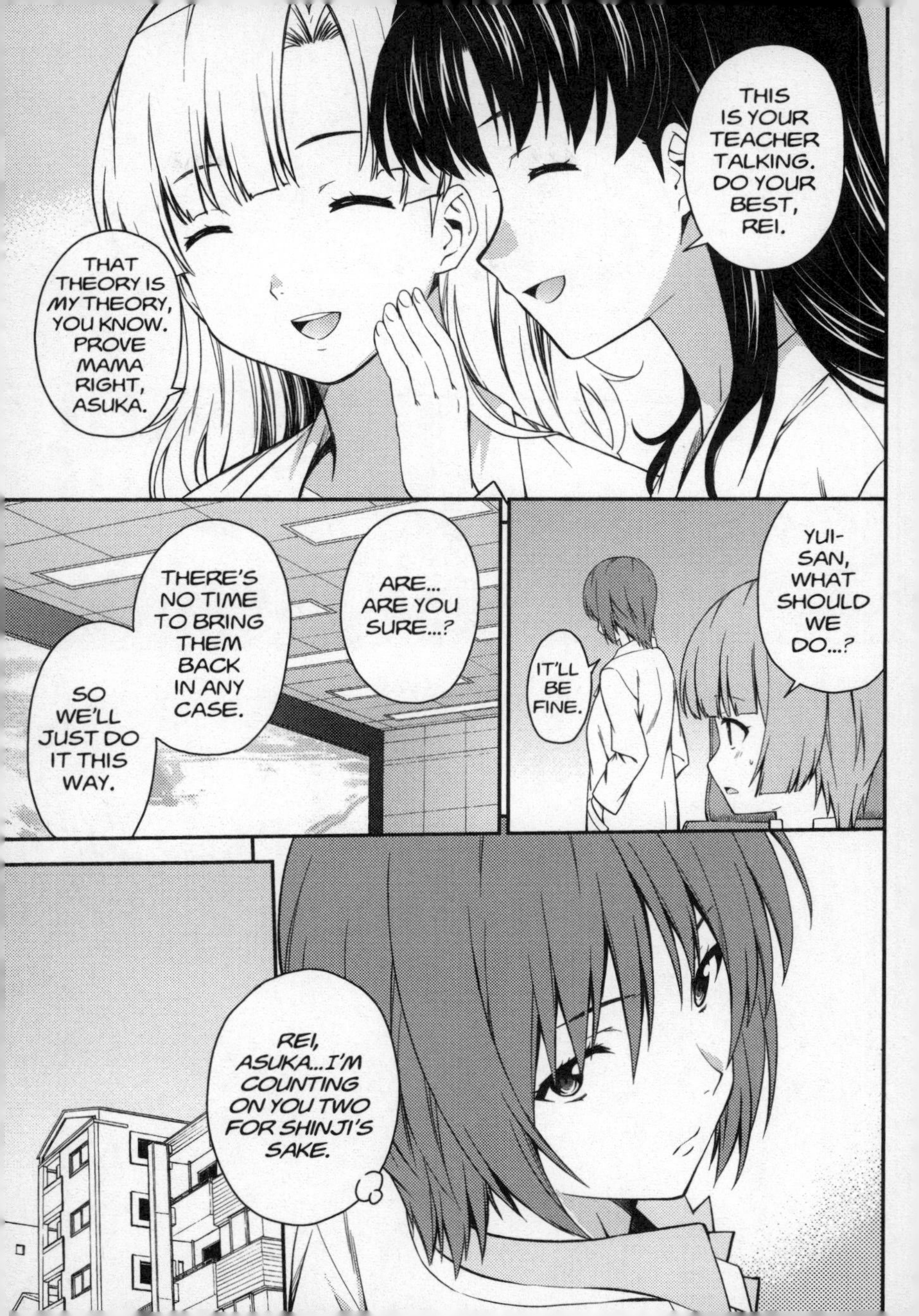
THIS IS YOUR TEACHER TALKING. DO YOUR BEST, REI.
THAT THEORY IS MY THEORY, YOU KNOW. PROVE MAMA RIGHT, ASUKA.
YUI-SAN, WHAT SHOULD WE DO...?
IT'LL BE FINE.
ARE... ARE YOU SURE...?
THERE'S NO TIME TO BRING THEM BACK IN ANY CASE.
SO WE'LL JUST DO IT THIS WAY.
REI, ASUKA...I'M COUNTING ON YOU TWO FOR SHINJI'S SAKE.

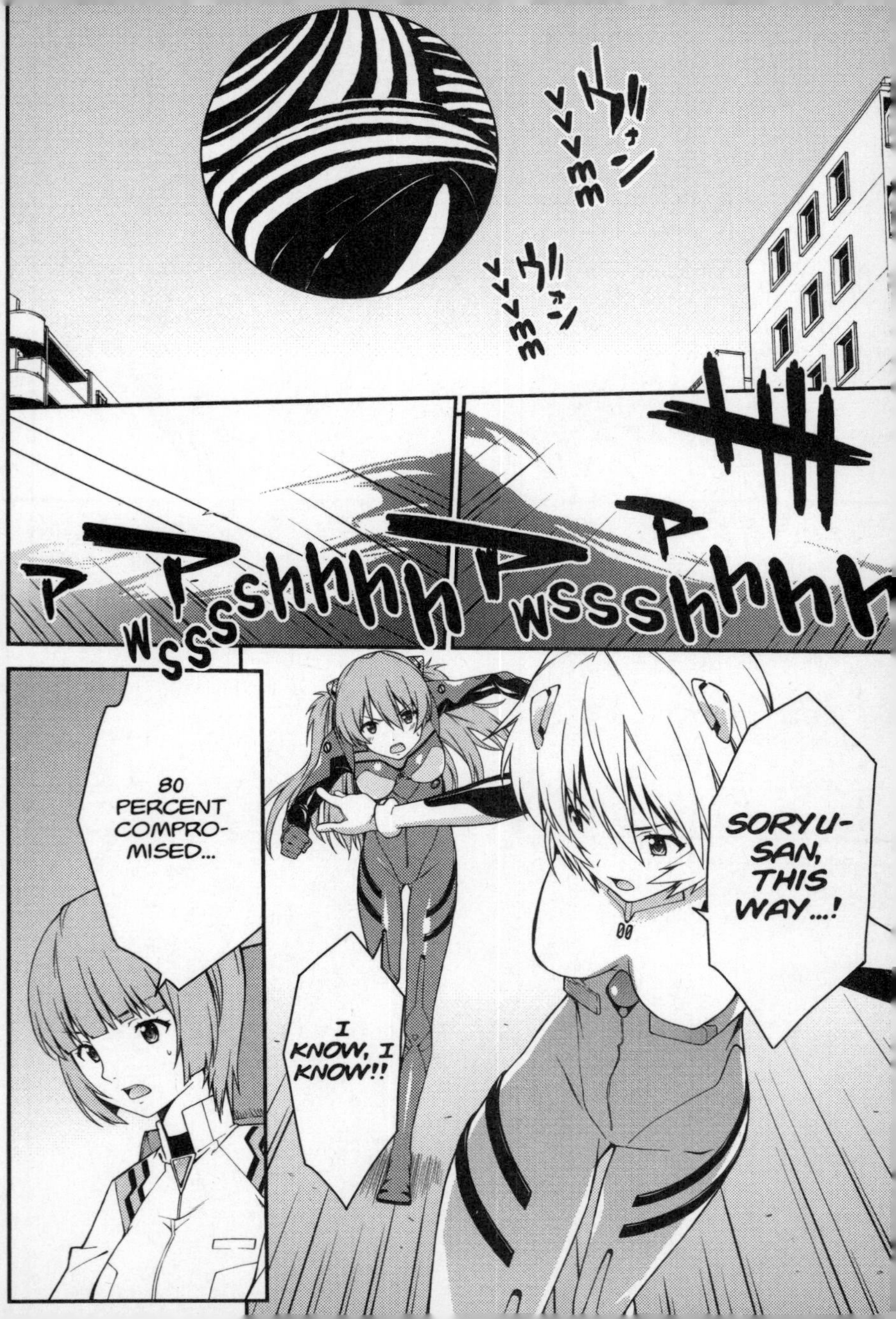
ヴォン vvvmm
ヴォン vvvmm
P wssshhhh
P wsssshhhh
SORYU-SAN, THIS WAY...!
I KNOW, I KNOW!!
80 PERCENT COMPROMISED...

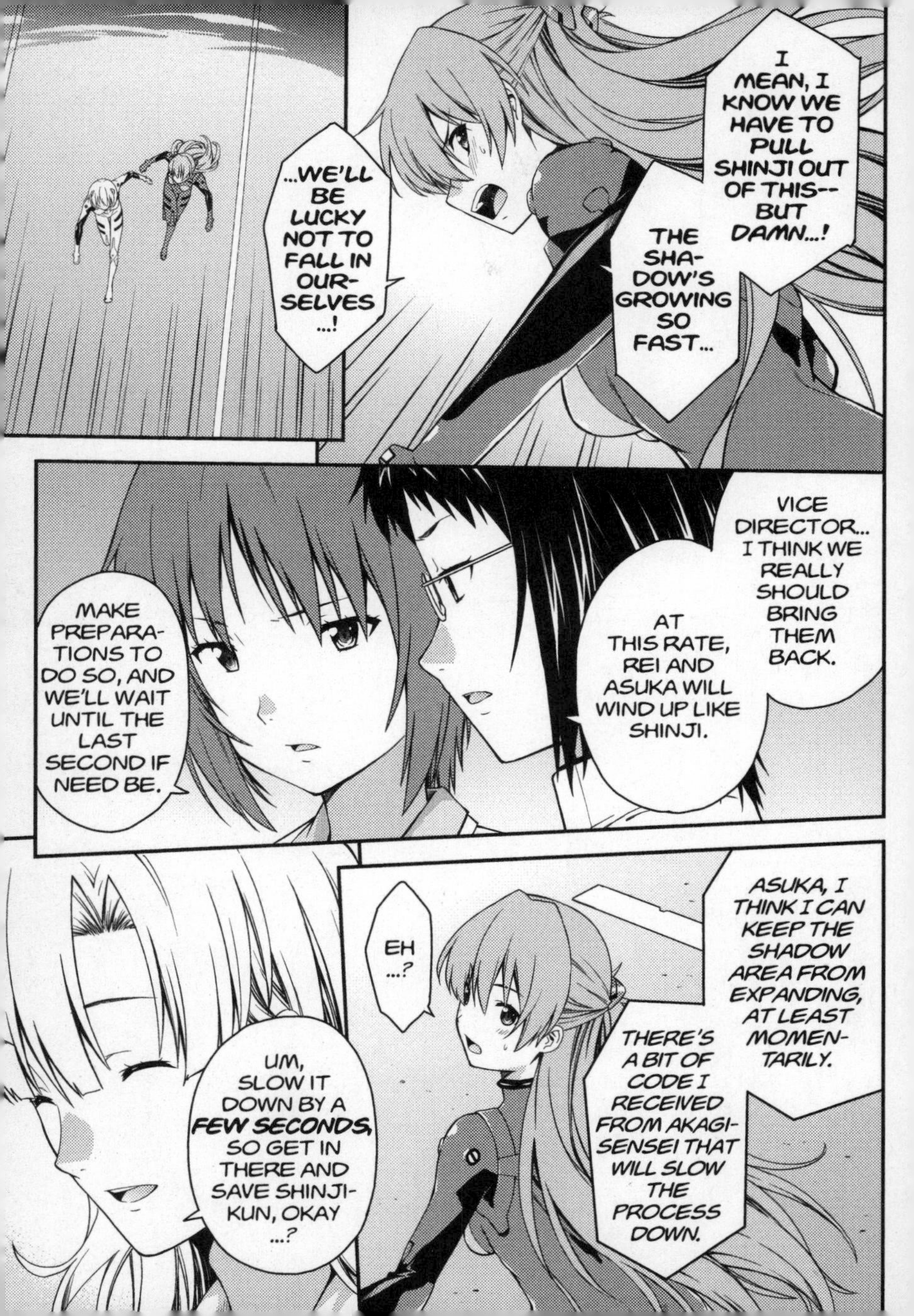
I MEAN, I KNOW WE HAVE TO PULL SHINJI OUT OF THIS-- BUT DAMN...!
THE SHADOW'S GROWING SO FAST...
...WE'LL BE LUCKY NOT TO FALL IN OURSELVES...!
VICE DIRECTOR... I THINK WE REALLY SHOULD BRING THEM BACK.
AT THIS RATE, REI AND ASUKA WILL WIND UP LIKE SHINJI.
MAKE PREPARATIONS TO DO SO, AND WE'LL WAIT UNTIL THE LAST SECOND IF NEED BE.
ASUKA, I THINK I CAN KEEP THE SHADOW AREA FROM EXPANDING, AT LEAST MOMENTARILY.
THERE'S A BIT OF CODE I RECEIVED FROM AKAGI-SENSEI THAT WILL SLOW THE PROCESS DOWN.
EH...?
UM, SLOW IT DOWN BY A **FEW SECONDS,** SO GET IN THERE AND SAVE SHINJI-KUN, OKAY...?

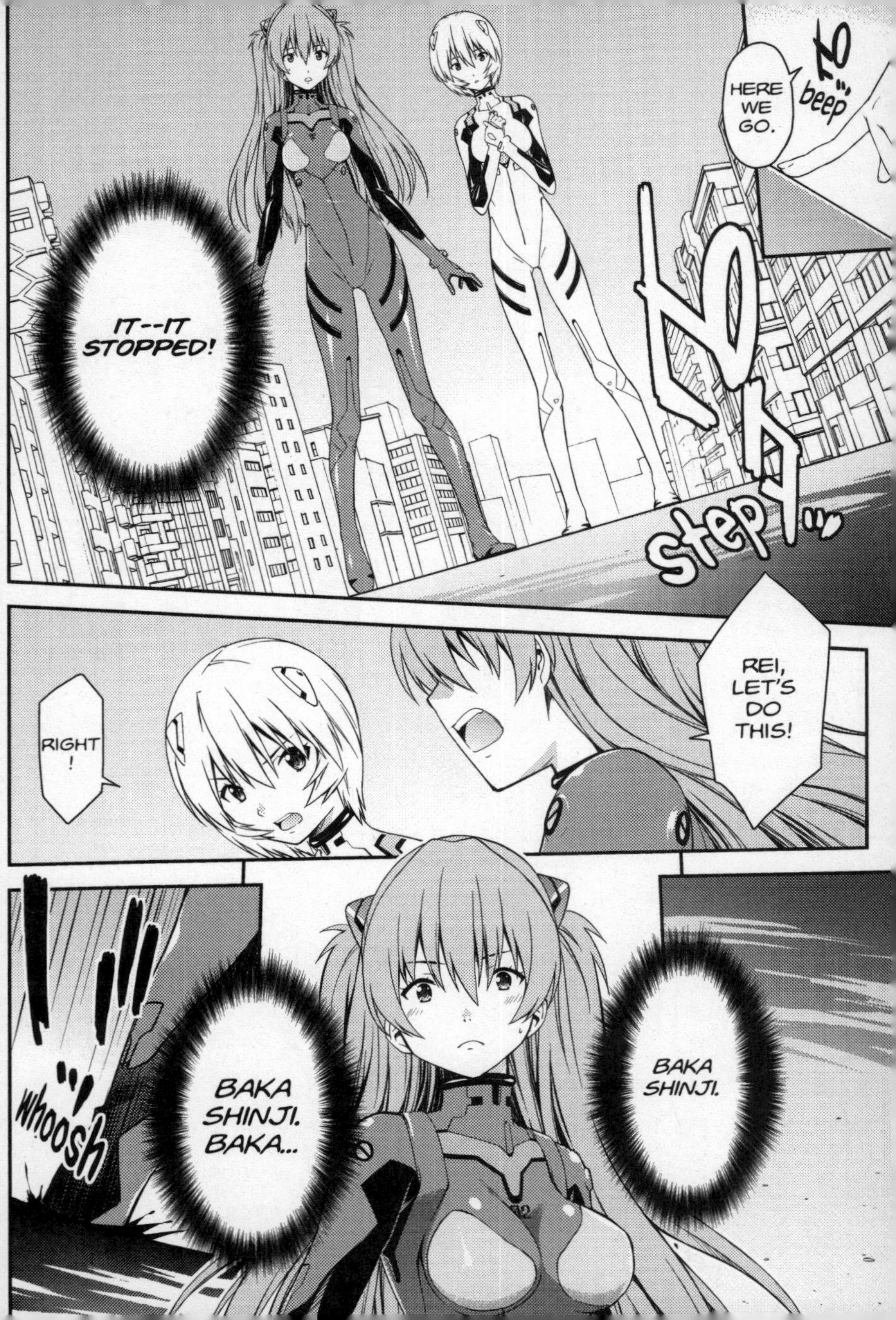
beep
HERE WE GO.
step
IT--IT STOPPED!
REI, LET'S DO THIS!
RIGHT!
BAKA SHINJI.
whoosh
BAKA SHINJI. BAKA...

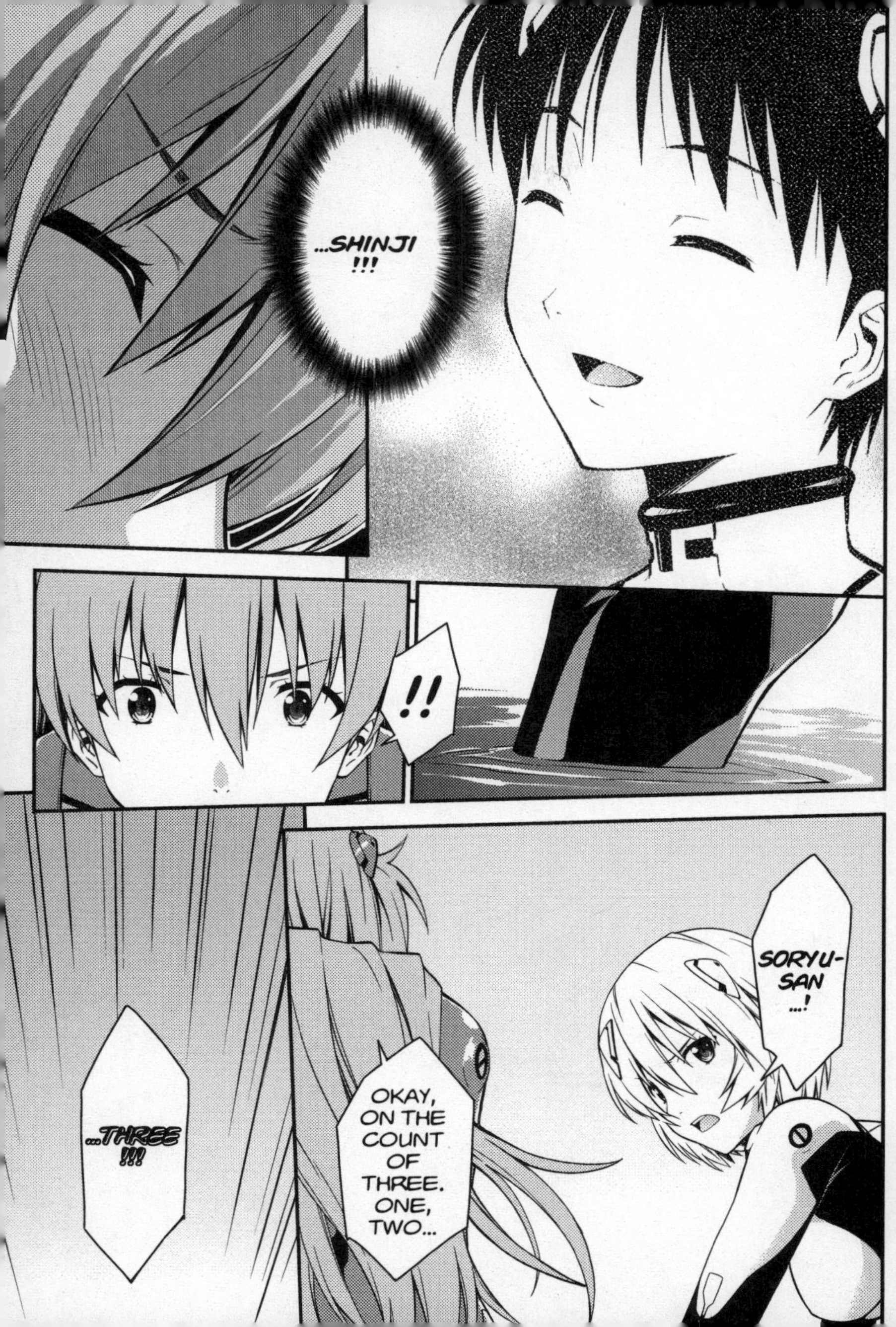
...SHINJI !!!
!!
SORYU-SAN ...!
OKAY, ON THE COUNT OF THREE. ONE, TWO...
...THREE !!!

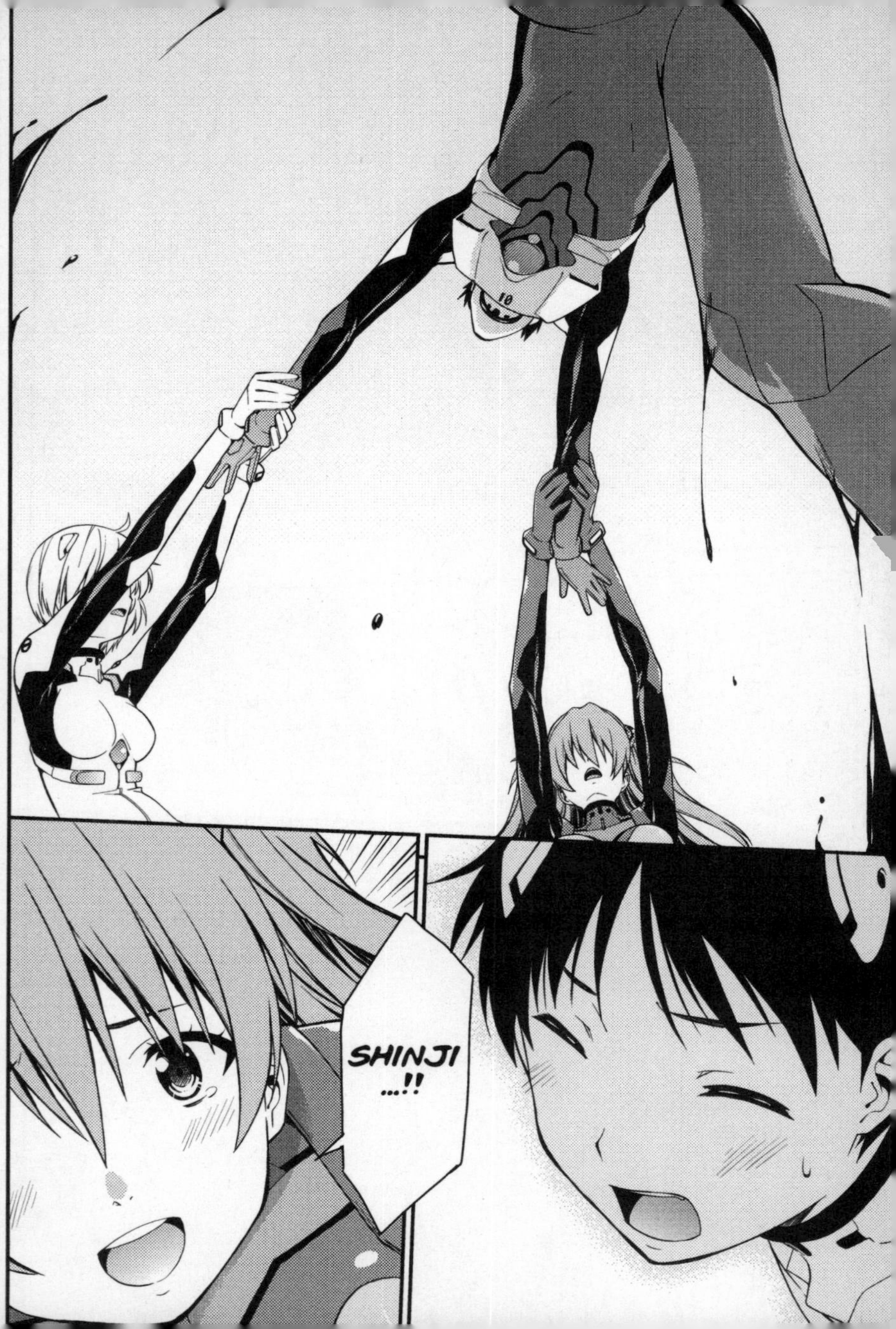
SHINJI ...!!

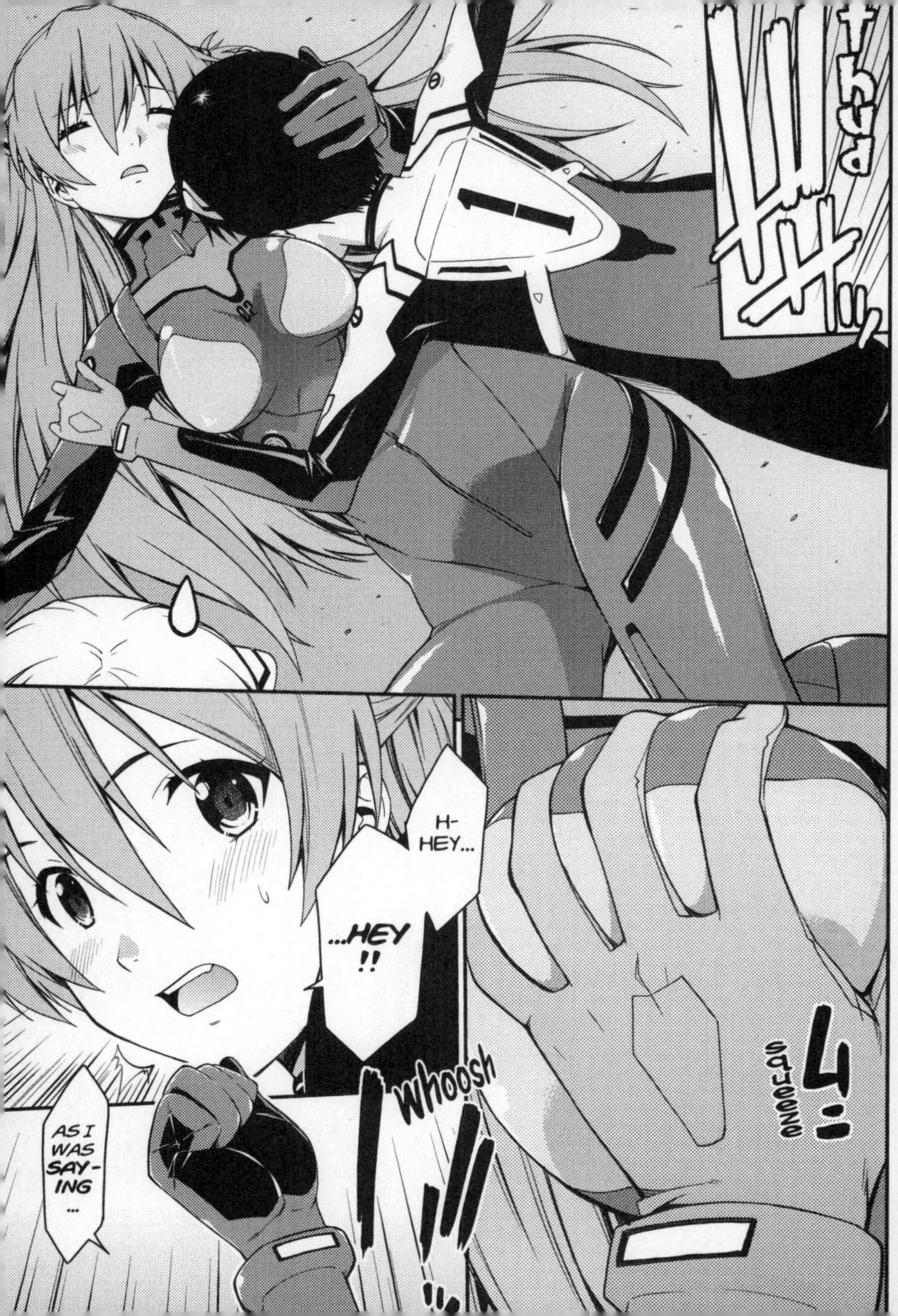
rub
squeeze
H- HEY...
...HEY !!
whoosh
AS I WAS SAYING...

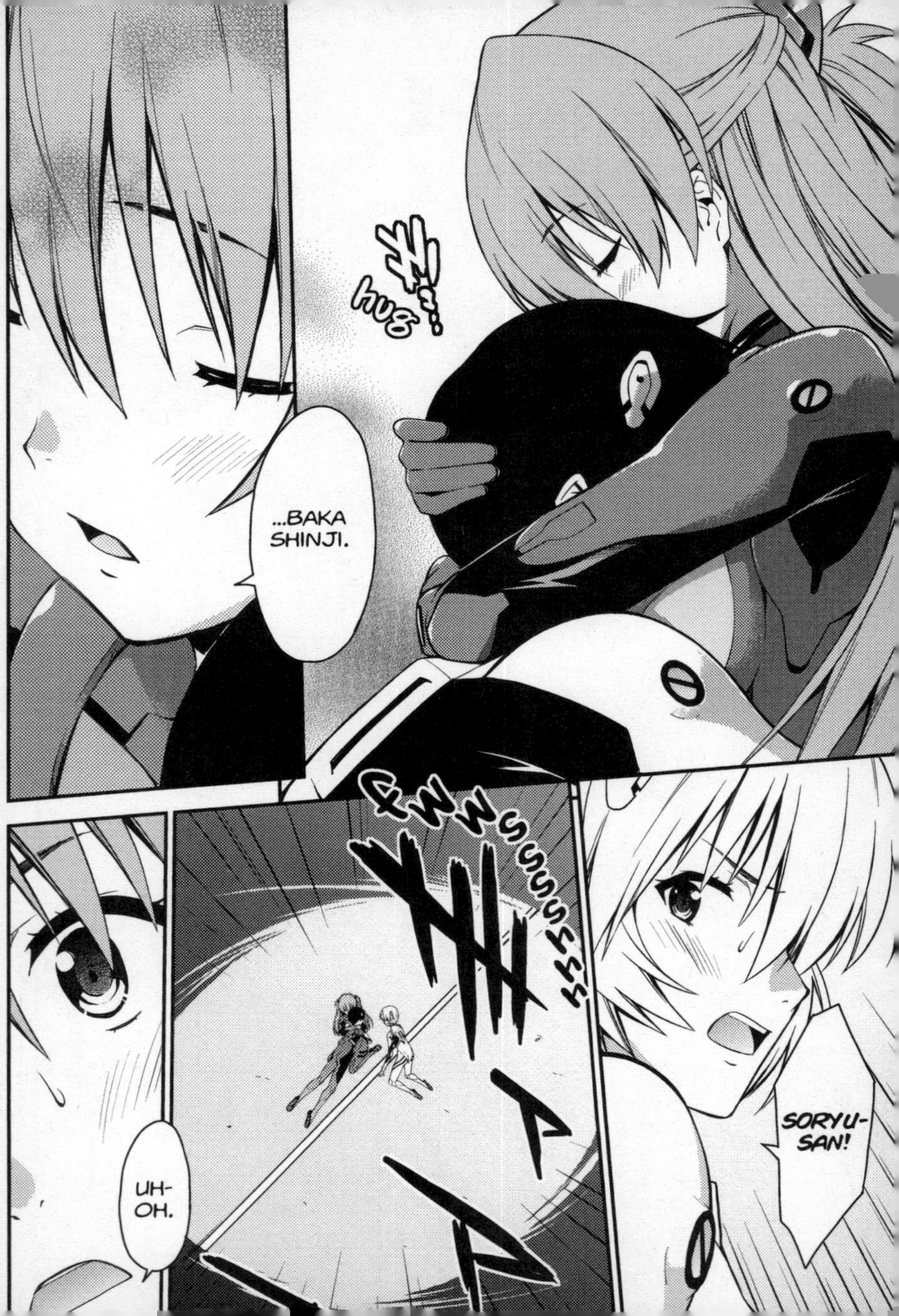
hug
...BAKA SHINJI.
SORYU-SAN!
FWSSSSSSSH
UH-OH.

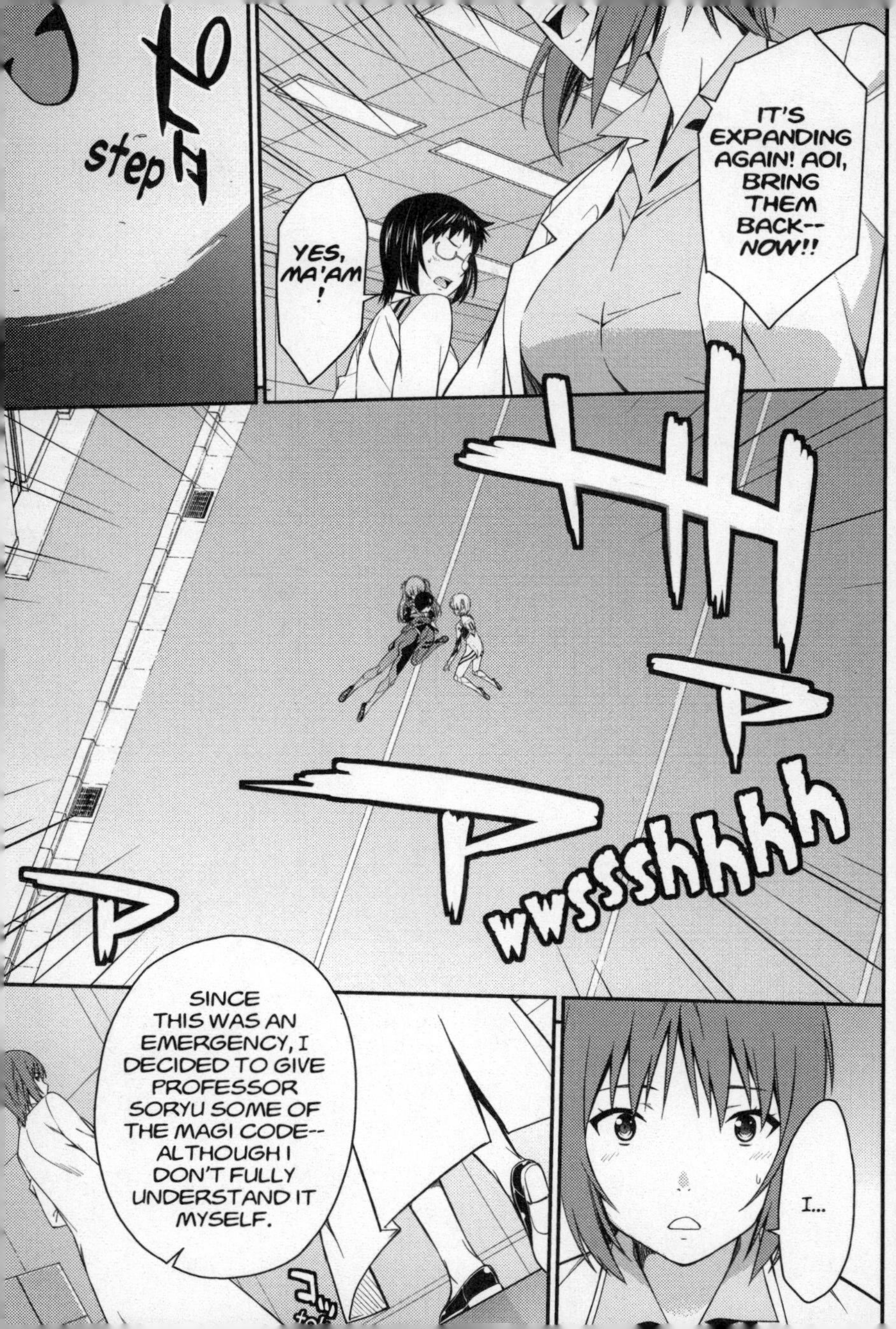
IT'S EXPANDING AGAIN! AOI, BRING THEM BACK--NOW!!
YES, MA'AM!
step
wwssshhhh
I...
SINCE THIS WAS AN EMERGENCY, I DECIDED TO GIVE PROFESSOR SORYU SOME OF THE MAGI CODE--ALTHOUGH I DON'T FULLY UNDERSTAND IT MYSELF.

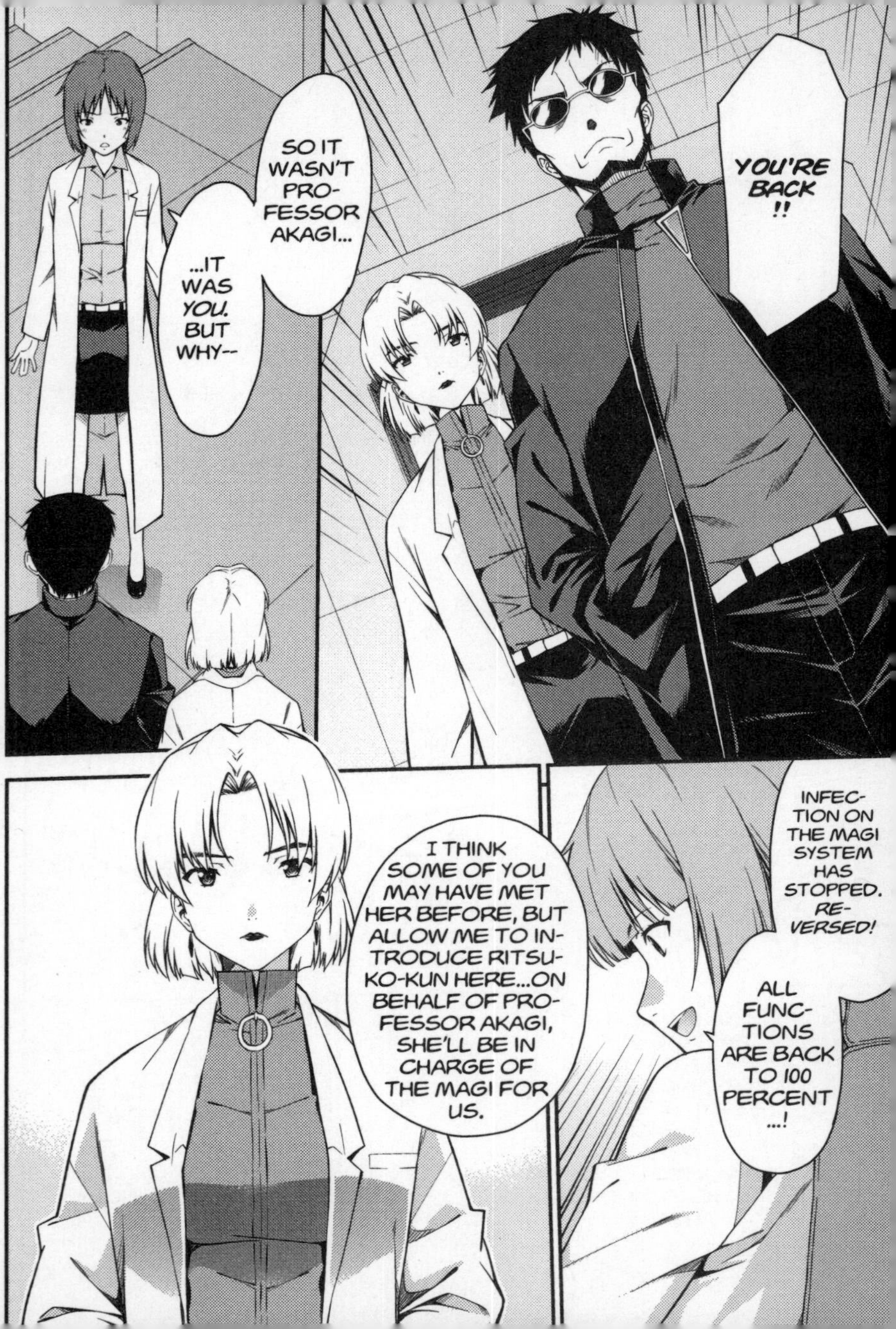
YOU'RE BACK !!
SO IT WASN'T PRO-FESSOR AKAGI...
...IT WAS YOU. BUT WHY--
INFEC-TION ON THE MAGI SYSTEM HAS STOPPED. RE-VERSED!
ALL FUNC-TIONS ARE BACK TO 100 PERCENT ...!
I THINK SOME OF YOU MAY HAVE MET HER BEFORE, BUT ALLOW ME TO IN-TRODUCE RITSU-KO-KUN HERE...ON BEHALF OF PRO-FESSOR AKAGI, SHE'LL BE IN CHARGE OF THE MAGI FOR US.

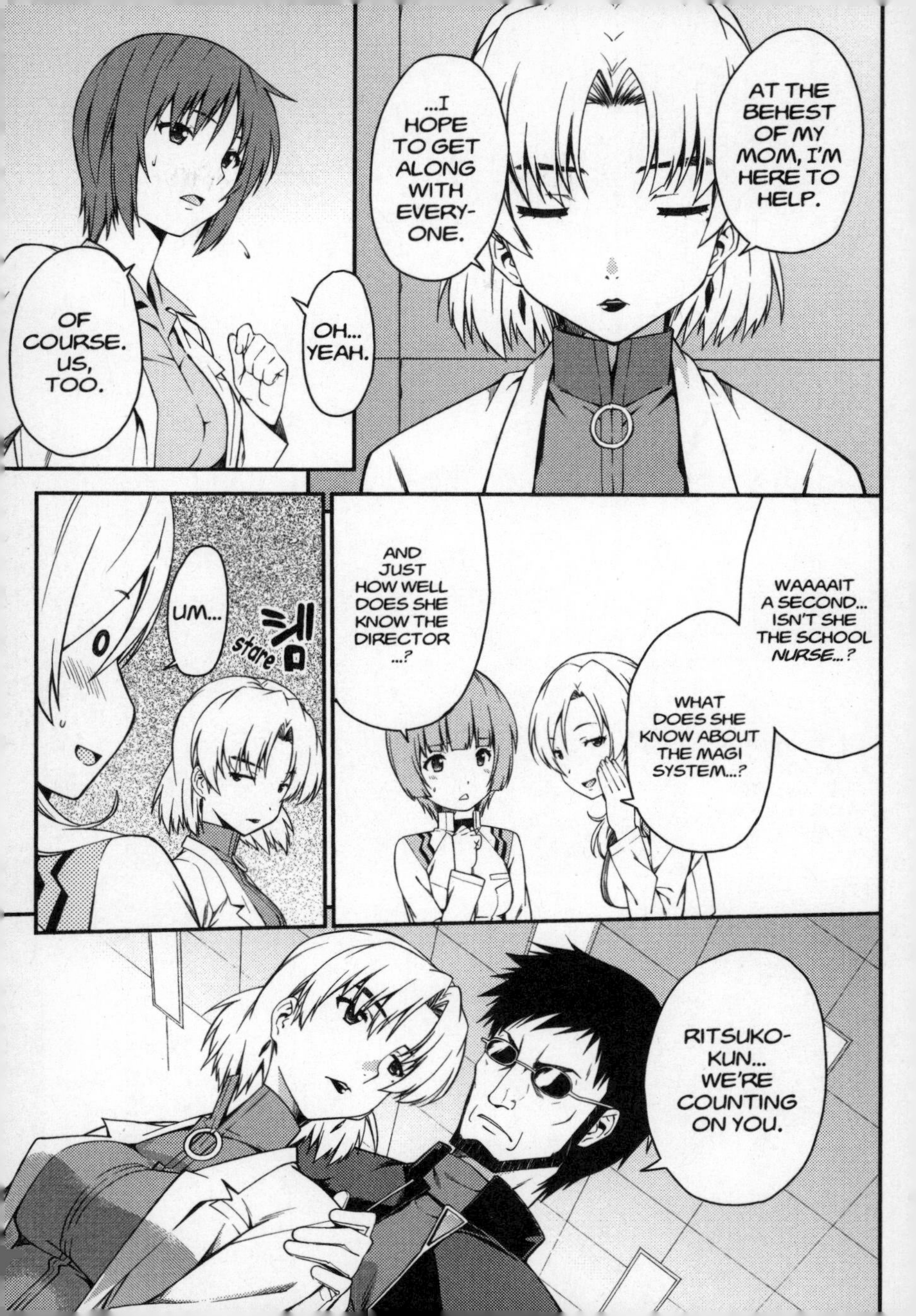
AT THE BEHEST OF MY MOM, I'M HERE TO HELP.
...I HOPE TO GET ALONG WITH EVERY-ONE.
OH... YEAH.
OF COURSE. US, TOO.
WAAAAIT A SECOND... ISN'T SHE THE SCHOOL NURSE...?
WHAT DOES SHE KNOW ABOUT THE MAGI SYSTEM...?
AND JUST HOW WELL DOES SHE KNOW THE DIRECTOR ...?
stare
UM...
RITSUKO-KUN... WE'RE COUNTING ON YOU.

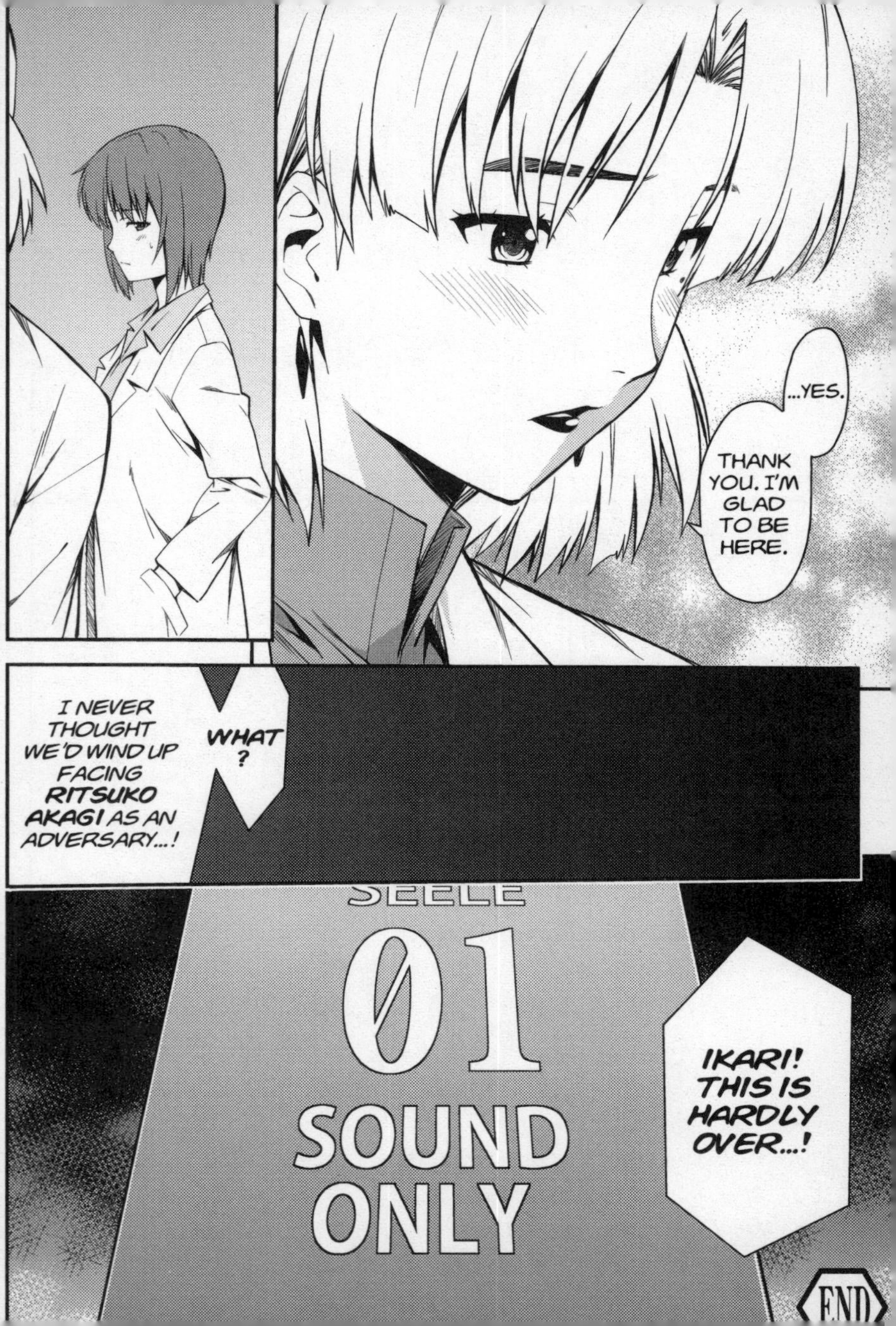
...YES.
THANK YOU. I'M GLAD TO BE HERE.
WHAT?
I NEVER THOUGHT WE'D WIND UP FACING RITSUKO AKAGI AS AN ADVERSARY...!
SEELE
01
SOUND ONLY
IKARI! THIS IS HARDLY OVER...!
END

the shinji ikari raising project

NEON GENESIS EVANGELION
THE SHINJI IKARI RAISING PROJECT

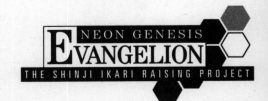

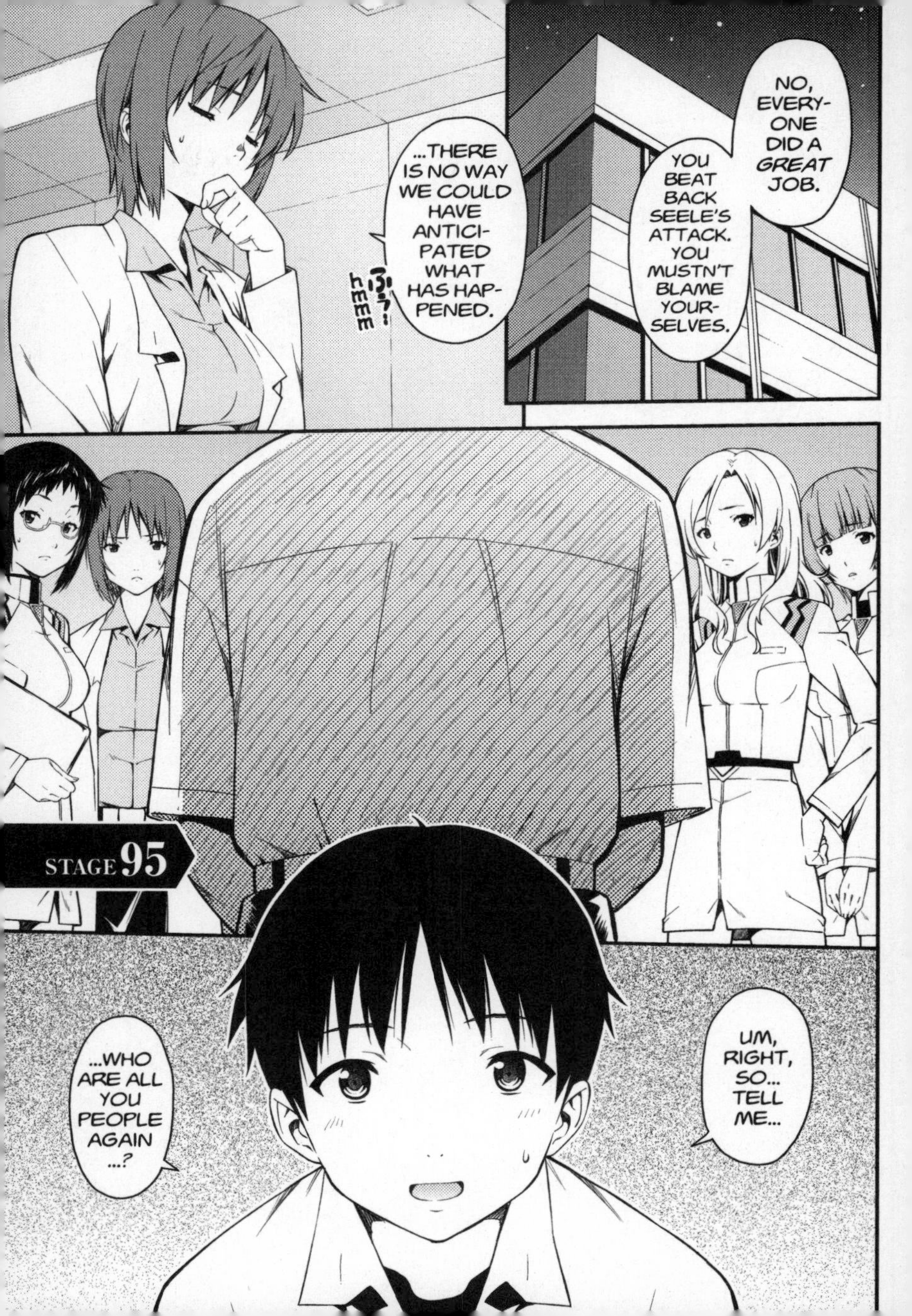
NO, EVERY-ONE DID A GREAT JOB.
YOU BEAT BACK SEELE'S ATTACK. YOU MUSTN'T BLAME YOUR-SELVES.
...THERE IS NO WAY WE COULD HAVE ANTICI-PATED WHAT HAS HAP-PENED.
HMMM
STAGE 95
UM, RIGHT, SO... TELL ME...
...WHO ARE ALL YOU PEOPLE AGAIN ...?

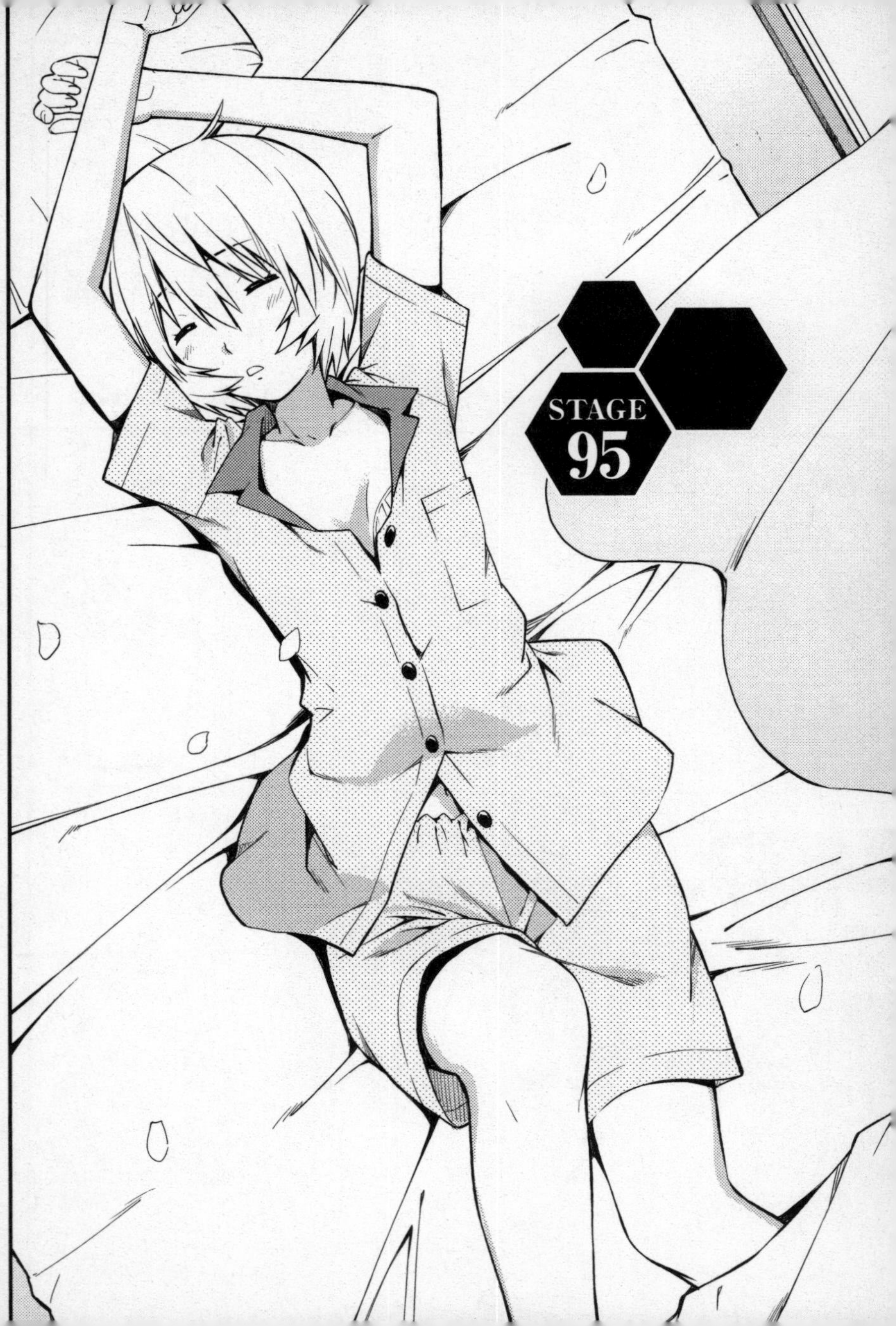
STAGE
95

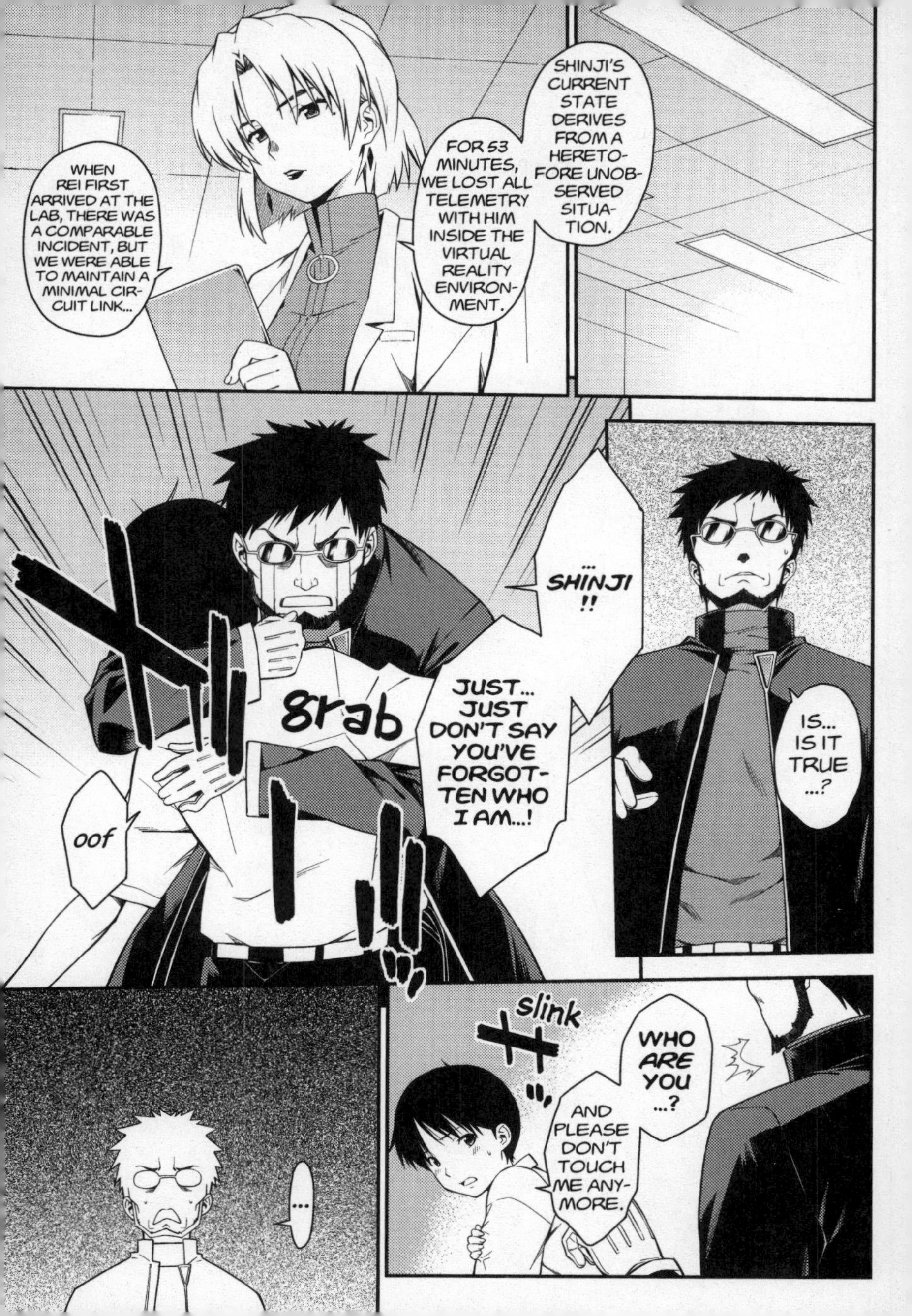
SHINJI'S CURRENT STATE DERIVES FROM A HERETOFORE UNOBSERVED SITUATION.
FOR 53 MINUTES, WE LOST ALL TELEMETRY WITH HIM INSIDE THE VIRTUAL REALITY ENVIRONMENT.
WHEN REI FIRST ARRIVED AT THE LAB, THERE WAS A COMPARABLE INCIDENT, BUT WE WERE ABLE TO MAINTAIN A MINIMAL CIRCUIT LINK...
IS... IS IT TRUE ...?
...SHINJI !!
grab
JUST... JUST DON'T SAY YOU'VE FORGOTTEN WHO I AM...!
oof
slink
WHO ARE YOU ...?
AND PLEASE DON'T TOUCH ME ANYMORE.
...

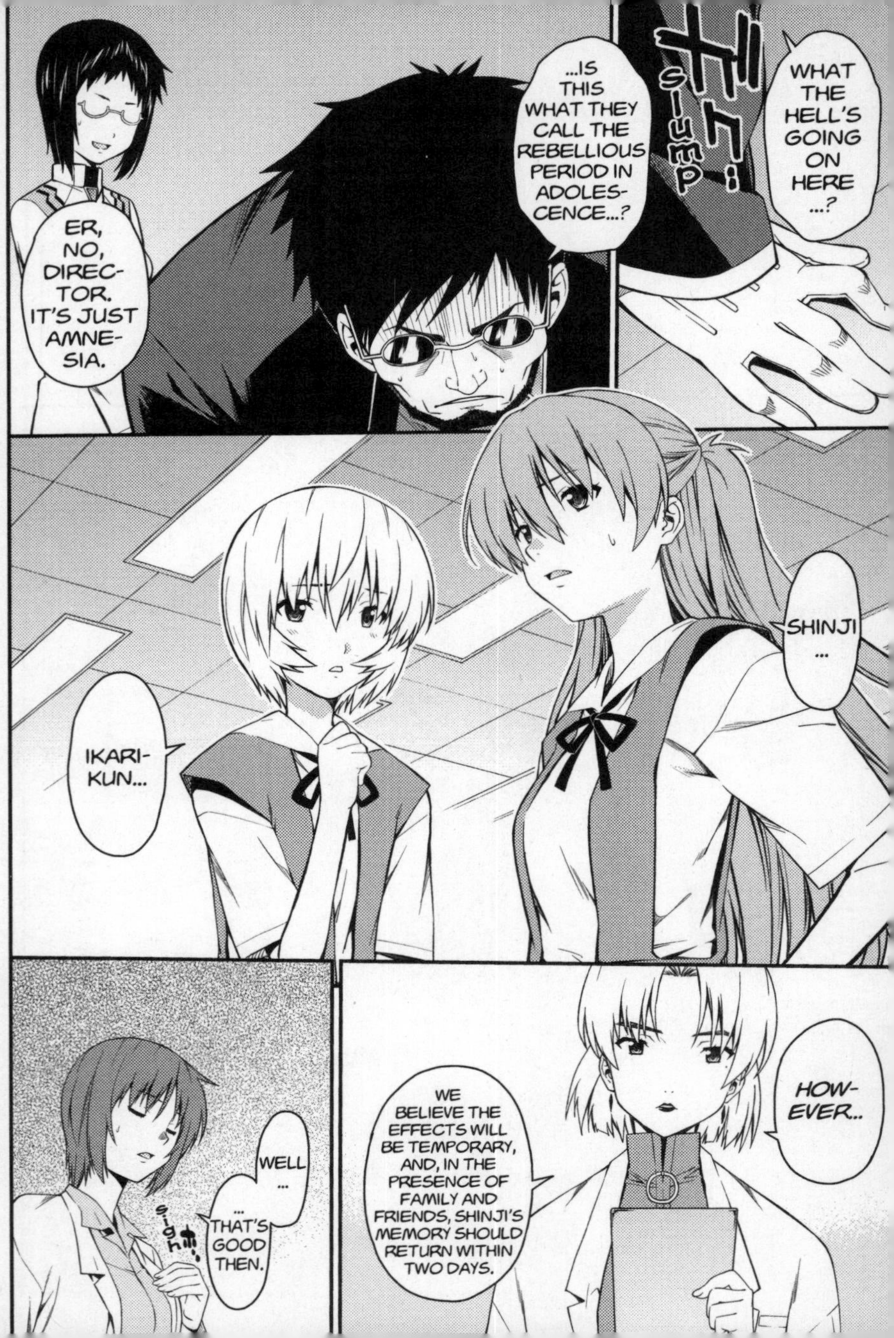
WHAT THE HELL'S GOING ON HERE ...?
slump
...IS THIS WHAT THEY CALL THE REBELLIOUS PERIOD IN ADOLES-CENCE...?
ER, NO, DIREC-TOR. IT'S JUST AMNE-SIA.
SHINJI ...
IKARI-KUN...
HOW-EVER...
WE BELIEVE THE EFFECTS WILL BE TEMPORARY, AND, IN THE PRESENCE OF FAMILY AND FRIENDS, SHINJI'S MEMORY SHOULD RETURN WITHIN TWO DAYS.
WELL ...
... THAT'S GOOD THEN.
sigh

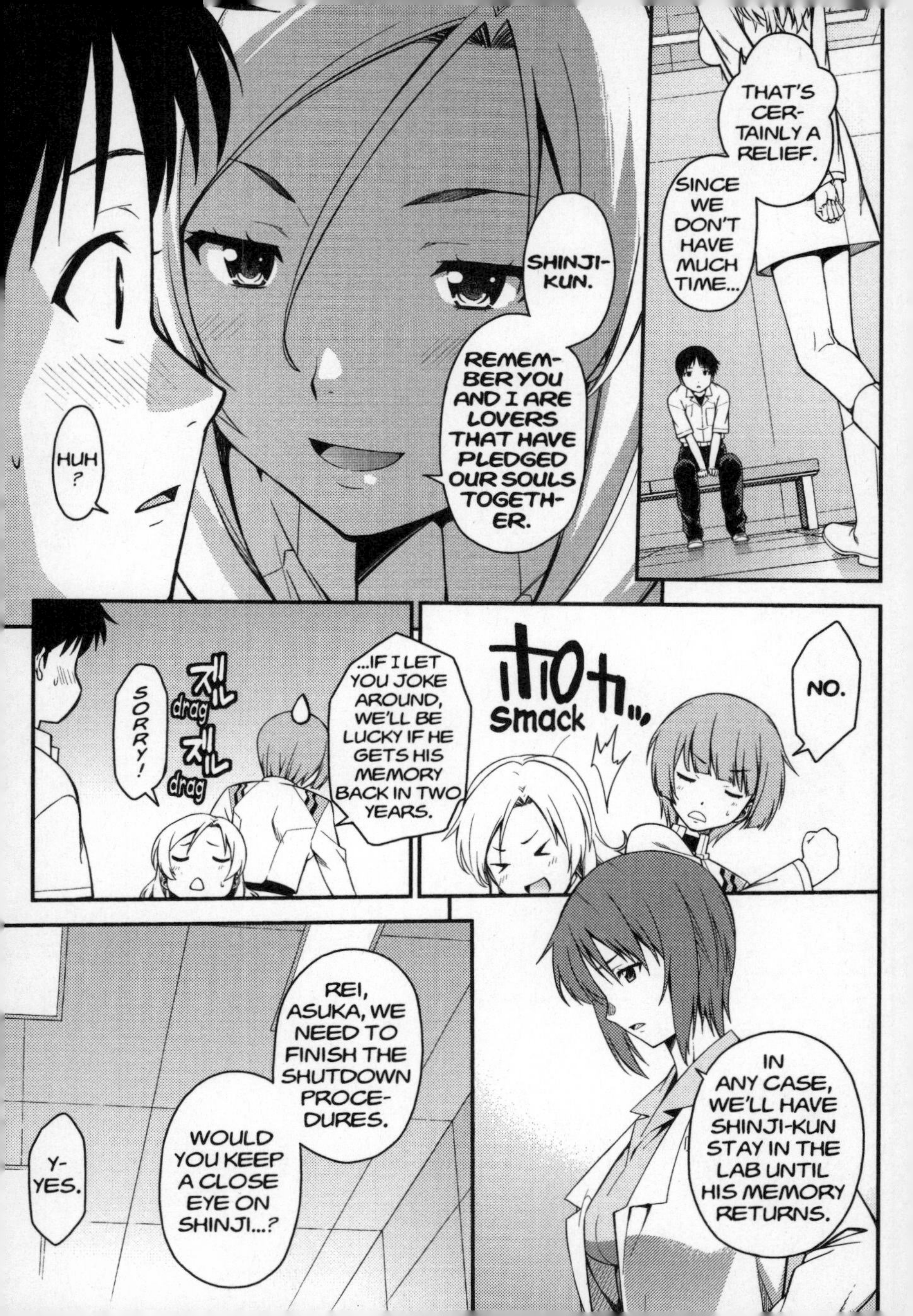
THAT'S CERTAINLY A RELIEF.
SINCE WE DON'T HAVE MUCH TIME...
SHINJI-KUN.
REMEMBER YOU AND I ARE LOVERS THAT HAVE PLEDGED OUR SOULS TOGETHER.
HUH?
NO.
smack
...IF I LET YOU JOKE AROUND, WE'LL BE LUCKY IF HE GETS HIS MEMORY BACK IN TWO YEARS.
drag drag
SORRY!
IN ANY CASE, WE'LL HAVE SHINJI-KUN STAY IN THE LAB UNTIL HIS MEMORY RETURNS.
REI, ASUKA, WE NEED TO FINISH THE SHUTDOWN PROCEDURES.
WOULD YOU KEEP A CLOSE EYE ON SHINJI...?
Y-YES.

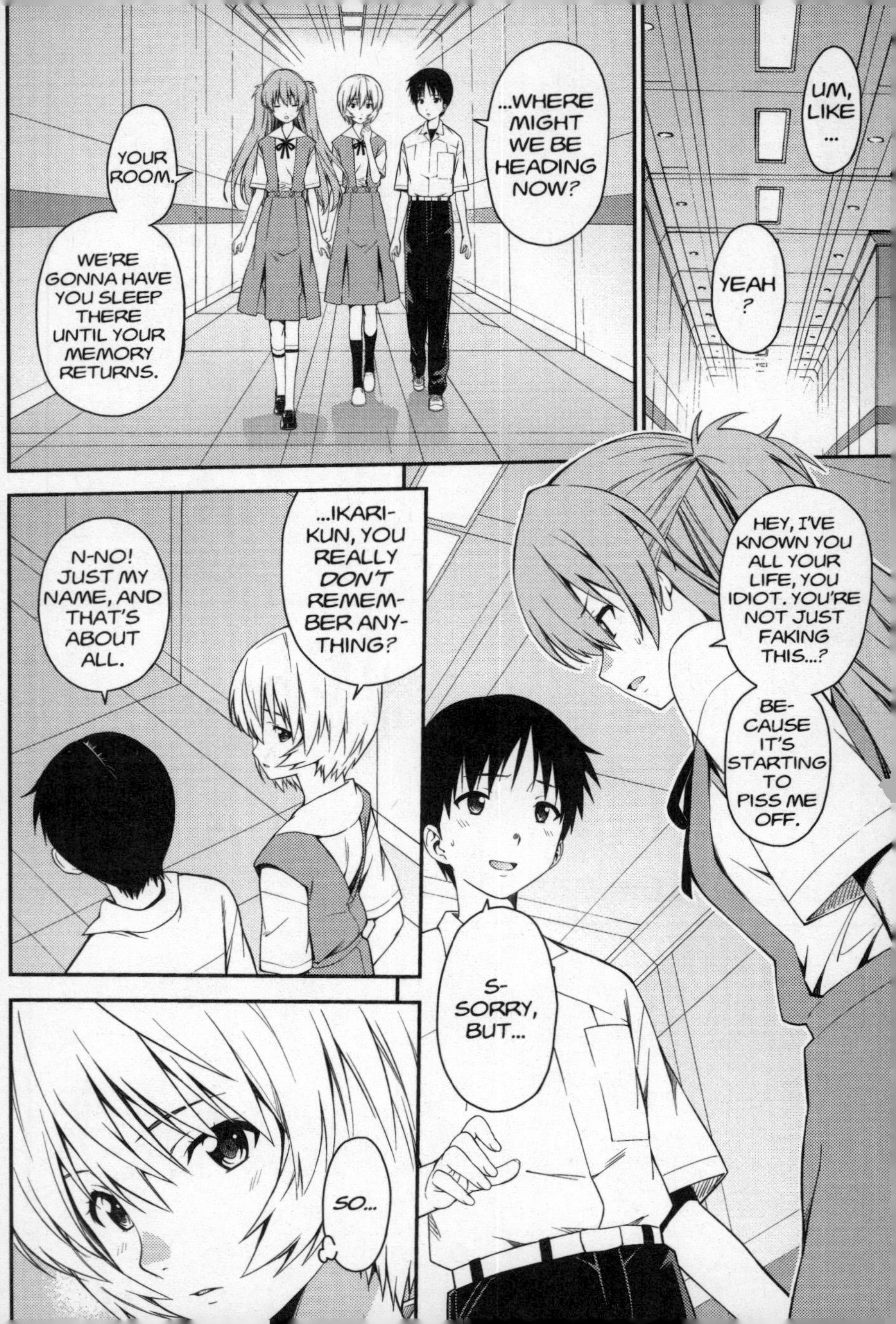
UM, LIKE ...
YEAH ?
...WHERE MIGHT WE BE HEADING NOW?
YOUR ROOM.
WE'RE GONNA HAVE YOU SLEEP THERE UNTIL YOUR MEMORY RETURNS.
HEY, I'VE KNOWN YOU ALL YOUR LIFE, YOU IDIOT. YOU'RE NOT JUST FAKING THIS...?
BE-CAUSE IT'S STARTING TO PISS ME OFF.
S-SORRY, BUT...
...IKARI-KUN, YOU REALLY *DON'T* REMEM-BER ANY-THING?
N-NO! JUST MY NAME, AND THAT'S ABOUT ALL.
SO...

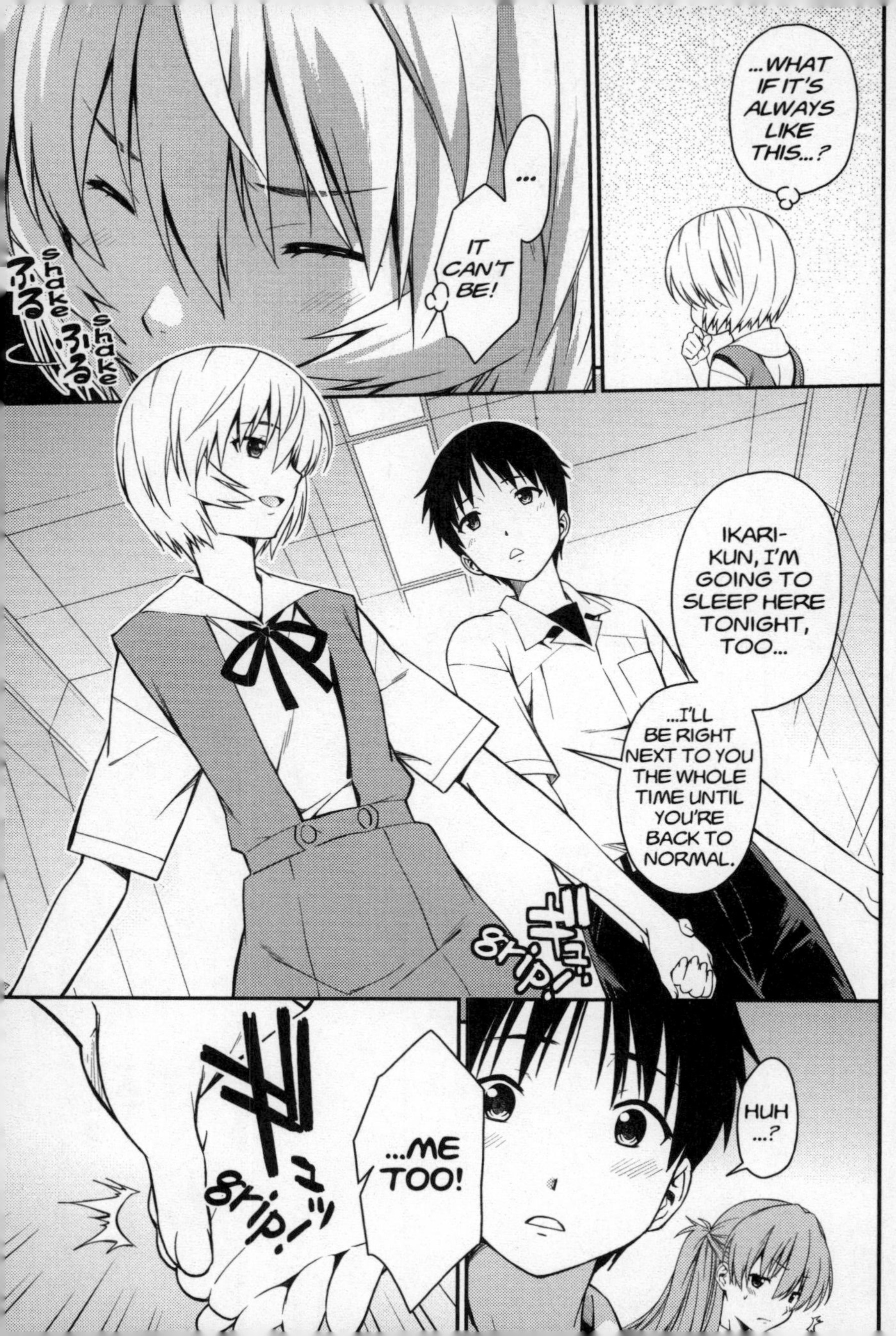
...WHAT IF IT'S ALWAYS LIKE THIS...?
...
IT CAN'T BE!
ふる shake ふる shake
IKARI-KUN, I'M GOING TO SLEEP HERE TONIGHT, TOO...
...I'LL BE RIGHT NEXT TO YOU THE WHOLE TIME UNTIL YOU'RE BACK TO NORMAL.
ギュ grip!
HUH ...?
...ME TOO!
ギュッ grip!

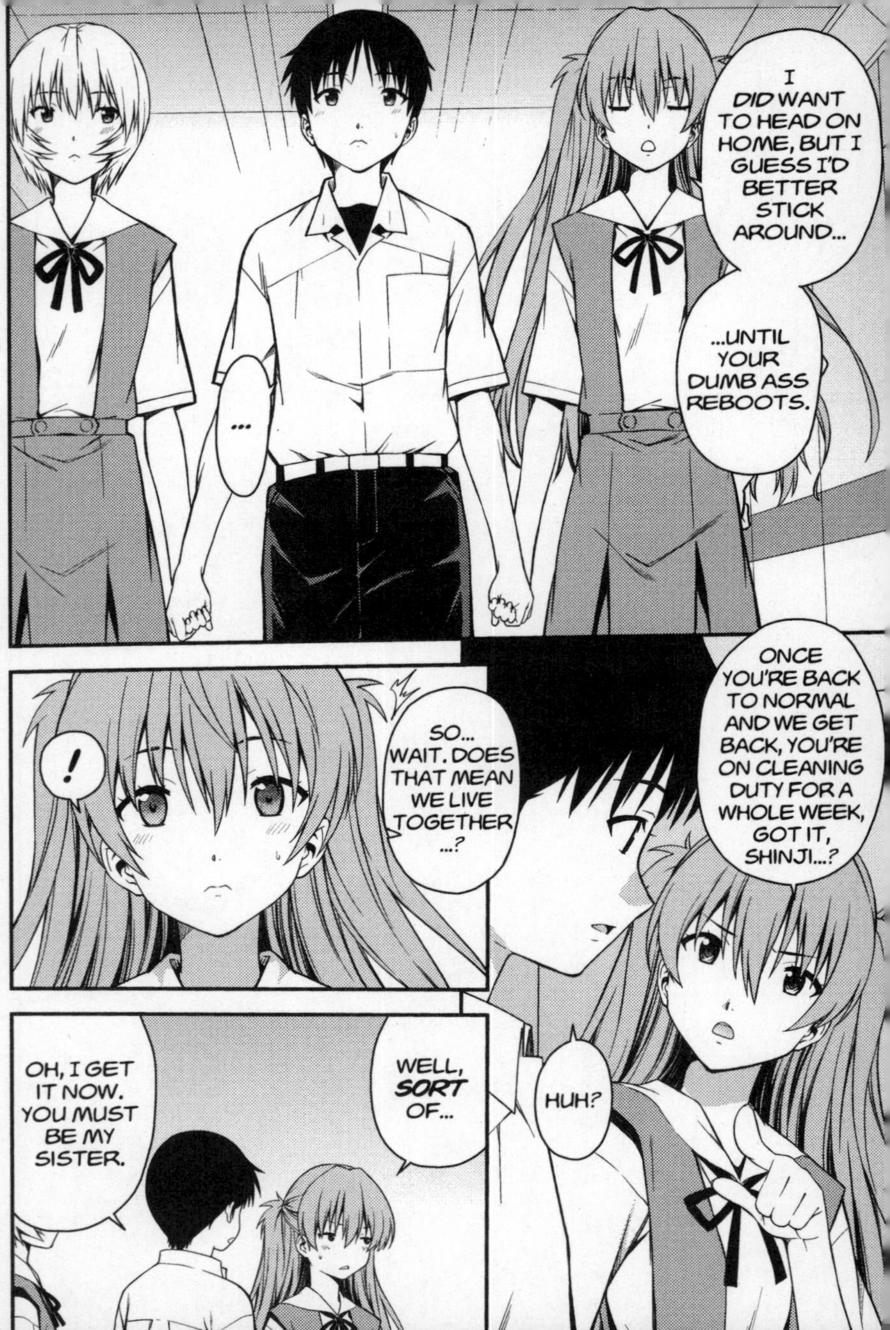
I *DID* WANT TO HEAD ON HOME, BUT I GUESS I'D BETTER STICK AROUND...
...UNTIL YOUR DUMB ASS REBOOTS.
...
ONCE YOU'RE BACK TO NORMAL AND WE GET BACK, YOU'RE ON CLEANING DUTY FOR A WHOLE WEEK, GOT IT, SHINJI...?
HUH?
!
SO... WAIT. DOES THAT MEAN WE LIVE TOGETHER ...?
WELL, ***SORT*** OF...
OH, I GET IT NOW. YOU MUST BE MY SISTER.

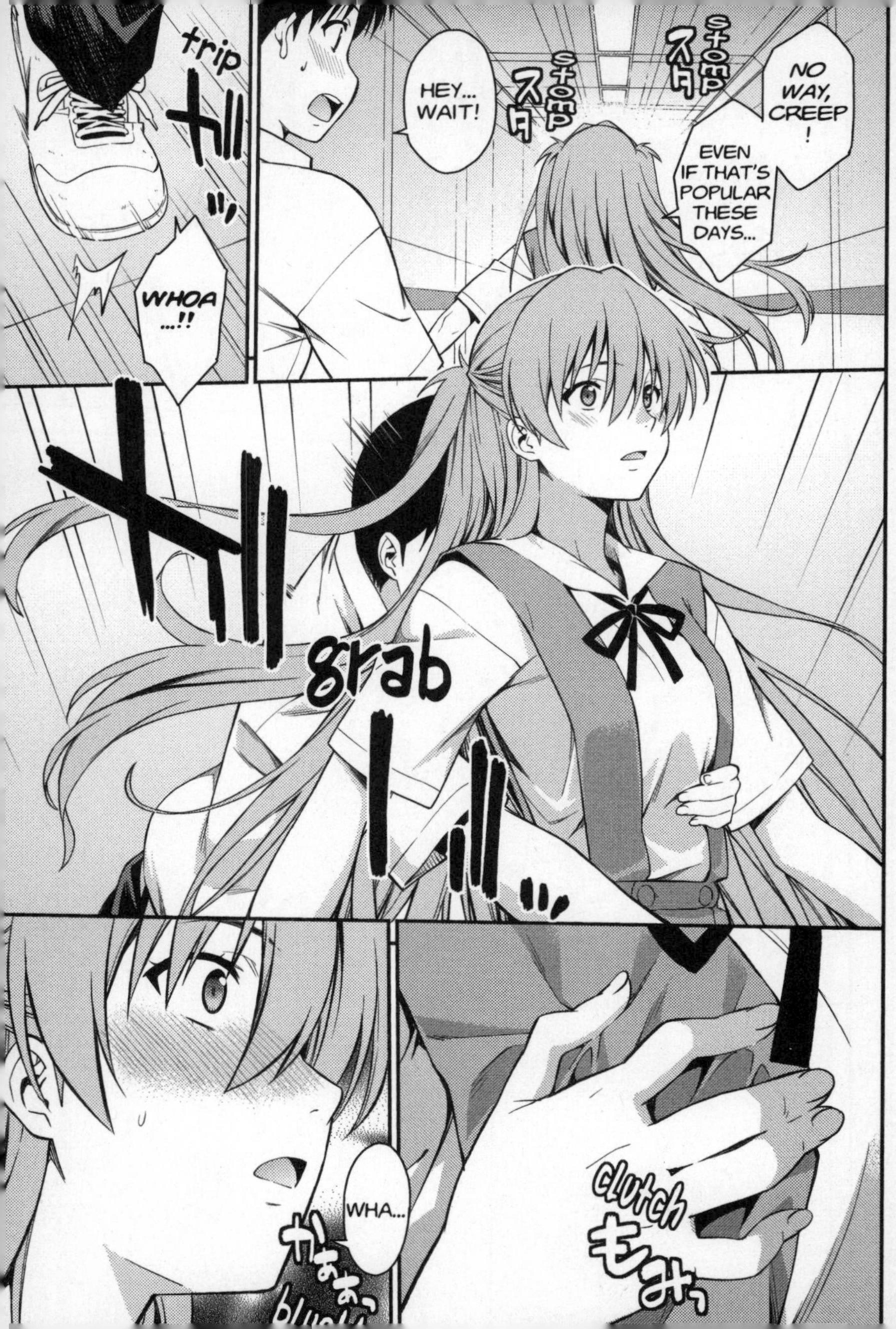
NO WAY, CREEP!
EVEN IF THAT'S POPULAR THESE DAYS...
stomp スタ
stomp スタ
HEY... WAIT!
trip
WHOA ...!!
grab
clutch もみっ
WHA...
かあぁっ

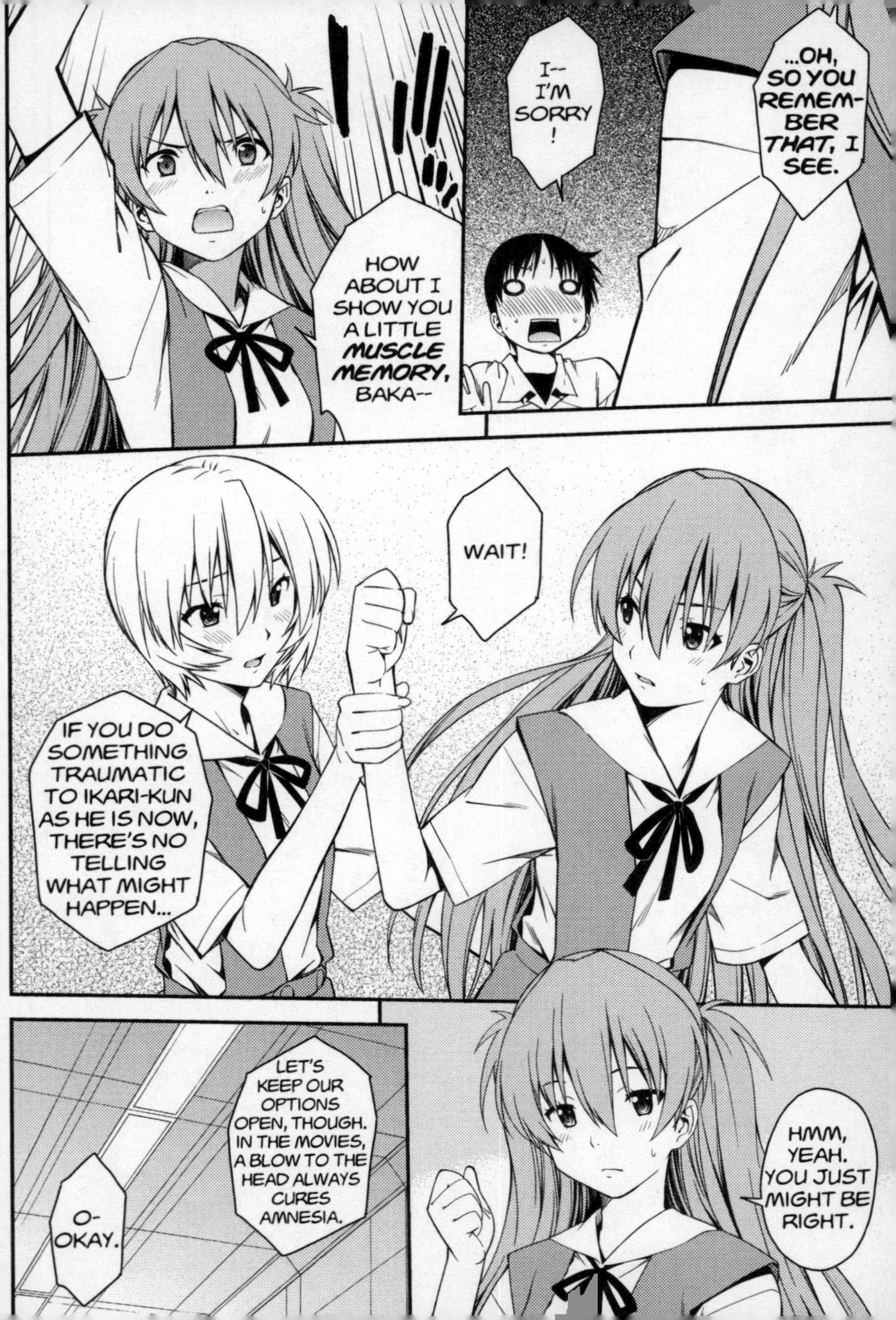
...OH, SO YOU REMEMBER THAT, I SEE.
I-- I'M SORRY!
HOW ABOUT I SHOW YOU A LITTLE MUSCLE MEMORY, BAKA--
WAIT!
IF YOU DO SOMETHING TRAUMATIC TO IKARI-KUN AS HE IS NOW, THERE'S NO TELLING WHAT MIGHT HAPPEN...
HMM, YEAH. YOU JUST MIGHT BE RIGHT.
LET'S KEEP OUR OPTIONS OPEN, THOUGH. IN THE MOVIES, A BLOW TO THE HEAD ALWAYS CURES AMNESIA.
O-OKAY.

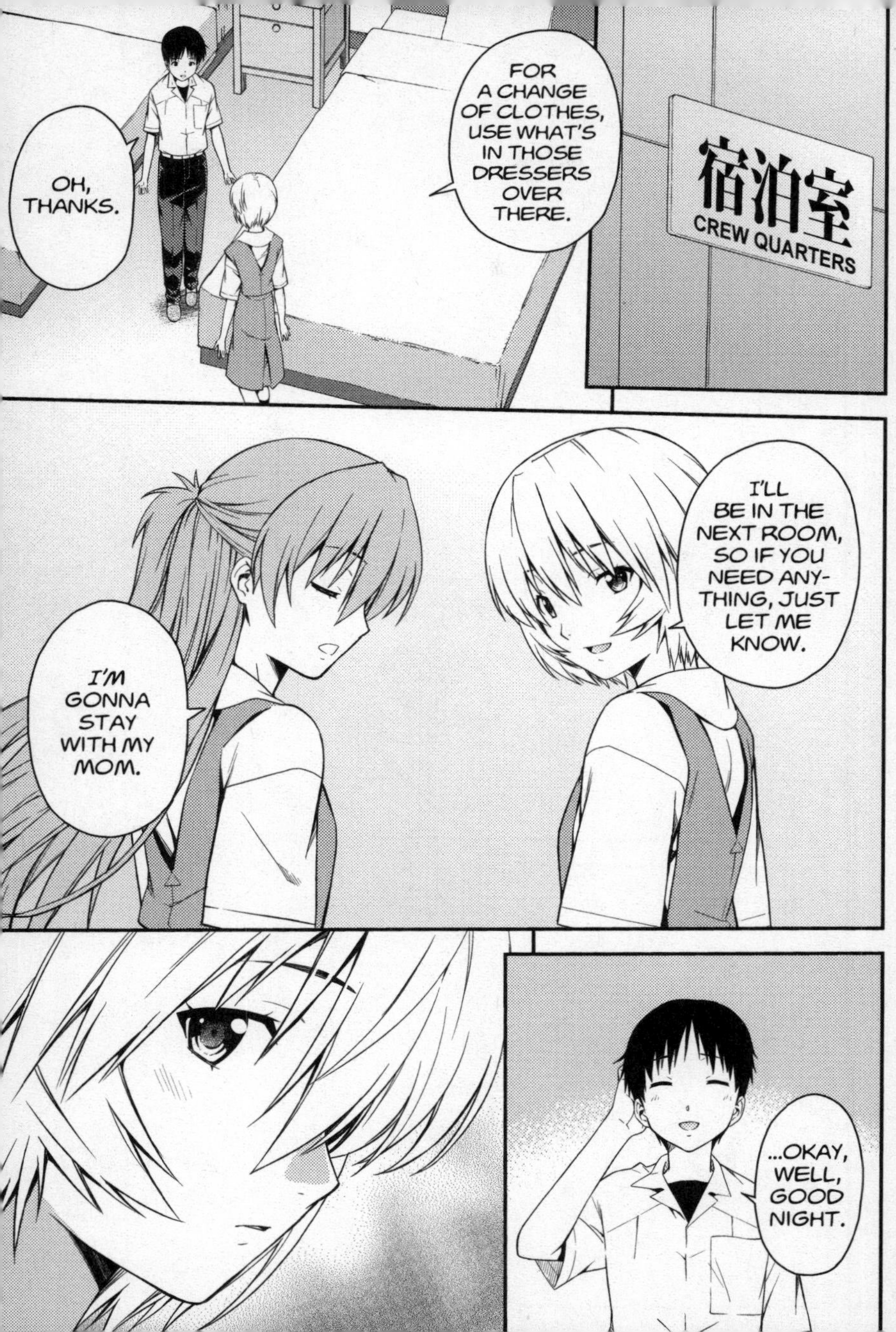
宿泊室
CREW QUARTERS
FOR A CHANGE OF CLOTHES, USE WHAT'S IN THOSE DRESSERS OVER THERE.
OH, THANKS.
I'LL BE IN THE NEXT ROOM, SO IF YOU NEED ANYTHING, JUST LET ME KNOW.
I'M GONNA STAY WITH MY MOM.
...OKAY, WELL, GOOD NIGHT.

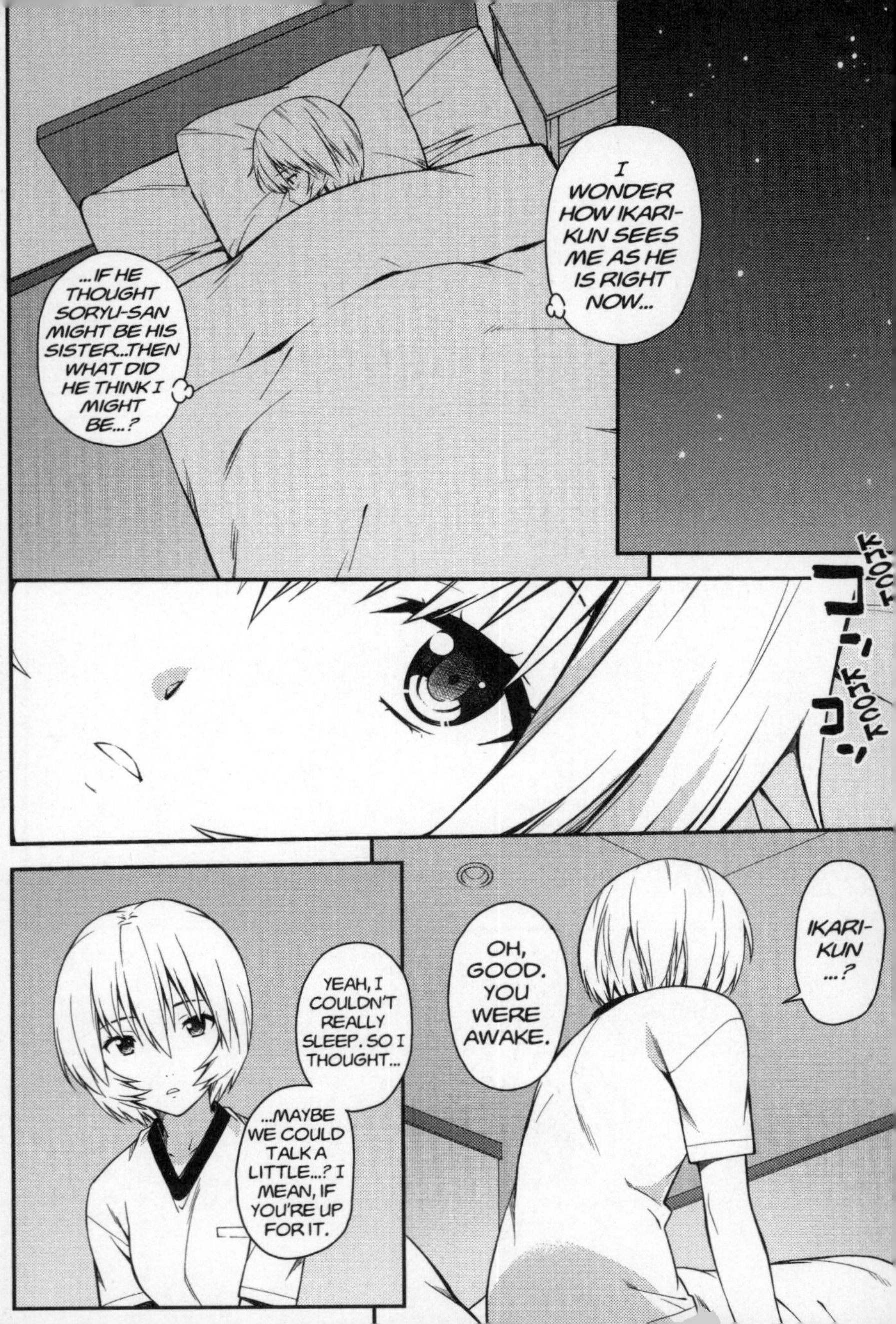
I WONDER HOW IKARI-KUN SEES ME AS HE IS RIGHT NOW...
...IF HE THOUGHT SORYU-SAN MIGHT BE HIS SISTER...THEN WHAT DID HE THINK I MIGHT BE...?
KNOCK
KNOCK
IKARI-KUN ...?
OH, GOOD. YOU WERE AWAKE.
YEAH, I COULDN'T REALLY SLEEP. SO I THOUGHT...
...MAYBE WE COULD TALK A LITTLE...? I MEAN, IF YOU'RE UP FOR IT.

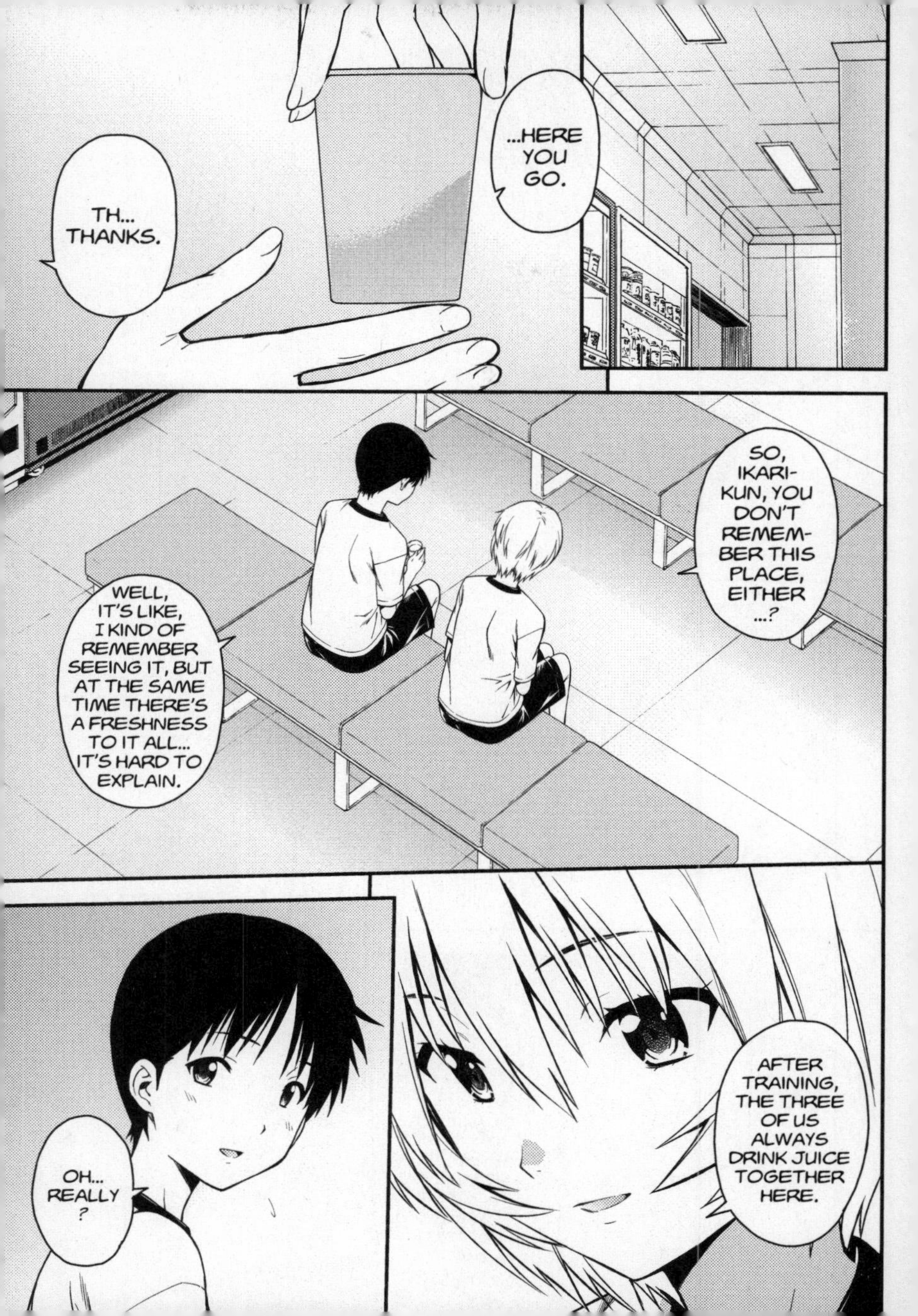
...HERE YOU GO.
TH... THANKS.
SO, IKARI-KUN, YOU DON'T REMEMBER THIS PLACE, EITHER ...?
WELL, IT'S LIKE, I KIND OF REMEMBER SEEING IT, BUT AT THE SAME TIME THERE'S A FRESHNESS TO IT ALL... IT'S HARD TO EXPLAIN.
AFTER TRAINING, THE THREE OF US ALWAYS DRINK JUICE TOGETHER HERE.
OH... REALLY ?

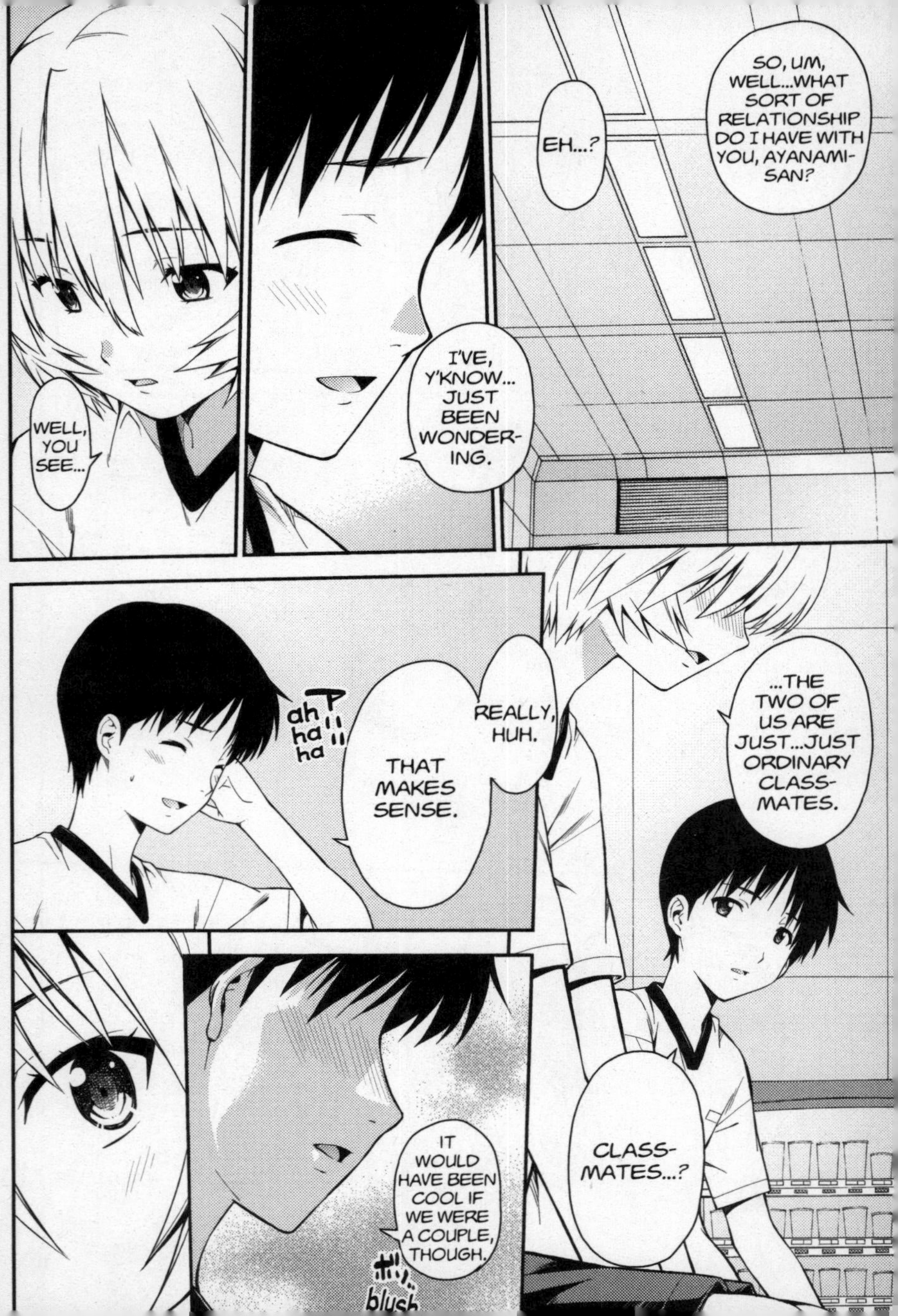
SO, UM, WELL...WHAT SORT OF RELATIONSHIP DO I HAVE WITH YOU, AYANAMI-SAN?
EH...?
I'VE, Y'KNOW... JUST BEEN WONDERING.
WELL, YOU SEE...
...THE TWO OF US ARE JUST...JUST ORDINARY CLASSMATES.
REALLY, HUH.
THAT MAKES SENSE.
ah ha ha
CLASSMATES...?
IT WOULD HAVE BEEN COOL IF WE WERE A COUPLE, THOUGH.
ポッ..
blush

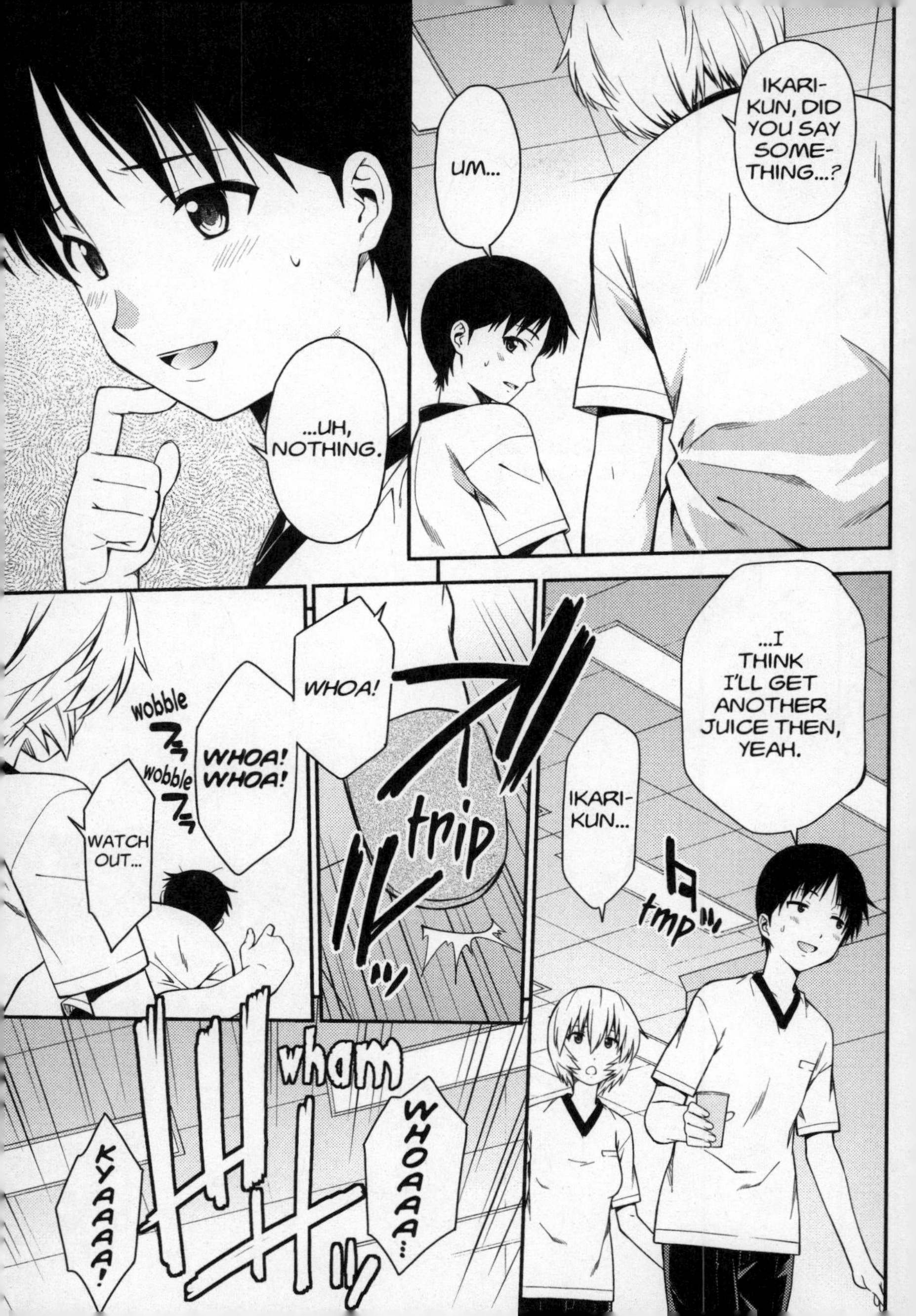
IKARI-KUN, DID YOU SAY SOME-THING...?
UM...
...UH, NOTHING.
...I THINK I'LL GET ANOTHER JUICE THEN, YEAH.
IKARI-KUN...
tmp
WHOA!
trip
WHOA! WHOA!
wobble
wobble
WATCH OUT...
wham
WHOAAAA...
KYAAAA!

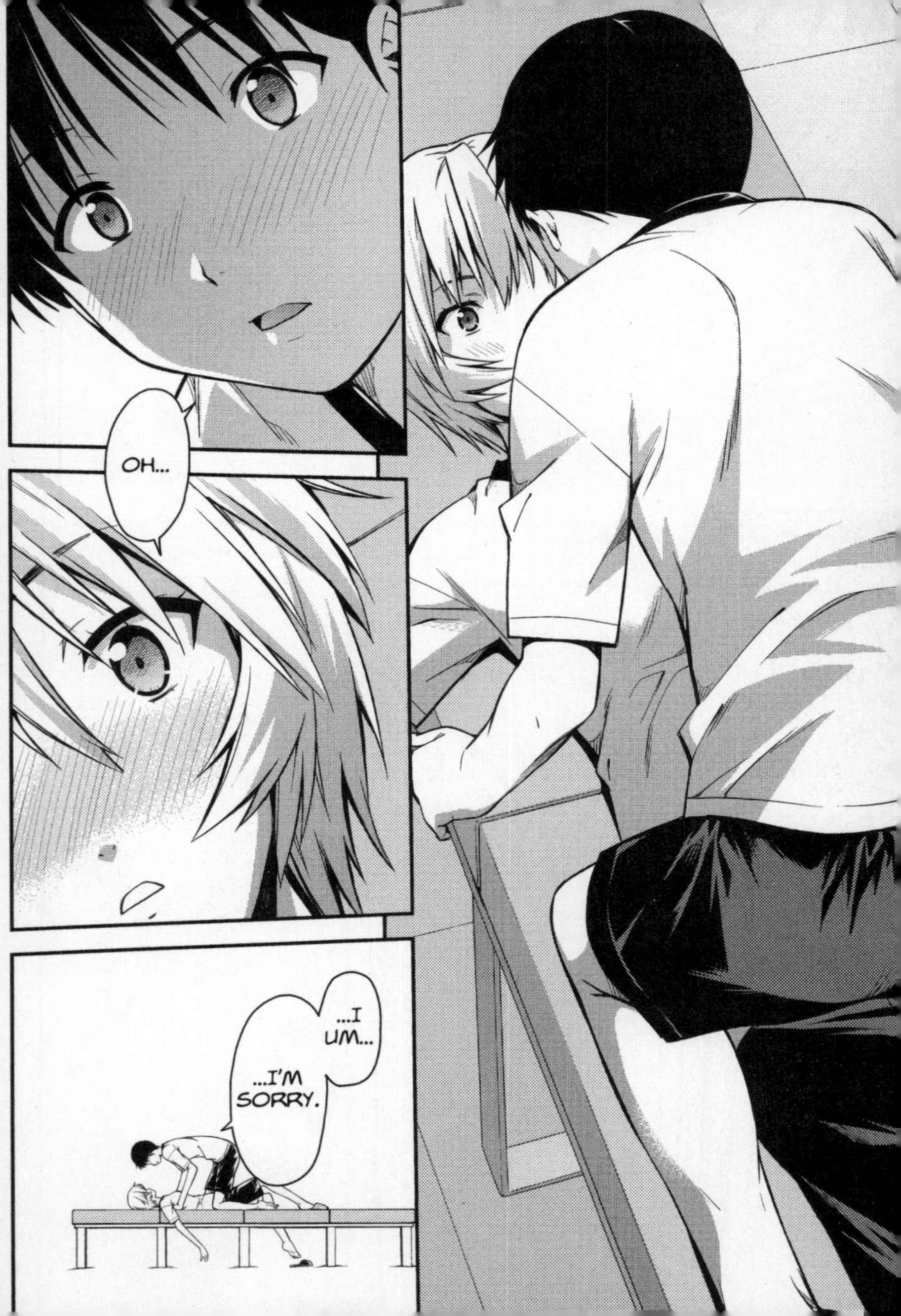
OH...
...I UM...
...I'M SORRY.

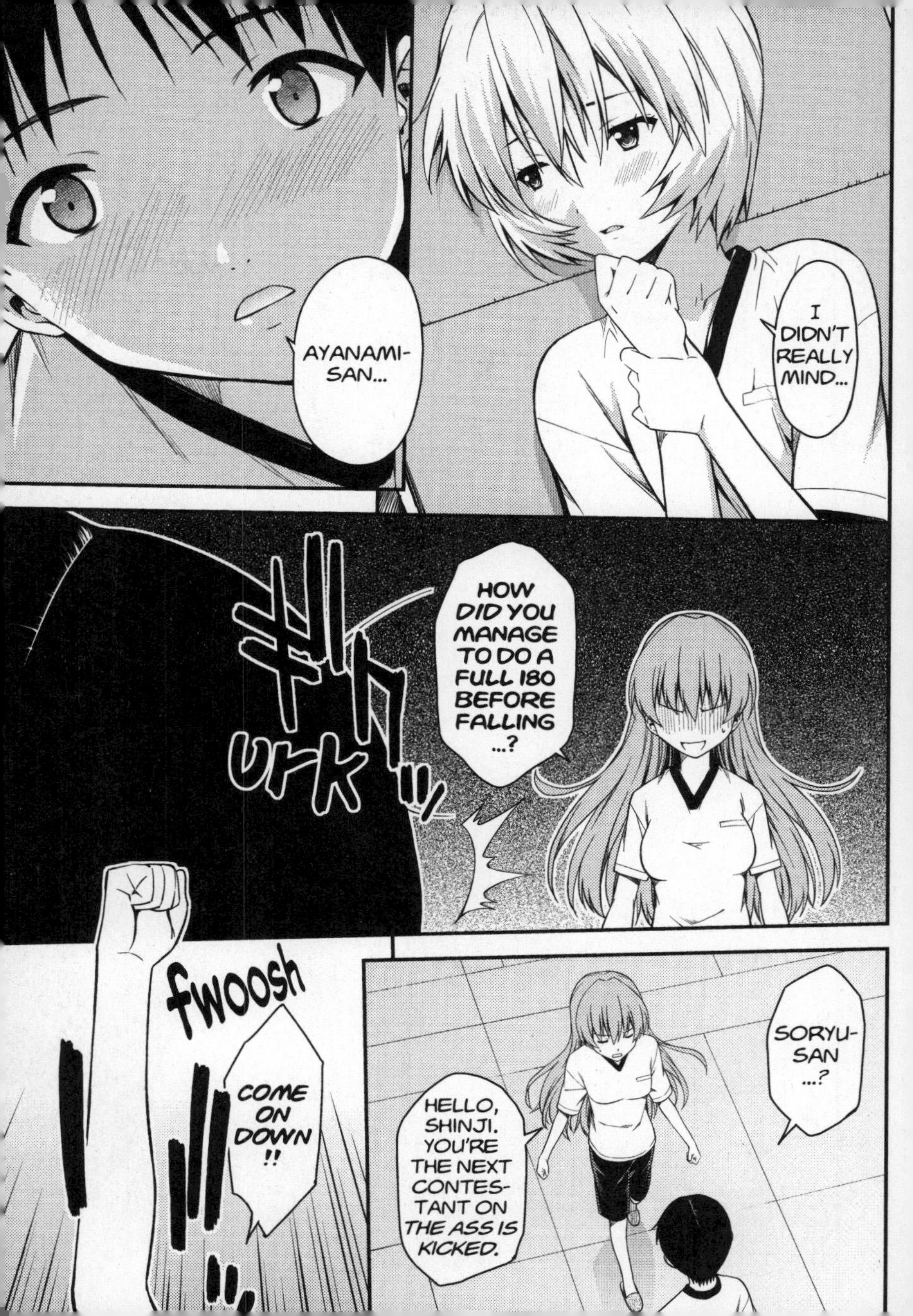
I DIDN'T REALLY MIND...
AYANAMI-SAN...
HOW DID YOU MANAGE TO DO A FULL 180 BEFORE FALLING ...?
urk
SORYU-SAN ...?
HELLO, SHINJI. YOU'RE THE NEXT CONTESTANT ON *THE ASS IS KICKED.*
fwoosh
COME ON DOWN !!

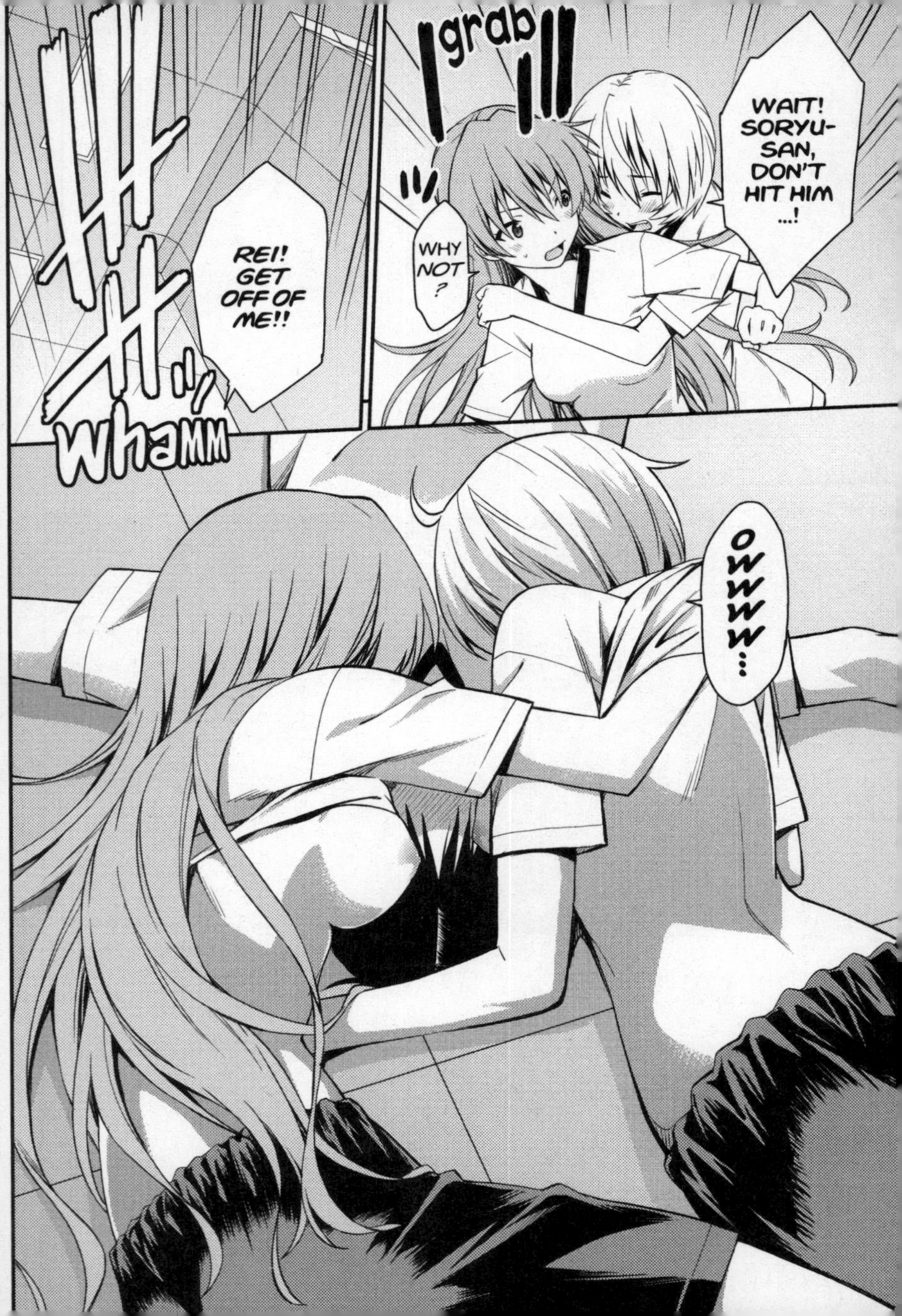
grab
WAIT! SORYU-SAN, DON'T HIT HIM ...!
WHY NOT?
REI! GET OFF OF ME!!
WHAMM
OWWWW...

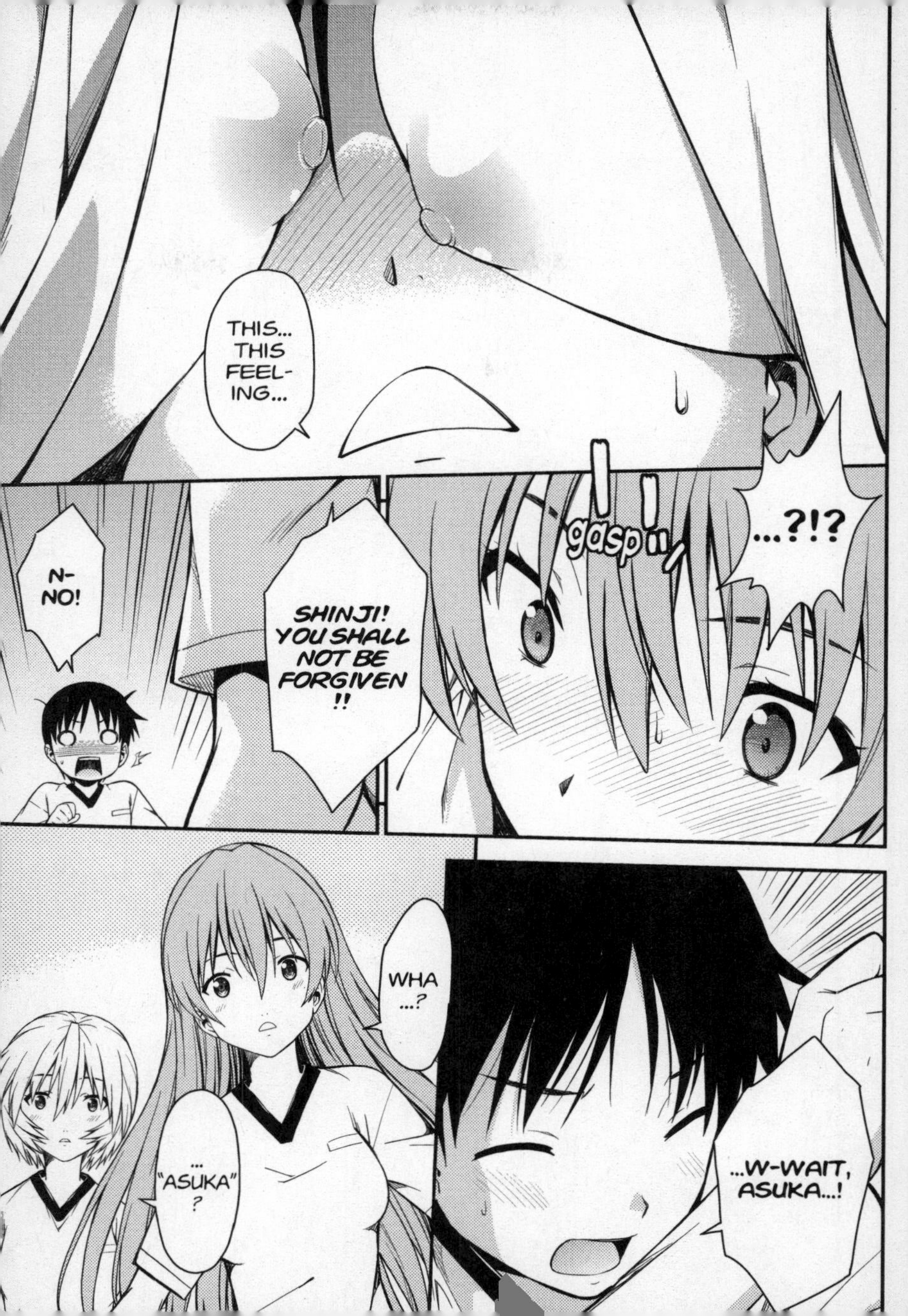
THIS... THIS FEEL- ING...
...?!?
gasp!!
SHINJI! YOU SHALL NOT BE FORGIVEN!!
N- NO!
...W-WAIT, ASUKA...!
WHA ...?
... "ASUKA" ?

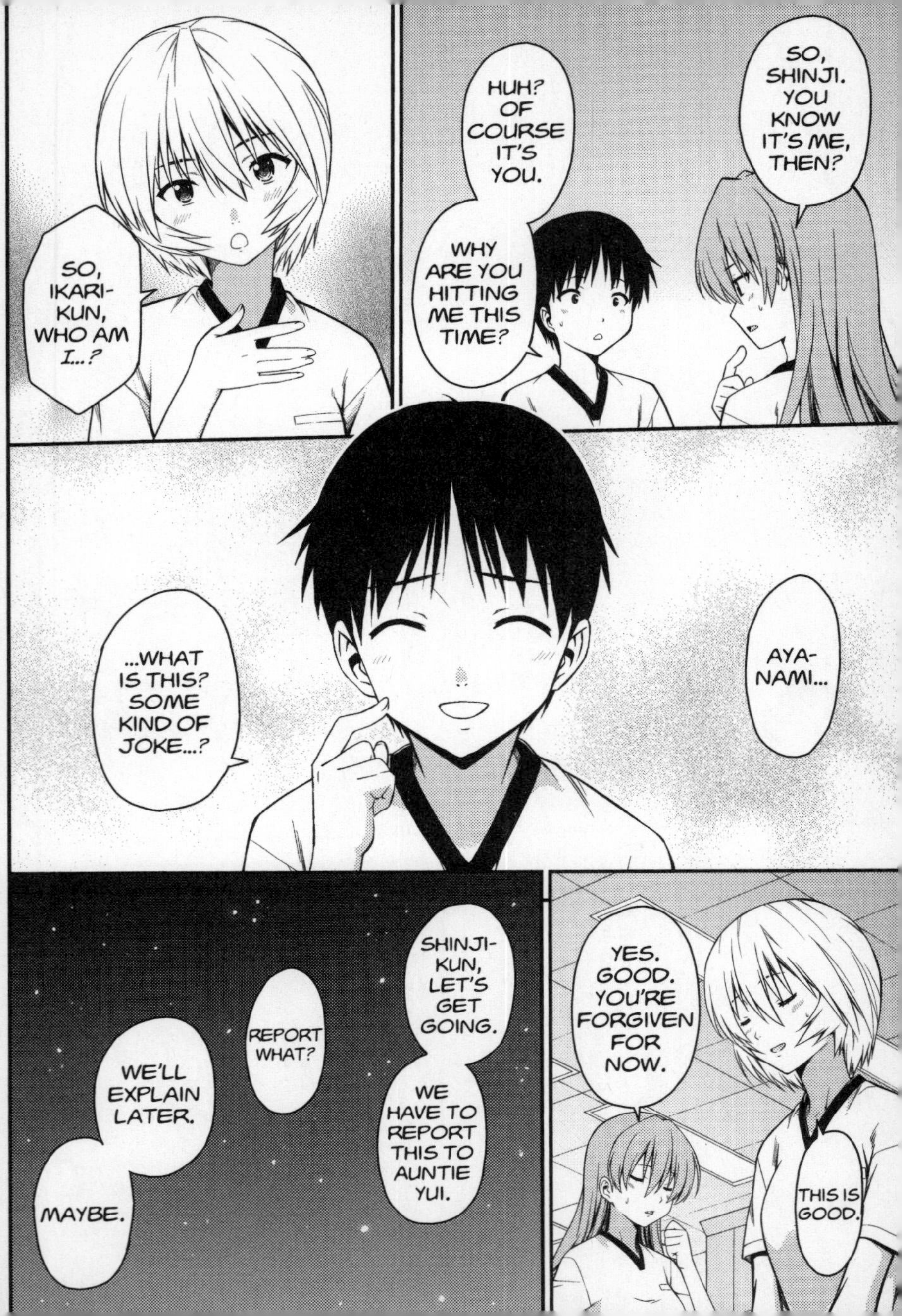
SO, SHINJI. YOU KNOW IT'S ME, THEN?
HUH? OF COURSE IT'S YOU.
WHY ARE YOU HITTING ME THIS TIME?
SO, IKARI-KUN, WHO AM I...?
AYA-NAMI...
...WHAT IS THIS? SOME KIND OF JOKE...?
YES. GOOD. YOU'RE FORGIVEN FOR NOW.
THIS IS GOOD.
SHINJI-KUN, LET'S GET GOING.
WE HAVE TO REPORT THIS TO AUNTIE YUI.
REPORT WHAT?
WE'LL EXPLAIN LATER.
MAYBE.

the shinji ikari raising project

NEON GENESIS
EVANGELION
THE SHINJI IKARI RAISING PROJECT

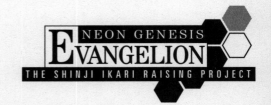

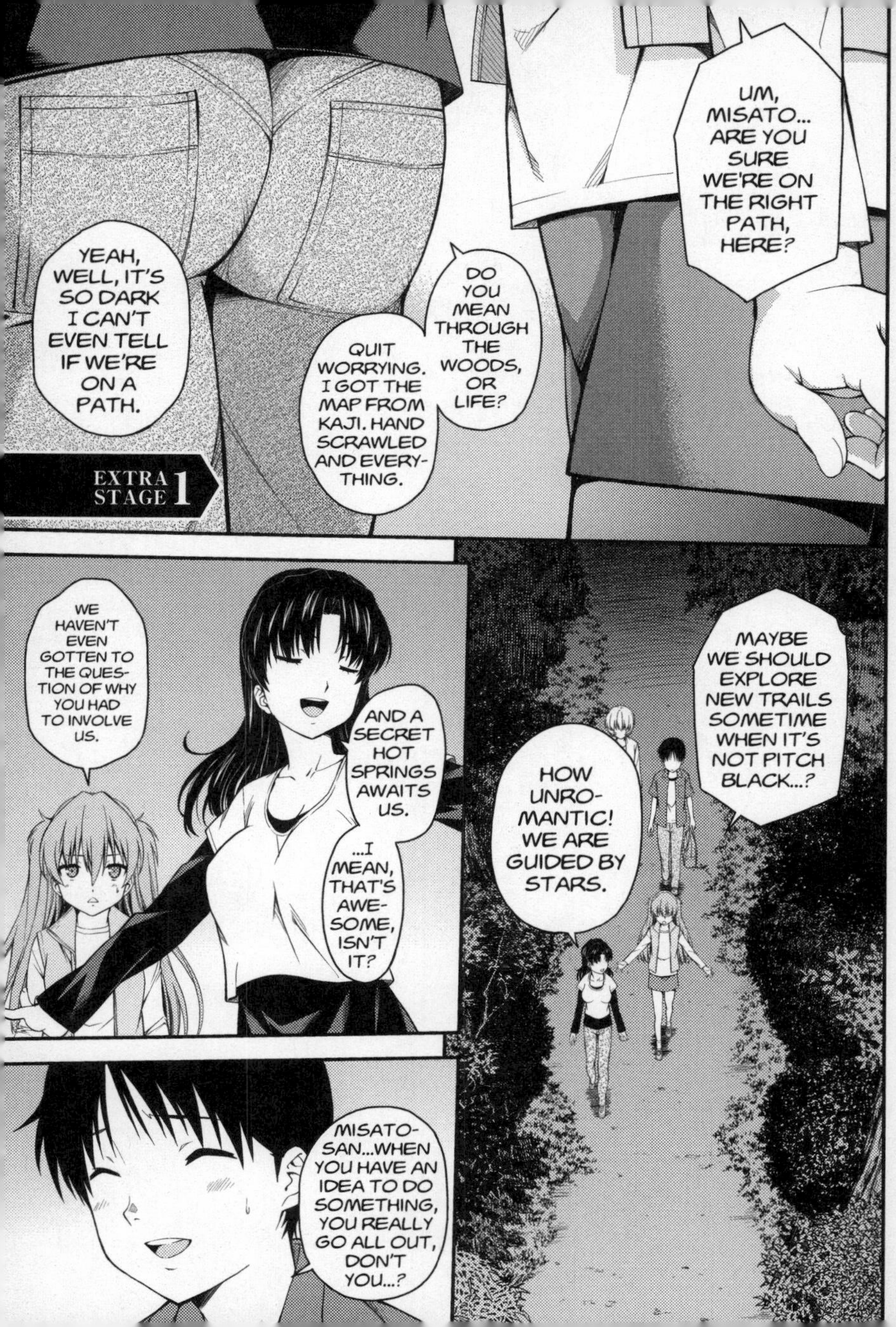
UM, MISATO... ARE YOU SURE WE'RE ON THE RIGHT PATH, HERE?
DO YOU MEAN THROUGH THE WOODS, OR LIFE?
QUIT WORRYING. I GOT THE MAP FROM KAJI. HAND SCRAWLED AND EVERY-THING.
YEAH, WELL, IT'S SO DARK I CAN'T EVEN TELL IF WE'RE ON A PATH.
EXTRA STAGE 1
MAYBE WE SHOULD EXPLORE NEW TRAILS SOMETIME WHEN IT'S NOT PITCH BLACK...?
HOW UNRO-MANTIC! WE ARE GUIDED BY STARS.
AND A SECRET HOT SPRINGS AWAITS US.
...I MEAN, THAT'S AWE-SOME, ISN'T IT?
WE HAVEN'T EVEN GOTTEN TO THE QUES-TION OF WHY YOU HAD TO INVOLVE US.
MISATO-SAN...WHEN YOU HAVE AN IDEA TO DO SOMETHING, YOU REALLY GO ALL OUT, DON'T YOU...?

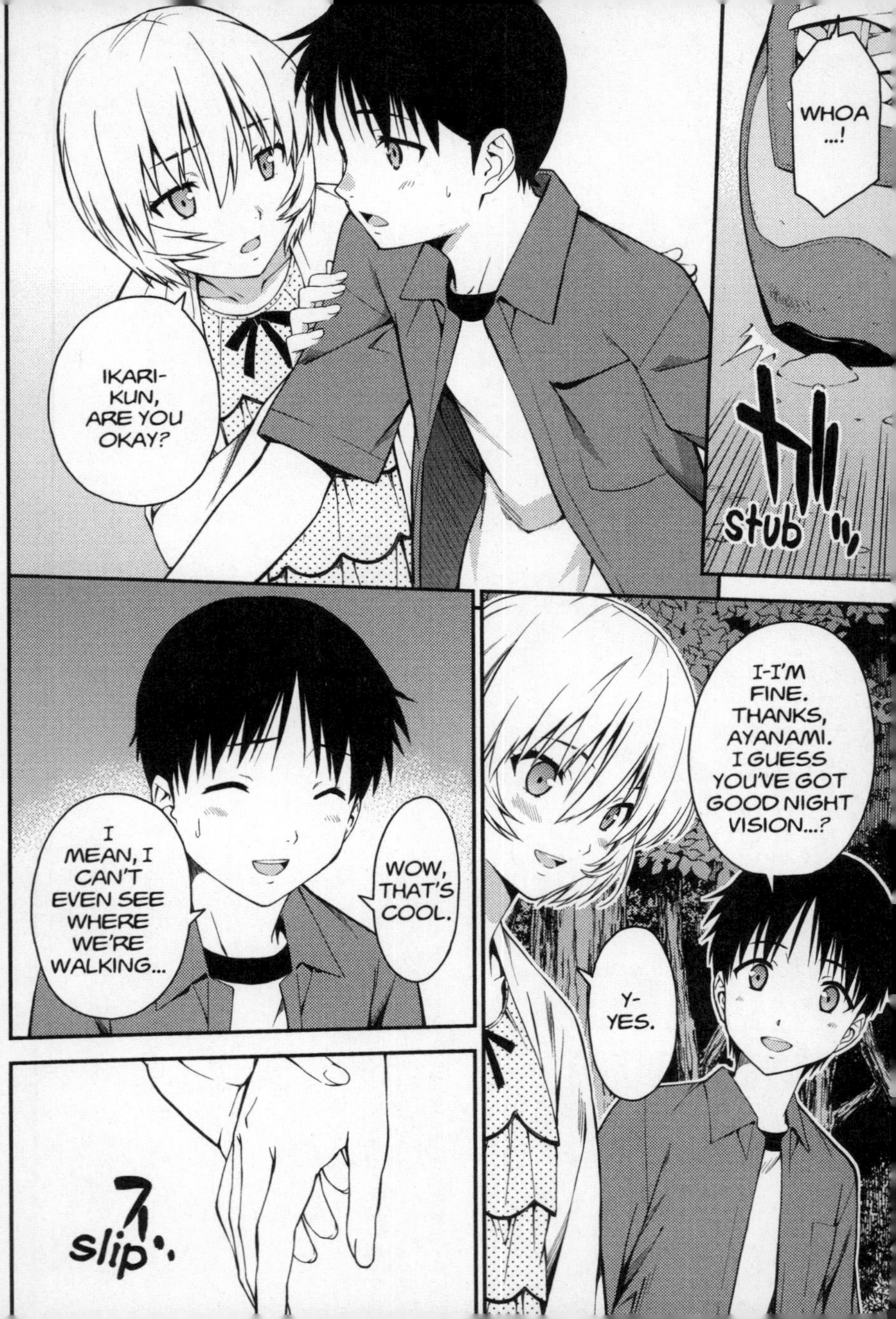
WHOA ...!
stub
IKARI-KUN, ARE YOU OKAY?
I-I'M FINE. THANKS, AYANAMI. I GUESS YOU'VE GOT GOOD NIGHT VISION...?
Y-YES.
WOW, THAT'S COOL.
I MEAN, I CAN'T EVEN SEE WHERE WE'RE WALKING...
slip

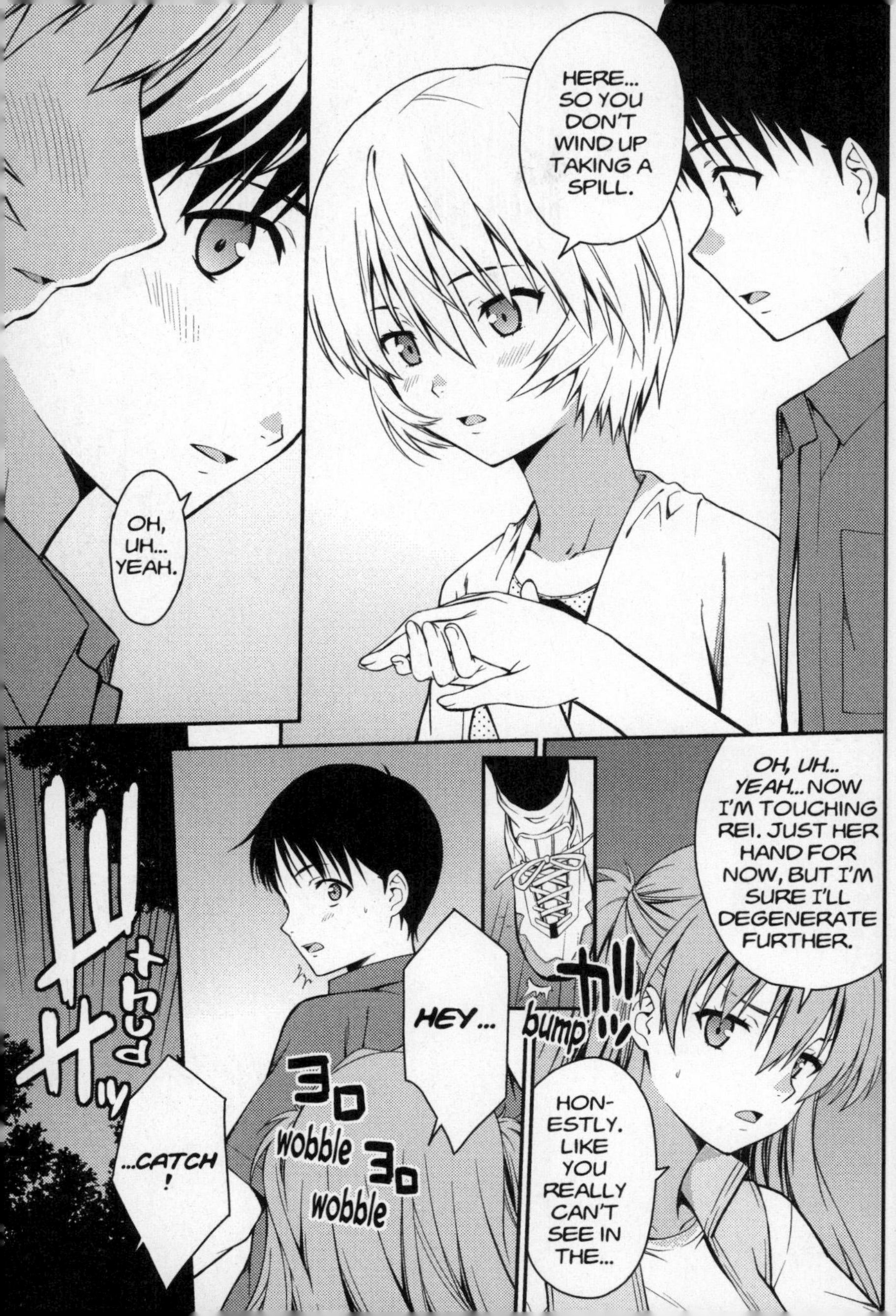
HERE... SO YOU DON'T WIND UP TAKING A SPILL.
OH, UH... YEAH.
OH, UH... YEAH... NOW I'M TOUCHING REI. JUST HER HAND FOR NOW, BUT I'M SURE I'LL DEGENERATE FURTHER.
bump
HON-ESTLY. LIKE YOU REALLY CAN'T SEE IN THE...
HEY...
wobble
wobble
...CATCH!
thud

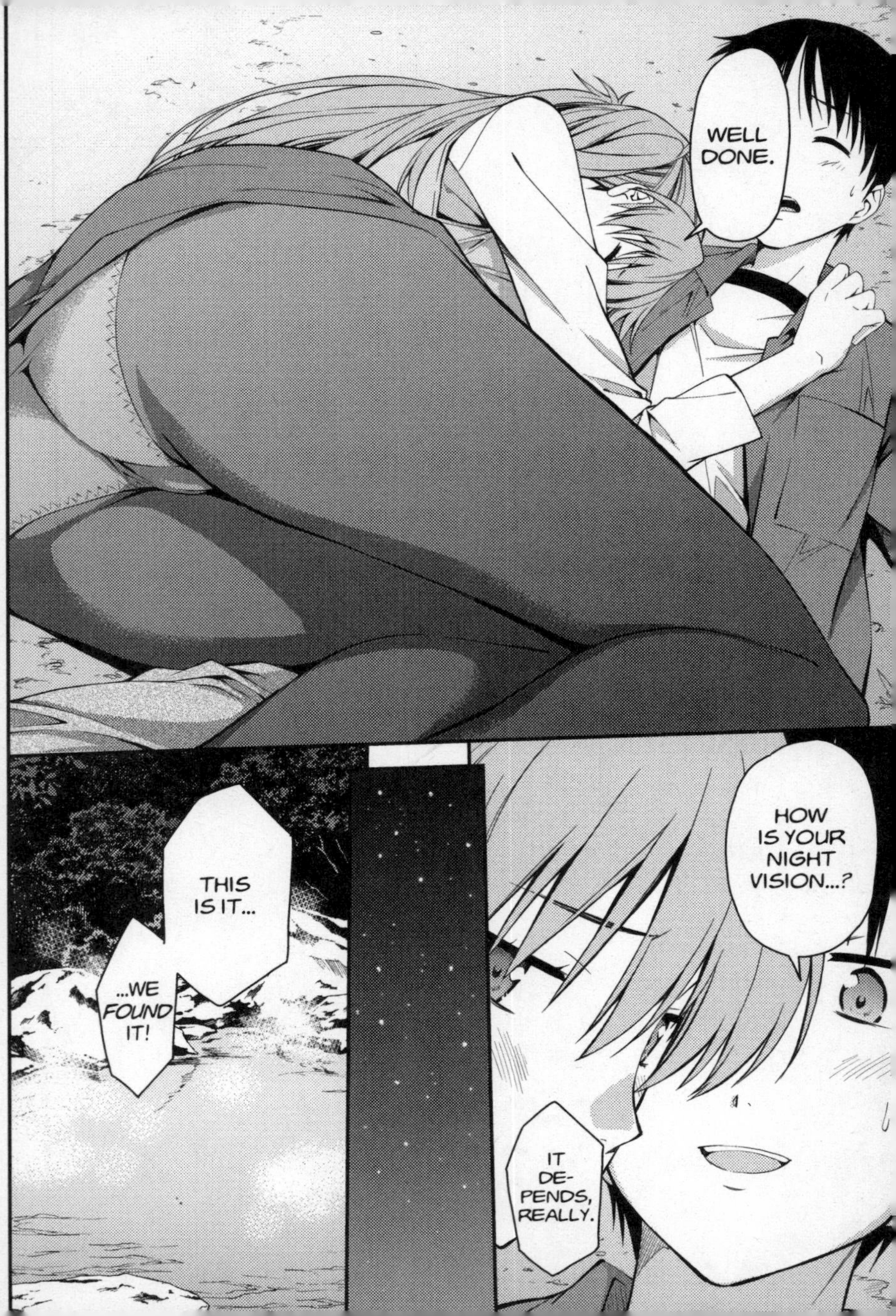
WELL DONE.
HOW IS YOUR NIGHT VISION...?
IT DEPENDS, REALLY.
THIS IS IT...
...WE FOUND IT!

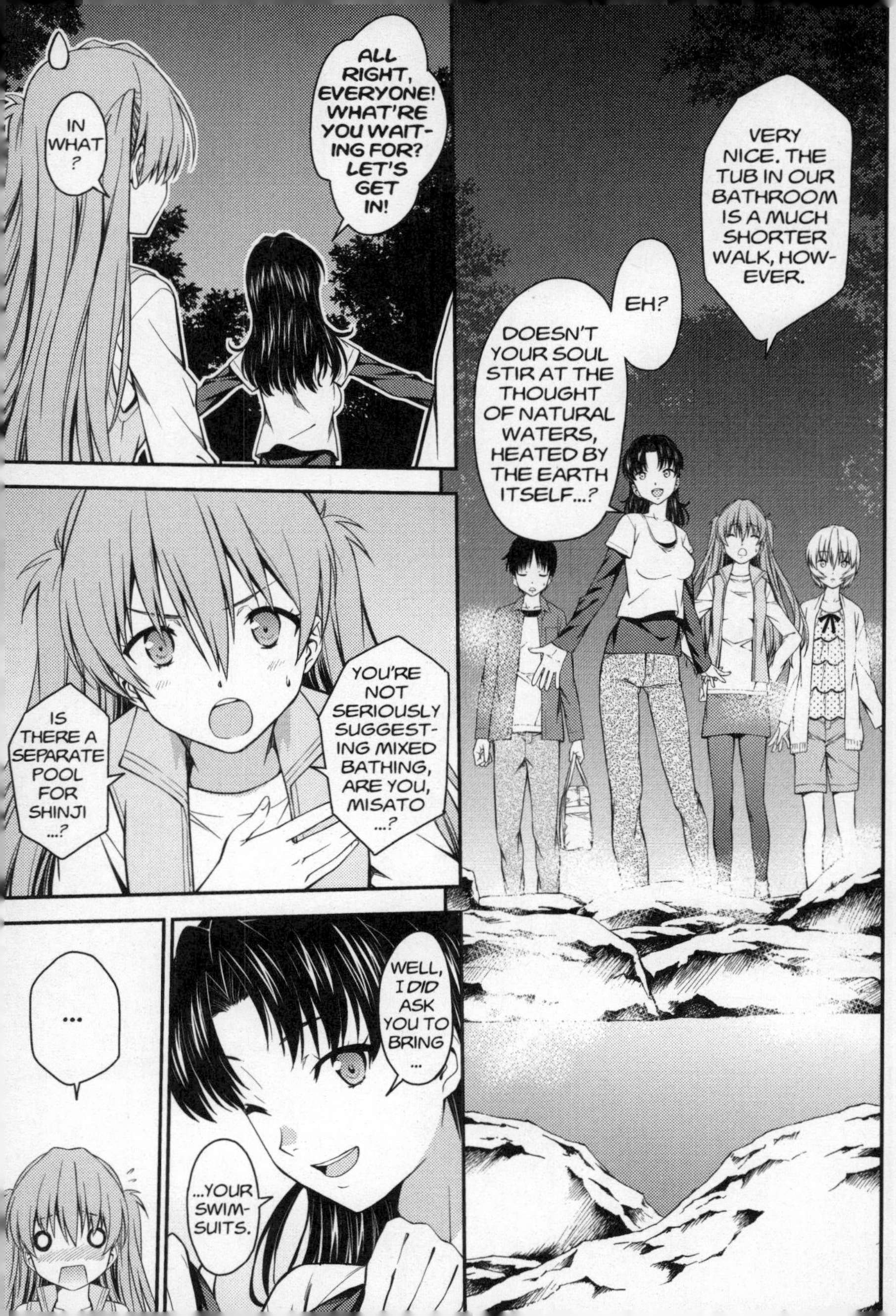
VERY NICE. THE TUB IN OUR BATHROOM IS A MUCH SHORTER WALK, HOWEVER.
EH?
DOESN'T YOUR SOUL STIR AT THE THOUGHT OF NATURAL WATERS, HEATED BY THE EARTH ITSELF...?
ALL RIGHT, EVERYONE! WHAT'RE YOU WAITING FOR? LET'S GET IN!
IN WHAT?
YOU'RE NOT SERIOUSLY SUGGESTING MIXED BATHING, ARE YOU, MISATO ...?
IS THERE A SEPARATE POOL FOR SHINJI ...?
WELL, I *DID* ASK YOU TO BRING ...
...YOUR SWIMSUITS.
...

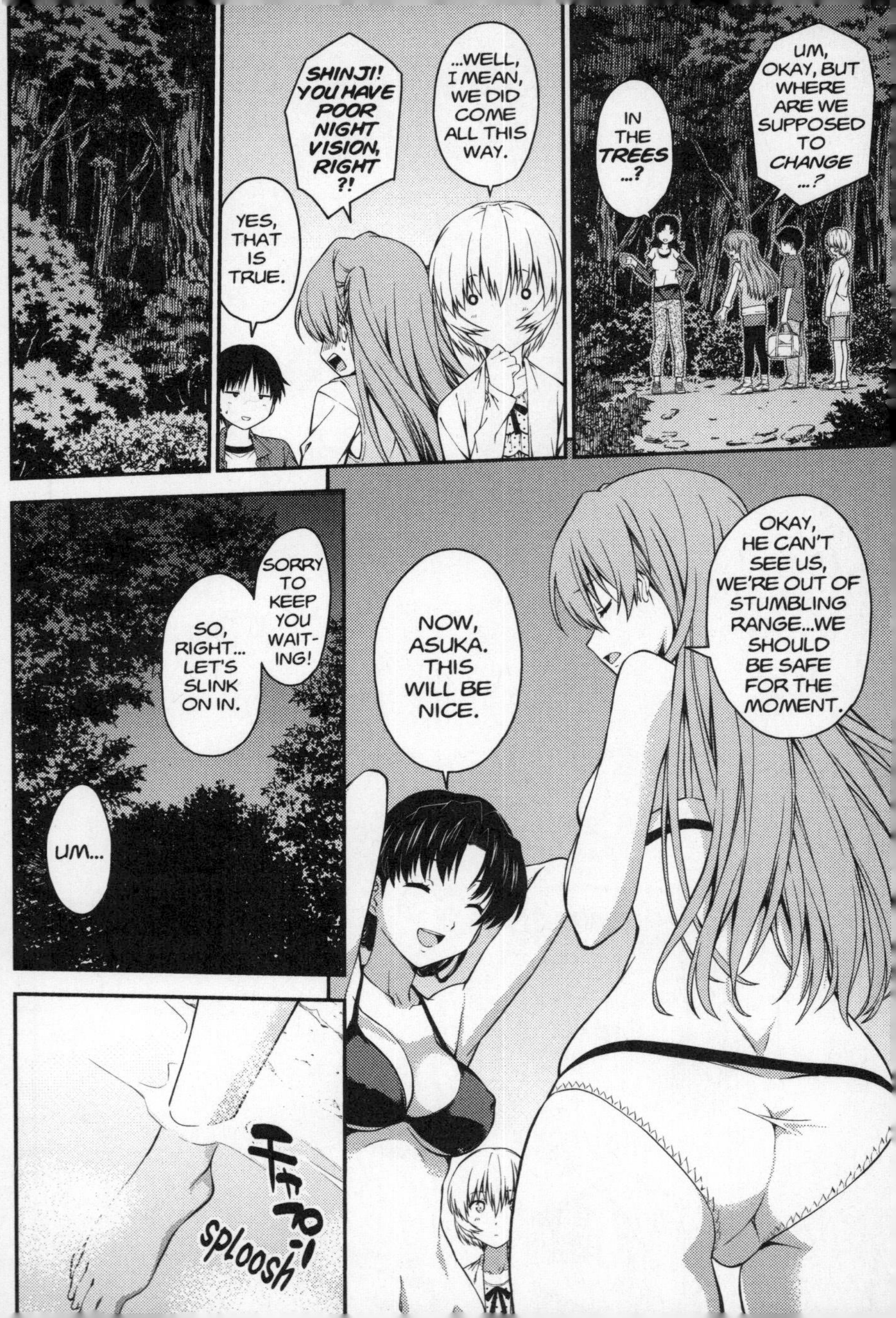
UM, OKAY, BUT WHERE ARE WE SUPPOSED TO CHANGE ...?
IN THE TREES ...?
...WELL, I MEAN, WE DID COME ALL THIS WAY.
SHINJI! YOU HAVE POOR NIGHT VISION, RIGHT ?!
YES, THAT IS TRUE.
OKAY, HE CAN'T SEE US, WE'RE OUT OF STUMBLING RANGE...WE SHOULD BE SAFE FOR THE MOMENT.
NOW, ASUKA. THIS WILL BE NICE.
SORRY TO KEEP YOU WAITING!
SO, RIGHT... LET'S SLINK ON IN.
UM...
sploosh

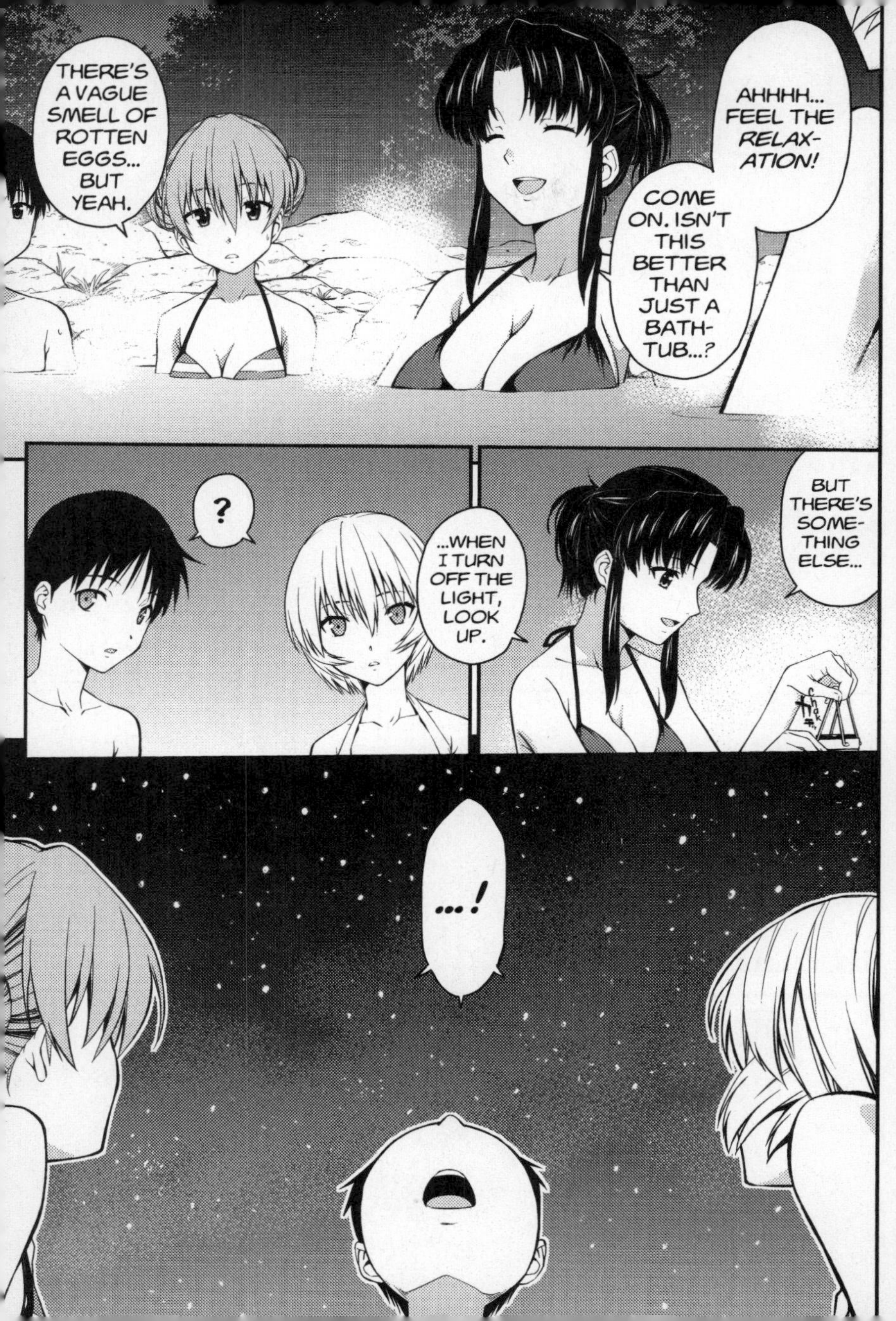
AHHHH... FEEL THE RELAX-ATION!
COME ON. ISN'T THIS BETTER THAN JUST A BATH-TUB...?
THERE'S A VAGUE SMELL OF ROTTEN EGGS... BUT YEAH.
BUT THERE'S SOME-THING ELSE...
...WHEN I TURN OFF THE LIGHT, LOOK UP.
?
...!

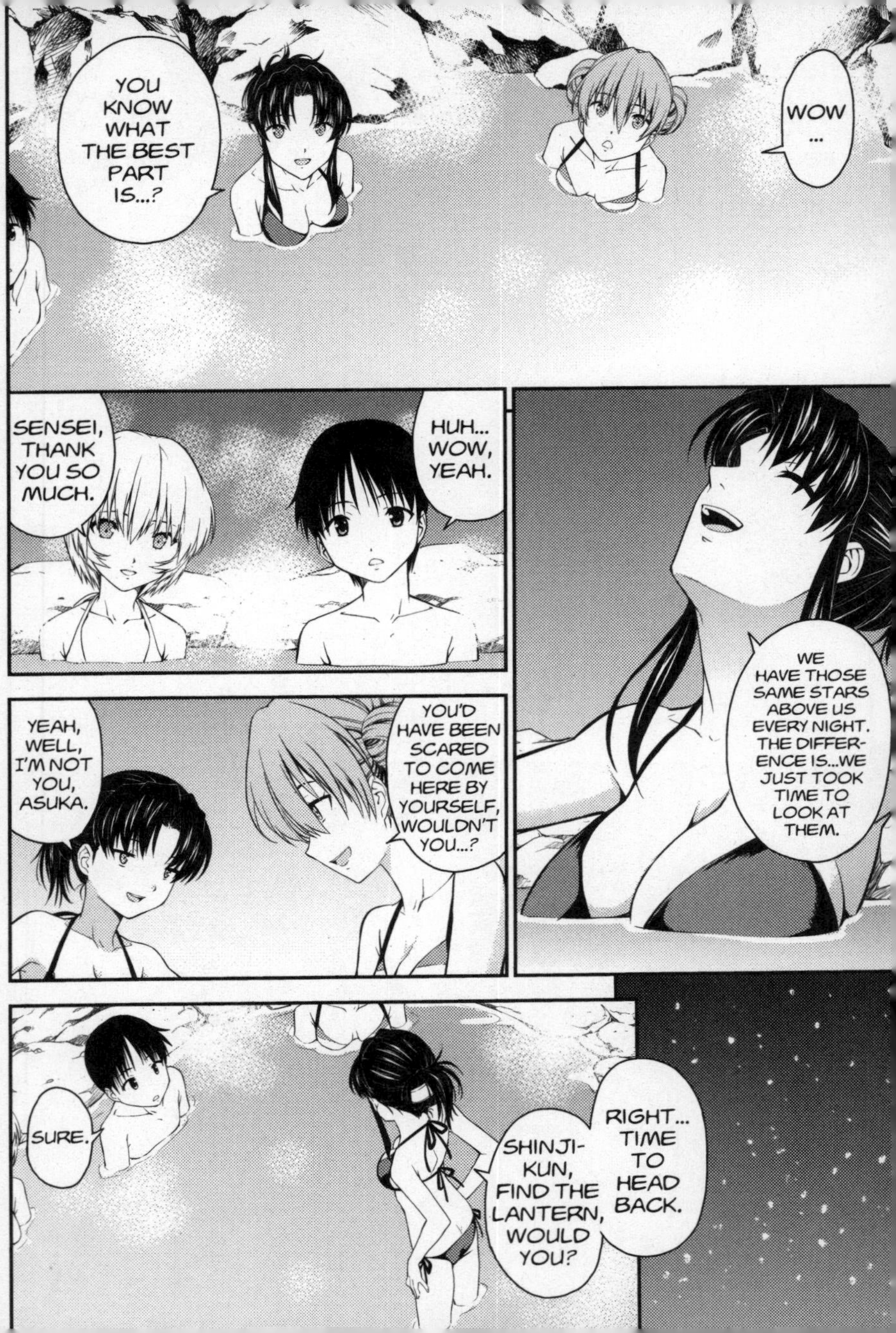
WOW...
YOU KNOW WHAT THE BEST PART IS...?
WE HAVE THOSE SAME STARS ABOVE US EVERY NIGHT. THE DIFFERENCE IS...WE JUST TOOK TIME TO LOOK AT THEM.
HUH... WOW, YEAH.
SENSEI, THANK YOU SO MUCH.
YOU'D HAVE BEEN SCARED TO COME HERE BY YOURSELF, WOULDN'T YOU...?
YEAH, WELL, I'M NOT YOU, ASUKA.
RIGHT... TIME TO HEAD BACK.
SHINJI-KUN, FIND THE LANTERN, WOULD YOU?
SURE.

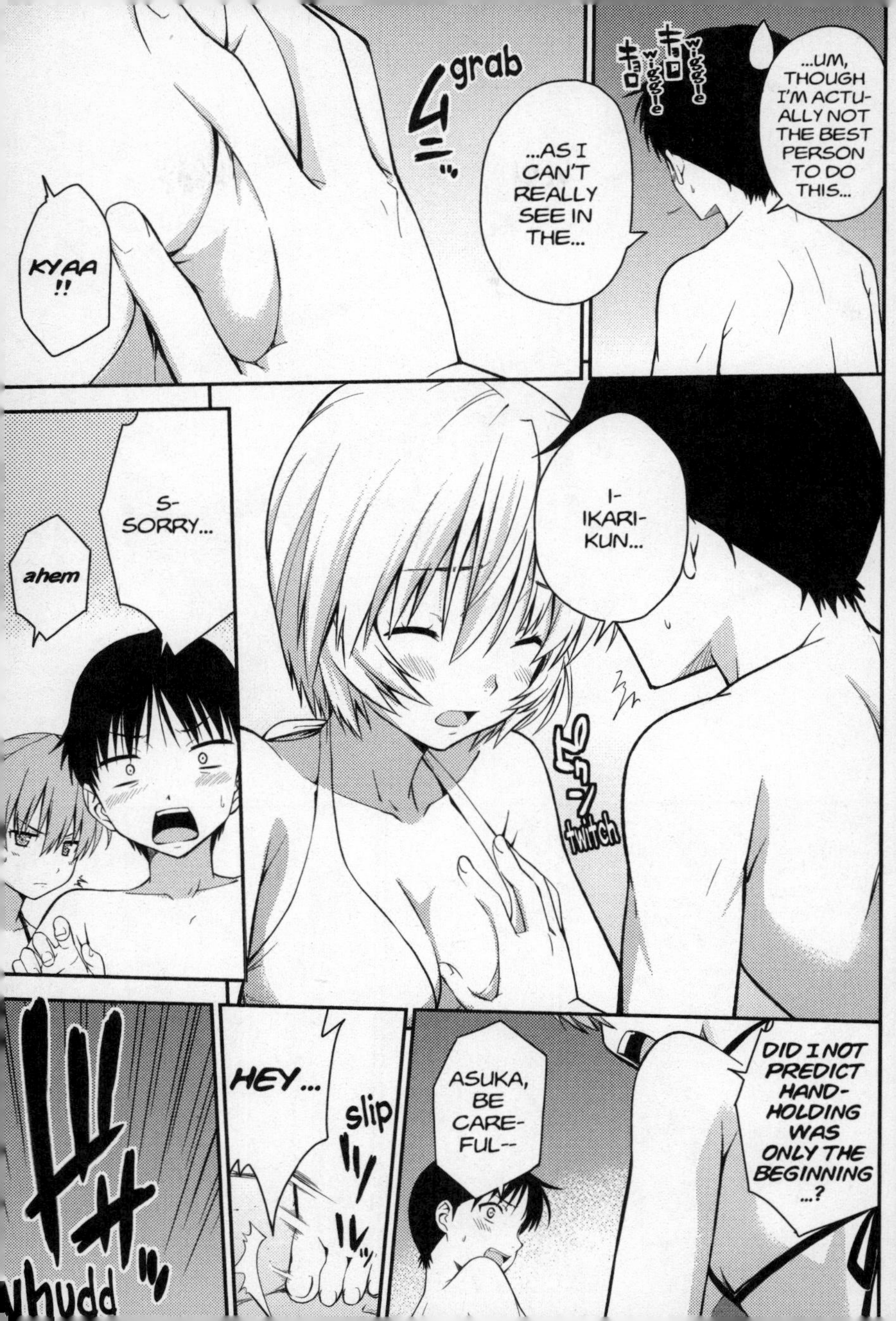
wiggle
wiggle
...UM, THOUGH I'M ACTU-ALLY NOT THE BEST PERSON TO DO THIS...
...AS I CAN'T REALLY SEE IN THE...
grab
KYAA !!
I-IKARI-KUN...
twitch
S-SORRY...
ahem
DID I NOT PREDICT HAND-HOLDING WAS ONLY THE BEGINNING ...?
ASUKA, BE CARE-FUL--
HEY...
slip
whudd

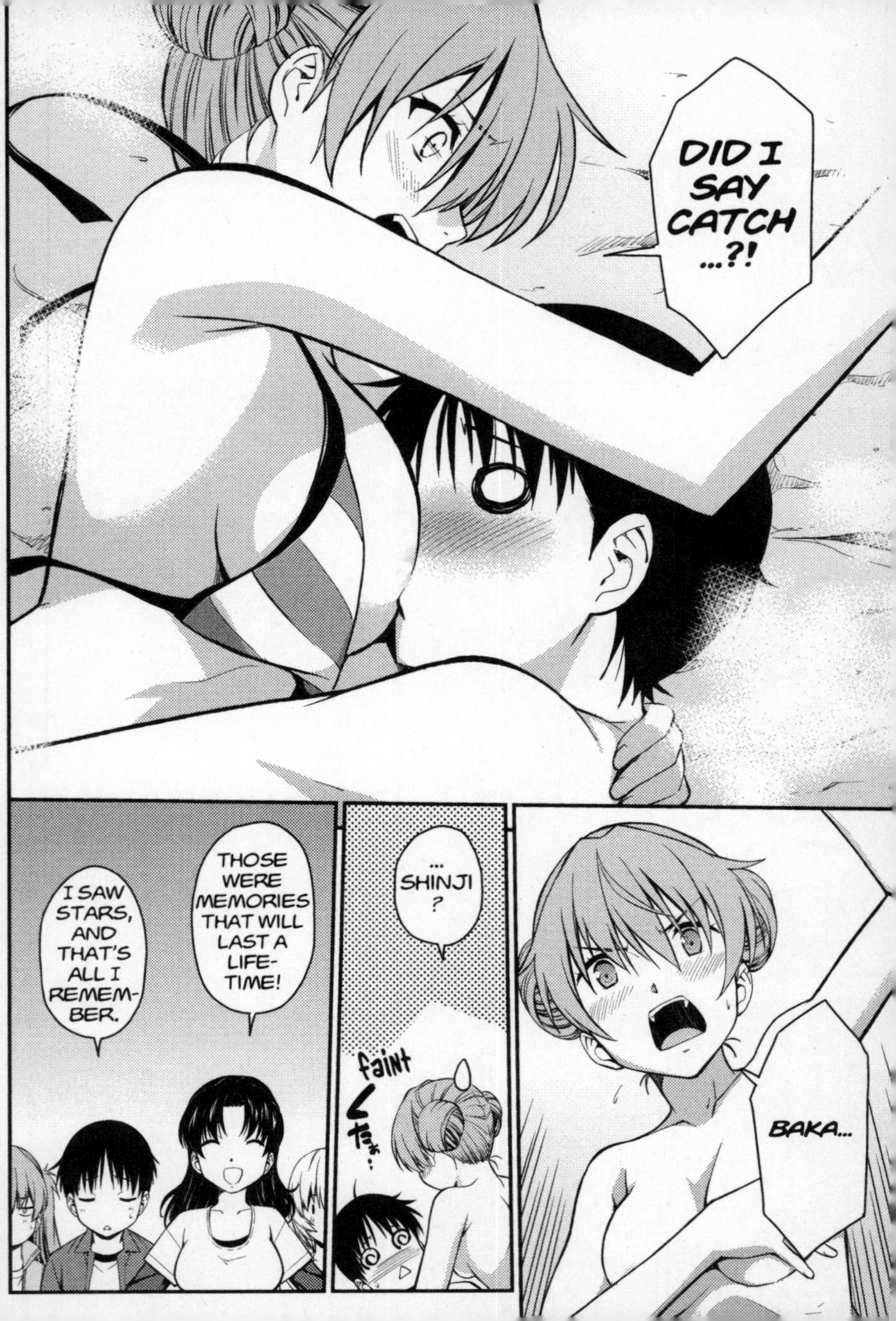
DID I SAY CATCH ...?!
BAKA...
... SHINJI ?
faint
THOSE WERE MEMORIES THAT WILL LAST A LIFE-TIME!
I SAW STARS, AND THAT'S ALL I REMEM-BER.

the shinji ikari raising project

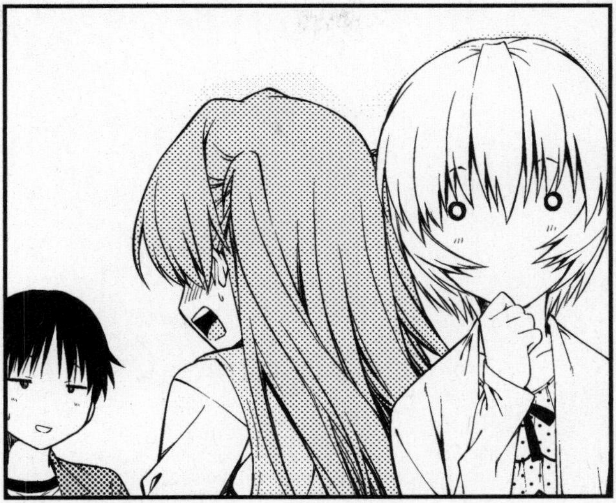

NEON GENESIS EVANGELION

THE SHINJI IKARI RAISING PROJECT

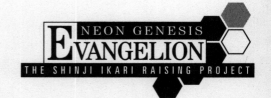

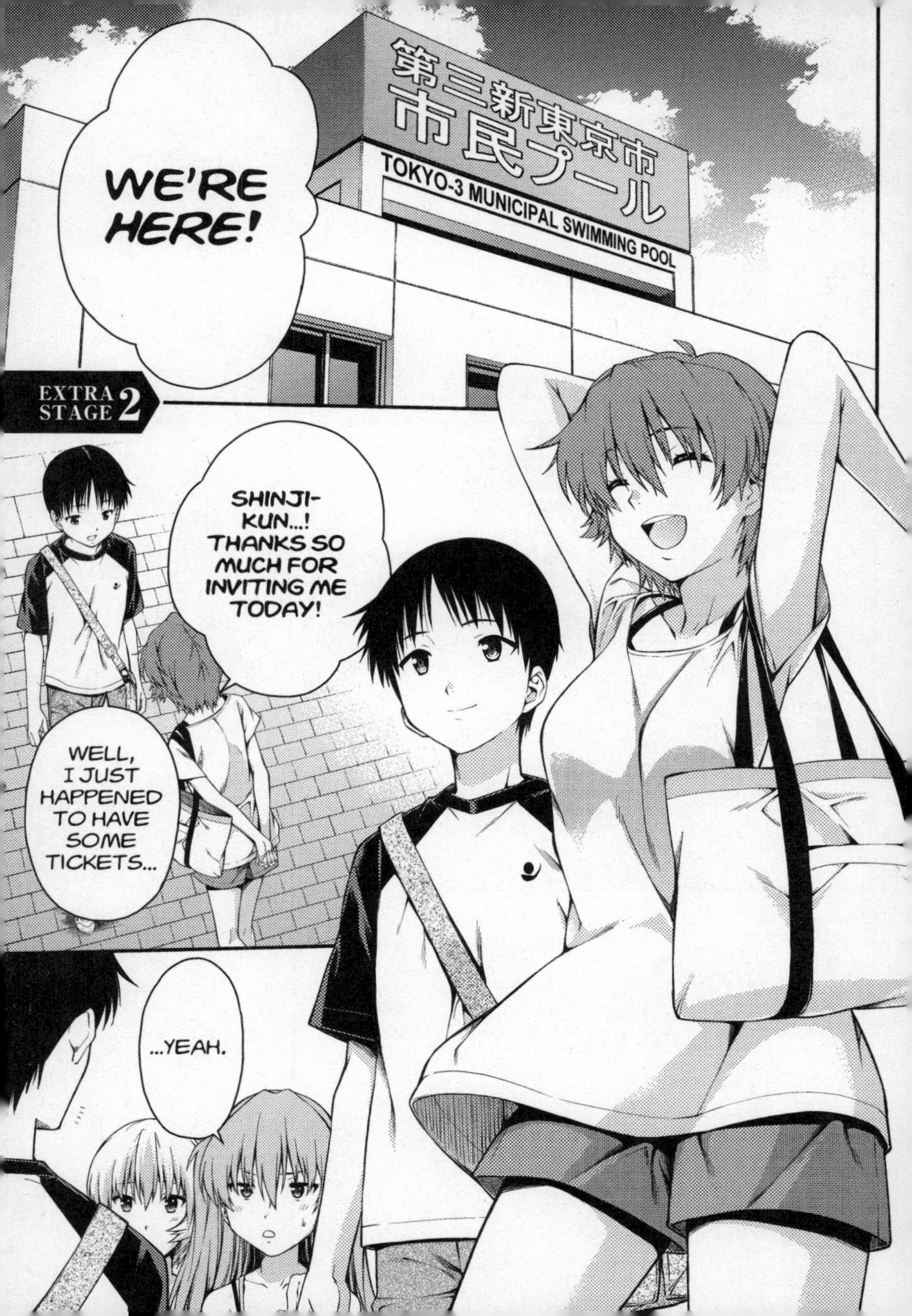

第三新東京市
市民プール
TOKYO-3 MUNICIPAL SWIMMING POOL
WE'RE HERE!
EXTRA STAGE 2
SHINJI-KUN...! THANKS SO MUCH FOR INVITING ME TODAY!
WELL, I JUST HAPPENED TO HAVE SOME TICKETS...
...YEAH.

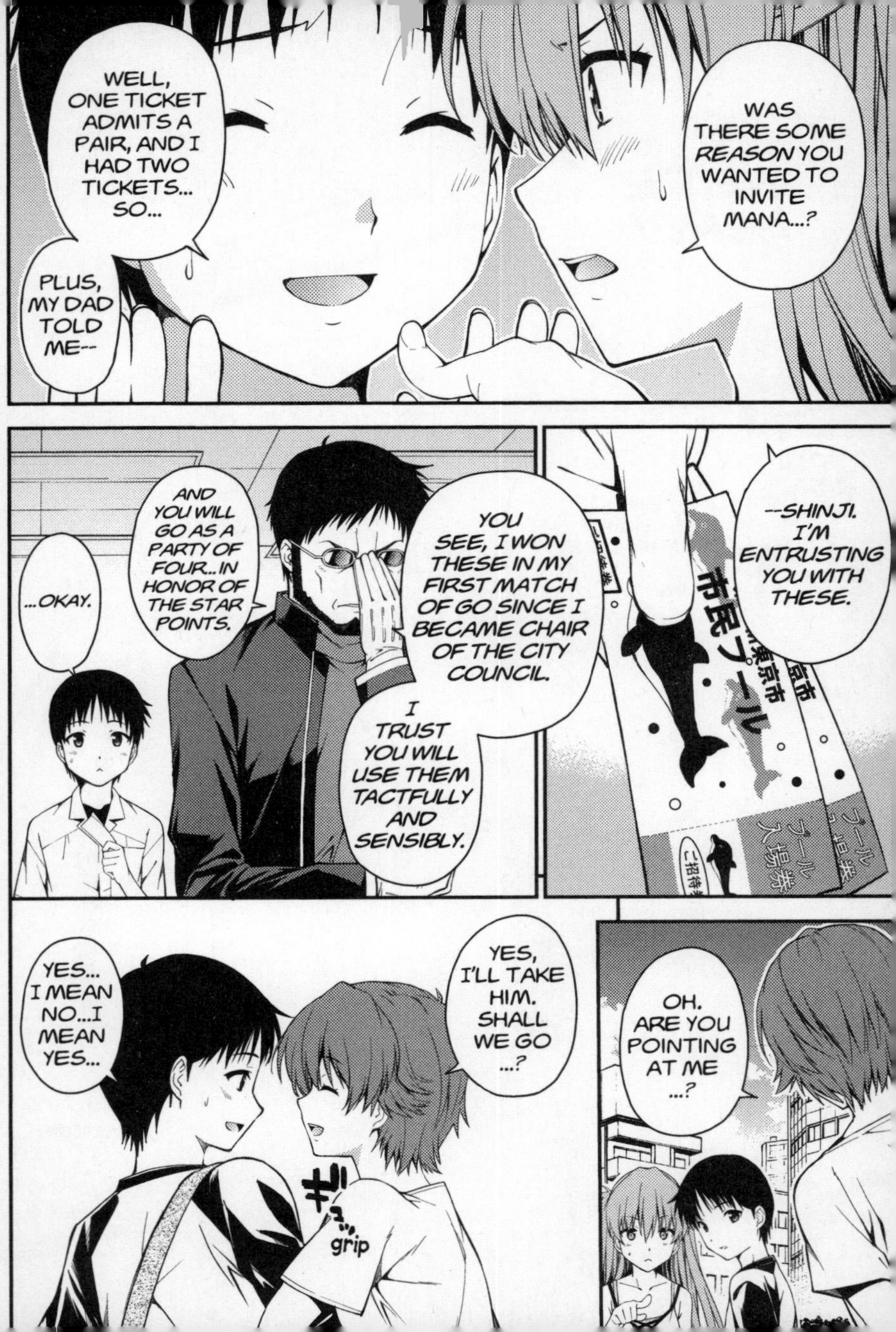
WAS THERE SOME REASON YOU WANTED TO INVITE MANA...?
WELL, ONE TICKET ADMITS A PAIR, AND I HAD TWO TICKETS... SO...
PLUS, MY DAD TOLD ME--
--SHINJI. I'M ENTRUSTING YOU WITH THESE.
市民プール
YOU SEE, I WON THESE IN MY FIRST MATCH OF GO SINCE I BECAME CHAIR OF THE CITY COUNCIL.
I TRUST YOU WILL USE THEM TACTFULLY AND SENSIBLY.
AND YOU WILL GO AS A PARTY OF FOUR...IN HONOR OF THE STAR POINTS.
...OKAY.
OH. ARE YOU POINTING AT ME ...?
YES, I'LL TAKE HIM. SHALL WE GO ...?
YES... I MEAN NO...I MEAN YES...
grip

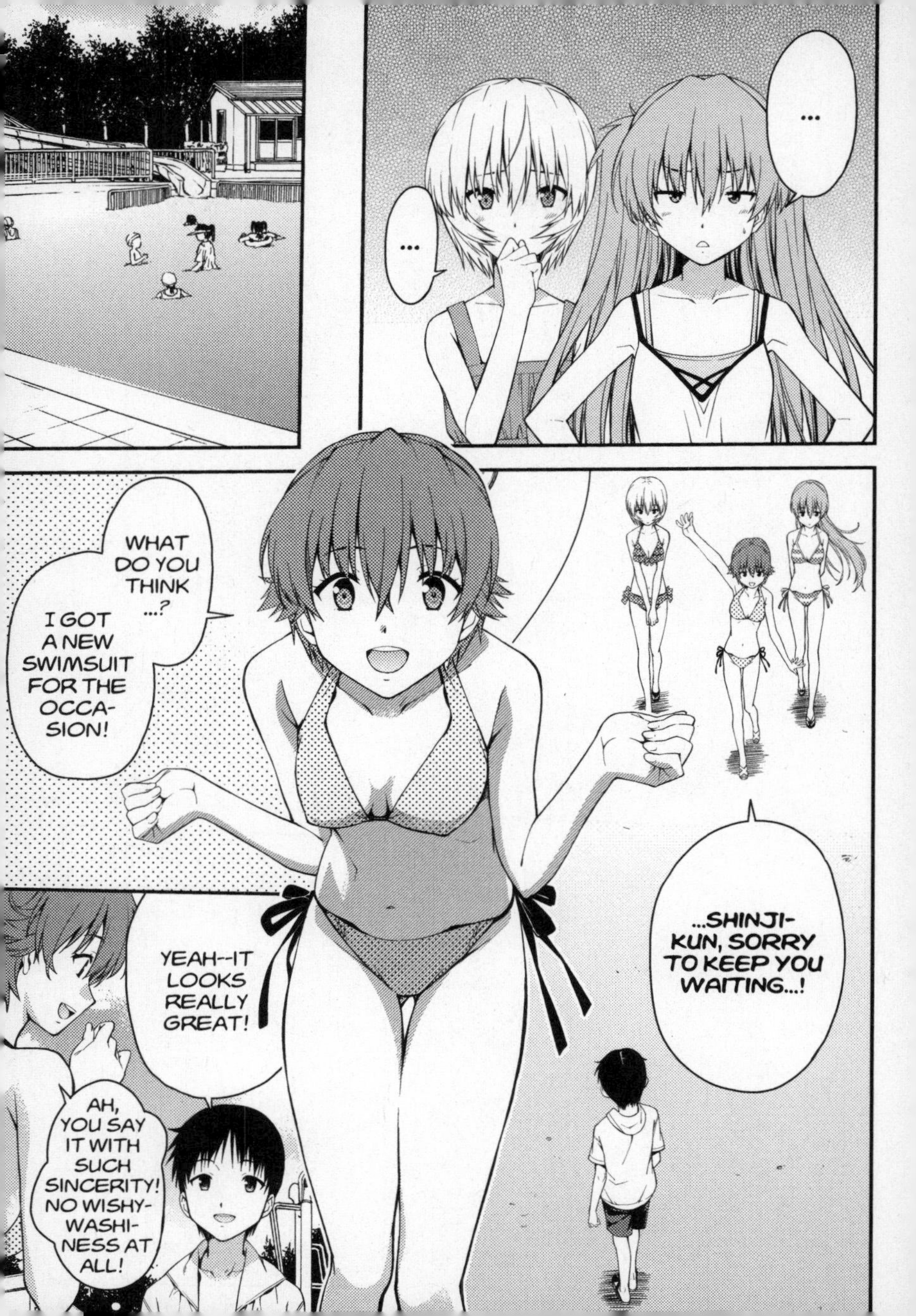
...
...
...SHINJI-KUN, SORRY TO KEEP YOU WAITING...!
WHAT DO YOU THINK ...? I GOT A NEW SWIMSUIT FOR THE OCCASION!
YEAH--IT LOOKS REALLY GREAT!
AH, YOU SAY IT WITH SUCH SINCERITY! NO WISHY-WASHINESS AT ALL!

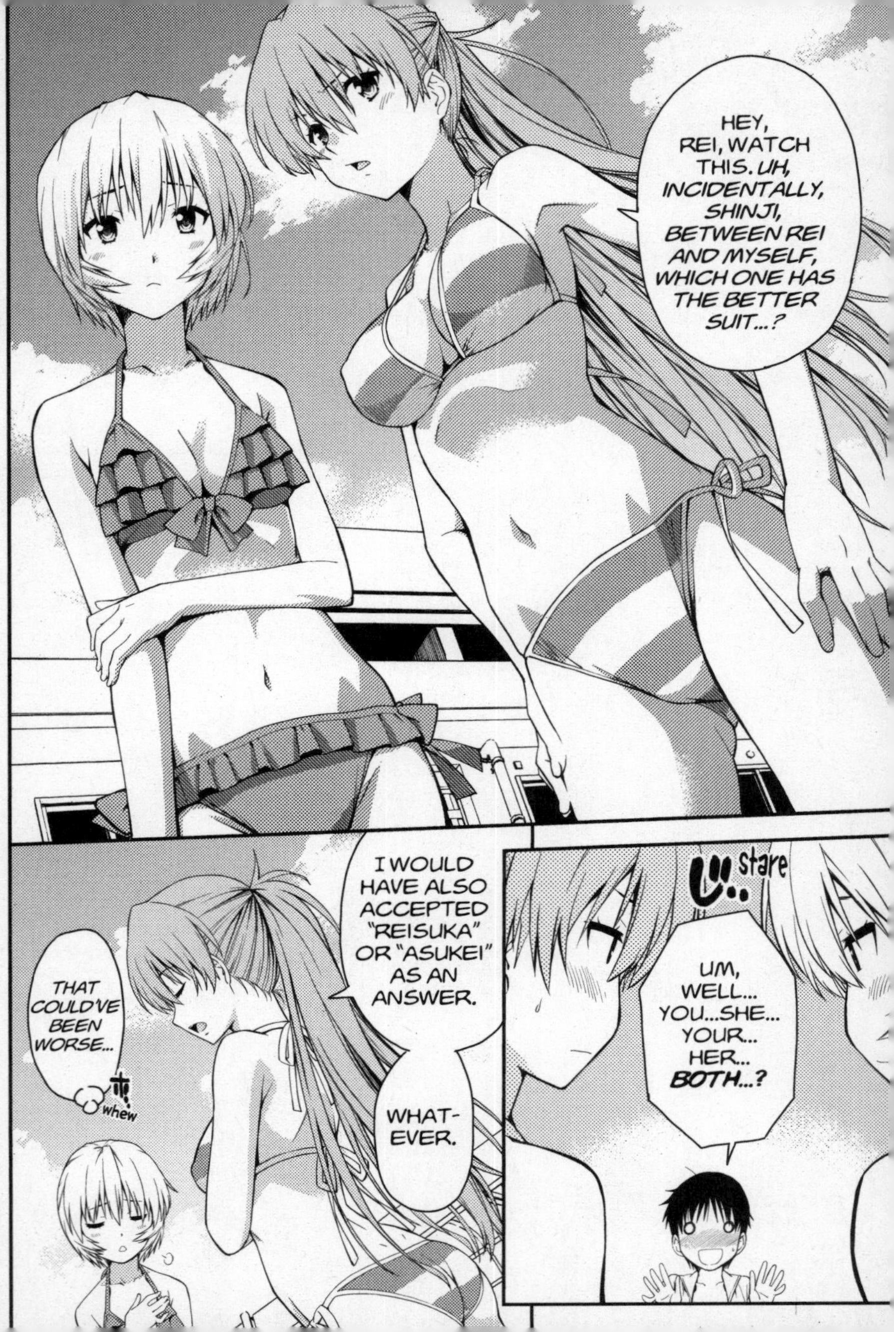
HEY, REI, WATCH THIS. UH, INCIDENTALLY, SHINJI, BETWEEN REI AND MYSELF, WHICH ONE HAS THE BETTER SUIT...?
stare
UM, WELL... YOU...SHE... YOUR... HER... BOTH...?
I WOULD HAVE ALSO ACCEPTED "REISUKA" OR "ASUKEI" AS AN ANSWER.
THAT COULD'VE BEEN WORSE...
whew
WHAT-EVER.

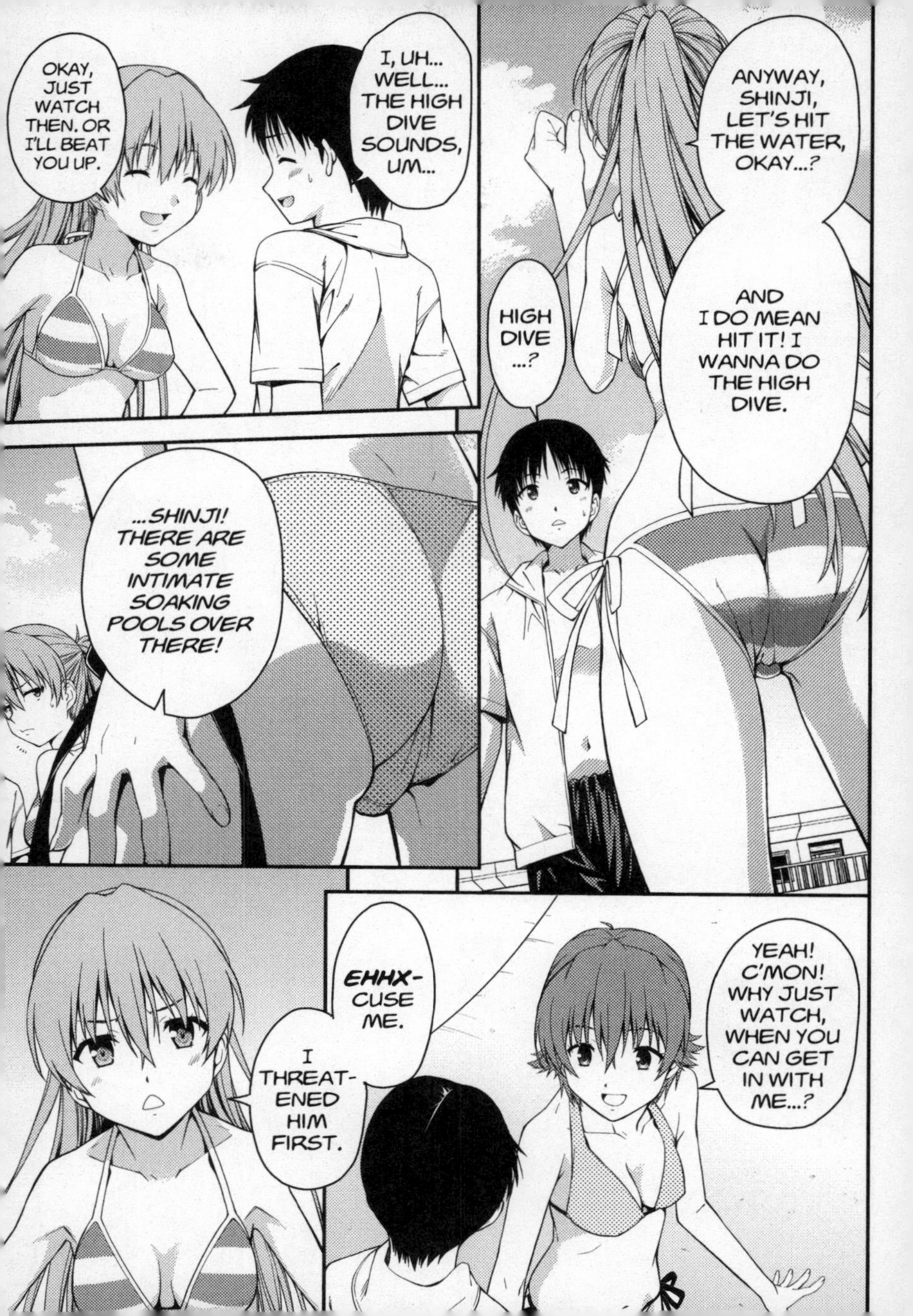
ANYWAY, SHINJI, LET'S HIT THE WATER, OKAY...?
AND I DO MEAN HIT IT! I WANNA DO THE HIGH DIVE.
HIGH DIVE ...?
I, UH... WELL... THE HIGH DIVE SOUNDS, UM...
OKAY, JUST WATCH THEN. OR I'LL BEAT YOU UP.
...SHINJI! THERE ARE SOME INTIMATE SOAKING POOLS OVER THERE!
YEAH! C'MON! WHY JUST WATCH, WHEN YOU CAN GET IN WITH ME...?
EHHX-CUSE ME.
I THREAT-ENED HIM FIRST.

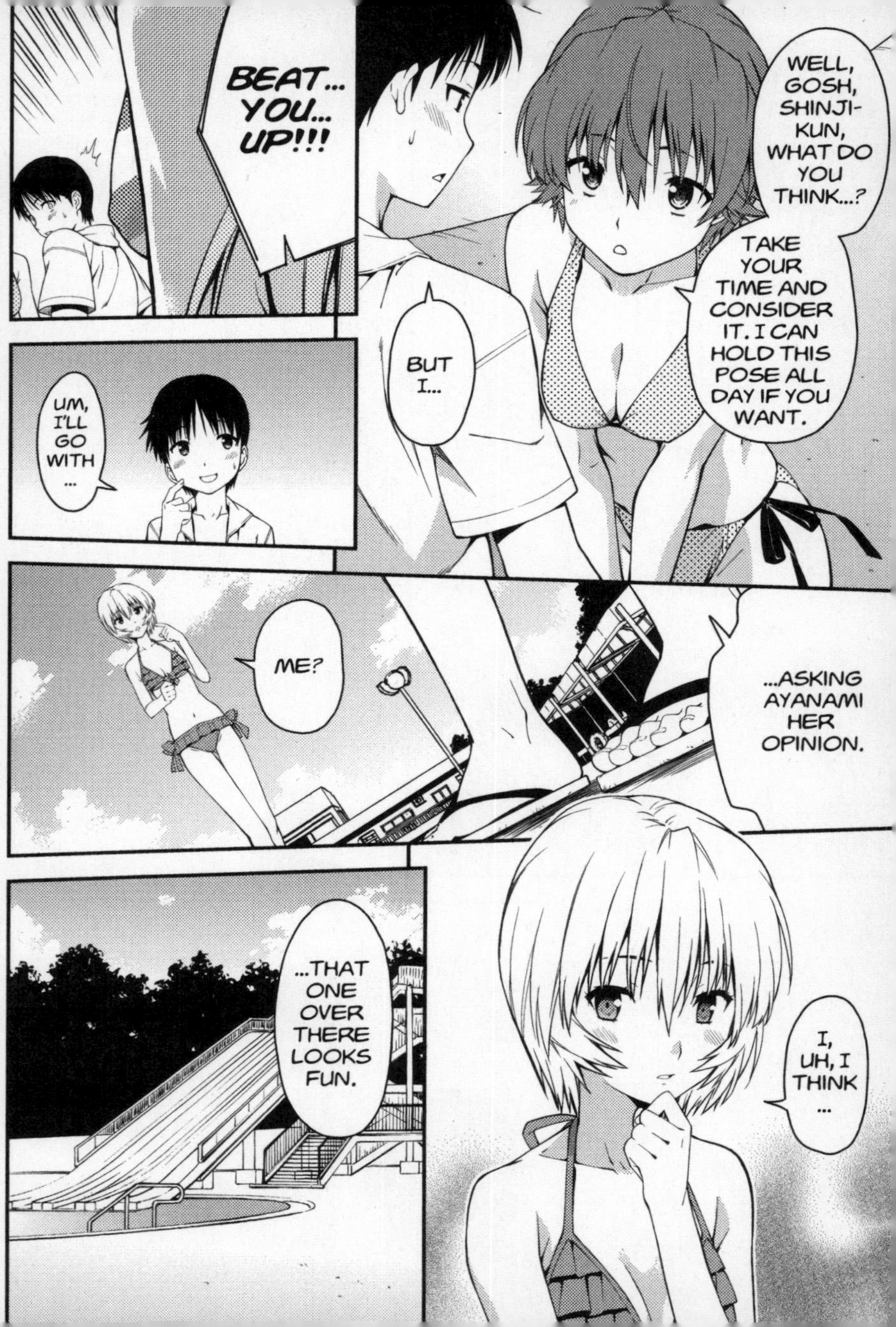
WELL, GOSH, SHINJI-KUN, WHAT DO YOU THINK...?
TAKE YOUR TIME AND CONSIDER IT. I CAN HOLD THIS POSE ALL DAY IF YOU WANT.
BUT I...
BEAT... YOU... UP!!!
UM, I'LL GO WITH ...
...ASKING AYANAMI HER OPINION.
ME?
I, UH, I THINK ...
...THAT ONE OVER THERE LOOKS FUN.

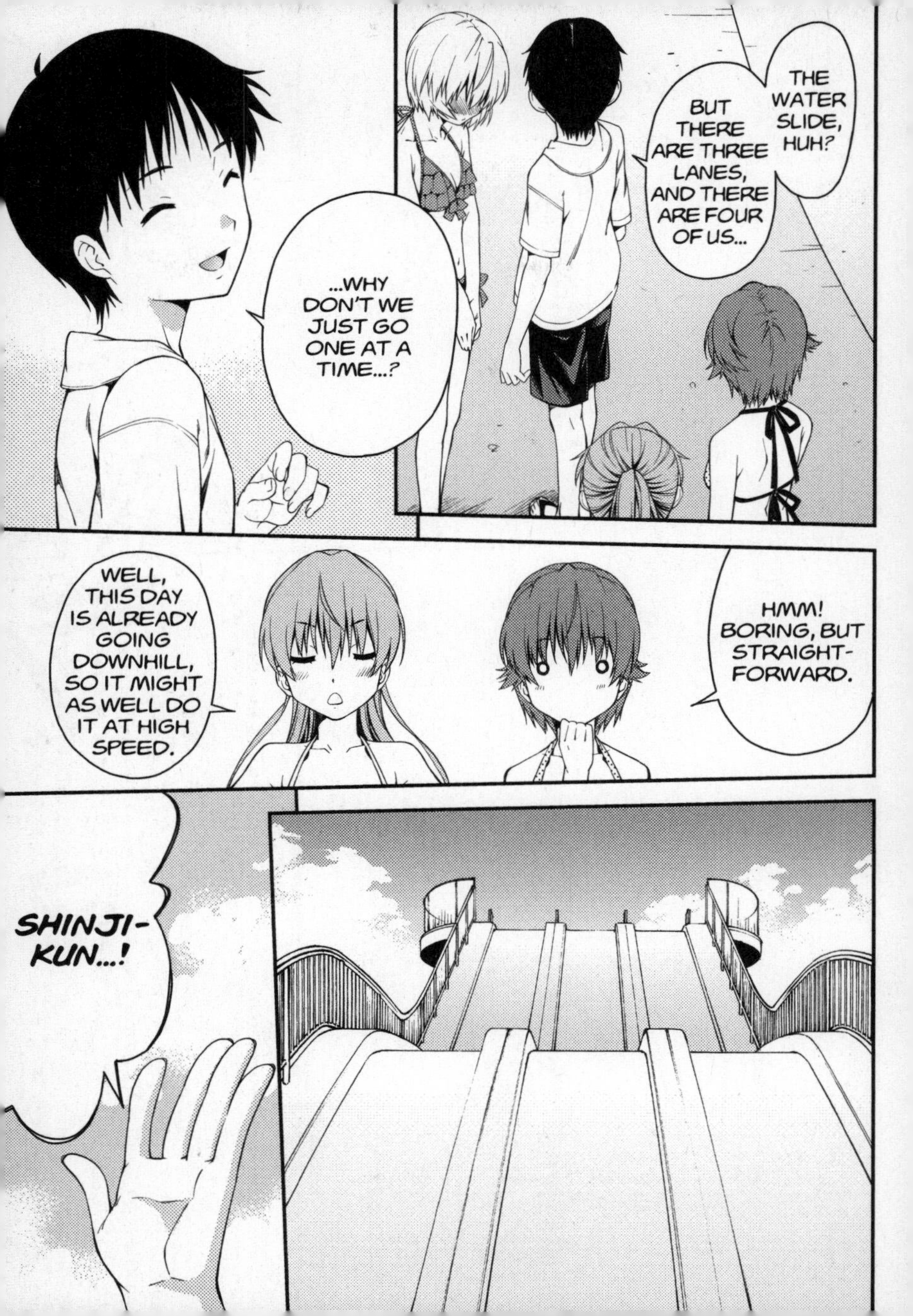
THE WATER SLIDE, HUH?
BUT THERE ARE THREE LANES, AND THERE ARE FOUR OF US...
...WHY DON'T WE JUST GO ONE AT A TIME...?
HMM! BORING, BUT STRAIGHT-FORWARD.
WELL, THIS DAY IS ALREADY GOING DOWNHILL, SO IT MIGHT AS WELL DO IT AT HIGH SPEED.
SHINJI-KUN...!

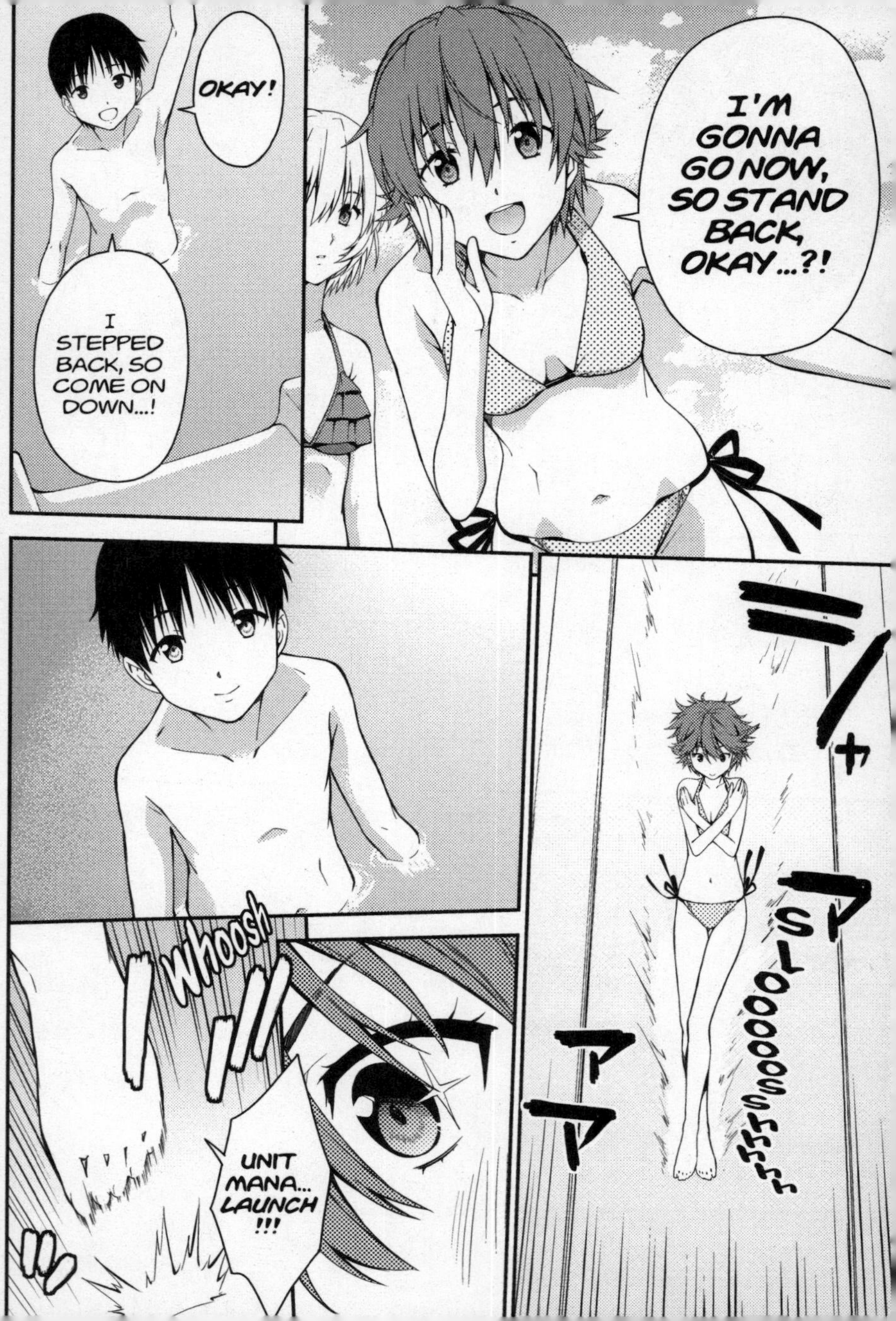
I'M GONNA GO NOW, SO STAND BACK, OKAY...?!
OKAY!
I STEPPED BACK, SO COME ON DOWN...!
シャア
SLOOOOSSHHHHH
アア
whoosh
UNIT MANA... LAUNCH!!!

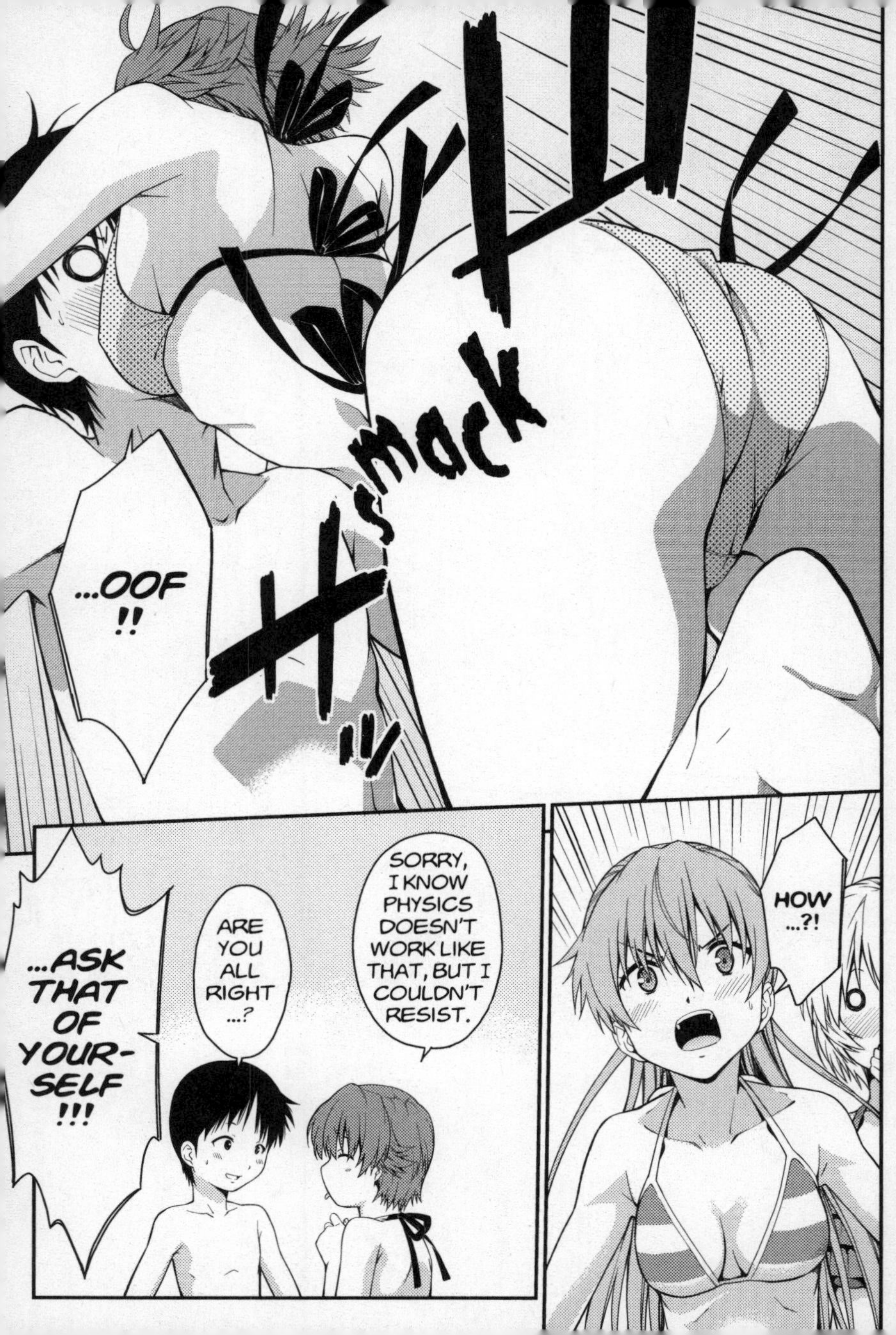
smack
...OOF !!
HOW ...?!
SORRY, I KNOW PHYSICS DOESN'T WORK LIKE THAT, BUT I COULDN'T RESIST.
ARE YOU ALL RIGHT ...?
...ASK THAT OF YOUR-SELF !!!

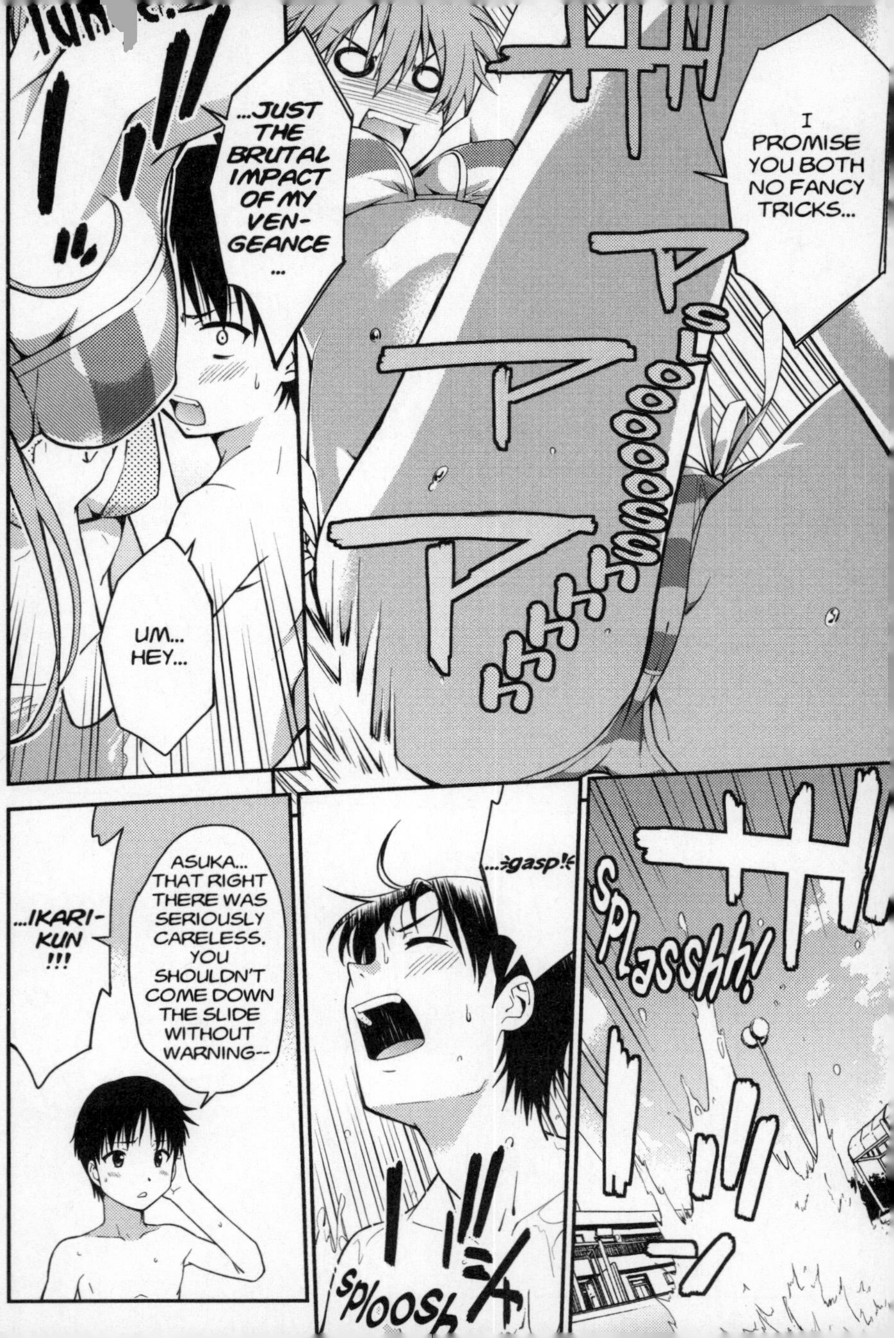
I PROMISE YOU BOTH NO FANCY TRICKS...
...JUST THE BRUTAL IMPACT OF MY VEN-GEANCE...
UM... HEY...
SPLASSHH!
...gasp!
sploosh
ASUKA... THAT RIGHT THERE WAS SERIOUSLY CARELESS. YOU SHOULDN'T COME DOWN THE SLIDE WITHOUT WARNING--
...IKARI-KUN!!!

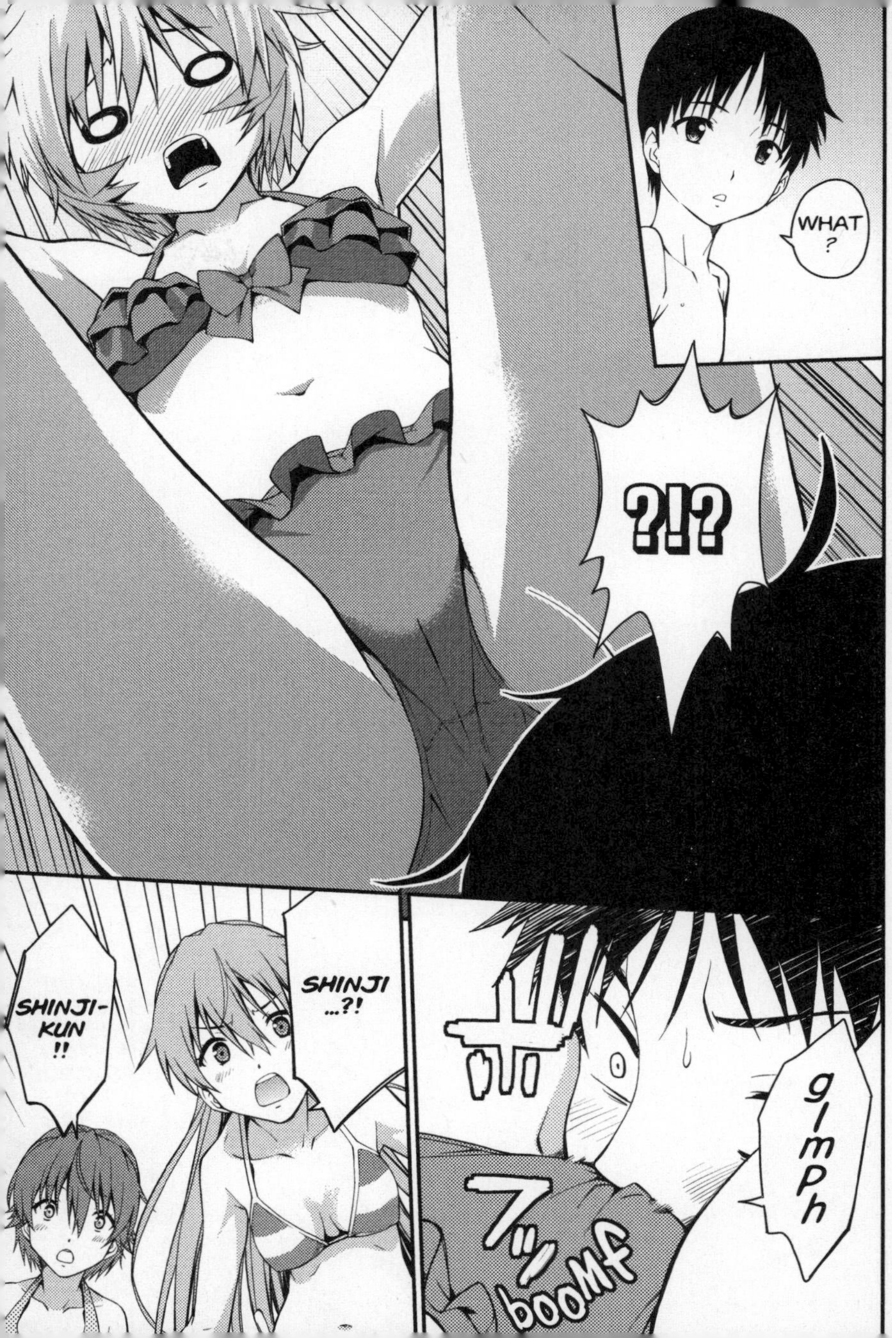
WHAT?
?!?
glmph
booMf
SHINJI...?!
SHINJI-KUN!!

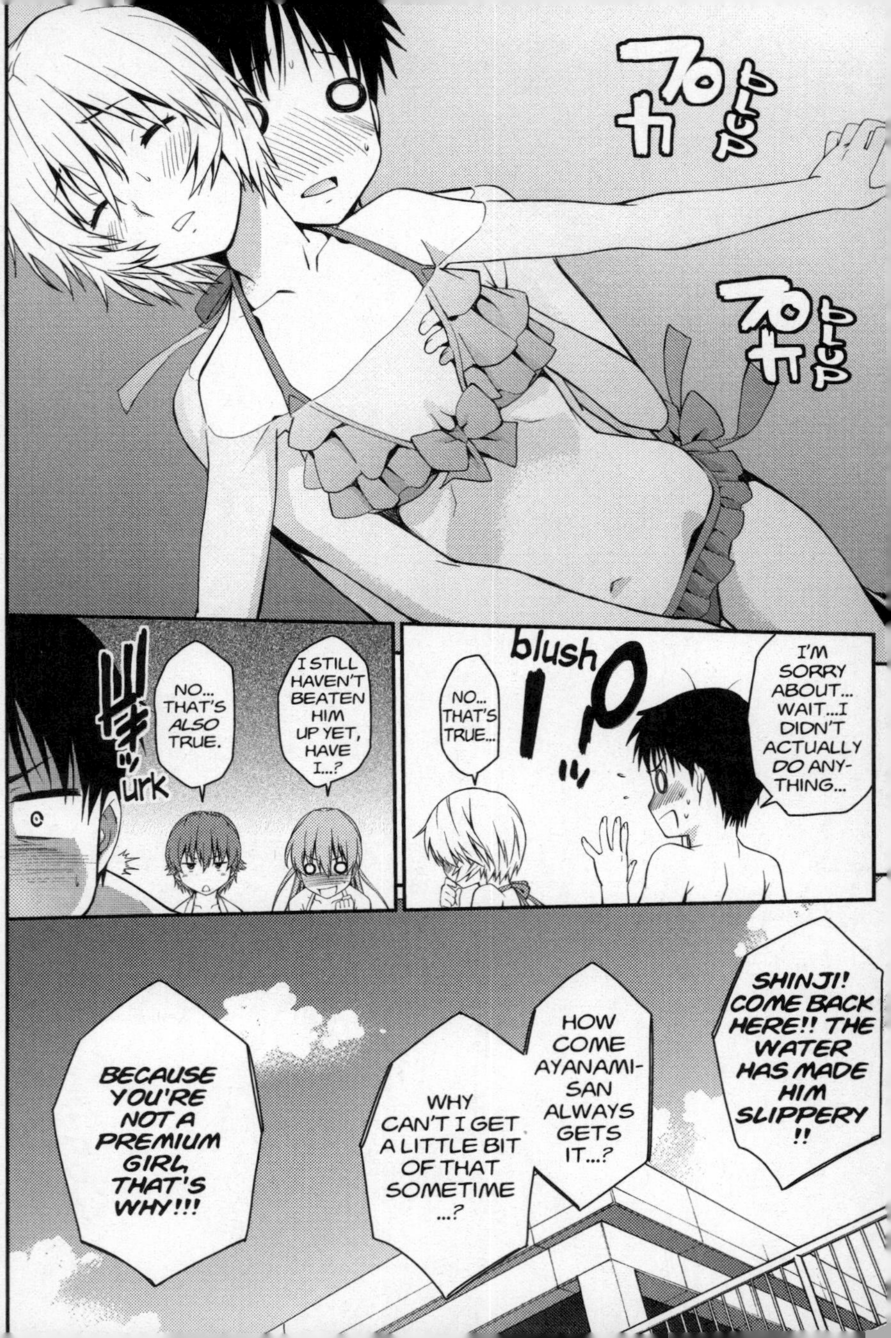
plup
plup
I'M SORRY ABOUT... WAIT...I DIDN'T ACTUALLY DO ANYTHING...
blush
NO... THAT'S TRUE...
I STILL HAVEN'T BEATEN HIM UP YET, HAVE I...?
NO... THAT'S ALSO TRUE.
urk
SHINJI! COME BACK HERE!! THE WATER HAS MADE HIM SLIPPERY!!
HOW COME AYANAMI-SAN ALWAYS GETS IT...?
WHY CAN'T I GET A LITTLE BIT OF THAT SOMETIME...?
BECAUSE YOU'RE NOT A PREMIUM GIRL, THAT'S WHY!!!

the shinji ikari raising project

NEON GENESIS
EVANGELION
THE SHINJI IKARI RAISING PROJECT

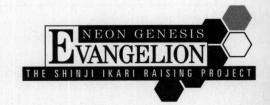

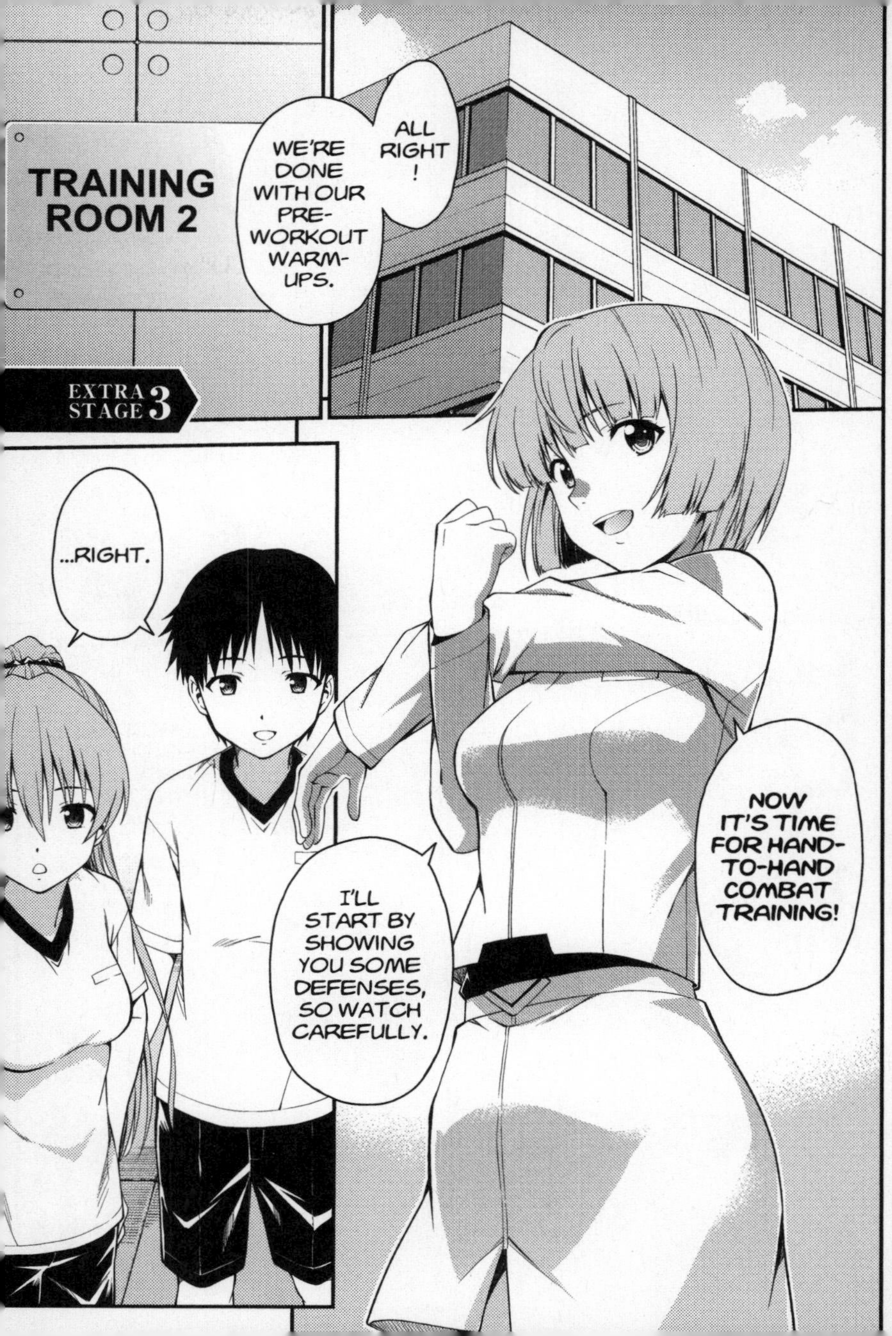
TRAINING ROOM 2
ALL RIGHT!
WE'RE DONE WITH OUR PRE-WORKOUT WARM-UPS.
EXTRA STAGE 3
NOW IT'S TIME FOR HAND-TO-HAND COMBAT TRAINING!
I'LL START BY SHOWING YOU SOME DEFENSES, SO WATCH CAREFULLY.
...RIGHT.

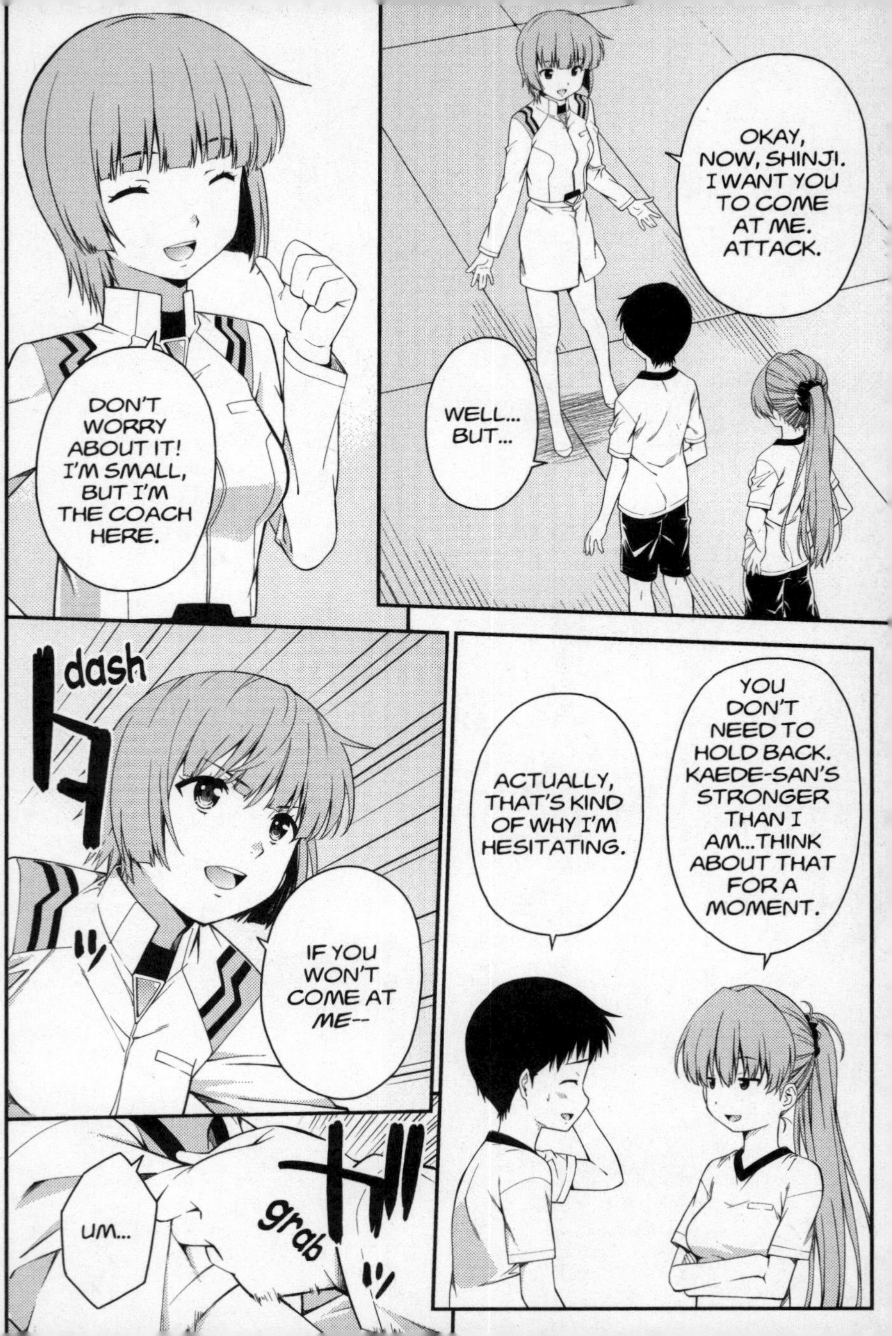
OKAY, NOW, SHINJI. I WANT YOU TO COME AT ME. ATTACK.
WELL... BUT...
DON'T WORRY ABOUT IT! I'M SMALL, BUT I'M THE COACH HERE.
YOU DON'T NEED TO HOLD BACK. KAEDE-SAN'S STRONGER THAN I AM...THINK ABOUT THAT FOR A MOMENT.
ACTUALLY, THAT'S KIND OF WHY I'M HESITATING.
dash
IF YOU WON'T COME AT ME--
grab
UM...

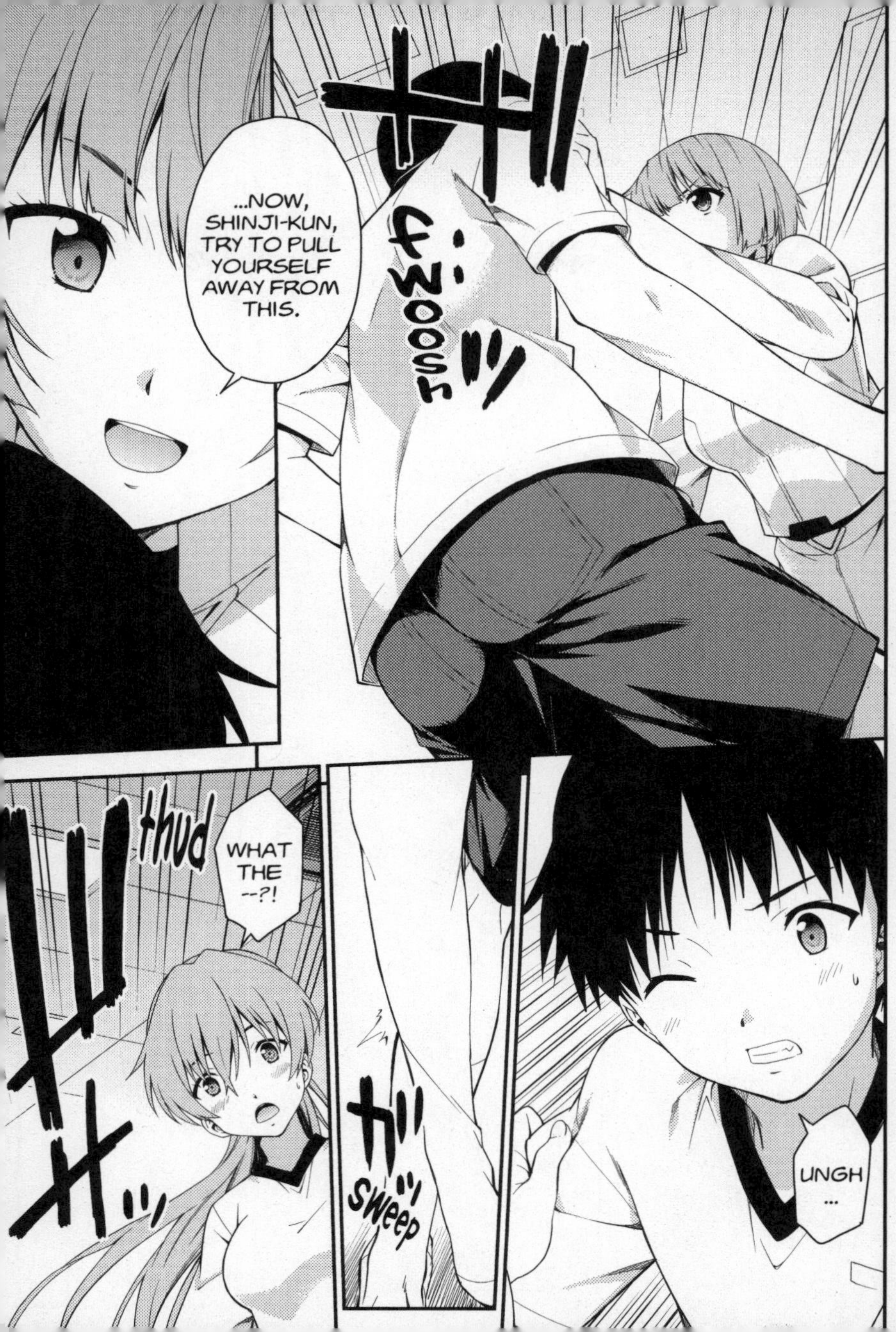
fwoosh
...NOW, SHINJI-KUN, TRY TO PULL YOURSELF AWAY FROM THIS.
UNGH ...
sweep
thud
WHAT THE --?!

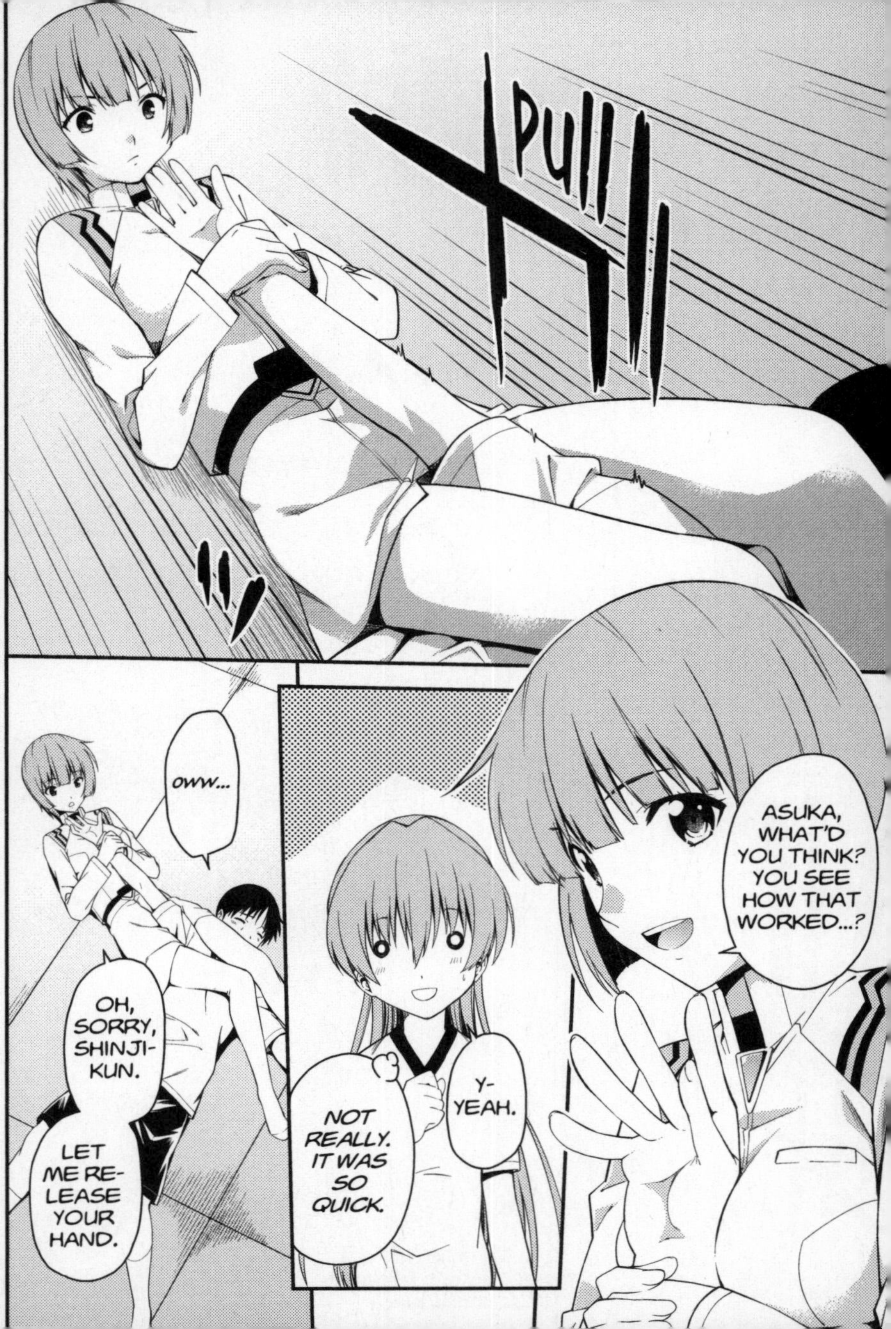
PULL
ASUKA, WHAT'D YOU THINK? YOU SEE HOW THAT WORKED...?
Y-YEAH.
NOT REALLY. IT WAS SO QUICK.
OWW...
OH, SORRY, SHINJI-KUN.
LET ME RE-LEASE YOUR HAND.

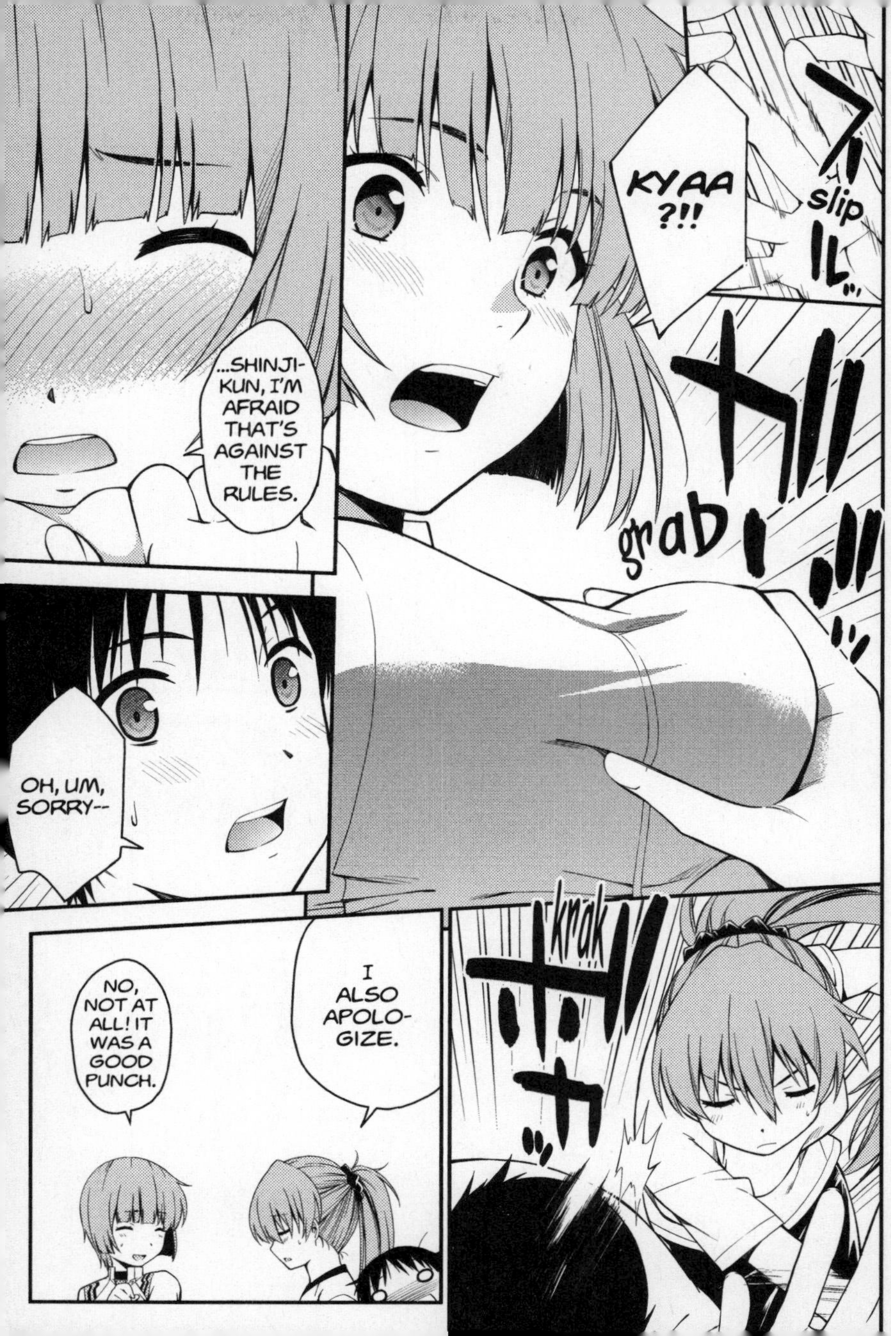
KYAA ?!!
slip
grab
...SHINJI-KUN, I'M AFRAID THAT'S AGAINST THE RULES.
OH, UM, SORRY--
krak
I ALSO APOLOGIZE.
NO, NOT AT ALL! IT WAS A GOOD PUNCH.

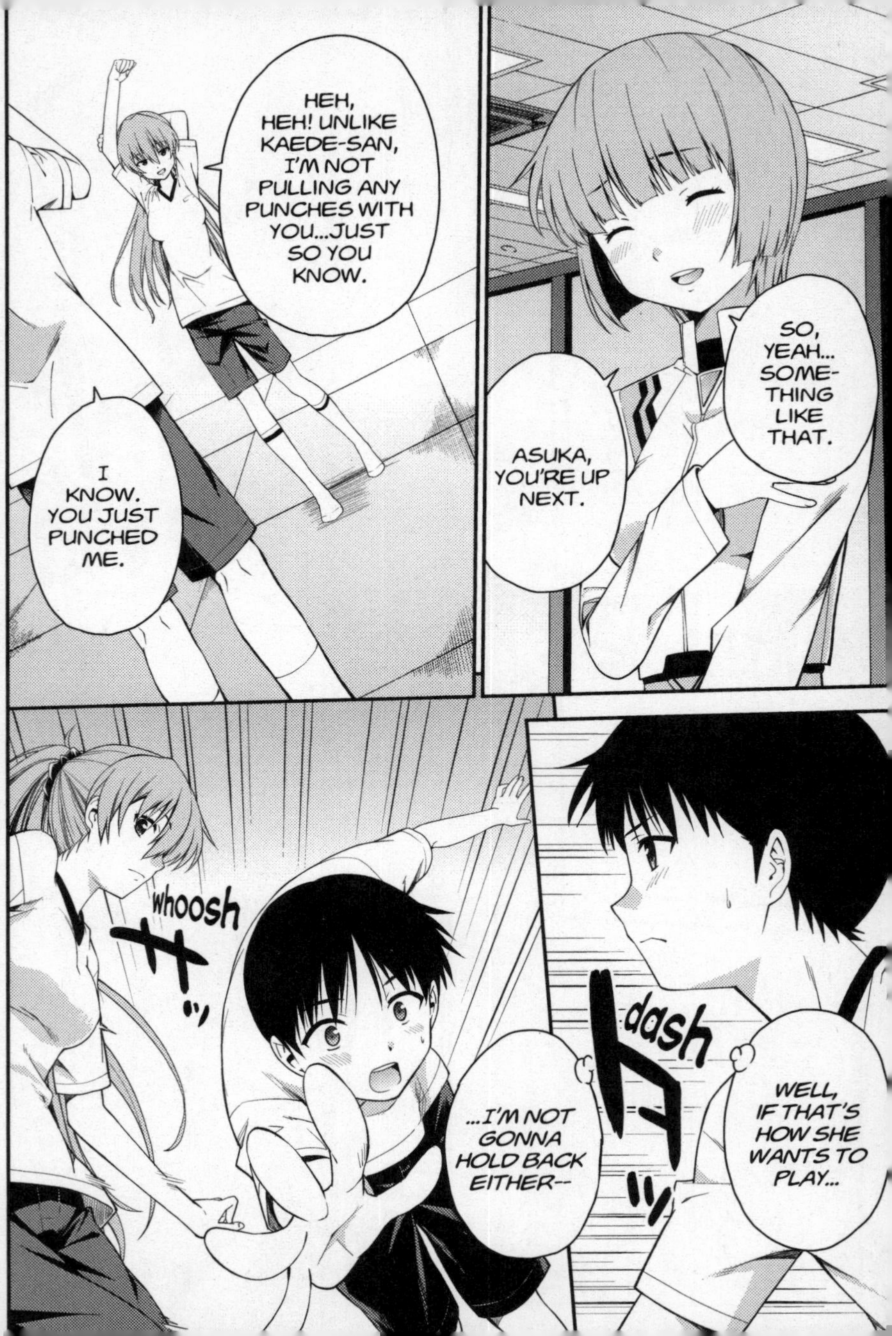
SO, YEAH... SOME-THING LIKE THAT.
ASUKA, YOU'RE UP NEXT.
HEH, HEH! UNLIKE KAEDE-SAN, I'M NOT PULLING ANY PUNCHES WITH YOU...JUST SO YOU KNOW.
I KNOW. YOU JUST PUNCHED ME.
WELL, IF THAT'S HOW SHE WANTS TO PLAY...
dash
...I'M NOT GONNA HOLD BACK EITHER--
whoosh

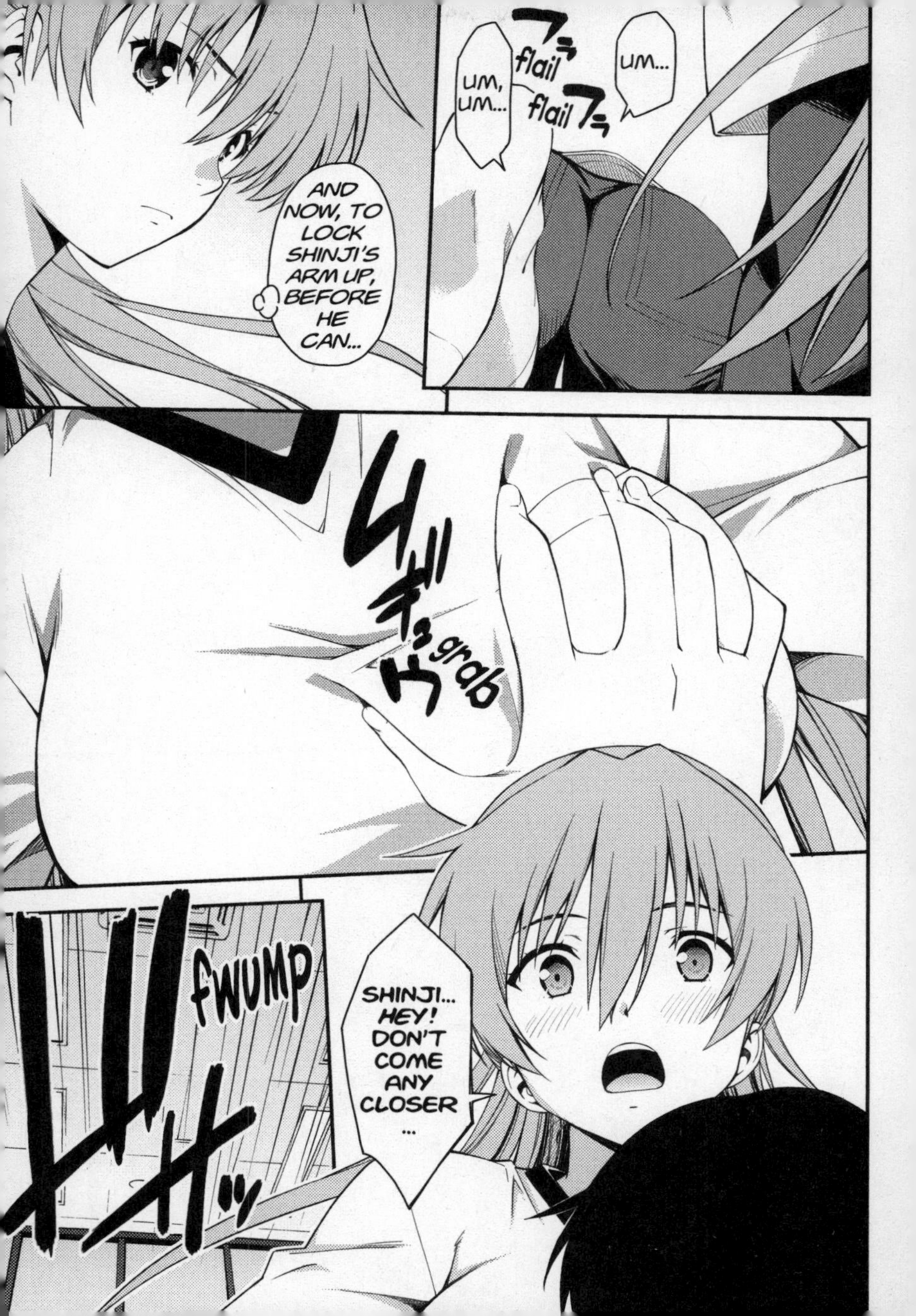
UM...
flail
flail
UM, UM...
AND NOW, TO LOCK SHINJI'S ARM UP, BEFORE HE CAN...
grab
SHINJI... HEY! DON'T COME ANY CLOSER ...
fwump

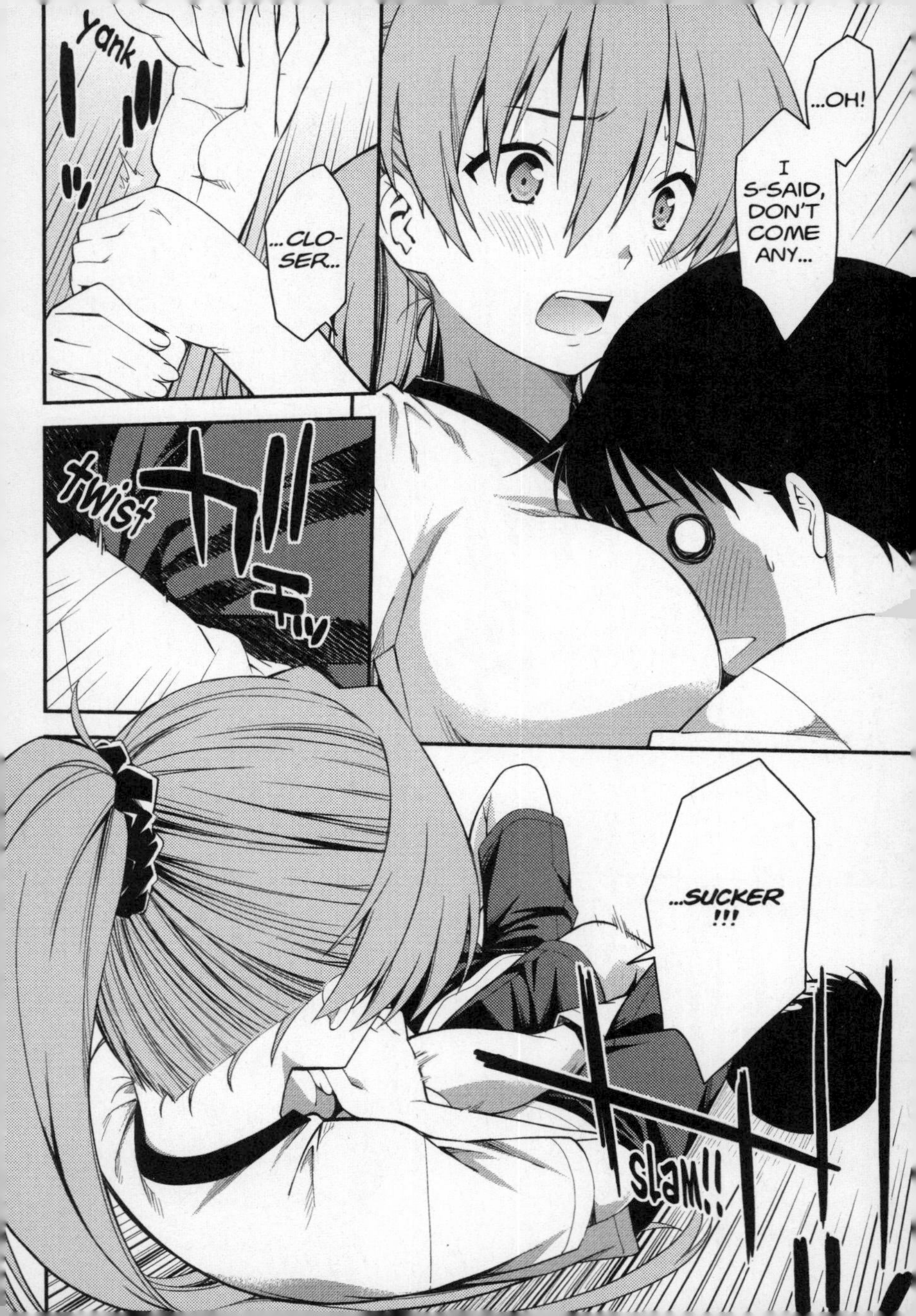
...OH!
I S-SAID, DON'T COME ANY...
...CLO-SER...
yank
twist
ガチャッ
...SUCKER !!!
slam!!

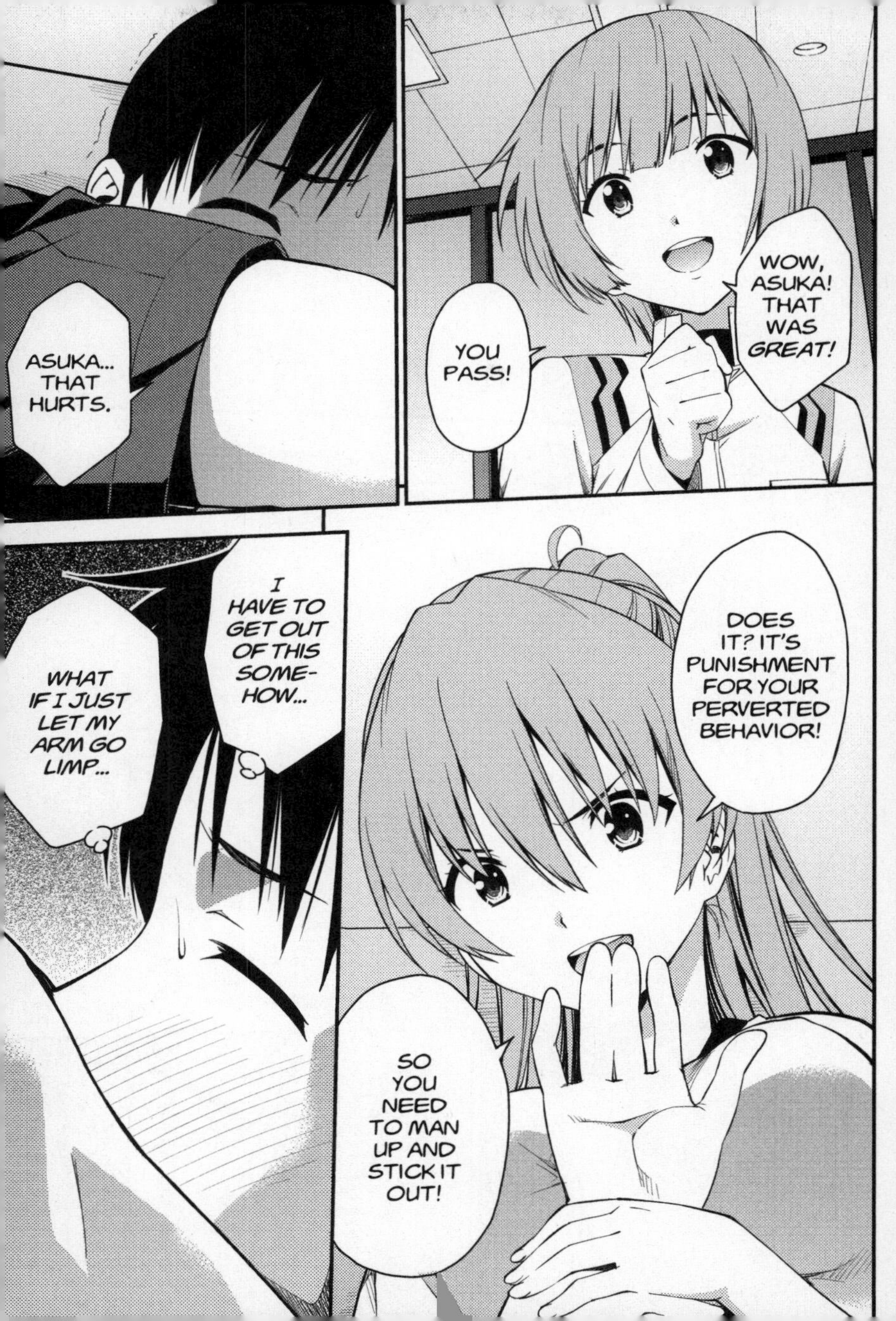
WOW, ASUKA! THAT WAS GREAT!
YOU PASS!
ASUKA... THAT HURTS.
DOES IT? IT'S PUNISHMENT FOR YOUR PERVERTED BEHAVIOR!
SO YOU NEED TO MAN UP AND STICK IT OUT!
I HAVE TO GET OUT OF THIS SOME-HOW...
WHAT IF I JUST LET MY ARM GO LIMP...

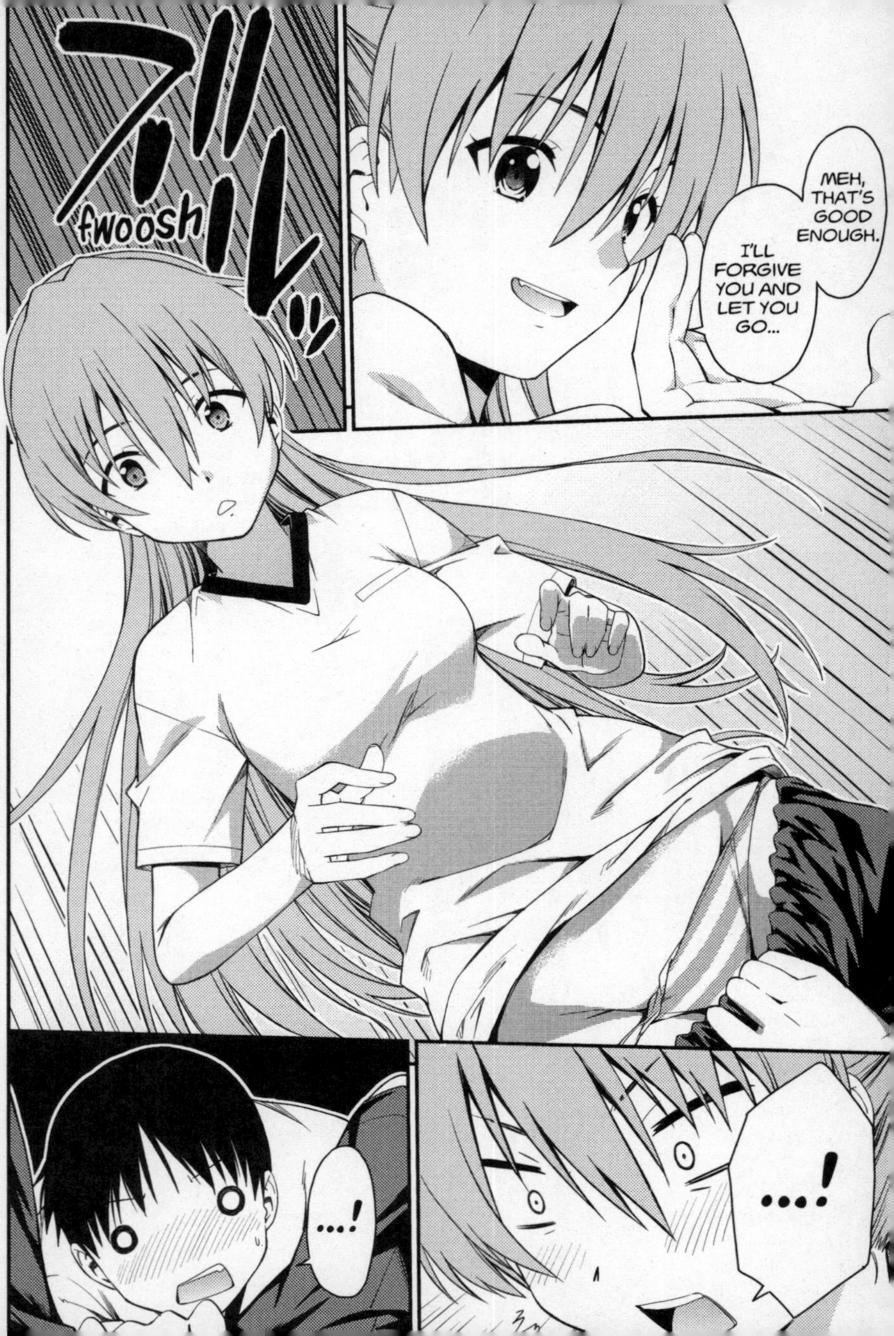
MEH, THAT'S GOOD ENOUGH.
I'LL FORGIVE YOU AND LET YOU GO...
fwoosh
...!
...!

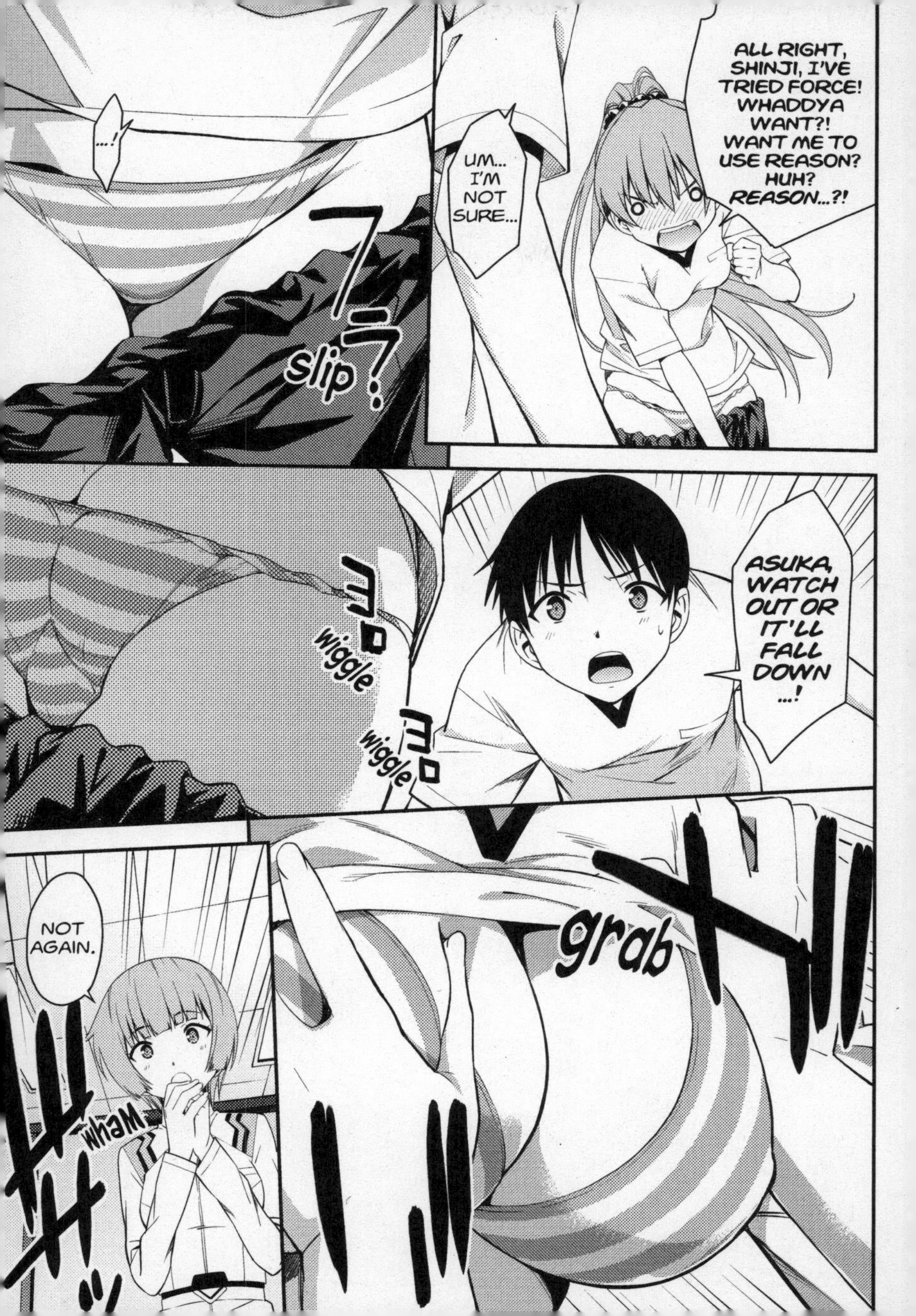
ALL RIGHT, SHINJI, I'VE TRIED FORCE! WHADDYA WANT?! WANT ME TO USE REASON? HUH? REASON...?!
UM... I'M NOT SURE...
...!
slip
ASUKA, WATCH OUT OR IT'LL FALL DOWN ...!
wiggle
wiggle
grab
NOT AGAIN.
wham

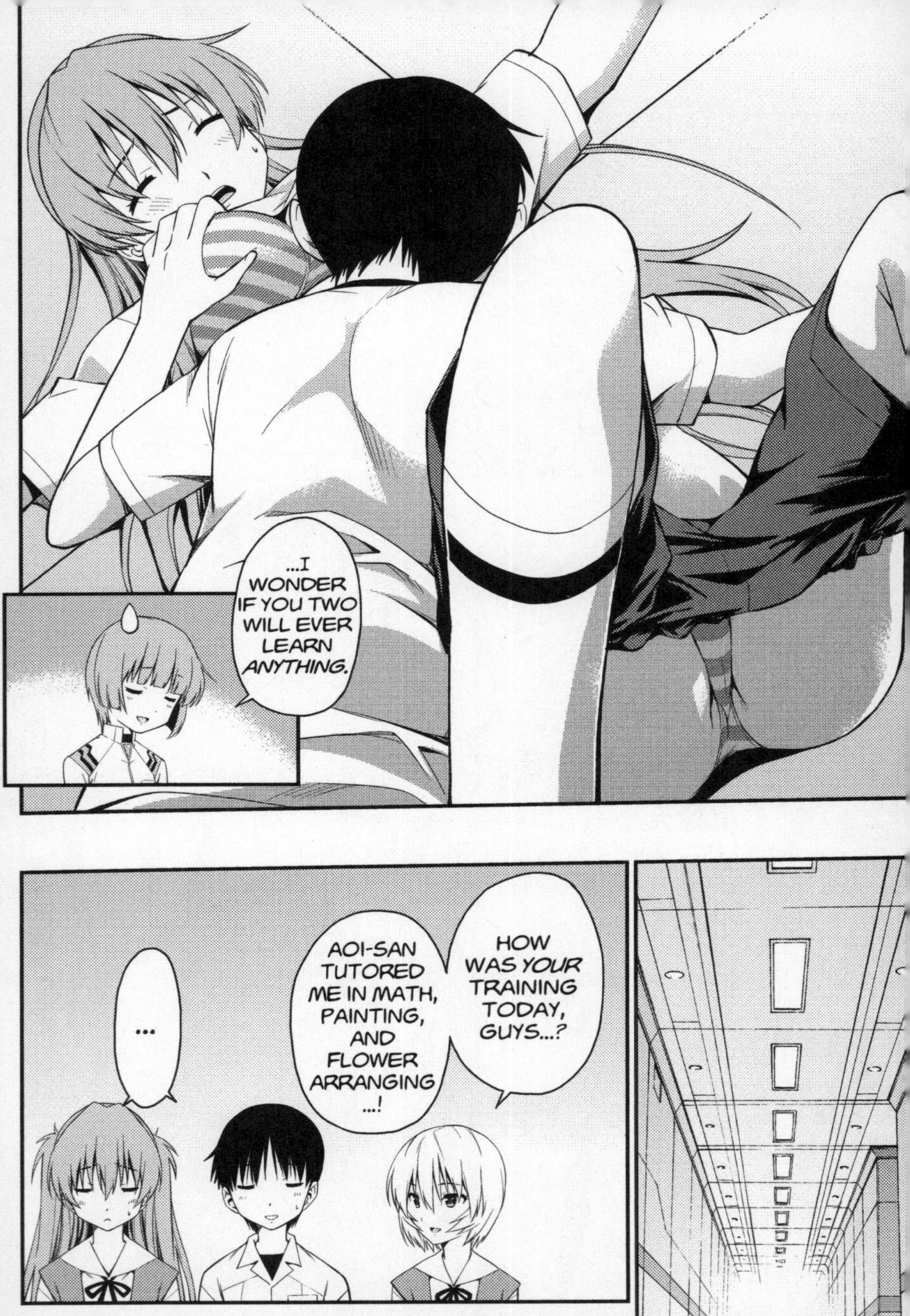
...I WONDER IF YOU TWO WILL EVER LEARN *ANYTHING*.
HOW WAS *YOUR* TRAINING TODAY, GUYS...?
AOI-SAN TUTORED ME IN MATH, PAINTING, AND FLOWER ARRANGING ...!
...

the shinji ikari raising project

NEON GENESIS
EVANGELION
THE SHINJI IKARI RAISING PROJECT

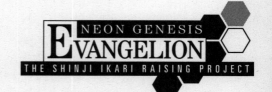

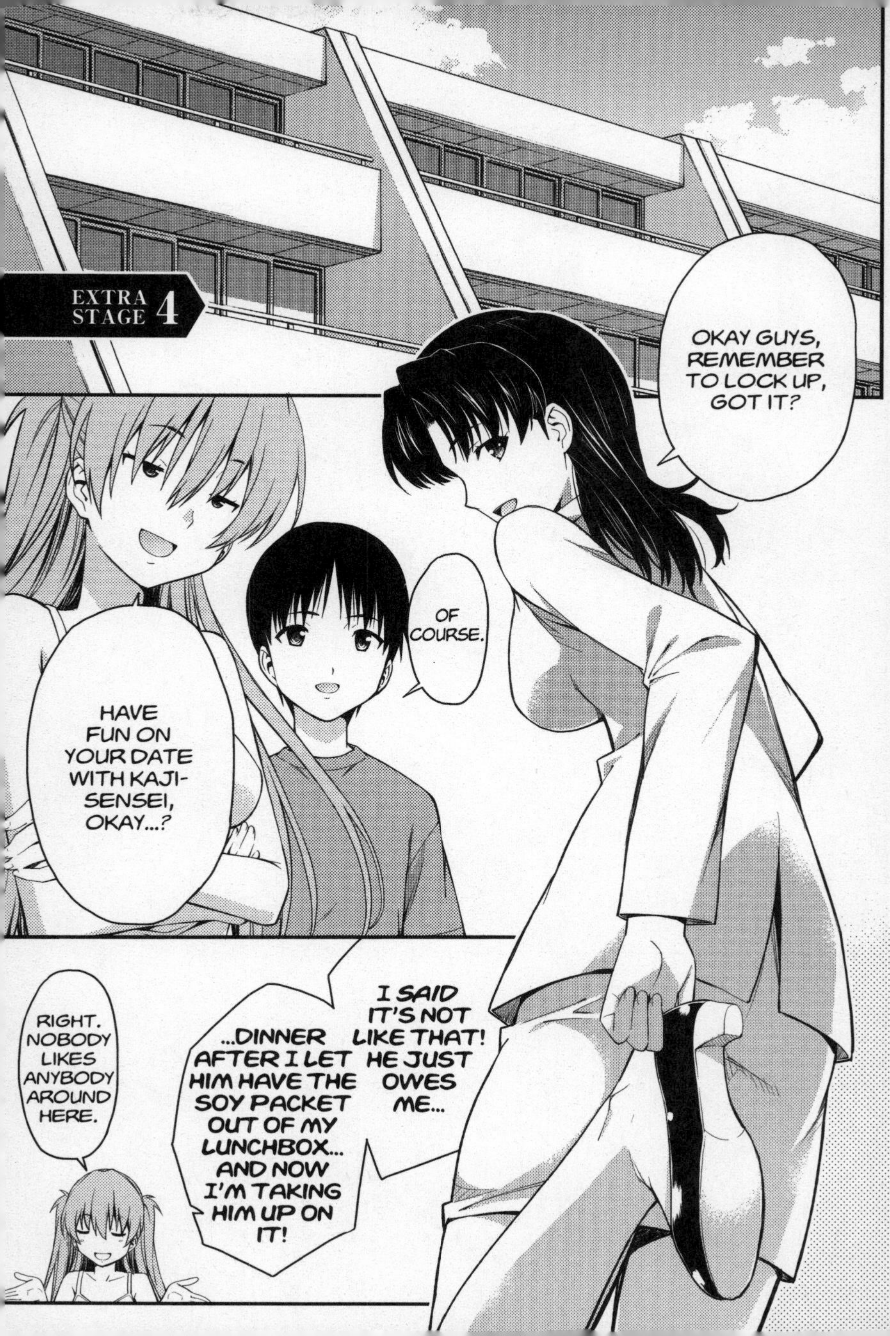
EXTRA STAGE 4
OKAY GUYS, REMEMBER TO LOCK UP, GOT IT?
OF COURSE.
HAVE FUN ON YOUR DATE WITH KAJI-SENSEI, OKAY...?
I SAID IT'S NOT LIKE THAT! HE JUST OWES ME...
...DINNER AFTER I LET HIM HAVE THE SOY PACKET OUT OF MY LUNCHBOX... AND NOW I'M TAKING HIM UP ON IT!
RIGHT. NOBODY LIKES ANYBODY AROUND HERE.

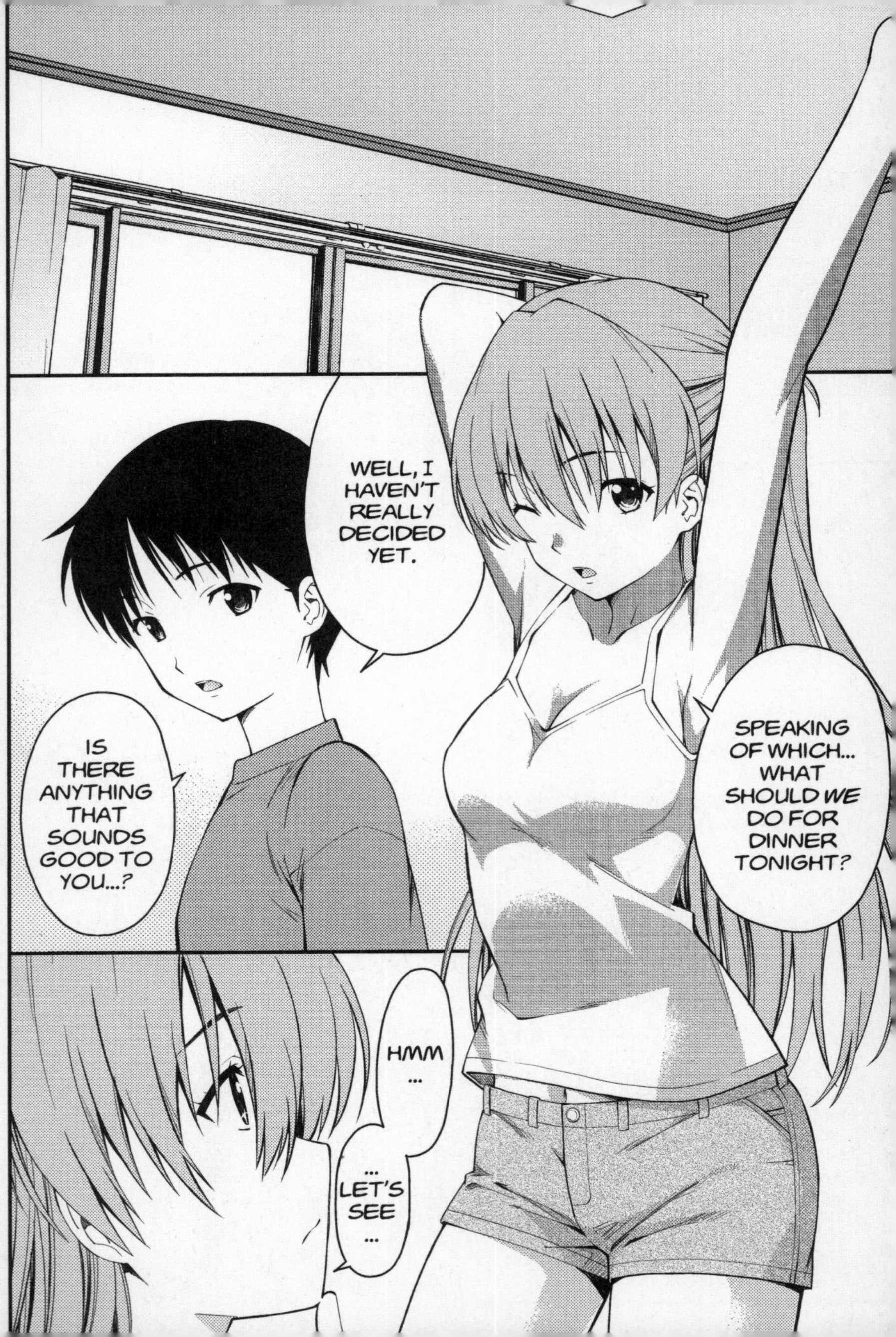
SPEAKING OF WHICH... WHAT SHOULD WE DO FOR DINNER TONIGHT?
WELL, I HAVEN'T REALLY DECIDED YET.
IS THERE ANYTHING THAT SOUNDS GOOD TO YOU...?
HMM... ...LET'S SEE...

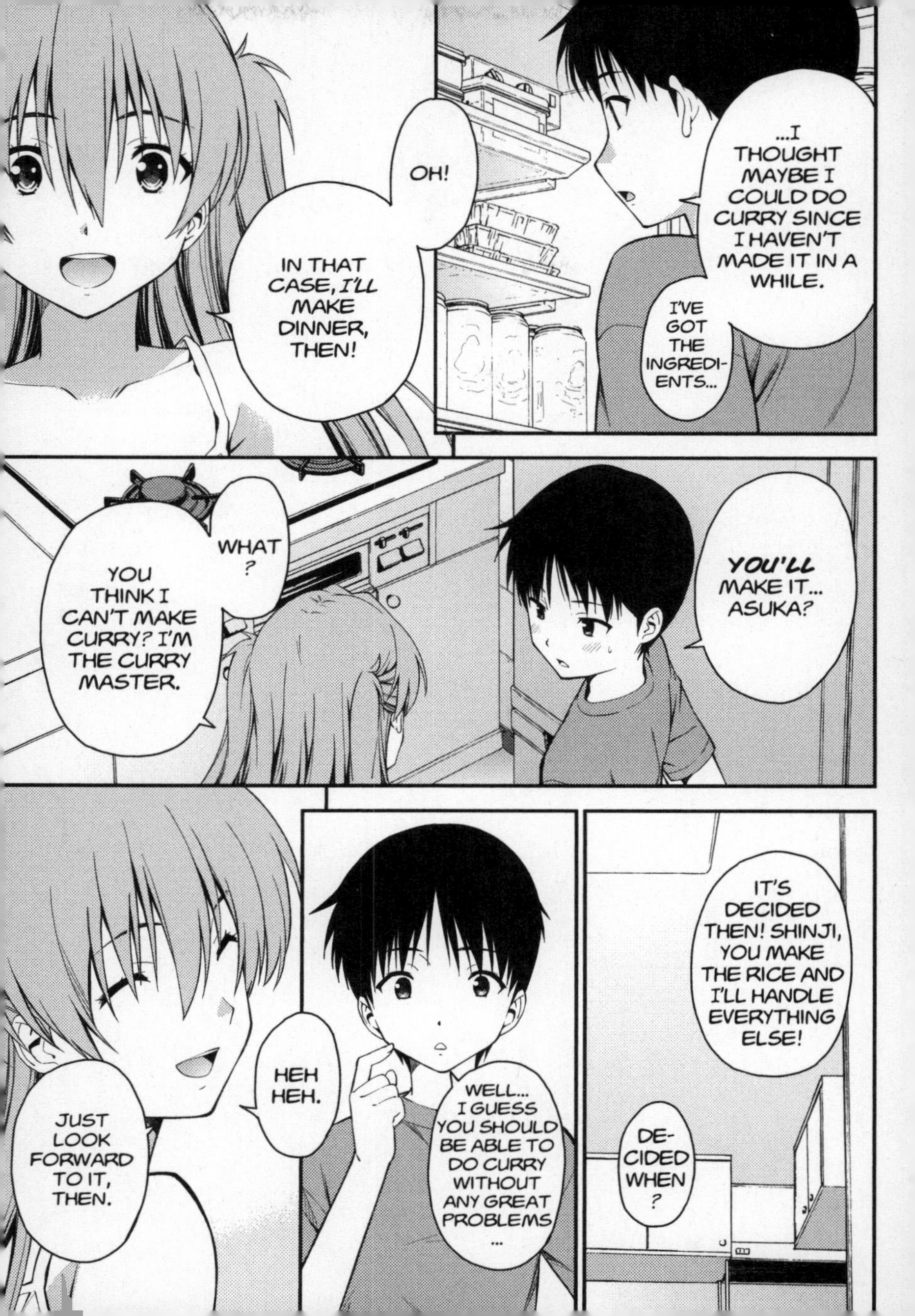
...I THOUGHT MAYBE I COULD DO CURRY SINCE I HAVEN'T MADE IT IN A WHILE.
I'VE GOT THE INGREDIENTS...
OH!
IN THAT CASE, I'LL MAKE DINNER, THEN!
YOU'LL MAKE IT... ASUKA?
WHAT?
YOU THINK I CAN'T MAKE CURRY? I'M THE CURRY MASTER.
IT'S DECIDED THEN! SHINJI, YOU MAKE THE RICE AND I'LL HANDLE EVERYTHING ELSE!
DECIDED WHEN?
WELL... I GUESS YOU SHOULD BE ABLE TO DO CURRY WITHOUT ANY GREAT PROBLEMS...
HEH HEH.
JUST LOOK FORWARD TO IT, THEN.

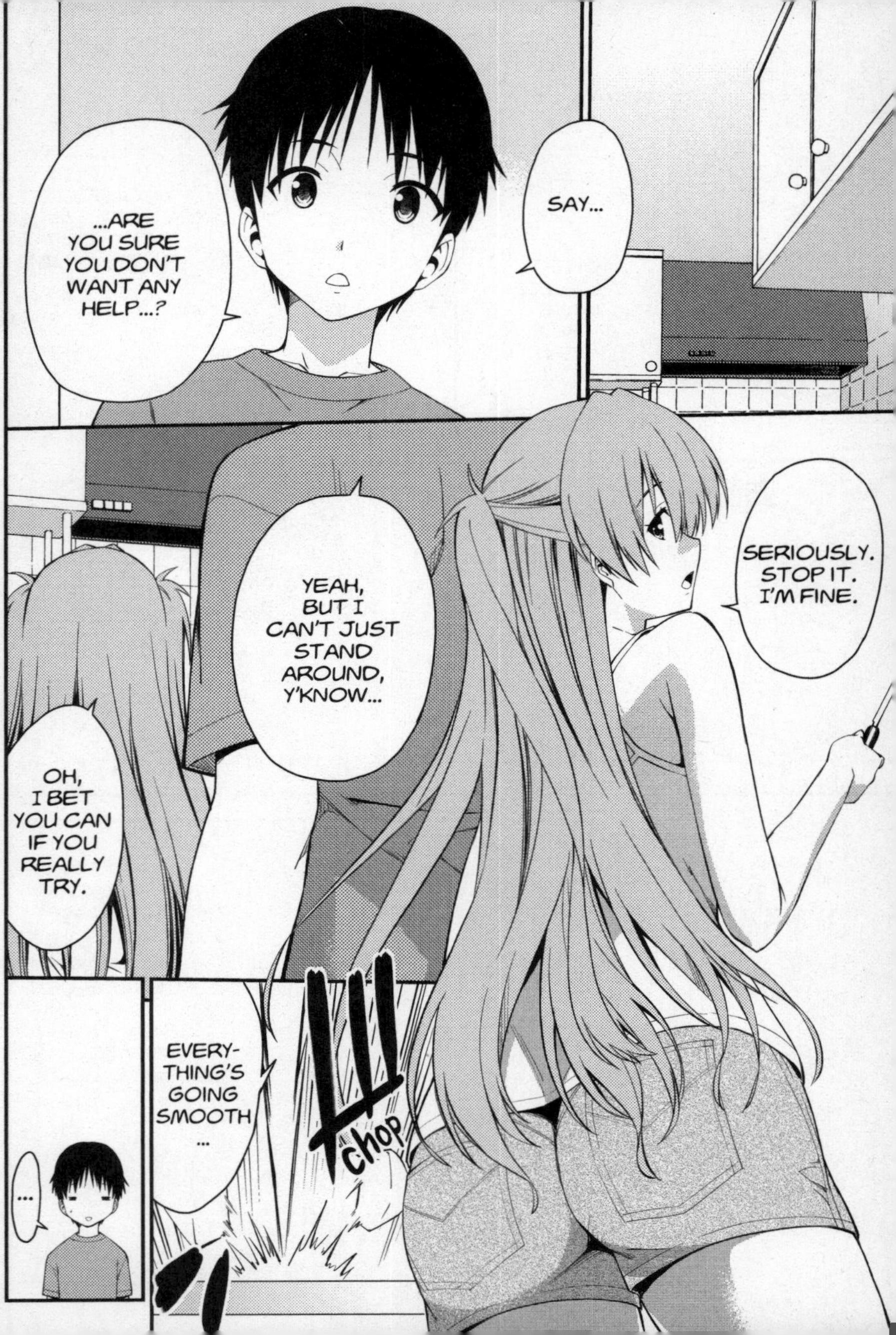
SAY...
...ARE YOU SURE YOU DON'T WANT ANY HELP...?
SERIOUSLY. STOP IT. I'M FINE.
YEAH, BUT I CAN'T JUST STAND AROUND, Y'KNOW...
OH, I BET YOU CAN IF YOU REALLY TRY.
chop
EVERY-THING'S GOING SMOOTH ...
...

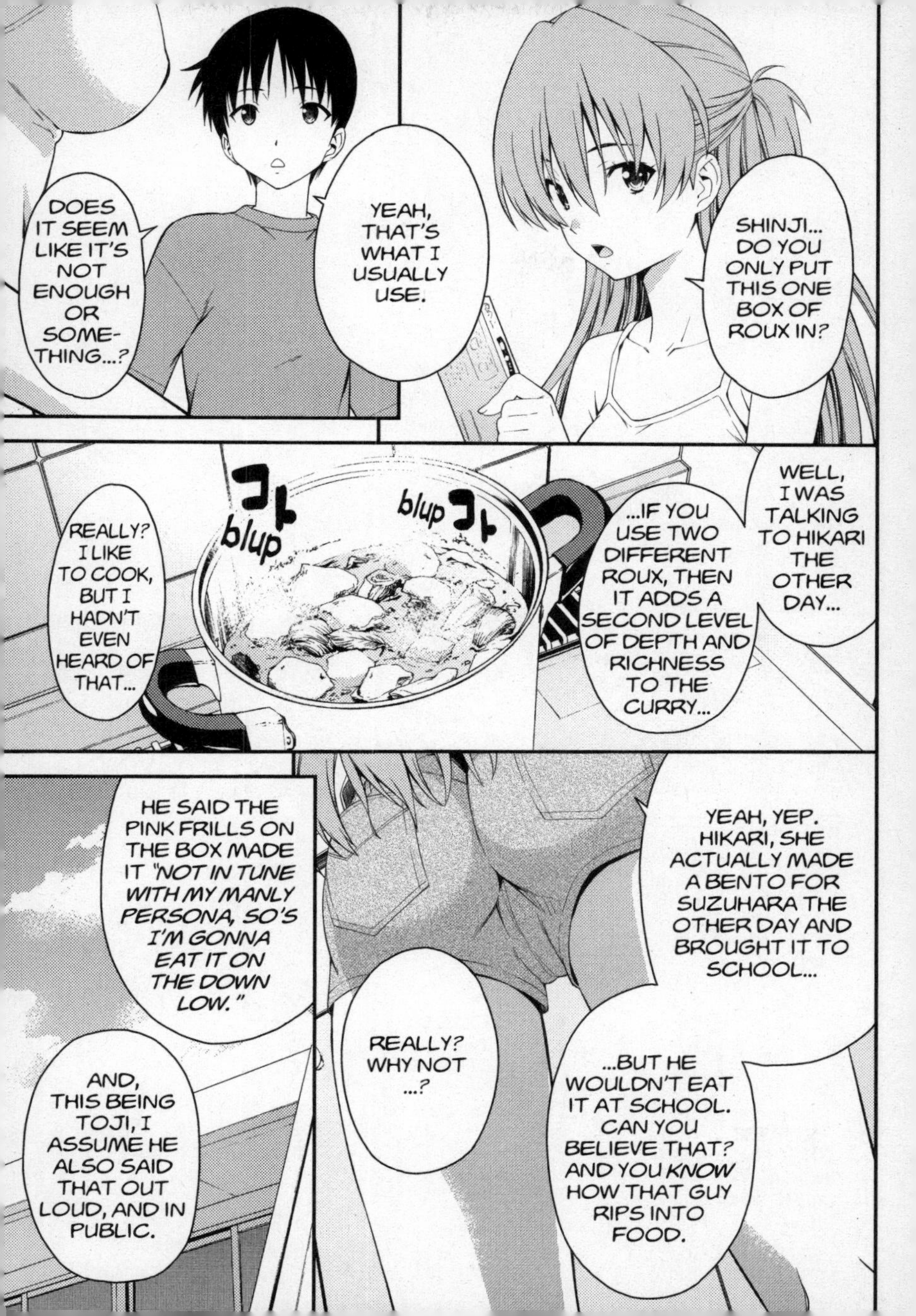
SHINJI... DO YOU ONLY PUT THIS ONE BOX OF ROUX IN?
YEAH, THAT'S WHAT I USUALLY USE.
DOES IT SEEM LIKE IT'S NOT ENOUGH OR SOME-THING...?
WELL, I WAS TALKING TO HIKARI THE OTHER DAY...
...IF YOU USE TWO DIFFERENT ROUX, THEN IT ADDS A SECOND LEVEL OF DEPTH AND RICHNESS TO THE CURRY...
blup コト
コト blup
REALLY? I LIKE TO COOK, BUT I HADN'T EVEN HEARD OF THAT...
YEAH, YEP. HIKARI, SHE ACTUALLY MADE A BENTO FOR SUZUHARA THE OTHER DAY AND BROUGHT IT TO SCHOOL...
...BUT HE WOULDN'T EAT IT AT SCHOOL. CAN YOU BELIEVE THAT? AND YOU *KNOW* HOW THAT GUY RIPS INTO FOOD.
REALLY? WHY NOT ...?
HE SAID THE PINK FRILLS ON THE BOX MADE IT *"NOT IN TUNE WITH MY MANLY PERSONA, SO'S I'M GONNA EAT IT ON THE DOWN LOW."*
AND, THIS BEING TOJI, I ASSUME HE ALSO SAID THAT OUT LOUD, AND IN PUBLIC.

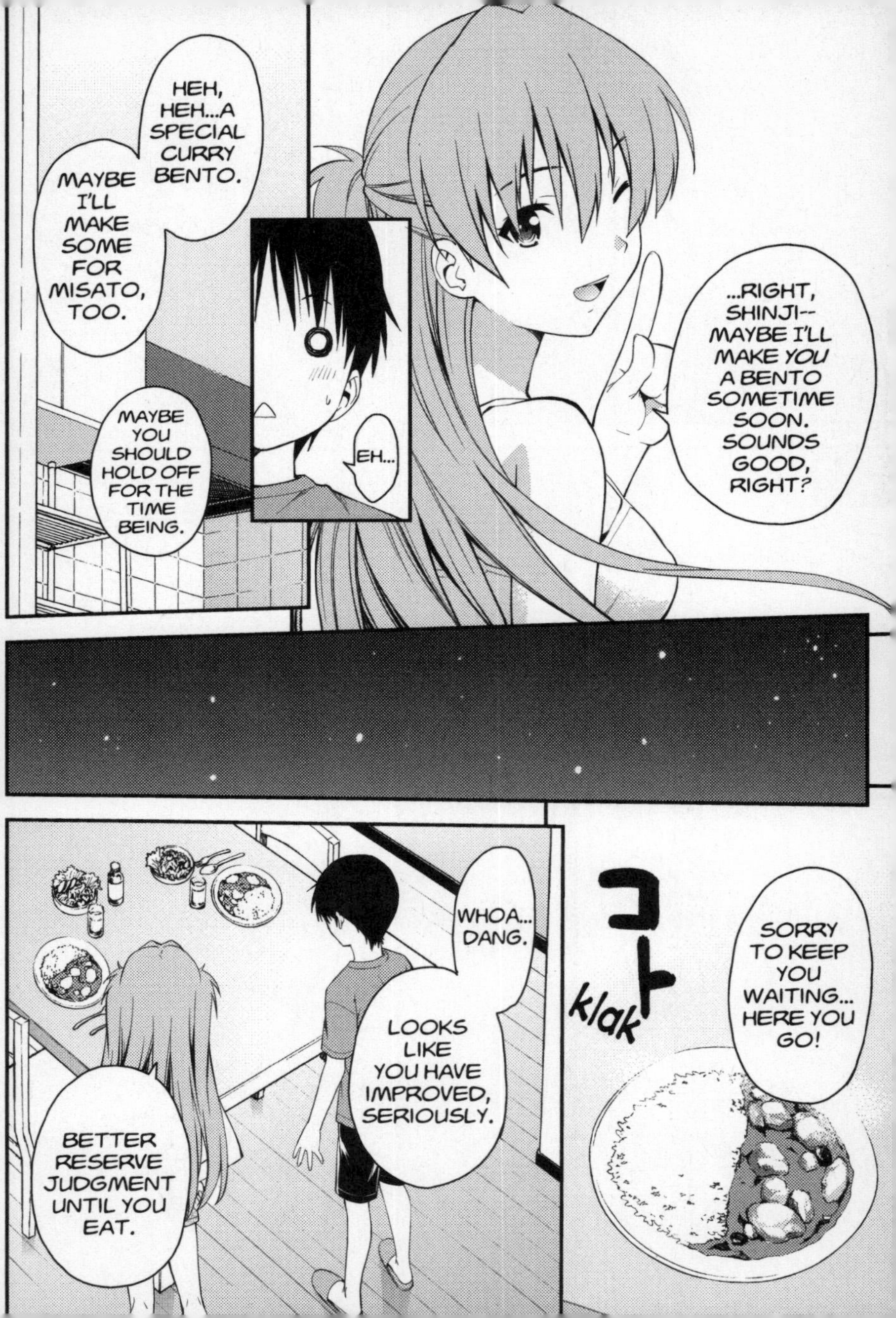
...RIGHT, SHINJI-- MAYBE I'LL MAKE *YOU* A BENTO SOMETIME SOON. SOUNDS GOOD, RIGHT?
EH...
HEH, HEH...A SPECIAL CURRY BENTO.
MAYBE I'LL MAKE SOME FOR MISATO, TOO.
MAYBE YOU SHOULD HOLD OFF FOR THE TIME BEING.
SORRY TO KEEP YOU WAITING... HERE YOU GO!
コト
klak
WHOA... DANG.
LOOKS LIKE YOU HAVE IMPROVED, SERIOUSLY.
BETTER RESERVE JUDGMENT UNTIL YOU EAT.

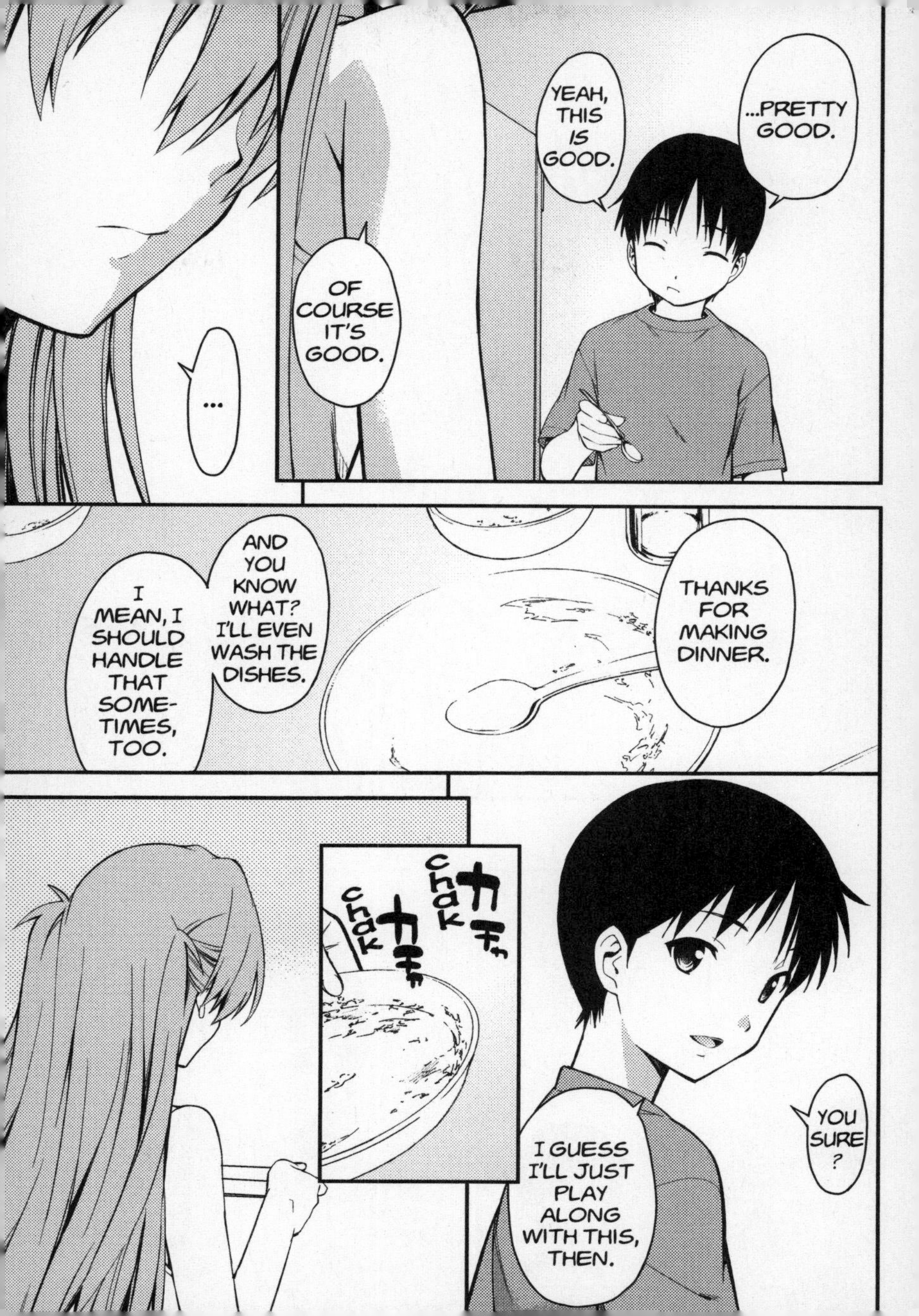
...PRETTY GOOD.
YEAH, THIS IS GOOD.
OF COURSE IT'S GOOD.
...
THANKS FOR MAKING DINNER.
AND YOU KNOW WHAT? I'LL EVEN WASH THE DISHES.
I MEAN, I SHOULD HANDLE THAT SOME-TIMES, TOO.
YOU SURE?
I GUESS I'LL JUST PLAY ALONG WITH THIS, THEN.
chak
chak

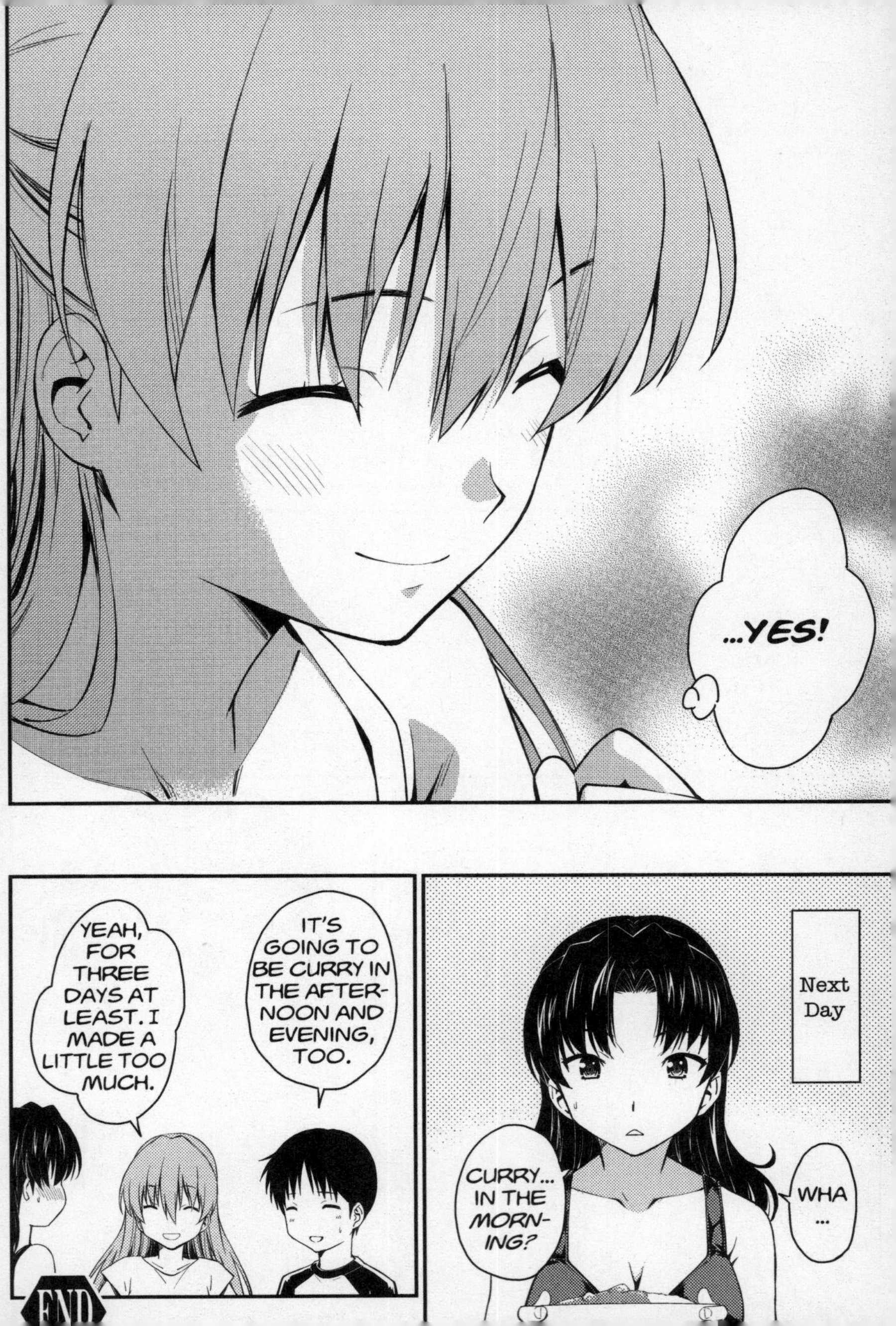
...YES!
Next Day
WHA ...
CURRY... IN THE MORNING?
IT'S GOING TO BE CURRY IN THE AFTERNOON AND EVENING, TOO.
YEAH, FOR THREE DAYS AT LEAST. I MADE A LITTLE TOO MUCH.
END

## AFTERWORD

So, in figuring out what sort of comment I should write here, I decided to look back on what I'd written in the past, and wound up with the following question:

How come my self-portrait is a shell?

-Osamu Takahashi

## ~STAFF~
Miki
and many others

## COVER DESIGN
Shiba Mitsuwo (Shindosha)

See you in vol. 17...

# MISATO'S FAN SERVICE CENTER

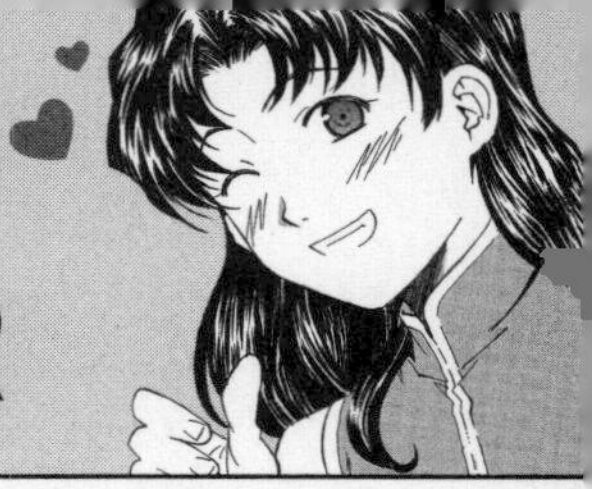

c/o Dark Horse Comics • 10956 SE Main Street • Milwaukie, OR 97222 • evangelion@darkhorse.com

It's been a while since the last volume of *The Shinji Ikari Raising Project*, but we here at Dark Horse haven't been idle on the *Evangelion* front—last year we released the one-shot manga *Tony Takezaki's Neon Genesis Evangelion* (check out the ad for it on the second-to-last page) by, well, Tony Takezaki, who was an Osaka high-school kid who met the founders of GAINAX while they were attending college there in the early 1980s. Takezaki not only knows *Evangelion* backward and forward; he has an uncanny

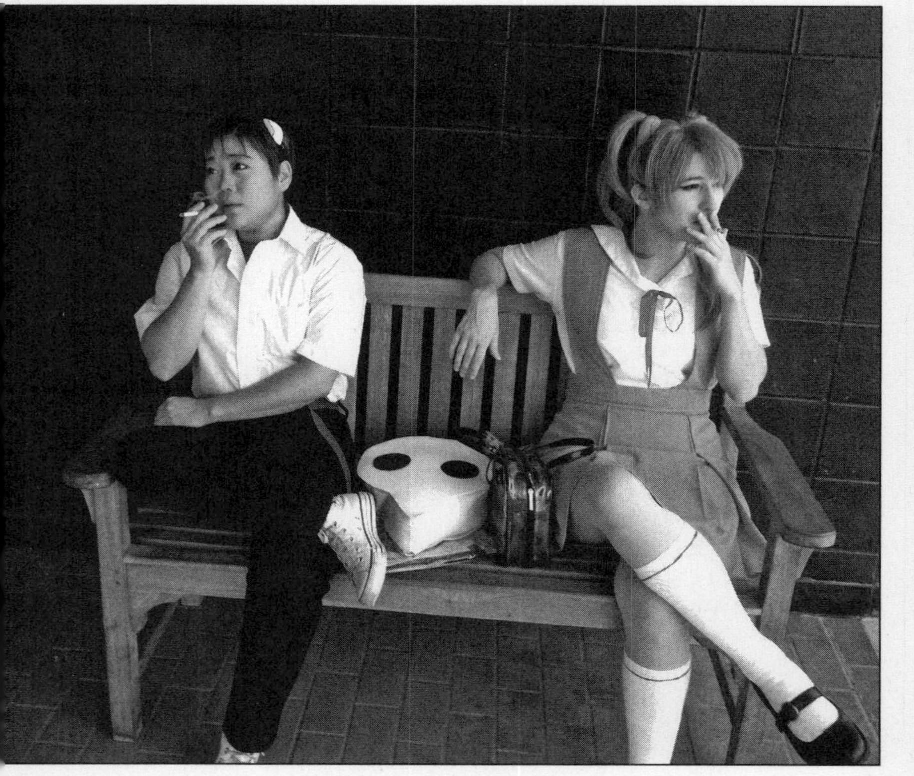

ability to imitate the art style of Yoshiyuki Sadamoto, making him the ideal *manga-ka* to be all sensitive and considerate toward our favorite series. You may remember some of Takezaki's stories from our earlier release *Neon Genesis Evangelion: Comic Tribute*; all the stories in *Tony Takezaki's Neon Genesis Evangelion* are new!

We also had two convention panels in 2015 at Anime Central and Otakon called—well, what else could we call them but "2015: The Year of *Evangelion*"? After all, it was not only the year the series itself took place, but also the twentieth anniversary of its premiere on Japanese television. But before the public got to see episode 1 on October 4, 1995, GAINAX had hosted a special sneak preview of the show earlier that summer for a small audience of fans at a mini con hosted by the studio, and our panel featured a retrospective presentation on that preview entitled "*Evangelion* Eve." Aaron Clark of EvaGeeks.org and EvaMonkey.com not only helped to get the panelists together at both cons; he prepared a short film that recapped everything that had happened with *Evangelion* the previous year.

At the Anime Central panel, Monk Ed from EvaGeeks was kind enough to participate and speak, whereas at Otakon, Aaron himself was there to moderate, and Andrew Todd and Sarah Myer joined in on the panel. We had a really good attendance at both cons, which just goes to show—if there was any doubt—that *Evangelion* not only retains its fascination twenty years after its debut; it is continuing to acquire new fans through the Rebuild films. Thank you so much, everyone, for coming by and bringing your comments and questions!

Spotted at Otakon waiting patiently for the fourth Rebuild film were Shinji and Asuka, a.k.a. our pals Sarah and Zelda. Now, I'm not necessarily recommending you light up yourselves, but let's face it—if you pilot an Eva, tar and nicotine are among the least of your worries. You can tell Maryland is a tobacco state by the sign posted in one of the hotels at Otakon, which solemnly stated that the penalty for smoking in the elevators is $25. Twenty-five dollars! In Portland, you would have been summarily shot. True story, as is the fact that a khara staffer visiting Otakon liked Sarah's Sachiel bag so much, he took a picture of it to bring home to show Yoshitou Asari, the Angel's designer. Don't forget to write in with your own comments, photos, and fan art for vol. 17, out in January!

—CGH

PRESIDENT AND PUBLISHER
**MIKE RICHARDSON**

DESIGNER
**JACK THOMAS**

DIGITAL ART TECHNICIAN
**CHRISTINA McKENZIE**

**English-language version produced by Dark Horse Comics**

**Neon Genesis Evangelion: The Shinji Ikari Raising Project Vol. 16**

First published in Japan as NEON GENESIS EVANGELION IKARI-SHINJI IKUSEI KEIKAKU Volume 16. Illustration by OSAMU TAKAHASHI © khara. Edited by KADOKAWA SHOTEN. First published in Japan in 2014 by KADOKAWA CORPORATION, Tokyo. English translation rights arranged with KADOKAWA CORPORATION, Tokyo, through TOHAN CORPORATION, Tokyo. This English-language edition © 2016 by Dark Horse Comics, Inc. All other material © 2016 by Dark Horse Comics, Inc. Dark Horse Manga™ is a trademark of Dark Horse Comics, Inc. All rights reserved. No portion of this publication may be reproduced or transmitted, in any form or by any means, without the express written permission of Dark Horse Comics, Inc. Names, characters, places, and incidents featured in this publication either are the product of the author's imagination or are used fictitiously. Any resemblance to actual persons (living or dead), events, institutions, or locales, without satiric intent, is coincidental.

Published by
Dark Horse Manga
A division of Dark Horse Comics, Inc.
10956 SE Main Street
Milwaukie, OR 97222

DarkHorse.com

To find a comics shop in your area, call the Comic Shop Locator Service toll-free at 1-888-266-4226

First edition: June 2016
ISBN 978-1-61655-997-7

1 3 5 7 9 10 8 6 4 2
Printed in the United States of America

# STOP!

止 ま れ

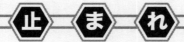

## THIS IS THE BACK OF THE BOOK!

This manga collection is translated into English, but arranged in right-to-left reading format to maintain the artwork's visual orientation as originally drawn and published in Japan. If you've never read comics this way before, take a look at the diagram below to give yourself an idea of how to go about it. Basically, you'll be starting in the upper-right-hand corner, and will read each word balloon and panel moving right to left. It may take a little getting used to, but you should get the hang of it very quickly. Have fun! If this is the millionth manga you've read this way, never mind.

1
WELL, THERE IS A CUTE GIRL SITTING NEXT TO YOU...
2
...SO I SUPPOSE IT'S UNDER-STANDABLE YOU CAN'T CONCEN-TRATE--
3
--BUT IF I CATCH YOU SPACING OUT AGAIN, YOUR NOVEL WILL BECOME REQUIRED READING.
4
MISATO-SENSEI...!!
5
JUST KIDDING! ♡
THUD!!
6
A NOVEL.

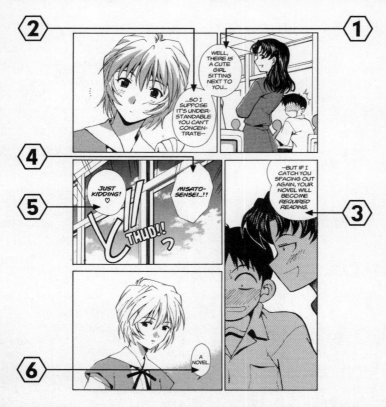